Esperanto and Languages of Internationalism in Revolutionary Russia

Esperanto and Languages of Internationalism in Revolutionary Russia

Brigid O'Keeffe

BLOOMSBURY ACADEMIC
LONDON • NEW YORK • OXFORD • NEW DELHI • SYDNEY

BLOOMSBURY ACADEMIC
Bloomsbury Publishing Plc
50 Bedford Square, London, WC1B 3DP, UK
1385 Broadway, New York, NY 10018, USA
29 Earlsfort Terrace, Dublin 2, Ireland

BLOOMSBURY, BLOOMSBURY ACADEMIC and the Diana logo are trademarks of
Bloomsbury Publishing Plc

First published in Great Britain 2021

Copyright © Brigid O'Keeffe, 2021

Brigid O'Keeffe has asserted their right under the Copyright, Designs and Patents Act,
1988, to be identified as Author of this work.

For legal purposes the Acknowledgments on pp. ix–xi constitute an extension
of this copyright page.

Cover Design: Ben Anslow

Cover image: Soviet propaganda poster for the Third International. The Communist International, abbreviated as Comintern and also known as the Third International (1919–1943), was an international communist organization initiated in Moscow during March 1919. (© Photo12 / Universal Images Group / Getty Images)

All rights reserved. No part of this publication may be reproduced or transmitted in any form or by any means, electronic or mechanical, including photocopying, recording, or any information storage or retrieval system, without prior permission in writing from the publishers.

Bloomsbury Publishing Plc does not have any control over, or responsibility for, any third-party websites referred to or in this book. All internet addresses given in this book were correct at the time of going to press. The author and publisher regret any inconvenience caused if addresses have changed or sites have ceased to exist, but can accept no responsibility for any such changes.

Every effort has been made to trace copyright holders and to obtain their permissions for the use of copyright material. The publisher apologizes for any errors or omissions and would be grateful if notified of any corrections that should be incorporated in future reprints or editions of this book.

A catalogue record for this book is available from the British Library.

Library of Congress Cataloging-in-Publication Data
Names: O'Keeffe, Brigid, 1979– author.
Title: Esperanto and languages of internationalism in revolutionary Russia / Brigid O'Keeffe.
Description: London ; New York : Bloomsbury Academic, 2021. |
Includes bibliographical references and index. |
Identifiers: LCCN 2020055613 (print) | LCCN 2020055614 (ebook) |
ISBN 9781350160651 (hardback) | ISBN 9781350160668 (ebook) |
ISBN 9781350160675 (epub)
Subjects: LCSH: Esperanto—History. | Esperanto—Social aspects.
Classification: LCC PM8209 .O34 2021 (print) | LCC PM8209 (ebook) |
DDC 499/.9920947—dc23
LC record available at https://lccn.loc.gov/2020055613
LC ebook record available at https://lccn.loc.gov/2020055614

ISBN: HB: 978-1-3501-6065-1
PB: 978-1-3502-4518-1
ePDF: 978-1-3501-6066-8
eBook: 978-1-3501-6067-5

Typeset by Newgen KnowledgeWorks Pvt. Ltd., Chennai, India

To find out more about our authors and books visit www.bloomsbury.com
and sign up for our newsletters.

For Zac, with love

Contents

List of Figures	viii
Acknowledgments	ix
A Note on the Text	xii
Introduction	1
1. A Universal Language for a Globalizing World	15
2. Pen Pals, Dreamers, and Globe-Trotters	47
3. Bolshevik Tower of Babel	81
4. Comrades with(out) Borders	113
5. Language Revolutions and Their Discontents	147
Epilogue: The Death of Esperanto	181
Notes	193
Bibliography	231
Index	247

Figures

1. L. L. Zamenhof (1859–1917)   24
2. Contact information for Dr. Esperanto in Warsaw as it appeared inside Zamenhof's first Esperanto primer, *Mezhdunarodnyi iazyk* (1887)   27
3. Postcard from A. H. Johnson of Melbourne, Australia to G. I. Tupitsyn, his Esperantist pen pal in late imperial Russia, 1912   76
4. Registration for Esperanto courses in revolutionary Petrograd, 1919   89
5. First Congress of the Third International (Comintern). Moscow, 1919   92
6. Ernest Karlovich Drezen (1892–1937)   117
7. Attendees of the 1926 SAT Congress held in Leningrad   132
8. Detail from the front cover of the SEU's journal *Mezhdunarodnyi iazyk*, 1926   151

Acknowledgments

My debt of gratitude spans the globe. I thank the many colleagues who have counseled me as I researched and wrote this book and who asked productive questions that led to a sharpening and refining of this project as it developed.

Several people have gone above and beyond to support me over the years. Yanni Kotsonis continues to be an ideal mentor, good friend, and indefatigable writer of letters. Jane Burbank's curiosity never fails to inspire me. I've been fortunate to benefit from her ideas about this project as well as the worlds it inhabits and the borders it has crossed. Steve Norris is truly one of the kindest and wisest people I know. Thank you, Steve, for always being generous with your advice, time, support, and good humor. Your students and colleagues are most fortunate, and your friends are luckier still.

Enormous thanks are owed to Jessica Reinisch, who welcomed me to join the Reluctant Internationalists project team at Birkbeck College, University of London, as a visiting fellow in the summer of 2015. Rarely have I so enjoyed scholarly collaboration and conversation of this high caliber. I thank Jessica Reinisch, David Brydan, Johanna Conterio, Dora Vargha, Ana Antic, Jessica Pearson, and Francesca Piana. It is also thanks to the generosity of Jessica Reinisch and the Reluctant Internationalists team that our Languages of Internationalism Conference convened at Birkbeck College in May 2017. I am grateful to all the participants of that incredible conference—for their superb papers, illuminating conversations, generous feedback, and the friendships made along the way.

Many colleagues have provided feedback and support of various kinds and without which I'd be far worse off. I offer particular thanks to Gleb Albert, Rachel Applebaum, Betty Banks, Peter Blitstein, Maurice Casey, Katie David, Bruce Grant, Faith Hillis, Sean Guillory, Kelly Kolar, Steve Maddox, Dave Rainbow, Josh Sanborn, Ben Sawyer, Andrew Sloin, Nick Underwood, Kate Antonova, and Ted Weeks. Special thanks are owed to Faith Hillis, who read the full draft of the manuscript. Humphrey Tonkin and Javier Alcalde demonstrated eager support and collegiality even from the earliest days of this project. Ulrich Lens generously shared his expertise.

In the years I worked on this book, I enjoyed the support of two incredible chairs who prioritized protecting my writing time whenever I was granted leave from teaching and/or service. May all academics be fortunate enough to have colleagues and friends like Chris Ebert and Gunja SenGupta. I thank you both for the wisdom and compassion with which you approached being our department's chair. Jocelyn Wills and Lauren Mancia provided camaraderie, made time for walks and ice creams, and offered the precious feedback that one is sometimes fortunate to receive from colleagues who work in quite distant fields of research. Phil Napoli anchored the Brooklyn College History Department at a crucial moment and has gone above and beyond to help colleagues and students alike. Thank you, Phil, for your kindness and leadership—you are the very best of Brooklyn College. My students remain an endless source of inspiration. I thank in particular two former students who served as my Kurz Undergraduate Research Fellowship assistants: Sergei Goz and Rabia Sirin. Sergei and Rabia, I will always be grateful and I cannot wait to see what you both do next. My thanks to Anna Law for giving my students this opportunity (and for sharing the most delicious cookies with the History Department on meeting days).

I am grateful for the generous financial and institutional support provided me by a variety of organizations. Without their crucial support, the research and writing of this book would simply not have been possible. PSC-CUNY Research Foundation grants funded trips to Russia and Poland. A Franklin Research Grant from the American Philosophical Society and a Tow Faculty Travel Fellowship generously funded research travel to Stanford and Moscow. A Whiting Fellowship afforded me time off from teaching so that I could travel to archives and begin writing. A Wolfe Fellowship could not have arrived at a better time in my career. It is thanks to the Ethyle R. Wolfe Institute for Humanities at Brooklyn College that I enjoyed a full academic year to devote almost solely to writing—a rare and precious opportunity in my corner of academia. The Advanced Research Collaborative at the CUNY Graduate Center welcomed me as a Distinguished CUNY Fellow in the fall of 2019. Here, I enjoyed the camaraderie of fellow writers from CUNY and elsewhere in a magical, teaching-free semester of writing and intellectual exchange. I offer special thanks to Donald Robotham—one could not have asked for a wiser or more welcoming head of the Advanced Research Collaborative. As a critical stage of writing this book, the Jordan Center for the Advanced Study of Russia at New York University welcomed me for a year as a writer in residence. I thank all the wonderful colleagues who make the Jordan Center such a transformative and delightful space in which to discuss research and debate ideas. The library privileges that the Jordan Center extended to me spared me no end of headache and frustration. On my home campus, the librarians at Brooklyn College's interlibrary loan office have heroically hunted down all manner of books and articles that CUNY—wracked for too many years now by immoral austerity budgets—cannot afford to house in its own withered collections.

I benefitted enormously from the opportunities to present my research as I worked on this manuscript and for the feedback I gained along the way. I am grateful for the generosity of the Max Kade Center for European and German Studies at Vanderbilt University; the Chicago Russian history *kruzhok*; the Havighurst Center at Miami University of Ohio; the NYU Jordan Center colloquium; the Honors College at the University of Houston; and the Tivadar Soros lectures hosted by the Esperantic Studies Foundation.

I thank the many archivists and librarians who helped me to research this project in Russia, the UK, Austria, Germany, and the United States. I consider myself especially fortunate to have been welcomed into the British Library, the Cambridge University Library, the Staatsbibliothek zu Berlin, the Österreichische Nationalbibliothek in Vienna, and the Rossiiskaia Natsional'naia Biblioteka, among others. I am grateful for the assistance provided me at every archive and library I visited, no less for the heartening reminder that archives and libraries are among the most hospitable and hopeful places to experience lived internationalism. I owe special thanks to Olga Kerziouk of the British Library and to Bernhard Tuider of the Department of Planned Languages and the Esperanto Museum of the Austrian National Library.

At Bloomsbury, I have enjoyed the immense expertise and generous guidance of Rhodri Mogford and Laura Reeves. My anonymous reviewers offered perceptive and helpful advice. The manuscript is much improved thanks to everyone who played a role in this book's production at Bloomsbury.

Friends have helped in ways both big and small. I offer heartfelt thanks to Joseph DeVeny, Iverson Long, Anya Ustivitskaya, Ludmila Borisovna, Nina Peskareva, Tatiana and Masha Shmigelskaia, Mobina Hashmi, Olga Livshin, Andy Janco, Desi Allevato, Karen Weber, Andrew Reinert, Krista Ream, Felix Zilberbrand, and Lisa Jill Anderson.

My family means everything and I thank them for their support and love, no less than their valiant attempts to express interest in my scholarly pursuits. These lines feel insufficient to express my gratitude and love for Sandi, Amy, and Deva; for Charlie and Mark; for Katie, Eoin, and Patrick. The MacMahons, Powers, Brymers, McMillans, Vencills, and VanKannels have offered support from near and far. Ernie, I dare say, knows full well how much he is loved. A better writing assistant would be hard to find. Special thanks to Rick for bringing new joys to our family. We couldn't be happier that you've joined us. To the O'Keeffe Girls, I owe more than I can ever repay. Thank you mom, Siobhan, and Deirdre.

I end these acknowledgments where I begin each day—thankful for Zac Centers. He speaks in a universal language of kindness, even when I cannot understand why or fathom how. I lack the words in any language to fully express how much I love him. It is to Zac that I dedicate this book.

Brooklyn, September 2020

A Note on the Text

I have used the Library of Congress system of transliteration for Russian except when referring to names and geographical places conventionally known to English readers in more familiar guise. I therefore refer to Tolstoy rather than Tolstoi and to Arkhangelsk rather than Arkhangel'sk.

Versions of the following chapters originally appeared in other publications, and I am grateful for permission to reproduce them.

An abridged version of Chapter 1 was first published as the article, "An International Language for an Empire of Humanity: L.L. Zamenhof and the Imperial Russian Origins of Esperanto," by Brigid O'Keeffe, in *East European Jewish Affairs* volume 49, issue 1, pp. 1–19. Copyright 2019 by Taylor and Francis. https://doi.org/10.1080/13501674.2019.1618165

An abridged version of Chapter 5 was first published as "Building a Communist Tower of Babel: Esperanto and the Language Politics of Internationalism in Revolutionary Russia," by Brigid O'Keeffe in Jessica Reinisch and David Brydan (eds.), *Internationalists in European History: Rethinking the Twentieth Century* (London: Bloomsbury, 2021).

Introduction

In 1887, an obscure Jewish eye doctor named L. L. Zamenhof launched Esperanto from the polyglot western borderlands of a tsarist empire in crisis. Esperanto was an international auxiliary language designed to revolutionize Russia and all of humankind. That this improbable global revolution had any chance of succeeding owed to the ordinary men and women throughout the Russian empire who heeded Zamenhof's internationalist call and learned Esperanto. In late imperial Russia, these hopeful cosmopolitans deployed Esperanto with the aim of conversing meaningfully with the wider world and transforming themselves into global citizens. They kickstarted a transnational movement to unite humankind in all its diversity by means of an international language. They engineered new types of social networks that transcended borders and linked Esperantists worldwide in a growing community of self-styled global citizens. In the era of globalization's "great acceleration," Esperantists embraced the revolutionary transformations of their age—revolutions in postal services, telecommunications, mass media, transportation, and the increasingly global exchange of goods, ideas, and people.[1] They personified a new type of grassroots internationalism in pursuit of a wide variety of ideological aims. They nurtured friendships with far-flung comrades, confidants, and pen pals—many of whom they would never meet face-to-face. Esperanto proved more than an international auxiliary language. Esperanto offered a transnational community and culture as a framework through which Esperantists fashioned for themselves new identities as patriotic cosmopolitans, as global moderns.[2]

And yet Zamenhof's vision of world revolution ultimately failed. It failed despite the fact that in the late nineteenth and early twentieth centuries, Esperanto energized people all over the globe in hopeful pursuit of a unified humanity. And today, well over a century since Zamenhof launched his global movement to unite humanity via an international auxiliary language, our world looks and feels all the more fractured, troubled, and inescapably interconnected than ever. As I write the introduction to this book, the COVID-19 pandemic has upended daily life the world over and wrought unprecedented suffering among the world's most vulnerable and least privileged in particular. Borders have been closed, international travel has slowed to a jaw-dropping trickle, international commerce has been disrupted, and international teams of scientists labor to produce a vaccine that can help save lives and allow the world to resume what remains of our pre-pandemic way of life. Perhaps we would do well to reconsider the Esperantists of an earlier, no less fraught era of globalization—to take seriously their histories and their visions of global citizenship, their hopes and their dreams, their successes and their failures as ordinary agents of internationalism.[3] Their concerns, as this book will reveal, remain very much with us today. The dilemmas they hoped to solve—the dilemmas of linguistic justice and effective international communication in a globalizing and unequal world, most prominently—have not been solved. Global citizenship and grassroots internationalism remain the ideal for some but a shameful scourge for others. The Esperantists of an earlier age are not historical outliers as has so often been assumed. They exemplify a particular engagement with globalization that perhaps looks small and much too niche from the vantage of a quick glance into a rearview mirror. Upon closer inspection, however, the history of Esperanto appears much more familiar, relatable, and illuminating than some might otherwise suspect.

This book is a study of Esperanto in revolutionary Russia—a period here understood broadly as spanning from late imperial Russia's era of Great Reforms through the deadly Purges and Terror of the late Stalinist 1930s. Its focus is on how men and women in revolutionary Russia variously contended with the challenges and opportunities of the evolving relationship between language and international communication in an avowedly global age. It seeks to show how the question of international language and international communication shaped revolutionary Russia's debates about its— and ordinary people's—place and role in an interconnected but divided world. The chapters that follow aim to bring to life the ordinary grassroots internationalism that linked Russia's Esperantists to comrades all over the world in an era of global transformation. It argues that the question of language and communication was at the heart of internationalism as it was experienced, practiced, and envisioned in late imperial and early Soviet Russia. This was an insistent question, an often bewildering one, and a nagging and noxious question to some. While Esperanto, in the end, did not prove to be the preferred solution to the apparent dilemmas of language diversity in the globalizing worlds that revolutionary Russia inhabited and shaped, Esperanto and its advocates framed key debates about internationalism, internationality, and what it meant to be a global citizen during this anxious era of revolutionary possibility and growing interconnection.

Esperantists in revolutionary Russia persistently posed what they called the international language question. In this era of increasing global entanglement and interconnectedness, how best should humanity communicate across the linguistic, ideological, cultural, socioeconomic, national, and imperial borders that divided it? Even while many of their contemporaries remained skeptical of the Esperantists' preferred answer to this international language question, few refused to acknowledge the question's relevance to the pressing needs of globalization as they were all the more keenly felt in the late nineteenth and early twentieth centuries. After the October Revolution, Russia's Esperantists persisted anew, this time with a question no less urgent, they claimed, for achieving the Bolsheviks' hoped-for "worldwide October." How could the global proletariat unite in the absence of a shared language in which to communicate, collaborate, and forge meaningful affective bonds? In their minds, proletarian internationalism demanded a *proletarian* international language and worldwide socialist revolution required a revolutionary and decidedly nonnational tongue.

Though dismissed by skeptical contemporaries and overlooked by historians, Esperantists spoke to their age—in Esperanto, but also in their native languages—and demanded an equitable solution to the dilemmas of linguistic diversity and linguistic injustice in a world whose webs of interconnection seemed to be irreversibly shrinking the globe and entangling the peoples who inhabited it. In revolutionary Russia, the Esperantists' mission crisscrossed and cross-fertilized—supplemented and intersected—more well-known ideological visions and campaigns to transform and rejuvenate Russia and the world. Esperanto began as Zamenhof's hopeful answer to the Jewish Question in the Russian empire and the wider world. The Esperantists who heeded his call in late imperial Russia represented a cross-section of educated Russian society—nobles and merchants, students and radicals, governesses and civil servants, daydreamers and believers in the possibility of utopian realization here on earth. In this late imperial era of breathtaking domestic crisis and ideological ferment, Esperanto appealed to all manner of Russian subjects aching to contribute to Russia's rejuvenation but also straining to find meaning and a real sense of place—a sense of home and belonging—in the wider world.

Late imperial Russia was Esperanto's birthplace and its anchor on Europe's outer periphery. Its homegrown Esperantists were exemplars of an educated public whose grassroots internationalism demanded effective languages of international communication, no less than a vocabulary of social justice and an expansive vision of a humanity liberated and united. Under the broad, ecumenical tent of fin de siècle Esperantism, globally conscious Russian subjects were in agreement on the need for an international auxiliary language to transform Russia and the world. They conversed and corresponded in this novel language of internationalism even if they disagreed over the ideological basis for the revolutionary transformation that they hoped Esperanto would enable them to achieve. Esperanto and Esperantists, then, offer us an entrée into the variety of global aspirations of educated imperial Russian society—from Jewish emancipation to equality of the sexes, from global friendship to postcard collecting, from conspicuous globe-trotting to exuberant one-worldism. Esperantists in late imperial Russia turned to Esperanto seeking, literally and figuratively, the world. This book turns to Esperantists in late imperial Russia to better understand their worlds—and, in particular, to better appreciate the politics, meaning, and experience of fashioning one's self a global citizen from their various corners of the fracturing tsarist empire.

In the wake of the revolutions that upended life in Russia in 1917 and burst the door open to new possibilities, young Esperantists joined in the imagining of a socialist world, of a proletariat united and emancipated. For them (though, fatefully, not for the Bolsheviks), this vision was utterly dependent on Esperanto being chosen as the rightful solution to an international language question that—in their eyes—took on fresh urgency under the conditions of hoped-for worldwide revolution. The global Esperantist community—already strained and undermined by the devastating circumstances of the Great War—fractured in near fatal fashion between Right and Left. Proletarian Esperantists hailed Esperanto as a weapon of socialist revolution, a necessary tool to smash capitalism and destroy the global bourgeoisie. Ideological divisions soon proved scarcely so neat in practice. Socialist Esperantists and anarchist Esperantists soon found themselves barely able to stomach conversation in any language, let alone in Zamenhof's language of hope and unity. In the interwar period, Soviet Esperantists struggled not only to achieve legitimacy at home but also to assert authority over the global proletarian Esperantist movement. As this book will show, they ultimately failed to achieve either. Soviet Esperantists were avid participants in and, ultimately, targeted victims of Stalin's revolutions. During Stalin's Purges and Terror, they found themselves trapped in the dangerous webs of the paradoxical Stalinist ideological blend of socialist internationalism and virulent xenophobia. By the close of the 1930s, the Soviet Union's leading Soviet Esperantists—with few, lucky exceptions—had been executed at the hands of the Soviet security police (NKVD), or banished to the Gulag for the alleged crimes of brazen espionage and anti-Soviet conspiracy conducted in an international language.

Esperantists and their distinctive internationalism in the late nineteenth and early twentieth century afford us a unique opportunity to take a global approach to modern Russian and Soviet history. Their movement was inconceivable outside of that era's globalization—a term used here to describe broadly the complex of processes that led to enduring political, cultural, economic, and social relationships and (inter-) dependencies on a global scale, no less than to conscious awareness of the global interconnections that increasingly knitted the world's peoples together in typically unequal and hierarchal fashion. Esperantists in revolutionary Russia were themselves obsessed with their place in the wider world. They understood that their global aspirations as well as their agency as global citizens were inescapably situated in and shaped by their imperial Russian and Soviet contexts. Esperantists in revolutionary Russia thus intuitively understood themselves and their world in a global perspective. They purposefully chose the international auxiliary language Esperanto as their means of crossing borders and sometimes transcending them, of traveling the world by railway or by envelope, of conversing and collaborating with foreigners, of coming closer to and potentially immersing one's self in an "abroad" that was at once both real and abstract. In all of these ways, revolutionary Russia's Esperantists demand of us that we anchor their history not only in their imperial Russian and early Soviet contexts but also in their global contexts. Historians have rightly called for "globalizing" how we study the Russian Revolution.[4] Perhaps there is no better place to turn than to revolutionary Russia's Esperantists. Ardent globalists and ordinary internationalists, they did not have to be prompted to consider their own and revolutionary Russia's place in the wider world.

Esperanto and the International Language Question

Zamenhof's was an age of technocratic scheming, of creative and often desperate searching for alternative futures among a European educated elite obsessed with the anxious gallop of globalization. International postal services, telegraph cables, railways, and steamships transformed the world with stunning rapidity in the late nineteenth century. For men and women like Zamenhof, the world was shrinking before their very eyes. Globalization drew them into new global circuits of exchange and pulled them into new border-crossing flows of people, goods, ideas, cultures, and conflicts. New technologies no less than a new emerging global consciousness transformed how and why the peoples of the world communicated over long distances and across borders.[5] For men and women like Zamenhof, the world seemed—very suddenly—to come within their reach. This stunning transformation in their relationship to space, time, and their own sense of self-in-the-world presented an array of new challenges of an international, universal scope. At one and the same time, this revolutionary globalization seemingly offered novel opportunities to reshape the world and how the peoples within in interacted. It inspired visions of alternative global futures. It invited what Vanessa Ogle has described as a mentality of "self-reflective globalization"—a palpable sense that ordinary people could act meaningfully on their own growing global (self-)consciousness and direct the flows and engineer the networks of the globalization that increasingly suffused their age.[6] There seemed to be no doubt that globalization was, at an accelerated pace, upending the world. Many, like Zamenhof, wanted to participate meaningfully in shaping an inescapably global future for all of humankind.

The historian Holly Case has recently described fin de siècle Europe as in the throes of a veritable "age of questions." Professional thinkers and the wider public obsessed over a series of dilemmas and debated their potential solutions. To pose a question, Case explains, was to declare a problem that urgently demanded a thoughtful but definitive solution. The Woman Question, the Jewish Question, the Polish Question and so many other upper-case queries—these were the rhetorical signposts of heady debates that preoccupied and reverberated across a widening, but still very Eurocentric, international public sphere in the so-called long nineteenth century.[7] Among these loaded questions there appeared the "international language question"—the question of what language (or languages) should be used for international communication in an age of keenly felt globalization. The very question itself—the international language question, that is—raised concerns of linguistic equity and fairness in what was a volatile age of ever more frequent global encounters and seemingly ever more divisive geopolitical rivalries.

Until recently, few scholars have so much as acknowledged the international language question in their studies of fin de siècle globalization. Historians have largely overlooked how the very idea of an international auxiliary language inspired women and men throughout the world in the late nineteenth and early twentieth centuries—a time when a variety of constructed languages competed as contenders for the solution to the many problems of international communication. If Esperanto registers at all in the historiography, it is as a mere footnote, an ornamental anecdote, or a fleeting reference to this quirky emblem of the global-mindedness of fin de siècle Europe.[8] This dismissiveness prevails despite the fact that Esperanto was the most successful of the constructed languages put forth as a solution to what was, in the late nineteenth and early twentieth centuries, considered to be the apparent problem of language diversity in an age of internationalism and global entanglement. This historiographical blindness to the "international language question" broadly, and to the phenomenon of Esperanto in particular, testifies to the endurance of the very dilemmas of language diversity in a shrinking world that people like Zamenhof hoped to solve. While historians of internationalism have yet paid scant attention to the crucial politics of language, scholars cannot take for granted that their subjects—even the avowed and eager agents of internationalism among them—were reliably able to communicate effectively across and beyond linguistic borders. The history of Esperanto reminds us not only of the perceived urgency of the international language question in an earlier era of globalization but also of the mundane struggles to understand, and to be understood, in a world that was shrinking before people's own widened eyes.

Zamenhof was among those aching to understand and to be understood in a fractured yet globalizing world. He came of age alongside the telegraph, international post, and the steamship. He grew up amidst the din of "the age of questions." Zamenhof was a member of an ever-growing global community of seekers of a solution to the international language question—to the myriad problems of living in modern-day Babel. He was neither the first nor the last to attempt to remake the modern world by means of a so-called international language. In the late nineteenth and early twentieth centuries, proposals for international languages flourished. Sometimes billed as "universal" languages, their proliferation heightened the perceived need for a global tongue in an increasingly global age. Advocates of an ever-growing list of international languages competed boisterously with one another, vying in the marketplace of ideas for their preferred solution to the chaos, inequity, and mundane miscommunication problems of modern Babel.[9]

In the decade prior to Esperanto's debut on this world stage, a Bavarian priest named Johann Martin Schleyer achieved unprecedented success in Europe for his own constructed international language, Volapük. The famously uncompromising Schleyer claimed that Volapük ("Worldspeak") had been delivered to him in mystical fashion as a seeming revelation from God. Launched in 1879, Volapük enjoyed a rapid ascent in central Europe in particular. Volapük clubs, textbooks, and courses helped to grow a movement populated largely by educated male Europeans who grafted their own practical and spiritual designs onto Schleyer's proposed world language. Yet Volapük's demise seemingly came on almost as quickly as had its rise. A decade after its launch, the Volapük movement shattered, with at least a few of its supporters having decamped to the new movement beginning to coalesce around Zamenhof's Esperanto. The collapse of the Volapük movement by 1890 owed less to divine intervention than to Schleyer's obsessive, tight-fisted attempt to micromanage the Volapük movement and to rigidly police the language that he had constructed. It suffered, too, from the outraged cries of scandalized patriots throughout Europe who insisted that Volapük was a mortal threat to their national pride and to the sanctity of the nation itself.[10]

This was, after all, an age of nationalism as well as internationalism—the two were, as historian Glenda Sluga has argued, mutually constitutive.[11] This tension between nationalism and internationalism imposed upon any proposal for an international language careful consideration of the tug-of-war between the practical needs of globalization and the ideological demands of nationalist sentiment. Among those willing to admit to the urgency of the international language question, few were willing to accept gladly a "world language" designed to displace the so-called national languages. Meanwhile, the notion that any one national language (at least any that was not one's own!) could be elevated to the role of a universal language was offensive and inflammatory. Today, native English speakers tend to take Global English for granted even if they might feel guilt and shame about it. Yet, as Michael Gordin reminds us in his study of how English came to be the lingua franca of international science, the idea that English might come to dominate science and every other global form of exchange remained "unfathomable" in the late nineteenth century. Gordin captures the dynamics of fin de siècle language politics (inextricable from the era's Eurocentric geopolitics) with this pithy explanation: "The French would never tolerate German; the Germans would never tolerate English; the English would tolerate nothing at all; and none of the rising nationalist movements would submit to any of these three."[12]

Esperanto proposed not only to solve the international language question but also to alleviate the fears that nationalists might have about the deracinating power of a universal language. As Zamenhof expressly conceived it, Esperanto was not intended to replace or displace the native tongues of the world's diverse peoples. Esperanto was designed to become everyone on earth's *second* language. This is why, from Esperanto's very launch, Zamenhof defined his language as an "international auxiliary language." That is to say, Esperanto was an international language in that it was designed to belong to everyone, to all of humanity, no matter their place of origin or native tongue. That Esperanto was an international *auxiliary* language meant that it was expressly designed to belong to *all* as a shared vehicle of effective communication between peoples who lacked a common native language. For Zamenhof and for the Esperantists who took up his language and heeded his internationalist call, no international language could succeed—at least not humanely, justly, and equitably—that was a pre-existing language that belonged natively to a dominant group. Neither English nor Japanese, neither French nor Portuguese could solve the international language question—at least not without chauvinism, inequity and hierarchy prevailing. International communication conducted in a national language elevated to the position of lingua franca would always disadvantage non-native speakers and privilege native speakers, thereby poisoning international relations. Zamenhof expressly built a vision of linguistic justice and equity into his international auxiliary language—although that vision no doubt overlooked the inherent advantage that speakers of dominant European languages would have in learning this international auxiliary language. Intended as everyone's second language, conceived as an international auxiliary language, Esperanto was designed to put everyone who spoke it on the same footing. By design, it would require *everyone* to put in the work of learning a second language—and namely, an international auxiliary language.

Some, indeed, would have to put more work into learning Esperanto as a second language than others. Esperanto was a constructed language—novel and sui generis, to be sure—but it certainly looked European. Esperanto was an a posteriori international language built from a variety of nuts and bolts that Zamenhof borrowed from other languages—primarily, the Romance languages, English, German, and Russian, but Latin and Greek too. Esperanto's European-ness can scarcely be denied. Consider the first line of the Lord's Prayer, which Zamenhof translated into Esperanto as *Patro Nia* and included in his first primer for his international language: *Patro nia, kiu estas en la ĉielo, sankta estu Via nomo* (Our father, who art in heaven, hallowed be thy name).[13] This was a language, Zamenhof and his acolytes insisted, that was profoundly easy to learn. Its grammar was clear-cut and neatly contained in sixteen unbending grammar rules. Esperanto launched in 1887 with a vocabulary comprising some 900 root words. These base roots enjoyed a nearly infinite elasticity thanks to the transformative affixes that would allow Esperantists to creatively make meaning and join in building the new language's stock of words. When Zamenhof declared his language to be astonishingly easy to master, he had first in mind European elites. His was a language, he wrote in an 1888 appeal to tsarist bureaucrats—that would be easily mastered by any "more or less educated European."[14] In this sense, too, Zamenhof and Esperanto were products of their time and their European milieu. Zamenhof belonged to an era in which many of the dominant debates about internationalizing or universalizing standards and practices across the globe presumed a "world" that first and foremost meant Europe and North America.[15]

Thus, it was not Esperanto's apparent Eurocentrism that troubled or perplexed most participants in debates over the so-called international language question. Rather, it was Esperanto's perceived threat to established borders and the states that encompassed them. And yet although Esperanto frightened and angered those in the fin de siècle who regarded Zamenhof's international auxiliary language as a mortal threat to the inviolable sanctity of nation and empire, it spoke meaningfully to many who understood themselves as faithful, patriotic members of overlapping communities. For the patriotic cosmopolitans of Esperantism, the very logic of Zamenhof's international auxiliary language affirmed that they need not divide their loyalties or choose between them. In considering the transformation of subjectivities during this era of palpable globalization, the historian Emily S. Rosenberg reminds us that "realms of the transnational, the national, the imperial and the local were not distinct; most people lived in them all at the same time."[16] Esperanto was designed to accommodate and complement this reality, to alleviate any sense of tension between the particular and the universal in pursuit of a global unity. This was one of the reasons why men and women around a rapidly changing globe were attracted to its linguistic no less than its subjective possibilities. In late imperial Russia, Esperanto appealed to a variety of constituencies within an educated public whose expanding global consciousness and grassroots internationalism has largely been overlooked by historians.[17] Esperanto offered the hope of an untroubled layering of identities in a world that threatened to flatten differences and to demand singular loyalties. When, in 1917, revolutionary Russia offered the world hope of a very different kind, Esperanto only became further entangled in the ideological struggles that spanned a globe upon which the Bolsheviks promised to refashion life via worldwide socialist revolution.

Revolutionary Russia in Global Perspective

In September 1919, a leaflet circulated in revolutionary Russia demanding that citizens of the Soviet republic take up their civic duty to study Esperanto. Without Esperanto, the revolution was doomed, the leaflet warned. Without Esperanto, the proletarians of all countries could never unite. A common language—a proletarian international auxiliary language—was necessary to realize a glorious Worldwide October.[18] Amidst the babel of revolutionary sloganeering in war-torn and devastated Soviet Russia, the Esperantists grasped onto the Bolsheviks' aspiration of global communism and their promise of an impending Worldwide October. They insisted again on raising the international language question and defended themselves as sober-minded pragmatists rather than starry-eyed utopians peddling a bourgeois fantasy better left off discarded in the rubbish bin of the past. The dilemmas of language diversity in a world in which the proletariat spoke in many different tongues demanded a solution now more than ever. Young socialist Esperantists throughout revolutionary Russia pinned the success of the Bolshevik Revolution on the fate of Esperanto—a language they now declared to be the most proletarian-friendly (because it was ostensibly so easy to learn) and the most purely internationalist (because it was an international auxiliary language) of all possible options for the lingua franca of global communism.

In the early years of their revolution, the Bolsheviks at best tolerated the Esperantists and their vision of international socialism without borders, of comrades without need of translators and interpreters, of global communism achieved in an international auxiliary language. During the 1920s, Soviet Esperantists struggled to prove Esperanto's value to the Bolshevik goals of international socialist revolution broadly conceived, and in particular to the needs and interests of the USSR's emerging approach to cultural diplomacy. As this book will explain, the Bolsheviks were at first little concerned with (and little impressed by) the Soviet Esperantists' endeavors by means of international post, radio, and transnational publishing to collaborate with the self-declared global community of proletarian Esperantists and the wider world of the embattled USSR's foreign friends and supporters. During the first decade of the Bolshevik Revolution, Soviet Esperantists reached out to the world and corresponded with comrades abroad in both creative and meaningful as well as in stilted and micromanaged ways. Only on the rarest of occasions did they enjoy tangible state support for their efforts. The most notable of these occasions was perhaps the Soviet Union's hosting in August 1926 of the Sixth World Congress of Proletarian Esperantists in Leningrad. Overall, however, early Soviet Esperantism was a movement fueled by the enthusiasm of its participants. These were Esperantists who adapted—sometimes rather crudely and sometimes unpersuasively—their sense of globalism and curiosity about the world to the evolving ideological priorities of the Bolsheviks.

After the launch of Stalin's revolution from above, the Soviet Esperantist movement faced ever greater and ultimately more dangerous struggles to secure within the constraints of Stalinist culture a viable niche for Esperanto and their transnational Esperantist networks. Party officials who had always looked upon the Esperantists skeptically began during the First Five-Year Plan to question if Esperanto was a language of subversion, class-enemy machinations, and potential espionage. The demands of feverish industrialization seemed to place a premium on teaching Soviet citizens the languages of the capitalist West—English, German, and French—rather than the seemingly lackluster and marginal Esperanto. Esperanto and Soviet Esperantists were nudged aside from even discussions of the future global language of the higher phase of communism—a future international language that Soviet linguistics insisted did not and could not yet exist under the conditions of building socialism.

The future of international socialism and socialist internationalism perhaps never seemed so much in doubt in the interwar period as it did during the years of Stalin's Purges and Terror in the late 1930s. As the historian Lisa Kirschenbaum reminds us, however, the worst and most dangerous years of Stalinist xenophobia coincided—however awkwardly—with the Spanish Civil War. International solidarity, she underscores, "coexisted, however uneasily and precariously, with the contemporary show trials and purges that promoted a very different vision of communist solidarity" during Stalin's Terror.[19] Even while Soviet soldiers fought in international brigades in Spain and even as the Soviet Union opened its doors to embrace the refugee children of war-torn Spain, at home a wave of xenophobic persecution crashed into communities of foreign communists who had built lives and careers for themselves in the Soviet Union and in the name of global communism.[20] The NKVD hounded Communist Party officials and ordinary people who had foreign connections, fluency in foreign languages, and even simply foreign-sounding last names. In this context of Stalinist xenophobia and rampant anxiety over the perceived threats of anti-Soviet conspiracy, espionage, and subterfuge, Esperantists appeared no longer as over-eager, language-loving eccentrics who liked to compose letters to foreign pen pals in an international auxiliary language. Instead, they were recast as dangerous internal enemies, as Trotskyite spies who deployed Esperanto to plot with conspirators abroad the Soviet Union's demise. Stalin's Purges and Terror did not destroy international socialism or put an end to Soviet internationalism. Stalin's Purges and Terror did, however, obliterate the Soviet Esperantist movement and with it, the Esperantists' vision of international socialism conducted in an international language designed to transcend all manner of borders, not simply linguistic ones. The demise of the Soviet Esperanto movement reflects in devastating fashion the tension between xenophobia and internationalism that predominated in the Soviet century. In particular, it emblematizes how foreign languages hung in the Soviet ideological balance as practical necessities of internationalism, conduits of desirable cultural and intellectual exchange, but also as dangerous tongues that could always potentially ignite in flames of subversion and espionage.

This book proposes that Esperanto provides a useful lens through which to examine how the global politics of language figured in the Russian Revolution and ultimately helped shape twentieth-century socialist internationalism. Scholarship on the Russian Revolution long took for granted the Bolsheviks' global pretensions. Historiographical debates within the field of modern Russian and Soviet history have focused most intensely on the domestic experiences and meanings of Russia's revolutions in 1917. In recent decades, however, scholars have endeavored to more thoughtfully place the history of Russia and the Soviet Union in global perspective and to consider the transnational and transimperial currents and relationships that have shaped Russian history. Most recently, the history of Soviet internationalism has enjoyed a veritable scholarly regeneration, opening productive avenues for understanding the construction of a twentieth-century socialist world.[21] This new scholarship on Soviet (and socialist, still more broadly) internationalism has helped to bring needed balance and perspective to international history's once overwhelmingly

Western focus.²² Scholars have illuminated the transnational networks of intellectuals, artists, and experts through which the Soviet Union channeled extraordinary efforts to exert world-historical leadership of cosmopolitan culture and international science.²³ They have revisited the vibrant history of foreign visitors' interwar pilgrimage to the Soviet Union, revealing it as a dynamic, mutual encounter and demonstrating the centrality of cultural diplomacy to the shifting goals of early Soviet internationalism.²⁴ Historians have breathed new life into the study of global communism as a way of life for ordinary men and women all over the world, a defining twentieth-century experience of proletarian internationalism that shaped individual life stories and the modern world.²⁵

Yet few scholars have asked how the dilemmas of language diversity and international communication impacted Soviet internationalism, let alone the grassroots currents of internationalism that took shape in the tumultuous late tsarist empire.²⁶ This book's uncommon focus on language politics widens the historiographical and chronological frames to consider how the late tsarist empire and early Soviet Union grappled with globalization's practical linguistic demands and the prospect of a global citizenry fluent in both an auxiliary language and shared values. Long before the Soviet Union consciously endeavored to establish Russian as a world language, Esperanto posed the option of collapsing the hierarchy of national languages on the global stage and giving ordinary people in the late tsarist empire and the early Soviet Union an international auxiliary language for communicating with comrades around the world. By exploring how Esperanto and other competing languages of internationalism shaped approaches to and imaginaries of international communication and transnational partnerships in revolutionary Russia, this book aims to highlight how the global politics of linguistic diversity distinctively shaped Soviet internationalism in its infancy. It shows how revolutionary Russia's grappling with the question of an international language sparked a variety of grassroots internationalisms among ordinary Esperantists who aspired to live as global citizens as much as Russian or Soviet ones. Revolutionary Russia's international language politics also helped pave the way for Soviet responses to Cold War contests over the power of global language and the linguistic reach and capacity of superpower status.²⁷

Esperantists may have "lost" the debates over the so-called international language question in late imperial Russia and the early Soviet Union. But they and the wider global Esperanto movement helped to generate far-reaching global conversations about language and international communication—conversations that shaped revolutionary Russia and a world that still struggles with the consequences of insistent globalization. In the hopes and the anxieties of Esperanto's first generations of acolytes, we hear echoes—albeit in an international auxiliary language long since drowned out by Global English—of precursors to our own age of internationality and entanglement.

Organization of the Book

Chapter 1 tells in a new way the story of Zamenhof and his launch of Esperanto in 1887. It explains Esperanto's imperial Russian origins, emphasizing Esperanto's underappreciated position as one of several utopian internationalist projects to compete for Russian society's attention and support in the twilight of the tsarist empire. It also situates the emergence of Esperanto against the broader backdrop of fin de siècle globalization and the keen sense of internationality that Zamenhof and many of his contemporaries in Russia and throughout the world felt in this age of anxiety and anticipation. For Zamenhof, Esperanto was always intended to serve humanity as more than a practical utility to facilitate international communication. Esperanto was the foundation for what Zamenhof envisioned as a future global moral community of new, emancipated people—comfortable with their differences and equipped with an international auxiliary language designed explicitly to transcend those differences rather than efface them.

Chapter 2 shifts to the ordinary Russian Esperantists who helped incubate Zamenhof's improbable global Esperanto movement and to create a distinctive culture of Esperantism. It explores how Esperanto provided its early adepts an outlet for epistolary and literal globe-trotting, the transnational exchange of ideas and expertise, and the forging of interpersonal relationships that defied linguistic, national, and cultural borders. In late imperial Russia and beyond its borders, Esperanto proved a ready-made vehicle for its adepts to fashion themselves into modern global citizens, at home and networked in the world. Chapter 2 explores the grassroots internationalism of the educated men and women in late imperial Russia who pioneered the social networking and publishing ventures that gave life to the early transnational Esperantist movement in the quarter century prior to the outbreak of the First World War. Theirs, I argue, was a patriotic cosmopolitanism that reflects a broader but typically overlooked ordinary internationalism that shaped late imperial Russian culture.

Russia's revolutions in 1917 opened the door to new possibilities for Russia and the world. The Bolsheviks pursued their revolution intending to unite the global proletariat in the construction of socialism. These plans for global revolution raised urgent practical questions about language diversity and international communication. Young socialist Esperantists were eager to deploy Esperanto in the service of world revolution and urged its adoption by the Communist International (Comintern) from the moment of its founding in 1919. In Chapter 3, I explain the Bolsheviks' evolving approach to the politics of language diversity in their struggle to kickstart global proletarian revolution in the interwar period.

While denied an institutional foothold within the Comintern, Soviet Esperantists worked tenaciously during the relatively hospitable New Economic Policy era (1921–8) to campaign for Esperanto's unique contributions to early Soviet cultural diplomacy. Chapter 4 examines how the Union of Soviet Esperantists endeavored to use Esperanto by means of emerging mass media, transnational Esperantist networks and institutions, and international postal services to promote Soviet achievements abroad. At home, they proudly declared themselves to be revolutionary comrades without borders— uniquely equipped to defy the linguistic and national boundaries that separated and buffered relations between ordinary Soviet citizens and the USSR's potential allies abroad. Yet, as I show in the chapter, the Esperantists' theoretical "borderlessness" proved dangerously out of sync with the official goals of Soviet cultural diplomacy, which was *premised* on the very real borders—ideological, linguistic, and national—that the embattled Soviet state was increasingly invested in surveilling, policing, and upholding.

Chapter 5 explores the Stalinist endeavor to master foreign language learning. It examines an overlooked aspect of Stalin's industrial revolution—the Soviet state's launch in 1928 of its "Foreign Languages to the Masses!" campaign. Industrialization demanded that Soviet citizens be able to access and comprehend blueprints, manuals, and scientific expertise that was largely unavailable to them in the Russian language. Soviet citizens were exhorted to study English, German, and French—so-called living foreign languages deemed essential to Soviet industrial success. Throughout the Stalinist 1930s, the Soviet Union was engaged in wide-ranging debate over foreign language study and methods of international communication. Soviet considerations of language, international communication, and the transnational exchange of expertise revolved around the practical needs of Stalin's five-year plans. Yet ideological concerns loomed large. During these years, Soviet linguists, officials, foreign language enthusiasts, and even Stalin himself engaged in a robust theoretical discussion about Marxism-Leninism's prediction of a coming international language under the conditions of fully developed communism. Soviet Esperantists participated actively in these wider discussions—even as Esperanto was increasingly rejected as useful for the Soviet present let alone the global communist future. By the time the Communist Party of the Soviet Union (CPSU) and Soviet society caught up to the Esperantists in insisting on the urgency of deciding the Soviet Union's relationship to foreign language learning and questions of international language, the Esperantists were already on the defense, struggling to find a respectable even if small place for Esperanto in the Soviet march toward communism in an increasingly hostile and dangerous geopolitical climate.

In the late 1930s, the Stalinist state deemed Esperanto a language of treason and its adepts—traitors, Trotskyites, and spies. The epilogue provides a microhistory of the Soviet Esperantists who were either executed or banished to the Gulag for using Esperanto as an alleged language of espionage. The Purges and Terror marked an important shift in Soviet internationalism, one that foreclosed the Esperantists' prior dreams of camaraderie and collaboration transacted in an international language that defied earthly borders. The death of Esperanto under Stalin emblematizes in dramatic and tragic fashion the ambiguous premium placed on foreign languages and the often precarious position of their speakers in the larger history of Soviet internationalism.

1

A Universal Language for a Globalizing World

In 1887, the first Esperanto primer was published in Warsaw, having cleared tsarist censors for sale throughout the Russian empire. The book, *International Language: An Introduction and Full Textbook for Russians*, was modestly priced and pseudonymously authored by "Doctor Esperanto" (Doctor Hopeful). Doctor Esperanto was Lazar' Liudovik Zamenhof (1859–1917), a Jewish subject of the Russian empire. In the introduction to *International Language*, Zamenhof insisted that Esperanto would tear down the linguistic barriers dividing humanity, allowing the world's diverse peoples to better understand each other's values, customs, and worldviews. As a "neutral" and "auxiliary" language, it would make it possible for the world's "peoples to come together in one family."[1] His international language was the best solution to the modern dilemmas of Babel because it was uncommonly easy to master. "*The entire grammar of my language can be learned perfectly in the course of* one hour," Zamenhof boasted.[2]

In his pursuit of an international language that could solve humankind's spiritual and practical problems, Zamenhof was not alone. Zamenhof appealed to many of his contemporaries who believed an international language was necessary to overcome the curse of Babel. Fin de siècle Europe exhibited a widely shared craving for an international language that could facilitate commerce, travel, diplomacy, science, and the international exchange of ideas and expertise.[3] Zamenhof and his constructed language came of age, after all, in an era of keenly felt globalization and rapid social change. The late nineteenth and early twentieth centuries witnessed a marked "international turn" in how men and women asserted and imagined themselves in the world.[4] Among them were Zamenhof and his fellow Esperantists.

While Zamenhof belonged to an era of self-conscious globalization, he also belonged—however unhappily—to the imperial Russian political culture to which he was native. In the first Esperanto primer, Zamenhof tellingly wrote:

> Anyone who has attempted to live in a city inhabited by people of different, mutually antagonistic nations (*natsii*) has no doubt appreciated what an enormous service would be rendered to humanity by an international language that *does not interfere in the domestic life of peoples* (*narodov*) and that could, at the very least, serve as the language of government and community life in countries with a population that speaks different languages.[5]

This was the vision of not just any idealist in the late nineteenth century but of a young Jewish man whose politics were profoundly shaped by his imperial Russian milieu.

Zamenhof's politics were largely overlooked or downplayed in early accounts of Esperanto and its successes in late nineteenth- and early twentieth-century Europe. The first biographies of Zamenhof, written by admiring Esperantists, tended more toward hagiography than historicism. As such, they emphasized Zamenhof's personality as an idealist and humanitarian more than they diagnosed his politics or deconstructed the sources of inspiration of his politics.[6] Yet scholars seeking to better appreciate Esperanto's place in world history have recently reconsidered Zamenhof as a political actor—an ideologue as much as an idealist. In particular, they have placed Zamenhof's Jewishness at the center of their accounts of what motivated an obscure oculist in Warsaw to launch an international auxiliary language in a bid to transform humankind.[7]

This chapter tells a new history of Esperanto—one that places Esperanto and its Jewish creator squarely in their imperial Russian context. That Zamenhof was a subject of the tsarist empire, and that this fact mattered, has long been acknowledged in the lean literature on Esperanto's history. Yet it has scarcely been explained *why* and *how* Zamenhof's status as a Jewish subject of the Russian empire mattered. Scholarship on the history of Esperanto has largely presupposed an imperial Russia that was flatly autocratic, oppressive, and especially cruel to its Jews.[8] The late Russian empire thus registers in the historiography on Esperanto as a one-dimensional backdrop painted in the muted tones of "authoritarian essentialism."[9] This chapter will explore how and why Esperanto's ideological vision of a reconciled humanity was born in late imperial Russia's multiethnic and multiconfessional borderlands and shaped by this autocratic empire's layered fin de siècle crises.

As late imperial Russia's tsars and bureaucrats struggled to cope with the challenges of a globalizing and industrializing world, its growing intelligentsia pursued a variety of creative and radical attempts to reimagine the world and Russia's place within it. Zamenhof joined his fellow intelligentsia elites as they agonized over Russia's past, present, and future. With Esperanto, Zamenhof contributed his own utopian project to the Russian intelligentsia's litany of wide-ranging schemes and philosophical visions for a radically liberating future. An international language that all would need to learn in addition to their native tongue(s)—Esperanto—was Zamenhof's utopian vision for a harmonious empire of humanity, a moral community of global citizens.

Esperanto's Russian origin story also highlights a specific brand of fin de siècle internationalism that has long been overshadowed historiographically by its competing radical utopian visions in late imperial Russia, such as nihilism, populism, and Russian Marxism. Esperanto was, for many in late imperial Russia and Europe more broadly, an attractive utopian program for all the world's peoples to unite in a global moral community built on human equality and made possible by an international auxiliary language. Esperanto also offered an exciting means of participating in a rapidly globalizing world and making connections across its national, linguistic, and ideological borders. This chapter explains how the unique transnational encounters and internationalist visions that Esperanto inspired were rooted in the multiethnic, multilingual, and multiconfessional borderlands of an empire in crisis, an empire home to people like Zamenhof who were imagining alternative futures for Russia and the world.

Fathers and Sons

In 1859, Lazar' (Liudovik) Markovich Zamenhof was born into a Jewish family in the expansive, multiethnic Russian empire. Zamenhof was born in the town of Bialystok, to be precise. This was a fact of enormous consequence. In Zamenhof's telling, his birthplace fundamentally shaped both his evolving worldview and his drive to create for the world an international auxiliary language uniquely capable of reconciling the fractures dividing humankind. Located on the western edge of the Pale of Settlement, Bialystok was a growing industrial town populated by Poles, Jews, Germans, Lithuanians, Roma, and Ukrainians—by Catholics, Russian Orthodox, and Jews. The Bialystok of Zamenhof's youth was a bustling town of polyglots in an empire that, in 1859, was on the precipice of decades of profound transformation born of political, cultural, and socioeconomic tumult that shook that empire's very foundations.

Located just beyond the eastern border of Congress Poland and falling within Russia's Grodno Province, young Zamenhof's Bialystok was a rapidly growing regional center within the tsarist empire's Pale of Settlement. The stunning tempo of Bialystok's industrial and demographic growth in the nineteenth century owed to its status as a center of the textile industry in imperial Russia's western borderlands. At the time of Zamenhof's birth, multiethnic Bialystok was undergoing a striking demographic change. In the span of the nineteenth century, Bialystok's Jewish population "increased almost thirteen-fold."[10] Much of this population growth owed to the steam engine of Jewish business in the region which accelerated the growth of local capital, stimulated Jewish migration from outlying villages to Bialystok itself, and gave rise, in the late nineteenth century, to Bialystok's own increasingly self-conscious and vocal Jewish working class. By the late 1860s, Jews owned nearly half of Bialystok's textile factories. Jewish entrepreneurs also produced and marketed soap, leather, and beer. By century's end, Bialystok's Jews constituted a large majority within a city that was outfitted with two synagogues, three Jewish cemeteries, a large Jewish hospital, a Jewish old-age home, and a wide range of other Jewish communal and cultural institutions catering to a variety of religious and political outlooks.[11]

Zamenhof's family, however, was not represented in Bialystok's expanding Jewish business sector. Zamenhof's father, Mark Zamenhof, was a largely self-taught language teacher and, by all accounts, a stern paterfamilias. In Bialystok, he began his teaching career as a private tutor but later gained a post teaching languages at a Jewish school for girls.[12] Eventually, he would publish a German language primer, *A Textbook of the German Language for Russian Young People* (Warsaw, 1871).[13] One Zamenhof biographer has described Mark as a "Russophile" who "had abandoned the observances of Judaism and wished to see Jews assimilated into the Gentile community."[14] Another notes the Russian-language speech that Mark Zamenhof gave in in 1868 on the occasion of the opening of a new synagogue in Bialystok. Offering his gratitude to Alexander II for his just and wise rule, Mark Zamenhof also exhorted his fellow Jews of the tsar's empire to work toward their own good-faith integration into the imperial social order. "We should no longer distance ourselves from our brothers the Russians, among whom we live" Mark Zamenhof intoned, "but share with them, equally, all the rights of this country, for our happiness and well-being."[15] Reputed Russophile and self-identifying proponent of Jewish Enlightenment (Haskalah), Mark was a Jewish striver who believed his family, coreligionists, and fellow inhabitants of the Pale would do well to prove themselves "useful" to the empire to which they belonged. The Zamenhofs were among many Jewish families in late imperial Russia who, as historian Benjamin Nathans has shown, were looking "beyond the Pale" and seeking integration into a social order that, they hoped, would soon discontinue the empire's "castelike isolation" of its Jewish subjects.[16] Mark's early career and long-term professional trajectory reflects this commitment to assimilation—an assimilation that in his own life and career he never seems to have divorced from the question of language or the skills of multilingualism.

The Zamenhof family primarily spoke Russian at home, but all—parents and children—were also native speakers of Polish and Yiddish. This was a fact entirely unremarkable for the Zamenhofs' time as well as for their local and imperial milieus. Bialystok demanded of its inhabitants multilingualism as a basic fact of life. As Esther Schor so aptly puts it, in Zamenhof's Bialystok, "multilingualism was not the preserve of the educated; it was the way one bought eggs, greeted policemen, prayed, and gossiped."[17] Looking back on his childhood, however, Zamenhof would later more ominously claim that in the Bialystok of his youth, multilingualism served primarily as a mode of hurling insults and sowing mistrust. Bialystok's "daily life," he argued, "was poisoned by the bickerings and animosities that arose out of this diversity of tongues."[18]

Multilingualism provided the inhabitants of Bialystok, no doubt, with the skills necessary to effectively buy eggs *and* hurl insults. Bialystokers' polyglottism certainly also proved useful in an era that for many in the late nineteenth century felt, looked, and sounded ever more expansive, more global. People, goods, and ideas flowed into Bialystok in its bustling "long nineteenth century," entangling the city and its inhabitants in an array of novel transnational networks and imagined communities. As their horizons widened, many of Bialystok's inhabitants increasingly felt their lives pinched and constrained in this industrial hub in the borderlands of an empire that, for Jews especially, felt ever more inhospitable. Droves of native Bialystokers in these years also abandoned their hometown for alternative futures elsewhere and their language skills surely helped many of them on their way. Thousands of Bialystok's Jews migrated in search of new lives elsewhere in the Russian empire or, in the aftermath of the pogroms that rocked the Pale in the tsarist twilight, in Europe, Palestine, or the Americas.[19]

For their own part, the Zamenhofs departed Bialystok in 1873 when Zamenhof was just thirteen, but they did not move far. The family took up residence in the Jewish quarter of Warsaw, where the striver Mark had secured a post teaching languages.[20] The young Zamenhof enrolled in a prestigious gymnasium where he exhibited a love for languages that soon rivaled that of his father. In Bialystok, Zamenhof had studied both German and French in elementary school. In Warsaw, he was able to study Latin and Greek and, later, some English too. Before long, the young Zamenhof's love for languages began to worry his father.

While still in secondary school, Zamenhof first began scheming to create a universal language for all mankind. In a letter written to a colleague in 1895, Zamenhof explained that his study of Latin and Greek had moved him to near ecstasy. "I dreamt," he wrote, "that some day I should travel about the world and in fiery words persuade the nations to revive one of these languages for common use. Afterward, I do not remember just how, I arrived at the firm conviction that this was impossible and I commenced to dream of a *new*, artificial language." Zamenhof began tinkering with grammar and syntax, suffixes and roots. He obsessively studied and considered the characteristics of the languages in his repertoire: Russian, Polish, Yiddish, German, French, Latin, Greek, and English. The complexity of living human languages at times "terrified" him, he admitted, and even tempted him to do "away with dreams!" And still, Zamenhof explained, he dreamed and experimented with language construction.[21]

Before long, the schoolboy Zamenhof had actually created a language—a prototype for what would ultimately become Esperanto. Yet his father worried that his son had become an obsessive, distracted from the profitable use of his time on schoolwork. It did not help matters that a teacher told the elder Zamenhof that his son was clearly teetering on the edge of some "incurable madness."[22] The priorities of father and son, language lovers both, were at fundamental odds. While Zamenhof's precocious goal was to create an international language that would reconcile the world's fractured peoples, his father's unrelenting goal was for young Zamenhof to gain entrance to medical school in one of the empire's capitals, St. Petersburg or Moscow.

His son's university education was Mark Zamenhof's solution to the dilemma of being Jewish in the Russian empire. One of the many changes initiated by Alexander II in the Great Reform era was the decision, in 1861, "to grant Jewish university graduates the rights and privileges of their Gentile counterparts—including unrestricted residence and choice of occupation."[23] For Mark, his son's successful completion of university was more than a pathway to secular enlightenment and professional security. It was a pathway to integration—to freedom from the Pale and the wider complex of disabilities and restrictions traditionally placed on Jewish subjects of the tsarist empire. Mark was but one of many Jewish parents in late imperial Russia who, in the wake of Alexander II's monumental reforms, embraced their children's university education as a guarantor of relative freedom within, and civic belonging to, the Russian fatherland.[24]

Each in their own way, father and son sought to triumph over difference—linguistic, religious, cultural, and socioeconomic. They both felt the strain, and the humiliation, of the tsarist empire's structures of particularism. In imperial Russia, legal and social categories of difference—estate, confession, ethnicity—defined the terms of civic belonging, established tsarist subjects' obligations and privileges (if any), and set the parameters for their possible social, economic, and geographic mobility. Mark Zamenhof wanted his son to escape the Pale of Settlement and climb the social and professional ladders of the tsar's empire. Lazar' wanted to create a universal language that would tear down the social and ethnic hierarchies and antagonisms that he felt, even at this young age, to define his place in the tsarist empire and thus in the world. Both desires are representative of "the Jewish encounter with late imperial Russia" that Benjamin Nathans has shown was in large measure oriented toward assimilation and integration.[25] In Warsaw, both father and son were still looking for a way out of Bialystok, searching for a way into an empire and a world that did not insist on Jewish restrictions and the Pale.

In 1879, Mark's vision won out, and young Zamenhof departed Warsaw to begin his medical studies at Moscow University. Prior to his departure, his father demanded that he leave his notebooks of language construction behind for safekeeping—from distraction, from potential harm. It was time, the father instructed the son, to focus on his medical training and his professional future. He would have time after he completed his studies to return to his pet language project, preferably as a hobby. Zamenhof later learned that his father had promptly burned his notebooks after his departure for Moscow.

Burning Questions

In Moscow Zamenhof found new outlets for considering a complex of questions—personal and avowedly political—that had vexed him in one shape or another since his early childhood in Bialystok. These were the very same questions, he would later explain, that led him to pursue the creation of an international auxiliary language that would promote mutual understanding across the national, racial, linguistic, and socioeconomic walls that divided humanity. Zamenhof remembered the Bialystok of his youth as a town in which Jews were rejected and maligned by Polish, Russian, and German neighbors who looked upon one another with scarcely less distrust and enmity than they looked upon the Jews. From the window of his parents' humble house, he claimed, he regularly watched Bialystok's Jewish inhabitants spat upon and abused. At the marketplace, he witnessed sneers and jeers. Through his courtyard and on his streets, accusations of Jewish blood libel swirled.[26] Bialystok was the setting for Zamenhof's first conscious experiences of anti-Semitism and where he first grappled with Europe's larger Jewish Question.

Once in Moscow, Zamenhof found himself untethered from the Pale, Warsaw's Jewish Quarter, and his father's authority. He not only remained fixated on his international language goals but also for the first time entered public debates over what futures could and should lie ahead for Jews in Russia and throughout the world. Young Jews like Zamenhof, frustrated and humiliated by the anti-Semitism that structured their lives, urgently searched for a solution to the Jewish Question. In Moscow, Zamenhof began to actively participate in the local chapter of *Hibbat Zion* (Lovers of Zion).[27] As he explained to *The Jewish Chronicle* in 1907:

> I was always deeply interested in the social life of my people, and in my youth I was an enthusiastic political Zionist. That was long before Herzl came upon the scene, and before the idea of a Jewish State became popular among Jews. People mocked at me when I declared that we ought to have a land of our own.[28]

Zamenhof soon became convinced that the answer to his and his fellow Jews' plight was to build a new Jewish homeland in North America. Emancipation required building a home from scratch, far from the Old World that had so consistently denied Jews dignity and belonging.

In fall 1881, however, Zamenhof abruptly departed Moscow University and returned to his parents' home in Warsaw. He had excelled in his studies during his two years in Moscow; it was not academic failure that prompted his departure.[29] Although he claimed that this abrupt move owed to his father's financial difficulties, there can be little doubt that the upheavals in the Russian empire following the assassination of Alexander II in March 1881 prompted Zamenhof's transfer to medical school at the University of Warsaw.[30] These upheavals included the pogroms that swept the Pale of Settlement throughout the year 1881 and that continued into 1883, leaving in their wake not only physical destruction of Jewish homes, lives, and businesses but also growing Jewish disillusionment with the promise of integration into Russian society. Many within Russian society blamed Jews not only for the tsar's assassination but also for nearly all the societal ills afflicting the tsarist empire. This outbreak of anti-Semitic violence, unprecedented in Russia's nineteenth century, marked a turning point in modern Russian and world history, as the pogroms prompted many Jews throughout Russia to pursue an array of increasingly radical solutions to what appeared an ever more intractable Jewish Question.[31]

Young Zamenhof was among those Jews in the western borderlands of the Russian empire who not only faced the immediate threat of this anti-Semitic violence but also had their worldviews profoundly shaken by the pogroms. In late December 1881, a fresh wave of street violence broke out in Warsaw. Jewish bodies were bruised and beaten, windows were shattered, and broken furniture littered the city streets. Like many of their neighbors in Warsaw's Jewish Quarter, the Zamenhofs sought safekeeping from the violence and disorder. They hid in their cellar throughout the three days of chaos. Lazar' emerged from that cellar, it appears, outraged and emboldened. He channeled his anger through his pen.[32]

In January and February of 1882, an impassioned essay titled, "What, Ultimately, Is to Be Done?" appeared in serial form in one of imperial Russia's Jewish newspapers, *Razsvet*.[33] The essay's title was almost certainly a conscious nod to the most consequential work of radical literature published in imperial Russia during the era of Great Reforms: Nikolai Chernyshevskii's *What Is to Be Done?* (1863). The essay's author, writing under the pseudonym Gamzefon, was young Zamenhof. With palpable anguish, Zamenhof in his essay confronted the so-called Jewish Question—and the unsatisfactory solutions to it that his fellows Jews had proposed in Russia and throughout Europe more broadly. Assimilation was worse than a pipe dream, he argued. Even if it could be achieved in the manner its proponents claimed, assimilation promised to exterminate rather than liberate the Jewish people. A mass return of the world's Jews to Palestine was, Zamenhof argued, likewise a chimera rooted in efforts to "artificially sustain within ourselves memories of an ancient homeland."[34] The solution to Jews' plight of alienation and discrimination in modern Europe, Zamenhof insisted, was to relocate to an uninhabited territory that could be purchased and remade by Jews as their homeland. It was time, Zamenhof wrote,

> to gather our people, to transform them from vagrants to settled citizens, to give them a corner somewhere on this earth where they can become the predominant,

independent element, where the cities would be built by them, and the fields worked by them, and where industry would be in their hands, where they would be the proprietor, where their manners and customs would be indigenous (*mestnye*).[35]

More specifically, he proposed that the Jewish Diaspora relocate and settle in an unoccupied territory in North America, one that Jews could call their own. Such a promised land, he imagined, might be found along "the free shores of the Mississippi."[36]

In the wake of the recent pogroms, Zamenhof argued, it was time for Jews to take radical action to liberate themselves from the dead end of trying to make the best of living in tsarist Russia and its European counterparts. It was likewise painfully clear, he explained to his Russian Jewish readership, that "the Russian people do not love you, despite the fact that you have begun to name yourselves Vania and Kolia; they regard you as a plague that must be localized and from which they would be happy to be completely spared."[37] It was time to go, Zamenhof insisted. It was time for Jews, reviled and persecuted, to abandon the Russian empire that did not want them. It was time to build a homeland for Jews from scratch. Palestine—over which so much blood had already been spilled—was not a realistic answer for Jews' salvation. It was time, Zamenhof urged, to look to what he imagined might be some unpopulated, blank-slate territory in North America that could be refashioned into the Jews' own.

Zamenhof was not alone in his anguished response to the pogroms. In the tsarist empire's last decades, the fresh memory of the 1881–2 pogroms and the unabashed reality that new pogroms might break out at any time in Russia strongly influenced Jewish intellectuals and students. The Pale simmered with disaffection but also with idealistic longing for a better future for Jews and for all humanity. Jewish youth—Zamenhof among them—searched in grief and frustration for bold new solutions to the Jewish Question, which for them translated into the question of how to live with dignity in an empire that seemed to deny the very possibility of Jewish dignity. For those who did not pursue emigration as an answer to this plight, socialist and (proto-) Zionist ideologies proved ever more attractive.

The stubborn autocracy, meanwhile, proved as disinterested in reconciling with its aggrieved Jewish subjects as it did with its larger, ever-growing and ever-more-rebellious intelligentsia. The Temporary Laws of May 1882 saddled Jews in the Pale of Settlement with a new collection of punitive restrictions that proved anything but temporary.[38] In 1887, the tsarist government introduced quotas to restrict Jewish matriculation to all state-run universities and secondary schools. Given the apparent successes of higher education as a mechanism of Jewish integration in the Russian empire, the quotas were a cruel blow to those Jewish families, like the Zamenhofs, who had been doing their best to transcend the Pale and prove themselves "useful" to the autocracy.[39] "After 1882," the historian Benjamin Nathans explains, "What was true for Russian society held for the Jews as well: the government refused to make allies of, or even to prop up those Jewish elites who had been most favorably disposed to it, and thereby gave unintended nourishment to new ideas and new movements offering far more radical solutions to the Jewish predicament."[40] One of those solutions was Esperanto.

An International Language for Russia's Jews (and the World)

In an interview given to *The Jewish Chronicle* in 1907, Zamenhof reflected on the evolution of his Jewish politics as well as his mission to equip the world with a workable international auxiliary language. Candidly linking the two, he commented that "no body of men stands so much in need of an international medium of communication as the Jewish people."[41] By then, Zamenhof had been nurturing this conviction for at least two decades. With the publication of his first Esperanto primer in 1887—the same year that the tsarist government mandated quotas for Jewish matriculation at secondary and higher schools—Zamenhof seemed to have quietly exchanged his precocious dreams of Jewish salvation on the banks of the Mississippi for dreams of Jewish salvation in a world transformed by his international auxiliary language. The evolution of Zamenhof's ideological vision was, however, more complicated and zigzagged.

In the 1880s, Zamenhof's personal life and his politics were changing at what must have felt at times to be a dizzying pace. He graduated from medical school with his degree in 1885. For a couple of years, Zamenhof led a rather peripatetic life as he looked for a hospitable town in the Pale to set up his medical practice and establish a base for a hoped-for family of his own. His dream of a Jewish homeland in North America withered in the face of its harsh reception by his peers and fellow seekers of the best solution to the Jewish Question. Yet Zamenhof continued to wrestle with that question and attended *Hibbat Zion* meetings when in Warsaw. At one of these meetings, he met Klara Zilbernik—a woman from a well-off Jewish merchant family—whom he married in 1887. For a brief time, he campaigned to raise funds to help finance the construction of Jewish colonies in Palestine. All the while, his various efforts to establish a successful medical practice failed one after the other. Likewise, the proto-Zionist causes he entertained in these years reliably disappointed him and kept him in open-eyed pursuit of a better answer to the Jewish Question.[42]

All of these changes in Zamenhof's life and worldview came at a time in which the Russian empire was undergoing its own growing pains and worsening social fractures. Alexander III's so-called counter reforms accelerated the radicalization of politics across the ideological spectrum. Russia's youth, in particular, were becoming ever more engaged in what historian Richard Stites memorably described as "social daydreaming." They, and the Russian intelligentsia more broadly, contemplated their era of rapid technological, cultural, and intellectual innovation as well as the autocracy's stubborn inertia. Fed up with the status quo, they schemed creatively for an alternative future. This social daydreaming led to assassinations and arson, arrests and hangings, exiles and émigrés, but also to an array of experimental attempts to live a radical, liberating future in the tsarist here and now.[43] Zamenhof's coming of age in the 1880s coincided with the broader tumult of an empire undergoing profound socioeconomic and cultural changes—a fact that could not have been lost on Zamenhof himself. He soon emerged as one the more original of late imperial Russia's social daydreamers.

Although still a young man, Zamenhof seemed to be aging at a prematurely rapid pace. Social daydreaming was no doubt as exhausting as it was, at times, exhilarating.

Figure 1 L. L. Zamenhof (1859–1917). *Source*: Getty Images.

Zamenhof's failures to establish a moderately successful medical practice wore him down. As one biographer noted, "His hair was failing out; his never strong constitution was being undermined by overwork and trying conditions."[44] Yet his marriage to Klara Zilbernik in 1887 introduced to Zamenhof's life more than hope for domestic happiness. The couple took up residence in Warsaw, where he had recently begun an ophthalmology practice. Klara's father had pledged a substantial dowry and the family agreed that a large portion of this dowry should be used to finance the publication of the primer for Zamenhof's international auxiliary language. Mark Zamenhof, by now working as a censor of Hebrew language books in the tsarist bureaucracy, is said to have convinced a colleague that his son's manuscript was "no more than a harmless eccentricity."[45]

The prematurely aging Zamenhof was nearly 28 years old when his *International Language* was published in its Russian-language original in late July 1887. He all but immediately began working on translating the primer into Polish, French, and German. By early 1888, Doctor Esperanto's brochure had been published not only in Polish, French, and German, but also in the English language.[46] The Russian edition of the book went into its second printing within six months of the first. By 1890, Hebrew, Yiddish, Swedish, Lithuanian, Danish, Bulgarian, Italian, Spanish, and Czech editions of the primer had appeared.[47] Klara's dowry was exhausted. "At the end of 1889," Zamenhof wrote, "we were left without a kopeck."[48] Doctor Esperanto reached out to the world with an ever-widening embrace and ever more empty pockets. Privately, Zamenhof hoped his little book would especially come to the aid of his fellow Jews.

In his 1907 interview with *The Jewish Chronicle*, Zamenhof explained that it was in search of a solution to the Jewish Question that he pursued the publication of his international language project in 1887. Fellow Jews had laughed at his earlier vision of a Jewish homeland built anew in some uncharted North American territory. Despite his best efforts to be persuaded by its various proponents, Zionism struck him as a recipe for disaster for the Jewish Diaspora. In the years following the pogroms of 1881–2, Zamenhof had become convinced that what was needed was a solution for the Jewish Question that was rooted in a universal language and universalist ideals. An international auxiliary language would be the tool with which Jews would collapse ghetto walls, transcend the boundaries of the Pale, reach out to one another, and ultimately reconcile with the world's diverse peoples—including Jews' current oppressors. He explained to his interviewer, "Primarily it was in the interests of my coreligionists that I invented this language…. Had I not been a Jew, the idea of a future cosmopolitanism would not have exercised such a fascination over me." He had always been, he insisted, "a devoted son of my unfortunate Jewish people, and whenever my task seemed hopeless I had only to think of my coreligionists, speechless and therefore without hope of culture, scattered over the world, and hence unable to understand one another."[49]

Yet in 1887, Zamenhof muted his Jewish politics. In the publication of what Esperantists would later call the *Unua Libro*, the *First Book*, Zamenhof did not directly appeal to Russia's Jews or to Jews more broadly. He scarcely acknowledged that he had conceived of his international auxiliary language as anything more than a novel technology designed, like the telegraph or the railway, to facilitate the globalization of his patently modern, self-consciously international age. Zamenhof introduced his international language as the ideal form of a public utility that modern humankind needed to exchange information, goods, and ideas across borders.[50]

In the *Unua Libro*, Zamenhof only made oblique reference to the much broader political and spiritual agenda that he had invested in his language. He vaguely imagined a world made more harmonious by communication in an international auxiliary language. He spoke, indirectly, of the experience of living in a multiethnic city and a multiethnic empire and how such an experience would lead any reasonable person to crave an international auxiliary language to help promote domestic harmony among "a population that speaks different languages."[51] Zamenhof in 1887 held back from explaining how his personal experience as a Jew living in the tsarist empire had led him to invest his wife's dowry in a bid to improbably transform the world. Only once Esperanto gained adherents in his home country did Zamenhof begin overtly politicking for Esperanto as an intended balm for ethnic hatreds of the kind he had experienced as a Jew in imperial Russia.

Tsarist Babel, Bialystok Global

In addition to the *Unua Libro*'s explanation and justification for the international language offered within it, Doctor Esperanto included in the publication two pages of small, tear-out promissory notes. "I, the undersigned," the coupons read, "promise to learn the proposed language of Doctor Esperanto if it will be shown that ten million people publicly give the same promise." On their obverse were blanks in which the signatories were to write their names and addresses. Once completed, the promises were to be sent via post to Doctor Esperanto, care of L. Zamenhof of Warsaw. Extra coupons were to be shared with "friends and acquaintances" so that they, too, could make the pledge and join in the number of the ambitiously hoped-for first ten million pioneers.[52] At the time, Zamenhof's own city of Warsaw housed a population of little more than a half million. Doctor Esperanto was hopeful indeed.

As he waited for millions of promissory notes to arrive in his name, Zamenhof worked to build his ophthalmology practice and to support his growing family. He also regularly placed advertisements for "the international language Esperanto" and its original textbook in the popular Russian-language journal *Niva*. They appeared alongside ads for violins, chocolate, toilet water, and Parisian beauty creams.[53] He corresponded with enthusiastic adepts of his international language, including those who offered criticisms and suggestions for its improvement. He also cultivated relationships with potential benefactors who could help bankroll the growth of what was gradually emerging as an international Esperanto movement.

Zamenhof understood that while his language did not need to garner ten million personally signed promissory notes to succeed, it would require a widening community of adepts committed to ensuring Esperanto's success as a lived language. It needed a faithful following of men and women who, with every conversation spoken and every letter exchanged, breathed new life into the language. Thus, in addition to his work advertising the language, he scrupulously counted and organized the promissory

АДРЕСЪ АВТОРА:

Господину Д^{ру} Л. Заменгофу

ДЛЯ Д-РА Эсперанто

въ ВАРШАВѢ.

или:

Al sinjor,o D^{ro} L. Zamenhof'

POR D-R,O Esperanto

en Varsovi,o.

ГЛАВНЫЙ СКЛАДЪ НАСТОЯЩЕЙ БРОШЮРЫ
(НА РУССКОМЪ ЯЗЫКѢ)
въ книжномъ магазинѣ В. А. Истомина
въ Варшавѣ.

Figure 2 Contact information for Dr. Esperanto in Warsaw as it appeared inside Zamenhof's first Esperanto primer, *Mezhdunarodnyi iazyk* (1887).

notes he received. In 1890, Zamenhof produced the first directory of the names and addresses of those who would soon come to be known as Esperantists. The directory, known as the first *Adresaro*, listed one thousand Esperantists from 266 cities in twelve countries. The geographical distribution of these first pioneering Esperantists is striking, if not surprising. Thirty of the Esperantists hailed from Germany, twenty-two from Austria-Hungary, nine from Great Britain, six from France, and four hailed from Sweden and the United States each. Two of the first Esperantists were from the Ottoman Empire, while Spain, Italy, Romania, and China provided one adept each. Of the 1,000 Esperantists listed in the first *Adresaro*, 919 were from the Russian empire.[54] The five cities home to the greatest number of known Esperantists were, in descending order, St. Petersburg, Warsaw, Odessa, Kiev, and Moscow.[55] It has been estimated that 20 percent of the Esperantists appearing in the first directory were Jewish.[56]

The first serial Esperantist publication was nonetheless inaugurated in 1889 in Nuremberg, a city that was then home to only two Esperanto speakers (at least according to the statistical information provided in the first *Adresaro*). Bankrolled initially by Christian Schmidt, the president of Nuremberg's International Language Club, *La Esperantisto* (*The Esperantist*) was, in its fitful six years of publication, largely authored and edited by Zamenhof himself. The inaugural issue featured a prospectus replicated in three columns—one column each for the German, French, and Esperanto versions of the text. The remainder of the first issue's texts were produced in German and Esperanto, side by side. Despite its German financing and publication origins, however, *La Esperantisto* was an inconsistent serial that, throughout the entirety of its short existence, primarily attracted subscribers from the Russian empire.[57] An article that appeared in an 1893 issue of *La Esperantisto* even betrayed the nascent movement's self-conscious awareness of its overwhelming Russianness. The "anomaly" of the movement's concentration in tsarist Russia, *La Esperantisto* explained, could be explained easily by the fact that more resources had thus far been spent advertising Esperanto there than elsewhere. Esperanto's popularity in Russia was not, the article insisted, reflective of some essential quality of life in the Russian empire.[58]

Zamenhof recognized that Esperanto needed to attract more than his fellow Russians and more than his fellow Russian Jews. Yet, for Zamenhof, there *was* something avowedly Russian and imperial in the origins of the language he had created. During the 1890s, Zamenhof struggled to create an Esperantist community not only within Russia but also well beyond it. By definition, Esperanto's primary purpose was to connect its speakers and make possible communication and improved understanding among the world's peoples. Even while he worked rather desperately to expand Esperanto's reach during this time, he also grew more comfortable in publicly explaining the imperial Russian sources of inspiration that had motivated him since childhood to seek a solution to the scourge of Babel. Somewhat more slowly did Zamenhof begin to acknowledge that it was not just his experience as a subject of the Russian empire that had inspired Esperanto, but also his experience as a Jewish subject of the Russian empire in particular. He demonstrated early on a keen awareness of the need to control and hone what he called "the story of the *birth* of the language."[59] In time, he realized that this story could both help and hurt efforts to grow the Esperantist movement both within but also beyond his native Russian empire.

In 1895, Zamenhof wrote a letter to fellow Russian Esperantist, Nikolai Borovko.[60] This letter came to be nearly as canonical a text of the Esperanto movement as the *Unua Libro* itself. Though ostensibly a private missive, it was soon published in *Lingvo Internacia*, a periodical based in Sweden that had filled the void left by the recent collapse of *La Esperantisto*.[61] In this soon famed "Letter to Borovko," Zamenhof offered not only the origin story for Esperanto but also a selective autobiography in miniature. Of Bialystok, Zamenhof wrote, "this place of my birth and of my childhood years gave the direction to all of my future purposes." Zamenhof's letter, however, was no wistful hymn to a mourned homeland or childhood idyll. Bialystok is rendered an accursed city, pulsing with ethnic and religious hatred. On the streets of Bialystok, Zamenhof claimed, he heard a different language spoken every which way he turned his head. Every which way he looked, he saw humiliation, animosity, and bitter conflict. Bialystok, he explained, was home to "four diverse elements: Russians, Poles, Germans, and Jews."[62] In Zamenhof's telling, the peoples of Bialystok—Russians, Poles, Germans, and Jews—were foes, not friends. It was a tsarist Babel in miniature—hopeless, fractured, confused.

"In such a city," Zamenhof lamented, "a sensitive soul feels the heavy woe of polyglottism and becomes convinced at each step that the multiplicity of languages is the sole or at least the chief cause which divides human beings."[63] Zamenhof did not mention his native fluency in multiple languages, nor did he stress the sheer normalcy of Bialystokers' multilingualism. This was history written in the tragic vein, not the banal. He emphasized how the daily life of his childhood bred disillusionment and even traumatized him. "I was educated to be an idealist," Zamenhof explained, "I was taught that all men are brothers, and yet on the street and in the market place everything caused me to feel that people did not exist; that there were only Russians, Poles, Germans, Jews, etc. This always tortured my childhood's soul." As a young man in the ethnic jumble of imperial Russia's western borderlands, he explained, he had arrived at the conviction that an international language was needed to heal humankind's fractures, and that such a language needed to "be absolutely neutral, belonging to none of the now-living tongues."[64] Yet Zamenhof's narrative had nothing explicit to say about the anguish he had felt as a Jew growing up in late imperial Russia. Embedded silences did strategic work as in his cryptic account of how, as a student in Warsaw, he came to devise his early prototype for Esperanto.

In his soon-to-be canonical account of Esperanto's birth, it was the Russian-language storefronts of his milieu that inspired what he believed was the essential ingredient of Esperanto's success: its agglutinative principle. Strolling the streets of imperial Russia's borderlands, he saw signs for the local confectionary and porter's lodge, *konditorskaia* and *shveitsarskaia*, and focused on the declensions made possible by the ending "-skaia." He explained: "I saw that the suffixes gave me the possibility of making out of one word other words which one would not have to learn separately. … I suddenly found the ground under my feet."[65] Zamenhof created Esperanto with these linguistic and cultural inputs of his native Russian language and empire at the forefront of his imagination and linguistic repertoire. Soon, he claimed, "I had written the whole grammar and a small vocabulary." This vocabulary ultimately came to be devised largely on what he called a "romance-germanic" basis.⁶⁶ This decision arose from his undeniably Eurocentric conviction that there already existed what he called an "immense storehouse of ready words, already international" at the heart of Europe's dominant languages.⁶⁷

In closing his letter to Borovko, Zamenhof heightened the melodrama of his tale. He recalled keeping his language project a secret for fear of the inevitable ridicule it would inspire. The loneliness he felt was overwhelming. "During the five and a half years of my stay in university," Zamenhof wrote, "I never spoke to anyone about the matter. This period was for me very difficult. … I hardly went anywhere or took part in anything, and the most beautiful time of life—the years of a student—for me passed most sadly." Zamenhof did not mention *Hibbat Zion*, the 1881 pogroms, or youthful dreams of a Jewish homeland on the shores of Mississippi. In this famed letter to Borovko, Zamenhof obscured as much as he revealed about the origins of Esperanto. He muted the Jewish politics that inspired him and the anguish that plagued him still. He offered a decontextualized portrait of the tsarist Babel of his youth. For more than a century after the letter's publication, many of his acolytes and biographers followed suit.

Hillelism

In his letter to Borovko, Zamenhof reflected on how it was his "sensitive soul" that had made him so attuned to the linguistic, ethnic, and religious divides that had afflicted the Bialystok of his youth.⁶⁸ Yet in late imperial Russia, one need not boast a sensitive soul to appreciate the extent to which the question of "nationality" increasingly pervaded the intellectual, political, cultural, and bureaucratic life of this overwhelmingly diverse empire. In late imperial Russia, intellectuals and tsarist administrators waded through the messy thickets of language, estate, and religion in their varied efforts to understand, define, as well as to bureaucratically manage nationality. Like Zamenhof, they centered many of their discussions of nationality on the question of language. Yet nationality was as yet an amorphous category for potential use in bureaucratic management, elite self-understanding, and political mobilization. In tsarist Russia's fin de siècle, debate swirled over the relationship between language, estate, religion, and the nature of national difference.⁶⁹

These debates came into still sharper focus when, in 1897, imperial Russia executed its first modern census, hinging its efforts to capture the ethnic ("national") diversity of the empire on the question of its subjects' language. The census's explicit questioning of the native language of the empire's diverse inhabitants was an undisguised effort to statistically "know" its ethnic composition. The statisticians who designed the census and analyzed its results treated native language, and sometimes also confession, as indicative of nationality.⁷⁰ Yet what might the question of "native language (*rodnoi iazyk*)" statistically mean when posed to Zamenhof, a native speaker of Russian, Polish, and Yiddish who had primarily spoken Russian in his Jewish family home? It was precisely subjects of the empire like Zamenhof who emblematized the shortcomings of the census's attempt at reductive simplicity. Zamenhof had long been wrestling with the questions that the census results raised about what nationality might or could mean in the multilingual and multiconfessional tsarist empire.

Zamenhof's politics, and his campaign for Esperanto in particular, reflected late imperial Russia's increasingly emphatic insistence on the political and social significance of ethnicity, and thus of one's purported "national" or "native" language. At the turn of the century, as the politicization and institutionalization of ethnicity accelerated in imperial Russian life, Zamenhof continued his best efforts to promote Esperanto at home and abroad. He nearly drove his family into bankruptcy while doing so. He also, however, undertook a renewed effort to solve the Jewish Question in Russia. This effort, though pursued pseudonymously, was divorced neither from his mission to transform the world via Esperanto nor from the obsession with the national that then increasingly saturated imperial Russian, European, and global politics. Under the pen name "Homo Sum (I am Man)," Zamenhof in 1901 offered his fellow Russian Jews a program he named Hillelism in honor of the famed Jewish scholar and that he conceived of as "a project for solving the Jewish problem."[71] With Hillelism as with his related project of Esperanto, Zamenhof's politics could never be divorced from the dilemmas confronting the Jewish Diaspora as well as the Russian empire as a whole. Zamenhof understood these dilemmas as being dependent upon global solutions, premised on a practical mechanism of transcending, *not effacing*, linguistic, ethnic, and religious difference.

With the publication of *Hillelism (Gillelizm)* in 1901, Zamenhof ended a hiatus from actively participating in Jewish political debates—a hiatus that, in his own account, had begun in 1884. In this philosophical tract, Zamenhof reviewed the lamentable contours of the Jewish Question, explained the causes of Jews' historic plight in exile, and diagnosed the failures of the various assimilationist and Zionist solutions that his fellow intellectuals had offered in vain. He sought, he explained, "to show how the Jewish question could be more effectually solved."[72] In fact, many of the arguments Zamenhof presented in *Hillelism* were those he had articulated, albeit in shorter form, in the polemics he had published in *Razsvet* in the wake of the 1881–2 pogroms. As he had in his youth, Zamenhof again insisted that neither assimilation nor Zionism presented a realistic solution to the Jews' persistent alterity in a hostile world. "All who do not confess the Jewish faith are completely alien to us (*nam chuzhdy*)," Zamenhof wrote, "despite the hundreds of years that they have lived with us on one land, shared with us one conversational language."[73] The Jewish Question, Zamenhof insisted, owed to the fact that a people united by religion had come to be defined as a separate people, a nation.

Yet, Zamenhof pronounced, Jews were an "abnormal nation." By contrast, he argued, a "normal" nation was one that "typically" shared a single language, territory, polity, and faith.[74] Jews defied this description in all regards except one. At best, he argued, they were a group of people who were scattered throughout the world and lacking a common language to unite them. There was only a common religion to affiliate them and this inhered, despite the fact that many contemporary Jews were irreligious.[75] Zamenhof argued that Jews falsely insisted that they were a coherent "people," a so-called nationality. Those who scorned Jews as alien likewise insisted that Jews were a nationality like any other. In an age in which men and women ever more militantly insisted that every people belong to a nation and that the ideal to which all nations aspire was the nation-state, Zamenhof insisted that Jews were not a nationality and not a nation.[76] "As a matter of fact," Zamenhof said bluntly, "the Jewish nation as such ceased to exist 2,000 years ago and Judaism, rightly understood, is an idea—a creed."[77]

Throughout *Hillelism*, Zamenhof argued that Europe's Jews were neither here nor there but everywhere, and everywhere they were unwanted and unwelcome.[78] "Who are we exactly?" Zamenhof asked in apparent exasperation. "We—at least under current conditions—are not Russians, nor Poles, nor Germans…. And neither are we a Jewish nation (*narod*)."[79] Jews fatally denied the reality of their precarious position, their abnormality, their false claim to nationality. They were a "shadow people," he insisted.[80] Dreaming of an ancient past, they clung to an "illusion" of nationhood that robbed them of a promising future no less than a tolerable present. Moreover, Zamenhof argued, most Jews were too "benighted" to be persuaded otherwise, and thus the Jewish intelligentsia owed it to their illiterate brethren to figure out, at long last, an effective solution to Jews' ever-worsening plight.[81]

In Zamenhof's mind, the answer was simple: Judaism needed to be reformed. The point was to shear all that was unnecessary, embrace the fundamental ethical principles of the Jewish faith, and thus to establish what Zamenhof called "a philosophically pure creed." At its heart, this creed could be summed up in the Rabbi Hillel's dictum, "Do not do unto others what is hateful to you." As he told *The Jewish Chronicle*, Hillelism demanded that Jews "preserve the various Jewish customs and ceremonials, feasts and fasts; not, however, as laws, but as traditions—as beautiful symbols of eternal truths."[82] Those truths, those core moral precepts should guide them in all their actions and outlooks on earth: Be humane to your fellow humans. Empathize with and respect others. Act in accord with your conscience, as it is "the voice of God."[83]

Hillelism was more than a project to reform Judaism and rescue Europe's Jews from prejudice and alienation. Hillelism was Zamenhof's vision of creating new people—indeed, a new people from which humanity as a whole could take the lead in transforming itself into a harmonious community of global citizens. In fulfilling the Hillelist program, Zamenhof believed, his fellow Jews would be liberating themselves both from their own pernicious illusions and their marginalized, orphan-like positions in a modern world of nations and nation-states. In the near term, Hillelism would allow its adepts, unshackled from the false nationality of Jewishness, to become a new people, a "normal" people. Over the long term, Zamenhof imagined, Hillelism would provide the pioneering institutional and philosophical framework through which all of humanity—despite the linguistic, religious, and national differences that defined it—could find common moral ground, common understanding, and indeed, shared humanity. The Hillelists would create a global moral community in which all men and women—despite their ethnic, national, or religious origins—would find fellowship and "spiritual refuge."[84]

For Zamenhof, the essential key to Hillelism, and thus to both Jews' emancipation and to the creation of a global moral community, was language. Language, he argued, was the essential basis and core prerequisite of all human communities, be they national or international. As a project of Jewish emancipation, he argued, Hillelism needed a new language for the new people it would create out of Europe's humiliated, alienated Jews. Neither Hebrew nor Yiddish, Zamenhof argued, were viable contenders for what must become the "genuine native language" of the Hillelists. He dismissed both languages with unapologetic efficiency. Modern Jews, Zamenhof claimed, did not speak ancient Hebrew and Yiddish was a jargon, hardly befitting the serious task of transforming, elevating, and emancipating Jews.[85] The Hillelists needed a "neutral, artificial" language through which Jews would regenerate and transform themselves and, ultimately, the world. Fortunately, the pseudonymous author of *Hillelism* argued, recent history had shown that a richly expressive, neutral, and phenomenally easy-to-learn international auxiliary language had recently proven itself.[86] Esperanto was ready-made for the Hillelist program meant to rescue Jews and the world.

In Zamenhof's mind, Hillelism and Esperanto were inseparable. Both were essential and indeed mutually constitutive in his vision for emancipated Jewry *and* global unity. Zamenhof's project for "solving the Jewish Question" was also a scheme for unifying humanity in shared global citizenship without demanding the eradication or denial of diversity. Doctor Hopeful imagined a new world unity within reach and a universal ethics that could inspire and bind together all the world's peoples. He anticipated a reversal of roles for Jews in world history. Hillelism, Zamenhof argued, was the "great historical mission of the Jewish people." As Jews, the Hillelists would blaze the trail to a "great and glorious future" for which their fellow humans would one day thank them. This "people of the future" would use "the language of the future" to build the foundation for "a future united humanity."[87]

If Zamenhof explicitly addressed himself to all Jews in *Hillelism*, portions of this anguished yet hopeful text spoke, at least implicitly, to his fellow Jews of the Russian empire in particular. The author's searing sense of pain at never feeling welcome in his own homeland is scarcely disguised. And while Zamenhof never makes mention of the tsarist empire's recent census, it seems obvious that the 1897 census, and the broader politicization of ethnicity in contemporary Russia, inflamed his sense of outrage as a Jew who did not feel welcome in his own homeland. Hillelism, he claimed, was designed to make sure that Jews could one day answer with pride the patently modern questions: "Who are you? What is your native language? What is your homeland?" These were questions, Zamenhof insisted, that a Jew in the tsarist empire could not answer without a reddened face, tortured answers, and a humiliated heart. Jews, he argued, could not claim Russia as their homeland and the Russian language as their native tongue without inviting contempt, pity, and/or accusations of falsehood. The Jewish pioneers of the future—his fellow Jews of Russia, he hoped—would pave the way for a Jew to answer these modern questions of ethnic, civic, and linguistic belonging and self-identification "openly and proudly.... with a raised head and with self-respect." The world would know the Jewish Question was at long last solved when the future arrived and Jews could claim the land on which they and their ancestors lived as their rightful "home."[88] They would, Zamenhof argued, feel welcome in this homeland and among their fellow human beings, no matter their origins and ethnicities. The Hillelists' homeland would ultimately be the world. They would share the globe with their fellow human beings in a unity secured by mutual respect, nurtured in a culture of universal ethics, and transacted by a universal language.

With the publication of *Hillelism*, Zamenhof anticipated the launch of a new Jewish movement that would one day inspire the whole world to seek cover in the "spiritual refuge" it offered all of humanity. Yet, in the first decade of the twentieth century, the Esperantist community grew at ever-increasing speeds while Hillelism remained a party of one. Rarely did it garner even tepid support among the Esperantists of late imperial Russia or their contemporaries abroad. Esperantists throughout the world volunteered to join what most of them embraced as an international moral community centered on Esperanto, not the moral precepts of an ancient rabbi as remixed by a Warsaw oculist aching to break free from the tensions of his native Russian empire. These Esperantists revered Zamenhof as their "prophet of idealism" and hailed him as the beloved genius who created the language that variously inspired them.[89] Yet they rejected his Hillelism as a distraction at best and a mortal threat to Esperanto at worst.

Esperanto's "Inner Idea"

In August 1905, the First World Esperanto Congress convened in Boulogne-sur-Mer, France. Zamenhof traveled from Warsaw to speak to the 688 attendees who hailed from as many as twenty countries, nearly all of them European. It was his first public appearance at an international gathering of enthusiasts of the international language he had created. He was terrified.[90] Zamenhof was visibly nervous as he approached the dais and began speaking in Esperanto to the assembled crowd. With trembling hands, he gripped his prepared speech. "Respected ladies and gentleman," Zamenhof intoned in the language of his very own construction, "I greet you, dear colleagues, brothers and sisters from the great world family, who have come together from near and distant lands, from the most diverse states of the world, to clasp hands in the name of the great idea which unites us all."[91]

The great idea of which he spoke would come to be known as the "inner idea" of Esperanto and would be enshrined in the so-called Boulogne Declaration adopted by the Congress. Zamenhof had arrived at Boulogne-sur-Mer intent on establishing this so-called "inner idea" as the fundamental ideological premise of what was rapidly becoming a nonetheless widely ecumenical Esperantist movement. He had also come prepared to end his keynote speech by reading a poem of his own writing—one that scandalized the Congress's organizers. They frantically begged Zamenhof—practically right down to the moment that he approached the dais to deliver his keynote speech—not to read his lyric "Prayer under the Green Standard." In effect, they were begging Zamenhof to keep his mouth shut about his Jewishness, his Jewish politics, and his quixotic Hillelism in particular. "We'll be ruined and a laughingstock," one despaired.[92]

Earlier that year, Zamenhof had written a private letter to one of the Congress's organizers, the French Esperantist Alfred Michaux, in which he revealed, "My Jewishness has been the main reason why, from earliest childhood, I gave myself completely to one crucial idea, one dream—the dream of the unity of mankind."[93] The letter set off alarm bells for Michaux. He promptly alerted his fellow co-organizers of the upcoming World Congress that Zamenhof was likely to give a dangerous speech full of "mysticism."[94] The members of the Congress Committee demanded that Zamenhof submit the full text of his intended speech for vetting. Zamenhof complied and when the French organizers reviewed his intended speech, they exploded in desperation and disbelief at the certain ruin Esperanto's creator now portended to bring to the movement that was just gaining steam. "He's a Jewish prophet!" one cried, while another sputtered in angst: "That Slav! Michaux will never be able to control this crazy man!"[95]

In fairness, then, Zamenhof's visible anxiety upon approach to the Congress dais had more to do than with simple stage fright. Zamenhof had been personally wounded by the Congress Committee's insistence that he tone down what they regarded as his incendiary speech—one they believed would destroy the burgeoning movement as a whole. Zamenhof is said to have been reduced to tears. He had not been prepared for the upbraiding his French colleagues had subjected him to and the unrepentant anti-Semitism of which it smacked.[96]

Still, Zamenhof gave his speech largely as he had originally intended. Lengthy and heartfelt, the speech *did* tend toward sentimentality and a certain degree of mysticism, as when he declared:

This present day is sacred. Our meeting is humble … but through the air of our hall mysterious sounds are travelling, very low sounds, not perceptible by the ear, but audible to every sensitive soul: the sound of something great that is now being born. Mysterious phantoms are floating in the air; the eye does not see them, but the soul sees them; they are images of a time to come, of a new era. The phantoms will fly into the world, will be made flesh, will assume power, and our sons and grandchildren will see them, will feel them and will have joy in them.[97]

This future joy, Zamenhof explained, was the achievement of a reunited humanity, long ago fractured by linguistic difference and the enmity it ushered into the world. The seeds of that glorious future, Zamenhof said, had been planted right here in Boulogne-sur-Mer, at this very World Congress of Esperanto. The assembled Esperantists had proven Esperanto's viability. They had demonstrated that men and women from all over the world could speak to one another using this language of reconciliation and global harmony. Invited to the Congress to celebrate Esperanto, Zamenhof arrived intent on preaching Hillelism, even if not by name.

It was not only Esperanto's international quality that made this future reunited humanity possible, Zamenhof emphasized, but also its essential nature as an auxiliary language. A native language to none in the room, Esperanto created a neutral arena in which human beings could meet and converse on an equal, mutually respectful basis. "In our meeting there are no strong nations and no weak nations," Zamenhof declared. "No one with privileges or without, no one is humiliated, no one is embarrassed." Through Esperanto, the men and women assembled had "for the first time in human history" managed to achieve true brotherhood and international harmony. Esperanto had made it possible for them to transcend their differences—ethnic, linguistic, religious—rather than deny or argue over them. They had gathered and conversed as a family reunited after a long and painful separation. "Let us be fully conscious of the full importance of this day," Zamenhof demanded, "for today, within the hospitable walls of Boulogne-sur-Mer have met not French and English, not Russians and Poles, but men and men."[98]

With this ecstatic rhetoric, Zamenhof presented to all assembled the so-called inner idea of Esperanto—a core ideological premise that the Congress in subsequent days would distill and approve in the so-called Boulogne Declaration. Regardless of whatever use Esperantists might seek to gain from the deployment of the language, Esperanto was first and foremost

> a neutral, human language which, "not intruding upon the personal life of peoples and in no way aiming to replace existing national languages," would give to people of different nations the ability to understand each other, and would be able to serve as a conciliatory language of public institutions in those lands where different peoples fight amongst each other over language issues.[99]

The linchpin of the Boulogne Declaration was its stipulation that "every other hope or idea which any Esperantist may attach to Esperantism is a purely private matter."[100]

It wasn't Zamenhof's proposed "inner idea" of Esperanto—at least as articulated in his speech—that had scandalized the Congress's Organizing Committee. Zamenhof's references to phantasmagoria no doubt rankled, but in the organizers' eyes it had not spelled certain doom for the movement. What the organizers desperately hoped to avoid, above all else, was for Zamenhof to frame Esperanto and its inner idea in religious terms and, even more specifically, in Jewish terms. They wanted an Esperanto divorced from Zamenhof's Jewish politics and from his Hillelism in particular. Despite their vigorous protests, however, Zamenhof read his "Prayer under the Green Standard" at the conclusion of his speech, dedicating it vaguely, but in the spirit of Hillelism, to "that high moral Power, which every human being has in his heart."[101] He submitted, however, to his French colleagues' demands that he remove the prayer's final stanza: "Christians, Jews, or Mahometans, We are all children of God."[102] When he finished speaking, the crowd erupted in applause and boisterous cries of "Vivu Esperanto" and "Vivu Zamenhof!" The French Esperantists of the organizing committee breathed a sigh of relief.

For the moment, Zamenhof settled on a certain degree of ideological vagueness in his speech at the Boulogne Congress. In relenting to the demands of the Organizing Committee, Zamenhof merely continued his long-standing manner of politicking in the safe mode of decontextualized politics and careful silences. Yet in his much-feared speech, Zamenhof had celebrated the fact that here, in the "Esperantoland" that the congress had created, he did not feel himself "a member of any one nation, but a simple human being." Speaking Esperanto, he claimed, "I do not belong to any national or sectarian religion, but am a simple human being." Zamenhof and the members of the Organizing Committee knew that these were the hopes of a Jew who hoped yet to deploy Esperanto as a means of solving Europe's anguished Jewish Question in a simultaneous bid to transform humanity as a whole. In post-Dreyfus-Affair France, in Boulogne-sur-Mer in the summer of 1905, Zamenhof and his French colleagues agreed it was best to keep quiet about the inspiration for Esperanto's "inner idea."[103]

The Boulogne Congress was a pivotal moment in the history of Esperanto, and of a burgeoning global, transnational community of Esperantists in the early twentieth century. It was the first of the international Esperanto congresses that have, in a variety of organizational guises, convened nearly every year since.[104] The Boulogne Congress solidified Zamenhof's international celebrity—at least among a growing number of adoring Esperantists who, against his wishes, liked to refer to him as the "majstro," or master. Zamenhof's "exaggeratedly bookish" image was itself marketed to (and by) the Esperantists, for whom his "frail build, modest demeanour, neatly trimmed beard, [and] horned-rimmed eyeglasses" became iconic.[105] Despite the acrimony and hand-wringing behind the scenes, the Congress was also crucial in that it helped to further elevate its French organizers as leaders of the growing transnational Esperantist community in their own right. "In a short time," Roberto Garvia explains, "Esperanto had shifted its center of gravity from Russia to France." It had done so with serious implications for the movement as a whole. By the time the Boulogne Congress met in 1905, France was home to the greatest number of Esperantists; French names swelled the Esperantist directory that Zamenhof continued to regularly publish. France was also home to Hachette, the publisher that provided the Esperantists (including Zamenhof) with lucrative contracts that helped to subsidize and grow the expanding international Esperanto movement. Imperial Russia may have been Esperanto's birthplace and Russians the incubators of the Esperanto movement in its earliest and most vulnerable years, but in the early twentieth century it was France that was seen as the hub of global Esperantism.[106]

France's dominant role has had consequences not only for the growth of the Esperanto movement in the early twentieth century, but also for how its history has been narrated and understood ever since. France came to dominate not only the Esperantist movement but also attempts to historicize it. The Boulogne Congress indeed proved a crucial moment in the history of Esperanto and of Zamenhof's own life trajectory. Yet the historiography has underestimated why and how events back at home, in the Russian empire, must have weighed on Zamenhof during his dramatic time in France. While Zamenhof was tussling with his French comrades behind the scenes and celebrating the success of his international language with the Esperantists assembled in Boulogne, the Russian empire was consumed by revolution. Decades of widening societal fractures were laid bare for all to see in Russia's 1905 Revolution—a revolution that looked and felt to many who lived through it like a civil war. At the time of the Boulogne Congress in August 1905, revolution simmered in Russia while, in New Hampshire, Sergei Witte led Russia's delegation in the negotiations that would lead to the Treaty of Portsmouth and conclude the Russo-Japanese War.[107]

Russia's humiliating defeats in the Russo-Japanese War had, long before the Boulogne Congress met in France, inflamed Russian public opinion and ignited widespread outrage and exasperation with the autocracy. The political violence perpetrated by the tsarist authorities against peaceful protesters in St. Petersburg on what swiftly came to be known as Bloody Sunday in January 1905 shocked the Russian public but also sent its many segmented constituencies into furious revolutionary agitation. For Zamenhof, the revolutionary upheavals of his native empire shaped his experience of 1905's greatest historical significance. The Boulogne Congress was no doubt a triumph for Zamenhof, but it was also a temporary escape from his more mundane reality in 1905: that of an imperial subject experiencing a cycle of uncertainty, exhilaration, fear, disillusionment, and hope in a time of unprecedented political ferment in an empire in crisis. As Zamenhof prepared for the Boulogne Congress, his homeland convulsed with revolution as its divided population went on strike, lit fires, seized manorial property, creatively organized grassroots political organizations, and shouted anti-Semitic slogans in xenophobic, far-right demonstrations.

Against this backdrop of Russia's 1905 Revolution, Zamenhof concluded that it was time to unite the world family before it was too late. It was time to establish Esperantoland, a global community of Esperanto speakers that transcended humankind's divisive borders. It was time to widen Esperantoland's welcoming embrace, and to reunite humanity before it was irreparably torn apart.

From the Ashes of 1905: An Empire of Humanity

In November 1905, several months after returning to Warsaw from Boulogne, Zamenhof wrote to one of his Esperantist colleagues in Paris to politely decline an offer for personal refuge from the violence and strife of what would come to be known as tsarist Russia's 1905 Revolution. Zamenhof wrote, despairingly:

> Life in our country and especially in our city is now indeed terrible; we are all very overwrought, the whole day is full of anxieties and I am quite unable to do anything. I hope, though, that everything will come right. The mutual hatred of nations and religions, terrorism, hypocrisy, and so on are growing terribly.[108]

Zamenhof underestimated just how bad things would get in the aftermath of Nicholas II's issuance of his October Manifesto. In a matter of just a few weeks after the tsar had sought to defuse the revolution by promising the empire's subjects an array of civil and political rights, hundreds of pogroms had ignited in Russia's western borderlands. Thousands were injured. As a result of the pogroms that had swept through the Pale in October 1905 alone, as many as four thousand died. Several hundred more pogroms would follow before the close of 1906, including a particularly shocking outbreak of violence against Jews in Zamenhof's hometown of Bialystok.[109] Russia's 1905 Revolution dramatically shaped Zamenhof's politics. Few historians have fully considered how integral Russia's "dress rehearsals" in 1905—rehearsals of civil war and of revolution broadly conceived—were for this pivotal moment in Zamenhof's intellectual and philosophical trajectory at a time typically referred to in the literature as Esperanto's "French period."

The 1905 Revolution, more broadly, is essential for understanding the imperial Russian origins of Esperanto. The strikes, violence, and radical politicking that characterized the 1905 Revolution should be seen as the culmination of the socioeconomic, political, and ethnic fractures that had been eroding the stability of the stubborn autocratic empire for several decades. The 1905 Revolution was the result of the very same societal fractures in imperial Russia that had animated Zamenhof's avowedly political pursuit of Esperanto from the start. Late imperial Russia was a vast empire that historically had sought (and often found) political strength in the entrenchment and strategic celebration of its population's enormous variation by estate, confession, language, and ethnicity.[110] It was also an empire that, especially in the era inaugurated by the Great Reforms, energetically sought a revolution from above that was designed explicitly to reinforce and strengthen the bonds of civic unity seen as necessary for Russia's success in a modern world of industrialization, nationalism, and globalization.[111] In the late nineteenth and early twentieth centuries, Zamenhof and Russia's tsars were—broadly speaking—wrestling with the same question: how to unify people otherwise markedly divided by language, religion, ethnicity, estate, and class.

In the wake of Alexander II's shocking assassination, his successors Alexander III and Nicholas II stubbornly devoted themselves to the preservation of autocratic power. In the final decades of imperial Russia, the autocracy worked to viciously suppress the perceived sedition of a growing intelligentsia that yearned to participate in Russia's regeneration, to give voice to its growing schemes to save Russia and the world, and to secure a social unity that—across the political and socioeconomic spectrum of the empire—appeared ever more painfully beyond reach. Diverse constituencies throughout late imperial Russia ached to heal the divides that, nearly everyone agreed, had left it fatally fractured and weak. When viewed in this widened lens, Zamenhof and Esperanto rightly emerge as stark emblems of this painful time in Russia's history, a time when educated society obsessively anguished and schemed in a search for healing, unity, and a wide array of utopian dreams.[112]

Zamenhof appears to have characteristically responded to the 1905 Revolution and its bloody aftermath of pogroms with both hope and despair. The pogrom in Bialystok, in particular, seems to have reinforced Zamenhof's belief that Russia's Jews, Russia, and the world desperately needed the salvation promised by Hillelism. In the years between the 1905 Revolution and the outbreak of the First World War in 1914, Zamenhof endeavored more and more to use his widening Esperanto platform to urge the reconciliation of humanity he believed only possible through the evolutionary process he charted in his Hillelist program. He repackaged Hillelism so as to market it more effectively and widely to Esperantists and non-Esperantists alike as the desperately needed salve for worsening divides and conflicts afflicting and threatening the globe. During these years, however, the Esperantist movement enjoyed tremendous growth, while Zamenhof's Hillelism was dismissed by even those who idolized Esperanto's creator and were inspired by his idealism.

In renewing his campaign for Hillelism, Zamenhof again turned first to his compatriots. In January 1906, he pseudonymously published his "Tenets of Hillelism" in *Ruslanda Esperantisto*, the periodical of the "Espero" society of Esperantists based in St. Petersburg. Zamenhof began by addressing what he called "the ceaseless mutual struggle between the various tribes and religions of the vast Russian state" and which exemplified humanity's need for a new creed, a new culture, a new auxiliary language. In tsarist Russia, Zamenhof explained, "injustice and violence" reigned in a society in which "the majority" lorded over and oppressed its minority populations "at every step." This was Russia's lamentable reality, Zamenhof argued, despite the fact that its minority peoples "have the same moral right to their natural homeland as do the majority." It was long past due to arrive at "some kind of neutral foundation upon which people of different ethnicities (*narodnostei /gentoj*) and religions—or at the very least the sons of one and the same fatherland—could come together peacefully and fraternally, without mutual hostility, hatred, and injustice." The neutral foundation that could and would make this Russian (and ultimately global) unity possible was Hillelism.[113]

Zamenhof enumerated what he was now calling his "tenets of Hillelism" for *Ruslanda Esperantisto*'s readers and explained that this philosophical program had first been devised "specially for only one human group." Without explicitly naming that group, he proceeded to explain how time and experience—especially the experience of the recent Esperanto World Congress in Boulogne—had led to the realization that Hillelism was for *all* to inaugurate, and not merely for one "group" to kickstart on behalf of humanity as a whole. In Boulogne, he explained, "more than a thousand people, arriving from the most diverse countries of the world" had proven that it was possible for peoples of diverse faiths, cultures, and languages to "live together in the most sincere friendship and fraternity." The key to this unity was the fact that the Esperantists in Boulogne had "spoken with one another exclusively in a neutral, international language and confessed to exclusively neutral-human religious principles."[114]

Zamenhof thus attempted to reframe Boulogne as the First World Congress of Hillelists, and Esperanto as the helpmate of Hillelism. Zamenhof hailed the Boulogne Congress as a testament to the possibility that the world's diverse peoples could unite under the banner of a universal ethics—Hillelism—and thus "live together in the most peaceful and sincere fraternity." Zamenhof minced few words in laying out his plans for moving forward. "The striking success of the Boulogne Congress," he wrote, "convinced the initiators of Hillelism that absolute justice, equality, and fraternity among nations (*narodami / popoloj*) is fully possible in practice." Therefore, he announced, it was the Hillelists' intention to propose at the international congress of Esperantists in Geneva, to be held in September 1906, the establishment of a "general group," indeed a "section" among the Esperantists, to organize all those committed to the tenets of Hillelism and a future of international harmony and justice.[115] These political maneuvers of Zamenhof in early 1906 were exactly what the Boulogne organizers had so feared in the stormy lead-up to First World Congress of Esperantists only a few months prior.

Well in advance of the Geneva Congress, however, Zamenhof was directing this Hillelist appeal to his fellow subjects of the Russian empire—his fellow Jews and Esperantists in Russia, in particular. Today more than ever before, he argued, the peoples of Russia were poised to take the lead in building the foundation for not just a more harmonious Russia but also a united humanity. Owing to the revolutionary events of the past year, Zamenhof claimed, the peoples of Russia eagerly anticipated a "new life" and a new type of civic belonging in a renovated empire. Never before had a people so needed the tenets of Hillelism as Russia did now. Hillelism, he promised, would make it possible for Russia's diverse peoples to live in peace and harmony with one another. "At the present critical moment," Zamenhof wrote:

> when our fatherland needs all its strength, it is necessary to bring to life those tenets that will allow all the subjects (*grazhdanam / regnanoj*) of diverse tribes and faith to put an end to their reciprocal quarrels and calculations and sincerely unite for the salvation of our shared homeland, which must—it goes without saying—finally become an association of all its subjects, and not that of only one tribe or religion.[116]

If, in 1901, Zamenhof had named Jews as the pioneers of Hillelism who would create the foundations for a future global family, in 1905 he endowed the Russian people as a whole with the Hillelist mission. He likewise reframed that mission as one that would first save Russia and then save the world.

Hillelists, Zamenhof explained, believed that by means of using a neutral international language and embracing "neutral religious principles and customs," a new people would be created. This evolution would be achieved over the slow, patient crawl of time—so patient, so slow that few Hillelists would notice in their daily lives their subtle contributions to the transformation of humanity. Zamenhof's first Hillelist tenet began simply, "I am a human being, and for me there exists only purely humane ideals." The Hillelist, he explained, believed in the equality of all peoples and trusted that a just and equitable world was possible if built on the foundations of a "neutral" shared international language and a universalist ethics that prized and united all humanity. The Hillelist likewise believed that homelands belonged equally to all the peoples who natively inhabited them, without regard to religious or any other "tribal" difference. The Hillelist was committed to a world in which all were endowed with the full right to speak whichever language they wished and to confess to any faith they wished at home. Yet all would speak the international language and behave in accord with the Hillelists' universal ethics in their interethnic and international relations. Love of one's homeland and patriotic service to it were righteous acts, provided that one's government embraced all those who belonged to that homeland, regardless of ethnic, religious, or other difference among its native inhabitants. Love of one's homeland, for the Hillelist, meant love of *all* his compatriots. Morality, for the Hillelist, could be summed up neatly and simply as: "Do unto others as you have them do unto you, and always listen to the voice of your conscience." One day, the Tenets of Hillelism stipulated, the landscape of the world would be dotted with Hillelist temples at which all the peoples of the world would gather in peace and fraternity. Hillelists would visit them as frequently as possible so as to usher in the final era of a world made every day more humane and harmonious by the realization of the Hillelists' universal ethics.[117]

At the heart of Zamenhof's renewed campaign for Hillelism as with the heart of his original Esperanto project was his foundational critique of his homeland, the Russian empire. The tsarist state, Zamenhof made clear, was constructed on the untenable and cruel foundations of chauvinism and Russian (Orthodox) supremacy. Even while the tsarist state strived to establish a civic vernacular and shared belonging for all the empire's diverse peoples of faith, language, and custom, he argued, its simultaneous and unapologetic pursuit of privileges for some and restrictions for others rendered it inhumane, illegitimate, and doomed. Revised in the wake of the 1905 Revolution as a project for renovating the Russian empire (and later, the world), Zamenhof's Hillelism was his vision of humane empire—based in equality and fraternity—that in time would morph into an empire of humanity. Just as he had searched for a means of transcending Bialystok as a young man, Zamenhof in the twilight of the tsarist empire was still searching for a means of solving the dilemmas of a particular tsarist Babel as the first step toward redeeming humanity on a global scale.

Zamenhof, as promised, took his campaign to the World Congress of Esperantists in Geneva in September 1906. Yet his keynote speech at Geneva is typically remembered not for his bid to convert the Esperantists assembled there into Hillelists, but instead for his moral condemnation of the Bialystok pogrom of 1906 as further evidence for a divided humanity's worsening plight and ever more desperate need of Esperanto. "I come to you from a country where now many millions are having a difficult struggle for their freedom," Zamenhof intoned, "for the most elementary human freedom, for the rights of man." Although the Esperantists, he acknowledged, had met in Geneva to speak Esperanto and not to engage in politics, he could not help but call the attendees' attention to the interethnic bloodshed then plaguing his homeland—the land of Esperanto's birth. "When I was still a child in Bialystok," Zamenhof explained:

> I gazed with sorrow on the mutual hostility which divided the natural sons of the same land and the same town. And I dreamed then that after some years everything would be changed for the better. And the years have passed; and instead of my beautiful dream I have seen a terrible reality; in the streets of my unhappy native town savages with axes and iron stakes have flung themselves, like the fiercest wild beasts, against the quiet town-dwellers, whose sole crime was that they spoke another language and practiced another racial religion than that of the savage brutes. For this reason they smashed the skulls and stabbed out the eyes of men and women, of feeble old men and helpless infants! I do not want to tell you the dreadful details of the butchery of Bialystok; to you as Esperantists I want to say only that the walls between the peoples, the walls against which we fight, are still fearfully high and thick.[118]

It was time, he urged the Congress attendees, to break down the walls that had for too long fatally divided the peoples of not only Bialystok or the expansive Russian empire but also of the entire tormented globe. "Give them the possibility of meeting and communication on a neutral basis," he insisted, "and only then those atrocities which we now see in various places will come to an end." In the face of the widening divides between the peoples of Russia and the entire world, he argued, "we, the Esperantists, must work harder than ever."[119] Esperanto, he emphasized, was no mere utility to ease the practical dilemmas of a globalizing world. Its purpose was to do far more than maximize commercial profits and simplify international travel and communication. Esperanto's purpose was and had always been to transact the reconciliation of humanity, to bring the world's peoples together in harmony and peace.

In Geneva, Zamenhof's words were greeted with the already customary ovations and shouts of "Vivu Zamenhof!" from his adoring Esperantist crowd. Yet Hillelism was not what the audience was cheering for. The applause, rather, was for Zamenhof, Esperanto, and its "inner idea," broadly conceived. Although Esperanto and Hillelism may have been inseparable in Zamenhof's view, they were separate philosophies in the minds of those Esperantists, and especially those Esperantists leaders, who had consciously considered them both. Zamenhof had to some degree absorbed some of the worries and protests of those comrades who had already urged him not to use the congress as a platform for his wide-eyed vision of a "neutral" world religion. At the time of the Geneva Conference in autumn 1906, Zamenhof again bowed to pressure and folded his Hillelist vision into the more easily digestible "inner idea." He was, as

Esther Schor has suggested, "in fact trusting the Esperantists themselves to understand the *interna ideo* as the mandate for a modern, ethical community."[120]

Zamenhof seems by then to have well understood the resistance on the part of Esperantists both within and without imperial Russia to sign on to his "Tenets of Hillelism." In the pages of *Ruslanda Esperantisto*, Zamenhof was soon confronted with rebukes to the Hillelist campaign. In March 1906, an editorial written by A. Dombrovskii appeared to speak for most of imperial Russia's Esperantists when it rejected the Hillelist premise that linguistic and religious diversity was the root cause of contemporary conflicts throughout the world. Dombrovskii pointedly countered Zamenhof's program with the insistence that linguistic and ethnic diversities "are not the causes, but rather the pretexts for wars and persecutions."[121] Dombrovskii was not an outlier. Broadly throughout the Esperantist movement in Russia and abroad, Hillelism elicited dismay, ridicule, and sometimes anger. Even after Zamenhof moved, in early 1906, to widen Hillelism's appeal by renaming it "Homaranism (Homaranismo)" (with "homarano" in Esperanto meaning, as he explained to his fellow Russian Esperantists, "a member of the human family"), his campaign remained a lonely endeavor.[122]

Hillelism failed to gain traction either in Zamenhof's native Russian empire or anywhere else. Asked in 1907 whether Hillelism had attracted any adherents, Zamenhof replied, "No, the Russian Jews would have nothing to say to it. Many persons confessed to me that in their hearts they agreed with me, but they had not the courage to say so openly. I could not find a single person willing to help me in organising such a sect as I contemplated." The path forward in the face of this disappointment was simple. "My efforts," Zamenhof explained, "are now devoted to the cognate object of furthering the movement which I have called Esperantism."[123] Although Zamenhof would continue in subsequent years to try and publicize his Hillelist program, his advocacy on its behalf within the Esperanto community was encoded in what for many was his more palatable vision of *Esperantujo*—that is, "Esperantoland" where the "inner idea" reigned whenever and wherever Esperantists came together. In Esperantoland, as Zamenhof and the adepts then imagined it, men and women from across the globe would come together, as they did every year at the world congresses, and speak in a neutral international auxiliary language, making mutual respect and understanding possible. New international relations, for Zamenhof, foretold a new kind of future and the creation of a new people and a new world. He was willing, however, to mute discussion of the finer points, the so-called tenets, of this larger vision. At the Third World Congress of Esperantists, held in Cambridge in 1907, Zamenhof somewhat slyly told his audience that "Esperantoland will gradually become a school for the training of mankind reconciled in brotherhood, and in this will lie the chief merit of our congresses."[124]

Death, Hope, and Imperial Collapse

Until the outbreak of World War I in August 1914, Zamenhof worked to advance the causes of Esperantism and Hillelism alike. He also continued his ophthalmology practice in Warsaw. As he had since the earliest days of the Esperanto movement, he dutifully corresponded with close colleagues, admirers, and critics alike. He attended each year's World Congress of Esperantists and, until declaring a retirement of sorts in 1912, gave a galvanizing keynote speech at each congress. Perhaps most stressful of all in these years was the outbreak of a scandal and a schism that threatened—for a short time at least—to destroy the Esperantist movement as a whole. When Ido—a so-claimed perfected Esperanto—was presented in 1907 to the world as a rival to Esperanto by a once devoted and leading Esperantist, Zamenhof did his best to provide both moral and linguistic leadership in defending the Esperanto movement and stemming the initial tide of prominent defectors to the Idists' camp.[125] Meanwhile, he somehow managed to find time to translate and publish Esperanto editions of world literature—from Gogol to the Old Testament, from Schiller to Moliere.[126] A workaholic with heart problems and a smoking addiction, Zamenhof was by all accounts racing as quickly toward a premature death as he was toward his illusive Esperantoland. Yet he refused to discontinue his work on behalf of either Esperanto or Hillelism, let alone to retire from tending to his Jewish patients in Warsaw.

When the Great War erupted in summer 1914, Zamenhof was not in Russia but traveling en route to that year's World Congress of Esperantists in Paris, scheduled to open on August 2. He never made it to Paris and the entire event was ultimately cancelled owing to the exigent circumstances of Europe rushing headlong into war. Yet for Zamenhof and many of his fellow Esperantists, there could have been little surprise over the outbreak of what soon revealed itself as a new kind of total and global war. Zamenhof and many of the Esperantists whom he had inspired had spent the previous decades fervently calling upon humanity to more actively and energetically seek solutions to the worsening conflicts over ever more sharper divides conceived as ethnic, national, and racial in particular. In 1911, Zamenhof had been invited to participate prominently in the First Universal Congress of Races held in London, an international conference devoted to the question of ameliorating racial hatred in the pursuit of global peace and security for all humankind. He presented to the First Universal Congress of Races the "inner idea" of Esperanto that he had been advocating for decades in a variety of guises. He argued, too, on behalf of the philosophical core of Hillelism, although he did not acknowledge his universalist philosophy by name. "The diversity of peoples and the hatred of each other which they betray will not wholly disappear from the face of the earth until humanity has but one language and one religion." Until then, he warned, the nations' "deplorable itching for domination" would contaminate international relations and guarantee humankind's ultimate ruin.[127]

The Great War exceeded the horrified expectations of Zamenhof and others who, in the decades leading up to August 1914, had warned about humankind's dangerous proclivities for ethnic, national, religious, and racial hatred. In Warsaw, Zamenhof's health continued to decline during the war, but he nonetheless persevered, now in a wartime context, to campaign for his Esperantist and Hillelist ideals and to bring them positively to bear on plans for the negotiation of a hoped-for peace. In April 1915, Zamenhof issued a circular appealing to the diplomats who would attempt to put the world back together again on peaceful basis once "the end is reached of the wholesale mutual slaughter" of the Great War. A lasting peace, he predicted, could only be achieved once it was guaranteed "that every country morally and materially belongs to all its sons in perfect equality of right." It would be a grave error to parcel up territories as awards to dominant nationalities who would then impose upon minority peoples the humiliations and injustices historically reserved for minority religions, languages, and ethnicities. Such an approach would only make inevitable "explosions of interracial strife, or even fresh wars."[128] He urged the disempowerment of militant nationalism and active measures toward the establishment, in the not distant future, of a "United States of Europe." To continue to allow chauvinism to motor international relations was not a realistic option. The only way to ensure a lasting peace would be to eradicate the humiliation and violence that men and women for too long had meted upon those less powerful and of different ethnic, national, religious, racial, and linguistic origins.

A mere few months later, the German military occupied Warsaw and began their push further into Russian territory. The prospect of Polish independence after the war seemed ever more realistic. Now a seeming orphan of his native Russian empire, Zamenhof found himself neither here nor there in occupied Warsaw. Zamenhof was also ill, his already poor health "wrecked" by "grief and exhaustion."[129] He continued, nonetheless, to appeal to newspapers throughout the world with his Hillelist vision.[130] The news that the February Revolution toppled the tsarist autocracy reportedly gave Zamenhof hope for a coming peace, a new Russia, a better future for the world. Yet by then, he was gravely ill and his health only worsened as Russia plunged into revolution. On April 14, 1917, Zamenhof took his last breath in occupied Warsaw. Two days later, Warsaw's Esperantists escorted Zamenhof's family and his body to the Jewish Cemetery on Okopowa Street, where he was laid to rest.

Imperial Son, Global Citizen

In 1887, Zamenhof launched Esperanto as a means of doing battle and ultimately eradicating the ethnic, religious, and linguistic chauvinism that he believed inhered in a Russian empire predicated on a hierarchy of its diverse peoples' belonging. Zamenhof spoke to the world in an international auxiliary language of his own creation, but in a spiritual vernacular nurtured in the western borderlands of a Russian empire in crisis. As a child, Zamenhof dreamed of escaping Bialystok, the hometown that he would later lament as an accursed tsarist Babel in miniature. As a young man, he searched for a solution to the Jewish Question and, in particular, for one that would enable global human solidarity, rather than what he quickly came to regard as the illusory dead-end of Jewish nationalism. Zamenhof's life was spent in fervent dreams of transcending what he regarded as the false and inconsistent universalist promises of his native Russian empire. He imagined an alternative future in which all the world's diverse peoples would unite in a global moral community—an empire of humanity built upon a radical vision of equality and made by possible by his international auxiliary language. Esperanto's "inner idea" and Zamenhof's Hillelism did not emerge in an abstract plane of fin de siècle global-mindedness and Jewish questions. Zamenhof,

Esperanto, and Hillelism were products of their time as of their place of origin, their late imperial Russian milieu.

With its widening sociopolitical fractures and the radical "social daydreaming" of its aggrieved intelligentsia, late imperial Russia was fertile soil from which an array of novel ideological programs emerged to challenge not only the tsarist autocracy, but also the world. Esperantism was a locally sourced ideological vision. Like many of its competing utopian projects in late imperial Russia, Zamenhof's Esperantism sought the transformation of Russia that would pave the way for the salvation of the world. That Zamenhof's vision, so improbably launched in 1887, initially had any hope at all of coming to fruition owed to the fact that in his very own Russian empire, there were men and women eager to reach out to the world and, using Esperanto, to transform themselves into global citizens. It is to them, and their varied pursuit of grassroots internationalism in late imperial Russia, that we now turn.

2

Pen Pals, Dreamers, and Globe-Trotters

In September 1888, Zamenhof petitioned the director of imperial Russia's Main Administration of Press Affairs, requesting permission to publish a weekly Esperanto leaflet named "La internaciulo"—"that is," he explained, "The Internationalist."[1] Zamenhof was seeking government permission to publish in a language that was understood, at most, by a few hundred people and, presumably, by no one in the employ of the tsarist censorship offices. Yet, Zamenhof argued, there were good reasons to pursue such an unusual endeavor. "Knowledge of foreign languages is at the present time," Zamenhof explained, "an urgent demand for every even slightly educated person."[2] To be alive in 1888, Zamenhof argued, was to be tied into an inescapably international age. To be ignorant of foreign languages meant being left outside of civilization. Moreover, Zamenhof continued, this was an age not just of internationality, but also of rationalization. Given the growing demands of internationalism and the diversity of the world's peoples, it made little sense for people to vainly attempt to master multiple languages. It would be more rational if instead everyone studied—in addition to her or his native tongue—one international language, common to all. "The whole world would be opened to us," Zamenhof argued, "and the time that we almost fruitlessly waste on the study of various languages might then be spent more productively."[3]

Insisting that Esperanto was the solution to the dilemmas of modern Babel, Zamenhof explained that the language he had created was uniquely capable of serving the world's diverse peoples as an effective "mediator (*posrednik*)." Esperanto was extraordinary in the ease with which it could be learned, he claimed, no less than in its "naturalness, sonorousness, flexibility."[4] Every "more-or-less educated European," he argued, could easily parse and comprehend any Esperanto text, even without prior knowledge of this international language.[5] Therefore, a small publication like the one he was proposing was essential for the promotion of this international language from which so much unambiguous good could be expected. Both the need and the craving for Esperanto was real, he urged. It was evidenced by the heaps of letters he was receiving from all over Russia and from interested parties throughout the world. Esperanto's adopters believed in the language's promise and begged Zamenhof to produce an Esperanto periodical that would help grow the nascent global community of Esperanto speakers.[6]

In its reply to Zamenhof, Russia's Main Administration for Press Affairs did not deny the merits of Zamenhof's claims—either about the internationality of the age or about the promise of Esperanto. The matter, from the bureaucratic point of view, was simpler than all that. There were no censors in the tsar's employ who could read the new language that Zamenhof sought to promote. Therefore, there was no choice but to decline his request.[7]

Zamenhof's disappointing encounter with the tsarist government in his 1888 attempt to launch *The Internationalist* at first glance appears to be emblematic of what has long been assumed about Esperanto's fate in late imperial Russia. Esperantists in the early twentieth century and scholars who have studied Esperanto since its emergence have long lamented the seeming misfortune of Esperanto's launch from within what has been presumed the inherently "hostile environment" of repressive tsarist censorship and a broader autocratic heavy-handedness.[8] Characteristic of this dismissive view, British Esperantist Joseph Rhodes claimed in 1907 that "Russia, the birthland of Esperanto, is hardly a soil on which an artificial language could be expected to thrive."[9] For Rhodes, Esperanto had little chance in tsarist Russia—a land of despotism and an overwhelmingly illiterate, agrarian country besides. Such claims later found their mirror in a now outdated historiographic tendency to analyze late imperial Russian life through a prism of "authoritarian essentialism" that once blinded historians from seeing the creativity and purpose of an array of associations, groups, and individuals who energetically participated in public life and imagined alternative futures for themselves, Russia, and the world.[10] This chapter will show that late imperial Russia proved a largely hospitable environment from which the nascent Esperantist movement emerged in the late nineteenth century. Indeed, a study of the grassroots internationalism of Esperantists in late imperial Russia highlights educated society's varied pursuit of a patriotic cosmopolitanism that afforded them a new identity as global citizens.

Imperial Russia fostered vibrant Esperanto communities throughout the empire. The conditions of Russian autocracy (themselves in considerable flux in the first decades of Esperanto's growth) no doubt pinched and at times placed real and stifling restraints on Esperantist activity in the late empire, but Russia's Esperantists worked productively to work around and within those limitations. Moreover, as I will show, it was often Russian Esperantists themselves who hobbled the growth of the movement in their homeland, namely by committing to an untenable vision of institutional political "neutrality" in the post-1905 era. Despite these obstacles, late imperial Russia's Esperantists participated actively in the global community of *samideanoj* (fellow-thinkers) that Zamenhof inspired and that they helped to create.

This was a novel age of global and transnational social networking made possible by cheap international postage, mass publishing, tourism, and a tidal wave of revolutions in telecommunications. Esperantists were at the forefront of the global grassroots one-worldism that blossomed in the late nineteenth and early twentieth centuries.[11] Imperial Russia's Esperantists served as the pioneers and early builders of Esperanto's transnational social networks in the fin de siècle. They availed themselves of novel opportunities to not only participate in these social networks but also to fashion new global identities for themselves. Their grassroots internationalism helps to explain

Esperanto's widening appeal in fin de siècle Europe, as well as to highlight the global consciousness of educated society in late imperial Russia. From wealthy aristocrats to cash-strapped students, Esperanto appealed to an array of ordinary Russian subjects who creatively deployed the language as a means of participating in the internationality of their age and fashioning themselves as modern cosmopolitans.

Lonely Early Adopters

In 1888, Zamenhof made clear, "I do not want to be the *creator* of the language; I only want to be its *initiator*."[12] For Esperanto to thrive, Zamenhof needed to recruit *Esperantists*—men and women who were not only adepts of this language, but also proselytizers of its world-historic purpose. His was an appeal to educated society, and especially to elites with the time and money to spare on Esperanto. Zamenhof's was an unabashedly quixotic endeavor—but one with a potential ready-made appeal to an elite Russian society intoxicated by the power of ideas and the novel technologies that heralded their speedy transmission around the world.

In 1890, an author who revealed himself only by the surname Zinoviev published a Russian-language pamphlet titled *The International Language "Esperanto"* that sought to stimulate interest in Zamenhof's language. The Russian periodical press, he lamented, had largely ignored Esperanto despite the fact that it lived up to the key promises that Zamenhof had made for it. Esperanto was easy to learn, write, and speak. It was pleasant-sounding, logical, and uniformly regular in its rules. Zinoviev hailed Esperanto as a "cosmopolitan language" well-designed for a world that was rapidly becoming more interconnected, entangled, and networked.[13] "The paths of communication and galvanic wires have already considerably connected the entire world as one," Zinoviev argued. An international language was needed to simplify and hasten this international communication. Esperanto, Zinoviev noted, was a timely invention for a world ever more urgently seeking to standardize, on an international basis, systems of measurement, time, and scientific terminology.[14] The modern world, Zinoviev argued, needed a modern solution to the curse of Babel and Zamenhof's Esperanto fit the bill as a "neutral, international language that belongs equally to all."[15]

In 1891, V. L. Kravtsov published a pocket-sized booklet titled *An Important Matter* in which he made a Russian patriot's case for Esperanto. Kravtsov argued that too much time was being wasted in trying to teach—largely in vain—foreign languages to Russian youth. Kravtsov urged his fellow Russian elites to lobby the government for Esperanto, the international auxiliary language of the future, to be taught in Russian schools.[16] Russia, he pointed out, was the home to "multifarious nationalities" and therefore, its undertaking of adopting a universal language would simplify the empire's governance over its diverse population. Moreover, Kravtsov argued, if Russia took the lead in establishing a universal language for all of humanity, it would elevate the tsarist empire's "primacy, might, and glory among all the powers."[17]

Kravtsov underscored the patriotic impulse at the heart of Esperanto's cosmopolitanism. "Thoughtful people who are idealistic, humane, and who are imbued with strong desire to help their fatherland and all of humanity," Kravtsov intoned, "cannot help but sympathize with the great idea" of a universal language. Yet in recent times, Kravtsov noted, seekers of an international language had been seen by many not as humanitarians or patriots, but as savages and traitors. The followers of Volapük had been condemned as traitors and ne'er-do-wells willing to foreswear their sacred national tongue. Yet, he noted, Zamenhof had made it clear that no adopter of Esperanto would ever be expected to abandon their native tongue. Esperanto was a language of *international* communication; it did not seek to supplant the world's national languages, held dear by their native speakers.[18]

Kravtsov and other early adopters of Esperanto were convinced that Esperanto would beneficially transform their globalizing world. In working to popularize Esperanto, they seemed instinctively to realize the need to seize the self-conscious modernity of the moment and to take advantage of the revolutions in telecommunications, transport, and media. In order to translate their hopes into realities, Zamenhof and the early Esperantists endeavored to create new social networks, publications, and associations that would not only link Esperantists to one another, but also embed Esperanto into the rhetoric, institutions, and imaginations of educated elites throughout Europe and across the globe. In the closing decade of the nineteenth century, Esperanto's early adopters set out to build novel transnational social networks and global imagined communities linked by Zamenhof's international language.

Social Networking in Late Imperial Russia

In his autobiography, Lev Trotsky recalled his isolated childhood growing up on his father's farm in the tsarist empire. "It was twenty-three kilometers from Yanovka to the nearest post office, and more than thirty-five to the railroad," Trotsky reflected. "From there it was a long way again to the Government offices, to the stores and to a civic centre, and still farther to the world with its great events." A curious child, he marveled at the technology that made telegraphy possible and wondered at the world that so rarely—"only on special occasions"—arrived at his parents' farm in the form of a letter or a telegram. "A letter was an event," Trotsky wrote, but

> a telegram was a catastrophe. Someone explained to me that telegrams came on wires, but with my own eyes I saw a man on horseback bring a telegram from Bobrinetz for which my father had to pay two roubles and fifty kopecks. A telegram was a piece of paper, like a letter. There were words written on it in pencil. Did the wind blow it along a wire? I was told that it came by electricity. That was still worse.[19]

Worse, he explained, because he could not yet wrap his head around the fascinating but unfathomable science of telegraphy. Trotsky was not alone in finding the new technologies that made possible the era's self-conscious modernity to be dizzying, terrifying, but nonetheless irresistible.[20]

Young Trotsky was but 8 years old when Zamenhof published the *Unua Libro* in 1887 and invited the world to communicate in his novel international language. Only in recent decades had telegraphy seen the "wiring of the world" in novel ways that revolutionized how governance, war, and peace were conducted by the world's imperial powerbrokers. Telegraphy demanded, too, revolutions in how space and time were conceived, no less than how language itself could be remade to accommodate the new communications and the information infrastructure it made possible.[21] As Trotsky's memory of his youth suggests, the communication revolution of the late nineteenth century galvanized new ways for people to imagine the world and their place within it. It also prompted them to question technology's role in their lives. And while the idea of sending a telegram, let alone having the money to afford it, was beyond the reach of most by the time Zamenhof's international language made its debut in 1887, both Esperanto and the telegram were responses to a need increasingly felt in ever wider social circles across class, national, and imperial lines—the need for speedy long-distance and, ultimately, international communication.

The need to communicate quickly and effectively across borders was coupled with a growing desire to make connections with people and places that a young man like Trotsky, off in the countryside, could only imagine. The miles of cables and wires feverishly laid in the decades prior to Esperanto's launch were symbols as well as enablers of the international networking and communications infrastructure so increasingly prized by governments (especially so those with far-flung overseas empires to rule and maintain), businesses, international professional and scientific organizations (themselves growing rapidly in number and scope), and individuals too. The era in which Zamenhof launched Esperanto was one in which businesses and governments were eagerly revolutionizing the global telecommunications infrastructure.[22] New modes and networks of international communications quickly gave rise to new visions of world markets, world news, and world citizens—even while their use largely remained the exclusive preserve of elites.[23] Despite this relative exclusivity, telegraphy proved a booming enterprise. As Marsha Siefert notes, "By the turn of the century, telegrams numbered 300 million annually, with one-fifth crossing state borders." Throughout the world, millions of men and women—young Trotsky included—had witnessed this telecommunications revolution transform their imagination of the wider world despite the fact that the cost of sending a telegram would, for the remainder of the nineteenth century, remain prohibitively expensive for most.

The early adopters of Zamenhof's international language were relatively well-off men and women. Even those among them who could not afford to send telegrams or travel internationally for leisure purposes could readily afford to send correspondence by post. Esperanto entered the world in an era during which affordable national and international postal services facilitated globalization and inspired visions of world unity achieved by epistolary exchange.[24] Even more so than telegraphy, the normalization of postal exchange in the nineteenth century—and the affordable postage that made it possible—transformed not only how ordinary people imagined space and time, but also their sense of community across long distances. The post made it possible to build and sustain meaningful long-distance relationships via correspondence, to create intimacy by means of paper, ink, and envelope.[25] The establishment of the World Postal Union in 1874 soon allowed for men and women all over the world to take advantage of cheap, flat-rate international postage.[26] It is no surprise therefore that a reliance on post was built into Zamenhof's vision for Esperanto from the start. As explained in the previous chapter, Zamenhof's first Esperanto primer had included coupons for readers to tear out, complete, and return by post to Doctor Esperanto in Warsaw. Those mail-in coupons signaled the senders' solemn vows to learn Esperanto, but also included their addresses so that they could be networked into postal correspondence between Esperantists.

To facilitate this communication and Esperantist social networking, Zamenhof tended scrupulously to his growing *Adresaro*—his directory of Esperantists worldwide. In 1896, Zamenhof published an updated directory listing the names and addresses of those who had signed on to Esperanto between December 1893 and December 1895. The directory listed adepts who resided in Algeria and Egypt (one Esperantist in each), South Africa and Argentina (one and three Esperantists, respectively). The directory listed a George Hodson of Melbourne, Australia, a Jerome Landfield of Binghamton, New York, and a P. L. Castanachi in Constantinople, Ottoman Turkey. The nascent Esperantist movement as yet largely resided in Europe. The directory listed twelve new Esperantists in Germany and fifty-nine in France. Yet, as with the first *Adresaro*, the bulk of new Esperantists were drawn from all over the Russian empire. The 1896 *Adresaro* listed 479 new Esperantists from imperial Russia, many of them residing in Vitebsk, Kherson, Kiev, Moscow, and Odessa. The directory revealed these Russian Esperantists as students, teachers, pharmacists, and military officers. More than sixty were women.[27]

Zamenhof's directories were tools with which Esperantists found one another. They were essential for those who knew no other Esperantist in their town, city, country, or even continent. The directories were lifelines for Esperantists who wanted to reach out, make connections, or even just to test the waters of an international language that, for one reason or another, they thought it a good idea to learn. Zamenhof's *Adresaro* was more than an accounting of his invention's progress. It was the building block of an emerging social network that transcended national, linguistic, and cultural borders, while also circuiting within them. By means of pen, paper, and post, early Esperantists befriended one another and exchanged their life stories, ideas, and thoughts through the vehicle of Zamenhof's international auxiliary language. Esperantists not only gave life to the language but also creatively expanded the reach of this growing social network to suit their professional, ideological, or personal needs.

Early Esperantist networking also took on institutional forms. In March 1892, Russian Esperantists established the "Espero" society in St. Petersburg. Its founding charter declared Espero's purpose as "the facilitation of international relations: commercial, scholarly, literary, and others" so as "to further the spread of the international language 'Esperanto' and to provide to those who are interested in this language the opportunity for closer relations."[28] Espero conceived of itself as a civic association that would regularly organize Esperanto courses, public lectures, and literary evenings. It committed to opening a member library and, if permitted by the tsarist regime, to publish regular periodicals as well as brochures and books. Espero hosted a celebratory opening ceremony in May 1892 that was attended by some forty Esperantists and well-wishers.[29]

The Ministry of Internal Affairs registered the Espero society in St. Petersburg and granted it permission to establish filial groups throughout the tsarist empire. Yet Espero was not permitted to produce its own Esperantist periodical for subscribers in Russia and abroad. The tsarist censorship regime held fast to the logic invoked when denying Zamenhof's first bid, in 1888, to publish an Esperantist periodical in Russia: censors could not monitor a periodical written in a language unknown to them. The only choice that remained for those hungry for Esperantist literature was to subscribe to Esperantist periodicals produced abroad.[30]

Enterprising Esperantists willing to put their own financial resources behind the production of Esperantist texts in imperial Russia were repeatedly greeted with censors' refusal. When, in 1894, N. Borovko produced a translation of A. S. Pushkin's *The Stone Guest* and appealed to Odessa's censorship office for approval to publish it, the response was harsh. "Esperanto is not a language at all, and the censorship office is not at all obliged to conduct an investigation of these hieroglyphs. It must do nothing more and nothing less than to forbid their publication."[31] In that same year, the mathematician P. A. Bulanzhe appealed to tsarist censors for permission to publish in Moscow a semi-regular periodical named *Esperantisto* that would report on all matters Esperanto. It would also devote a special section to "general international life" that would feature news on international congresses and world culture.[32] Bulanzhe, too, was refused.

Until Russia's 1905 Revolution inaugurated relative freedom of the press in the tsarist empire, Russian Esperantists' multiple attempts to gain official sanction to publish Esperantist texts were refused. The censors' standard refusal to these applications for Esperantist publication approval was, time and again, the explanation that without a censor who could read Esperanto, censorship itself and therefore publication in Esperanto was not feasible. Peppered throughout these bureaucratic documents are judgments of Esperanto as little more than a cipher for use by those electing to engage in the silly pastime of exchanging ideas in an obscure code. Tsarist censors long refused to consider Esperanto a language worthy of official consideration, if a language at all. As one censor employed in the St. Petersburg office put it in plain bureaucratese: "The Esperanto language does not exist in the list of foreign languages."[33]

When considered in light of imperial Russian censorship practices generally, the tsarist censorship of Esperantist publications in the late nineteenth century is neither unusual nor particularly prohibitive. From a bureaucrat's perspective in late nineteenth-century Russia, denying an application from an otherwise respectable member of elite Russian society seeking permission to produce an Esperanto-language journal presented a question of logistics first of all. In the tsarist censors' view, there was no sense in granting permission to publish in a language unknown, and largely unrecognized, by the bureaucrats tasked with overseeing the Russian press.

Imperial Russia's Chief Administration for Press Affairs, as its censorship bureau was formally known after 1865, governed the tsarist state's relationship with the empire's growing number of writers, editors, and publishers. Reputed for "its pettiness and absurdity," the tsarist censorship administration was often presumed obscurantist and oppressive by contemporaries as well as by subsequent commentators on imperial Russian intellectual life. Representative of this view, historian Marianna Tax Choldin argued that the tsarist government sought to erect a "fence around the empire" that would guard against the importation of foreign ideas that could variously prove dangerous to autocratic authority and imperial stability.[34]

Others, however, have acknowledged the tsarist state's wariness about the spread and importation of potentially dangerous ideas via the printed word, but have demonstrated that by the late nineteenth century, censorship practices in imperial Russia were not exceptional or even as harsh as once commonly presumed. Censorship in late nineteenth-century Russia, Charles A. Ruud argues, was not dissimilar from that seen elsewhere in Europe at the time in that it was oriented toward deploying "administrative controls ... that would enable the government to grant a large measure of press freedom while reserving expeditious means to strike at 'dangerously oriented' publications."[35] During the period between the Great Reforms and the 1905 Revolution, Ruud shows, the tsarist government simultaneously introduced "an element of press freedom" that made possible the dramatic expansion of Russian publishing (and intellectual life, generally), while also endowing censors with "very strong powers."[36] These powers were, however, primarily used against a rather small number of publications deemed exceedingly radical. The press, in general, was allowed to publish all manner of social criticism in imperial Russia. The number and variety of periodicals and other publications produced in Russia grew even after the assassination of Alexander II. So, too, did the numbers of Russian subscribers to the domestic and foreign press.[37]

It should not be forgotten that Zamenhof's original Esperanto primer—a book written in the Russian language—cleared the Russian censorship office in 1887 without incident. The problem with Esperanto, from the censors' view, was not that it was inherently dangerous, seditious, or radical. The censors' initial problem with Esperanto, rather, was that it was unknown to them. It was only in 1895 that imperial Russia's Esperantist community came under heavy suspicion by tsarist censors. Even then, the problem was not so much Esperanto, but rather who was attempting to wield it to spread "heretical" views.

Heretics and Censors

In 1894, a coterie of Esperantists in Voronezh wrote to Lev Tolstoy—the world-famous author, philosopher, and rebel—seeking his opinion on Zamenhof's international language. To their great excitement, Tolstoy replied with a letter of support for Esperanto and the broader idea that an international language would enable mutual understanding of the world's divided and disparate peoples. Esperanto, Tolstoy claimed, was so easy to learn that he was able to freely read texts in Esperanto after spending only two hours studying Zamenhof's primer for the language. "I think," he wrote, "that for universality in the genuine sense of the world—that is, so as to unite the Chinese, African peoples, and others—a different language is necessary, but for a European person, Esperanto is extraordinarily easy." Yet even despite its potential limits, Tolstoy endorsed Esperanto as a project of inherent benefit to humanity. "The study of Esperanto and its dissemination are an undoubtedly Christian endeavor (*delo*), making possible the establishment of the Kingdom of God," Tolstoy wrote.[38]

Tolstoy had been introduced to Esperanto as early as 1889 when an energetic early adopter sent him a copy of the *Unua Libro*. At that time, Tolstoy had vowed to do his "best to propagate the language, and especially the belief in the necessity for it."[39] Yet, Tolstoy perhaps underestimated the eagerness of Esperanto's early adopters and how much such a promise would mean to them. Russia's Esperantists were seeking an international celebrity who would preach Esperanto's practical and humanitarian qualities and give the movement a needed signal boost. When Tolstoy wrote to the Voronezh Esperantists in 1894, he again aroused hopes for a celebrity endorsement of Esperanto. This time, Zamenhof—who now found himself in dire financial straits after sinking whatever money he had into the movement—sought to capitalize on a possible partnership with Tolstoy. Given the overlap between the spiritual and moral impulses that motivated Zamenhof and Tolstoy in their otherwise quite different pursuit of brotherhood among all peoples, a potential partnership appeared profitable in more senses than one.

By 1894, Zamenhof faced not only his own financial stress but also the prospect that further growth of the Esperanto movement was stalled, with the small community of Esperantists becoming increasingly divided. In the previous year, debate over whether or not Esperanto as a language needed fundamental reforms—with an eye toward "perfecting" it—had occupied the bulk of the discussion in the pages of *La Esperantisto*. Zamenhof was desperate to grow Esperanto's community of speakers unencumbered by divisive and distracting efforts to "perfect" the language. Zamenhof and many of Esperanto's early adopters had seen with their own eyes how the Volapük movement collapsed under the pressure of its creator's perfectionism and rigid authority. Zamenhof wanted to cut off the debate over linguistic reform before it could sink the nascent Esperanto movement. In November 1894, he called a referendum in which the subscribers to *La Esperantisto* were entitled to vote for or against reforms. Zamenhof's anti-reformist position narrowly won the referendum, a "victory" owing in no small measure to the support he carried from the Russian Esperantist community.

In a letter to a fellow Russian Esperantist, Zamenhof heaved a weary sigh of relief. "As a result of this debate about reforms we have wasted the whole year," he wrote. Yet he was flush with hope for moving forward, now with the license to focus energies on expanding Esperanto's ranks rather than debating the need for linguistic perfection. Yet, as Zamenhof quickly learned, the damage had already been done. Over the course of 1894, *La Esperantisto* lost half of its subscription base—a decimation that neither the movement nor the publication could afford. Many of those who had advocated reform abandoned the movement, leaving behind an overwhelmingly Russian base of support for Esperanto. Advocates of language reform primarily hailed from outside of the Russian empire, while those who were against reforms, like Zamenhof himself, were subjects of the Russian empire. After the referendum, *La Esperantisto* hemorrhaged subscribers, the Esperanto movement contracted, and financing both the periodical and the movement proved, as ever before, a nearly insurmountable challenge for Zamenhof.[40]

In response to this growing crisis, Zamenhof ventured an altogether risky move. In 1895, he contracted with *Posrednik*, the Tolstoyan publishing venture that produced Tolstoy's and related texts for relatively cheap consumption by the Russian reading public. The idea was to allow for the publication of Tolstoyan texts in Esperanto in a recurring column in *La Esperantisto*. This partnership immediately raised the hackles of the tsarist police who, in early January 1895, dispatched a warning memo to the censors within the Main Administration of Press Affairs. The police sniffed conspiracy, arguing that the Tolstoyans had plotted a "secret participation in the publication of the paper, 'Esperantisto,'" with the aim of transforming it into "an organ for the dissemination of the ideas of their false teacher (*lzheuchitel'*)."[41] A week later, the censor who had been responsible in recent years for inspecting *La Esperantisto* as a foreign publication reported on its latest issue. He explained that in the five years that *La Esperantisto* had been presented for preliminary censorship, nothing had prevented his office from approving it for delivery to its Russian subscribers (who, he noted, comprised the bulk of the Esperantist movement broadly). Despite the fears of the tsarist police, the first issue of 1895 likewise presented nothing objectionable to the tsarist censors and would be cleared just as the previous five years of issues had been.[42]

The second issue of *La Esperantisto* in 1895, however, soon arrived in the tsarist censorship office featuring Tolstoy's "Reason and Religion: A Letter to an Inquirer." In it, Tolstoy promoted the antiauthoritarian approach to Christian spirituality for which he was by then well known internationally and anathematized (and eventually, in 1901, excommunicated) by the Russian Orthodox Church. Every man, Tolstoy wrote, must "exert the whole strength of his mind to elucidate for himself the religious foundations on which he rests." The human capacity for reason, he argued, was given by God for its deployment in all matters, including in questioning the sources and tenets of one's faith. A man, Tolstoy argued, "must not check his reason by tradition, but, contrariwise, must check tradition by reason."[43]

Now the tsarist censors did have reason to declare the contents of *La Esperantisto* dangerous and to ban its delivery to its subscribers throughout the Russian empire. Tolstoy's "Reason and Religion" was a heretic's rabble-rousing attempt to refute the irrefutable truth of the Christian Gospel (or so the censor justifying *La Esperantisto*'s ban would claim in his report); in any language, this was objectionable material that could not be allowed to circulate freely in Russia. Zamenhof's risky partnership with the Tolstoyans proved fatal to *La Esperantisto* itself. Once it was banned by the tsarist censors, *La Esperantisto* lost, in one fell swoop, three-quarters of its subscribers. It was swiftly forced to cease its operations and close.[44] A major artery of the Esperanto movement's networking and popularization infrastructure was collapsed at a time when it, and Zamenhof personally, could not afford it. When Tolstoy received word of the debacle, he attempted to intervene on Zamenhof's behalf. In May 1895, Tolstoy appealed to an acquaintance who had ties to the censorship office in St. Petersburg. Zamenhof, he explained, "has suffered in part because of me." If the tsarist censors would reverse their ban on Zamenhof's journal, Tolstoy promised, he would in no way participate in the Esperantists' affairs moving forward.[45] The tsarist censors did eventually reverse the ban, but it was too late for *La Esperantisto*—an already modest operation decimated by the Tolstoyan affair.[46]

As discussed above, the degree to which the tsarist government imposed censorship restrictions on the printed word in late nineteenth century has often been exaggerated. "The autocracy granted extensive publishing freedom, governed by law," historian Charles Ruud writes, "and did so to a degree far greater than westerners realize."[47] Yet prior to the 1905 Revolution the autocracy did vigorously attempt to outlaw the publication or import of texts that were seditious or libelous. This caution is useful for evaluating the downfall of *La Esperantisto* in 1895. While tsarist censors had banned the publication for its objectionable and dangerous Tolstoyan contents, this did not mean a ban on Esperanto as an objectionable and dangerous language in and of itself. Ulrich Lins has argued that following the *La Esperantisto* debacle of 1895, "the Esperantists were engaged in an uphill battle to prove their sociopolitical loyalty to the authorities and counter suspicions that the language served conspiratorial goals."[48] Yet the archival record suggests instead a more prosaic interpretation of the Esperantists' continued struggle to publish Esperanto literature in Russia until the 1905 Revolution collapsed the tsarist censorship regime. The challenge for Russia's Esperantists in these years remained, first and foremost, persuading the Main Administration of Press Affairs that Esperanto was a language at all, and that their office should employ censors who could appropriately surveil what they promised would be their politically innocuous publications.

Case in point is *Esperanto*, Russia's first domestically produced Esperantist serial. Although the first issue of this short-lived publication did not appear until 1905, the Main Administration of Press Affairs granted permission to its editor, a Yalta-based doctor named I. D. Ostrovskii, to produce the periodical in 1904. Ostrovskii appears to have been paying keen attention to the censors' approach to Esperantist ventures. His application to produce *Esperanto* in 1904 reflects a savvy understanding of the censors' bureaucratic scruples and was a clear effort to anticipate and satisfy their possible objections to the Esperantist publication he proposed. In a matter of a few months, Ostrovskii had succeeded in obtaining official sanction to publish his journal. That the first issue did not appear until 1905, and that the journal quickly faltered, owed not to tsarist opposition to Esperanto but instead to unexpected twists of fate.

On February 9, 1904, Ostrovskii applied to the Main Administration of Press Affairs to publish *Esperanto*, a journal whose purpose would be to acquaint the "Russian public with the current status of the question of adopting an international, auxiliary, constructed language which, while in no way encroaching on the existence of living languages, must service the easing of the academic, literary, and commercial relations between people who speak different languages."[49] Ostrovskii assured the censors that "questions and considerations of a political, political-economic, and religious character absolutely will not have a place in the proposed publication." The focus would strictly be placed on what was presented as the non-political, purely objective "academic, literary, technical, and commercial" concerns of an educated Russian public with the clear need to be in conversation with the rest of the modernizing world.[50] All material in *Esperanto* would be presented as parallel texts in the Russian and Esperanto languages. Ostrovskii also proposed a solution to a major stumbling block that had gotten in the way of previous efforts to publish Esperanto publication in imperial Russia: the lack of censors capable of reading Esperanto. Ostrovskii offered the name of Grigorii

Nikolaevich Liubi, a censor of foreign periodicals employed in St. Petersburg's Main Post Office who was fluent in Esperanto and willing to assume pro bono responsibility for censoring Esperanto publications.[51]

Ostrovskii likewise emphasized Esperanto's legitimacy and respectability, underscoring that forward-thinking experts throughout Europe had embraced it. He included with his application copies, in Russian and in English, of the Declaration of the Delegation for the Adoption of an International Language.[52] This declaration was the outcome of a commission established during the Universal Exhibition in Paris in 1900 to examine the question of an international auxiliary language. Signed on January 17, 1901, the declaration asserted its signatories' belief that the world did need an international auxiliary language—one, they insisted, that must meet three requisite conditions:

> First Condition: It must fulfill the needs of the ordinary intercourse of social life, of commercial communications, and of scientific and philosophic relations;
>
> Second Condition: It must be easily acquired by every person of average elementary education, and especially by persons of European civilization;
>
> Third Condition: It must not be one of the national languages.[53]

The declaration stopped short, however, of affirming any one constructed language as the logical choice for the international auxiliary language it otherwise deemed necessary. All possible competitors, of which Esperanto was but one in this age of galloping popularity of the idea of an international language, would be considered and evaluated accordingly by the delegates who represented academic, professional, and commercial interests throughout the world.[54]

Ostrovskii appealed to the tsarist government to recognize that Esperanto could not be ignored by any modern state seeking integration into the intellectual, scientific, economic, and cultural life of the global elite. To ignore Esperanto or worse, to frustrate its spread in Russia, was to hinder Russia from participating in an important global conversation. Ostrovskii noted how Esperanto publications were growing all throughout western and central Europe as well as in North America. In Russia, the very birthplace of Esperanto, the educated public lacked access to Esperanto publications and was shut out of discussions of one of the more pertinent questions for the global community of educated business, literary, and scientific leaders.[55]

The Collegiate Assessor Ostrovskii (a physician by trade) had compiled a generally faultless application and the Main Administration of Press Affairs approved Monsieur Liubi to take on the pro bono responsibility for surveilling Ostrovskii's proposed Esperanto journal.[56] On May 11, 1904, Ostrovskii's petition to publish *Esperanto* in Russia was formally approved.[57] All appeared to have fallen into place—until that is, Liubi died unexpectedly. In late October, Ostrovskii wrote to the Main Administration for Press Affairs again, suggesting that another St. Petersburg Esperantist in the tsar's employ, V. I. Krivosh, be employed to serve as the censor of Esperanto publications. By year's end, the Main Administration for Press Affairs approved Krivosh for the task.[58]

Once Ostrovskii's *Esperanto* finally made its appearance in Russia in 1905, circumstances had changed drastically both for Ostrovskii and the tsarist empire. Against the backdrop of Russia's worsening domestic and military crises, Ostrovskii managed to produce three issues of *Esperanto* before various practical and personal barriers to further publish the periodical led him to shut it down. By then, the 1905 Revolution had largely nullified the need for Russia's Esperantists to clear their Esperanto publications with tsarist censors before hitting the presses.

Navigating "Neutrality" and Politics in Post-1905 Russia

The 1905 Revolution galvanized Russia's civil society and Nicholas II's concessions to the Russian public widened the opportunities for civil society's expansion as well as the range of types of civic engagement. The years between the 1905 Revolution and the outbreak of World War I witnessed the general revitalization of Esperantism in imperial Russia. Russia's Esperantists managed to (re)organize themselves and deploy extraordinary effort to propagate Esperanto throughout the empire and abroad. Newfound press freedoms combined with the inspiration many Russian Esperantists found in the rapidly expanding global community of Esperantists to energize further growth of the movement. In the arenas of publishing, travel, study, transnational social networking, and international exchange of expertise, Russia's Esperantists avidly pursued opportunities to reach out to a world that increasingly proved willing to communicate with them in Esperanto.

As a result of the 1905 Revolution, Esperanto publishing (and publishing generally) flourished in the last decade of the tsarist empire, unhindered by prior censorship hassles. As Ruud explains, the tsarist censorship regime was practically disempowered during the course of the revolution when the Russian press took it upon its own authority to "publish largely what it pleased," regardless of the law. In 1906, Nicholas II agreed to "the complete withdrawal of preliminary censorship."[59] Thereby, he effectively dismantled the empire's censorship bureaucracy, allowing for a press that would now be checked by the judicial system, not the Ministry of the Interior. Those seeking to publish periodicals in Russia would no longer need prior approval from the Ministry of Interior's Administration of Press Affairs.[60]

The removal of press restrictions led all but immediately to the rapid production and marketing of Esperantist texts in late imperial Russia: from translations of literary works, to Esperantist journals, to proselytizing material written in Russian but intended to recruit new Esperantists to the cause. By 1912, an "Esperanto" bookstore opened on Tverskaia, Moscow's central boulevard.[61] One leading Russian Esperantist referred proudly to the "hundreds of brochures about the language of Esperanto that are appearing and disappearing in the book market."[62] Print capitalism, of course, helped to inspire and solidify a variety of "imagined communities"—the modern nation-state most famously.[63] The history of Esperanto shows how essential print capitalism was to the forging of a different type of imagined community—one that was fully compatible with the nation-state (and/or empire) while centered on a vision of global citizenship.[64] In these years, Esperantist publishing helped to cultivate its consumers' distinctive "planetary consciousness."[65] It also helped to build and network Esperantists' emerging global movement. Through the Esperantist press, much of which circulated transnationally, Esperantists forged tangible links with one another but also accessed a community-based means to imagine the wider world and their place within it. The surge in Esperanto publishing and its consumption that was witnessed in imperial Russia after the 1905 Revolution vividly underscores how, in this era of globalization, ordinary people around the world were fashioning new global identities for themselves while rooting the very same in their particular experiences of empire, nation, region, and/or town.

Esperanto texts arguably flew from shop stores during these years because more and more Russians were attuned to the globalization of their era and therefore inspired to at least take an interest in the international language movement, if not to join it themselves. After 1905, there was a marked growth in the number of local Esperantist societies and clubs. Espero, in St. Petersburg, served as a flagship. Esperanto societies also grew in Kiev, Moscow, Odessa, Saratov, Tiflis, Tomsk, Warsaw, Vladivostok, Yalta, and many other cities and towns throughout the vast Russian empire.[66] By 1910, according to one official report, there were eighty-six Esperanto clubs in Russia.[67] Efforts were first made in that same year to unite in a central Russian League of Esperantists.[68]

The coveted Esperantist periodical press that Russia's Esperantists had longed for in the pre-1905 years also began to take shape. Although it faced problems of funding and organization, this fledgling periodical culture helped in some measure to provide further institutional shape to the Russian Esperantist movement. Espero launched its own journal, *Ruslanda Esperantisto* (The Russian Esperantist) in April 1905 and, despite some interruptions, it was published through March 1910. Its subscription base was small, however, at an estimated three hundred in total.[69] While its issues had the potential to reach many more than its individual subscribers, *Ruslanda Esperantisto* surely also faced stiff competition from the Esperantist press that was being produced elsewhere in Europe, and especially in France. The journal's contents reveal, however, an imperial Russian inflection of the effort to advocate what Esperantists argued was the patriotic cosmopolitanism necessitated by their modern, international age.

Ruslanda Esperantisto's first issue launched with a preface addressed, in Russian and in English, to all *samideanoj*—fellow-thinkers. It acknowledged that in the land of Esperanto's birth, the movement had stalled while at the same time "Esperanto achieved colossal successes abroad."[70] *Ruslanda Esperantisto* urged a redoubling of Russian efforts to "catch up" with the movement in France and western Europe more broadly. E. Radvan-Ripinskii of St. Petersburg argued that promoting Esperanto in tsarist Russia was especially urgent given that "international life is pulsing with such sheer feverishness and haste."[71] The telegraph and the railway had already linked the world in astonishing new ways. The contemporary world, Radvan-Ripinskii claimed, was swiftly becoming unrecognizable to those not paying attention to the globalization that proceeded apace with revolutionary changes in science, geopolitics, and the increasingly global economy. Recently, he noted, the Japanese had emerged as a formidable new power on the world stage (a claim whose gravity could not have been lost on Russian readers during the humiliating Russo-Japanese War). Tomorrow, he wrote, it might be the Hawaiians, and then "maybe, the inhabitants of the Congo, the Ammanese, the Persians, and the Siamese." A rapidly globalizing world demanded an international language, but also the educated public's appreciation of the sheer rapidity with which their world was changing and becoming more entangled and competitive.

In line with this vision, a regular feature of *Ruslanda Esperantisto*'s programming was its "Esperanto Movement" pages. In each issue, the journal reported on news received from Esperantist clubs and individuals in countries around the world. These pages offered ready appeal to those already inclined to imagine themselves as citizens of the world. The "Esperanto Movement" feature allowed Russian Esperantists to visualize and internalize connections to "fellow-thinkers" in Nicaragua and Holland, in Mexico and the United States, in Sweden and Japan. *Ruslanda Esperantisto* delivered the world into the hands of the Russian Esperantists so eager to imagine and embrace it. In the fashion of Zamenhof's original *Adresaro*, *Ruslanda Esperantisto* also regularly published the addresses of Esperantists interested in corresponding with "fellow-thinkers" throughout the world. The journal's first issue printed the contact information of Esperantists in Madagascar, Trinidad, Canada, Brazil, the United States, New Zealand, Indochina, Belgium, England, and elsewhere. *Ruslanda Esperantisto* made it possible for Russia's Esperantists not only to imagine themselves as part of a wide world, but also to correspond with Esperantists on all continents.[72] These activities were central to their self-fashioning not only as Esperantists, but also as global citizens networked into a growing transnational culture.

Ruslanda Esperantisto endeavored in a variety of ways to satisfy its readers' Esperantism and cosmopolitanism generally, and understood these as inextricably aligned with their elite status in the Russian empire. *Ruslanda Esperantisto* offered modish art nouveau illustrations in addition to its standard fair of Esperantist poetry, reviews of Esperantist literature, and a regular stream of articles on the shape of the Esperantist movement, Russian art, science, technology, and sport. One repeated half-page ad that appeared in several issues, and which was paid for by a prominent St. Petersburg Esperantist, featured an image of an attractive young women with long, flowing hair and a crown of flowers. Alongside this alluring image of an "Esperantistka" appeared a more severe Russian-language text that accused those who had not yet taken up the study of Esperanto of "committing a crime against your homeland and all of cultured humanity."[73] This ad captures well the intensity of feeling many Esperantists (within Russia and without) felt for their internationalist cause—one they understood as patriotic in its very cosmopolitanism.

The commitment of Esperantists to growing the movement often awed their contemporaries. Enthusiasm and even single-minded devotion to the cause were never in short supply. Moreover, Esperantists who had personal wealth at their disposal had the capacity to profoundly affect the direction that the Esperantist movement took globally and locally. In early twentieth-century Russia, this type of investment power was seen in the ultimately short-lived efforts made by V. V. Bitner, the publisher and editor of imperial Russia's popular science journal *Vestnik znaniia* (Herald of Knowledge) on behalf of the Esperanto movement.

A journal that enjoyed a broad circulation, *Vestnik znaniia* catered to the ethos that science, technology, and knowledge were the clear pathways to civilizational progress. Bitner envisioned his journal as a method of teaching Russia's increasingly literate public about new technologies and the latest scientific developments, as well as of instructing them more broadly in Russian and world history, the natural sciences, and the arts. Prior to launching *Vestnik znaniia*, Bitner had contributed frequently to another popular scientific illustrated journal in late imperial Russia, *Priroda i liudi* (Nature and People)—a publication that, as Anindita Banerjee notes, "compelled its readers to constantly reimagine their own sense of being in the world."[74] For *Priroda i liudi*, Bitner wrote frequently on themes of astronomy and space travel, even venturing to imagine life on Mars and the topography of the earth's moon.[75] For this work, Bitner had earned considerable popularity among readers.

As *Vestnik znaniia*'s editor and publisher, Bitner was willing to take financial and intellectual risks in furthering the intelligentsia-led vision of the future that he vigorously promoted in the journal's pages. In 1905, Bitner came to see in Esperanto a curious experiment and was excited about its potential for uniting humanity. He therefore decided in 1906 to send all of *Vestnik znaniia*'s subscribers a free Esperanto textbook as a gratis supplement. He also created a special "Esperanto department" within *Vestnik znaniia*'s regular issues.[76]

Subscribers' vocal responses to his preliminary campaign to integrate Esperanto into *Vestnik znaniia*'s program surprised Bitner. Few readers emerged as staunch advocates of Bitner's Esperantist vision, and he received several letters of protest from those anticipating that valuable space in the journal would be squandered on Esperanto text that few subscribers would, or could, read. In 1906, Bitner wrote to readers explaining that while his sympathies did lie with Esperanto and that he firmly believed in its potential to profitably revolutionize commerce, science, and international relations, he could not move forward with his plans to integrate Esperantism into *Vestnik znaniia* without support from the journal's readership.[77]

Fearful of losing their chance to take advantage of Bitner's unprecedented sponsorship and wide readership, prominent Esperantists in St. Petersburg hurried to persuade Bitner to invest in popularizing Esperanto by means of his influential journal. Despite the fact that he himself had not yet learned Esperanto, Bitner placed faith in his readers' intellectual curiosity and soon announced plans to publish a supplement to *Vestnik znaniia* that he would call "Espero" and that would feature parallel texts in Russian and Esperanto. He hoped that doubting subscribers would discover in this free supplement the worthiness of Esperanto's aims, and primarily, its intended contribution to the "unification of peoples on the basis of cultural reciprocity."[78] Despite this, Bitner himself had still not learned Esperanto.

With its inaugural issue appearing in early 1908, "Espero" presented itself as a social experiment. Bitner believed that Esperanto was a powerful tool of human progress that could satisfy the very real demands of international relations in modern global society. He also believed that in the hands of Esperantists themselves, Esperanto was likely to fail—at least in Russia, that is. The very St. Petersburg Esperantists who had convinced him to publish "Espero" were in his mind poor leaders of, and campaigners for, the movement they claimed to represent. Moreover, their unrepentant elitism blinded them from seeing the merits in democratizing their movement—in welcoming into their movement Russia's "proletarian intelligentsia."[79] A core constituency of *Vestnik*

Znaniia's subscribers were from the growing ranks of imperial Russia's increasingly literate non-elites who were committed to self-improvement and informal education. These were, Bitner believed, the people who could transform Esperantism from a narrow elite pastime into a popular movement capable of realizing Zamenhof's dream of a universal language. Bitner thus hoped that his "coercive" (*prinuditel'nyi*) effort would result in persuading the majority of *Vestnik znaniia*'s estimated one hundred thousand readers to learn Esperanto.[80]

For nearly a year, *Vestnik znaniia*'s subscribers received their free "Espero" supplement. Within it, they found poetry and prose; articles on atheism and alcoholism; debates about (and a great deal of advocacy for) women's equality; proposals for a United States of Europe; meditations on the meaning of life and death; essays on astronomy, aeronautics, psychology, and pedagogy; and damning accounts of European colonialism. Relatively little space was reserved for narrow Esperantist concerns. The supplement asked a progressive readership to relate their concerns for humanity's future to Esperanto's internationalist promises. In December 1908, however, Bitner announced he was shuttering "Espero" in a lead article titled, "Goodbye, Esperantists—Long Live Esperanto!" He remained a believer in and supporter of Esperanto, he explained, but had no interest in further trying to collaborate with the leaders of St. Petersburg's 'Espero' society. They had failed to see what Bitner had seen: the urgency of persuading non-Esperantists of how Esperanto synced with humanist and humanitarian ideals, with a vision of a better global future.[81]

Bitner's frustration with the elite Russian Esperantists' narrow and often milquetoast approach to campaigning for their movement was not misplaced. Scholars of Esperanto have blamed the repressive tsarist regime, and its censorship practices in particular, for stalling the growth of the Esperantist movement in Russia.[82] In overstating the case for the tsarist autocracy's suffocation of Esperantism in late imperial Russia, scholars have allowed themselves to overlook the tactical mistakes and political choices made by the institutional organizers of Russian Esperantism themselves. Even after the 1905 Revolution, the leaders of tsarist Russia's organizational bases of Esperantism were loath to engage in overt political debates and were generally allergic to hitching Esperanto advocacy to that of any specific ideological base along late imperial Russia's widening and diversifying political spectrum. They, and many of their elite counterparts elsewhere in the global Esperantist movement, embraced a vision of ostensible political "neutrality" and one that they interpreted as being the very premise of the so-called Boulogne Declaration. This "myth of neutrality," as Esther Schor has termed it, insisted that Esperanto must be apolitical to thrive.[83]

As the organizational center of Russian Esperantism, St. Petersburg's "Espero" society attempted in its activities and publications to set the tone for the Esperantist movement in Russia as a whole. In the heady days following the October Manifesto, Espero's leaders hailed the 1905 Revolution, and the political and civil rights the tsar promised, as the long-awaited opportunity not only for Russia to regenerate itself, but also for the Esperantist movement in Russia to thrive and grow under the new conditions of political and civil freedom. In the pages of *Ruslanda Esperantisto*, they welcomed this "new era" in which Russian Esperantism "will, free and unhindered, take gigantic steps forward" in "a new, progressive, free Russia."[84] A. I. Asnes, *Ruslanda*

Esperantisto's editor and a St. Petersburg physician, exhorted Espero's members to "energetically work for Esperanto and to participate in the reconstruction of an old rotten regime."[85]

Espero's leaders' seeming euphoria for this "new era" proved short-lived. They soon committed to a sclerotic, decidedly apolitical approach to their work. In the years following the 1905 Revolution, they campaigned for Esperanto's practical utility in a globalizing world rather than on its potential as an ideological basis (in its own right) for reimagining and reconstructing Russia, let alone the world. *Ruslanda Esperantisto* remained a specialist periodical with a miniscule readership and circulation. Its pages were devoted almost exclusively to narrow Esperantist affairs. Poetry, short stories, book reviews, and regular reports from France—the unofficial world headquarters of the Esperanto movement—filled *Ruslanda Esperantisto*'s pages. Russia's leading Esperantists typically avoided anything that hinted even remotely of political activism.

Bitner thus saw Espero's leaders as out of sync with the impulses of Russian civil society in the post-1905 Revolution era. In his view, they peddled one narrowly conceived idea—the international auxiliary language Esperanto—without integrating it into any larger ideological vision or visions. As Joseph Bradley has argued, educated society in early twentieth-century Russia was increasingly defined by a spirit of self-conscious *obshchestvennost'*—"a sense of public duty and civic spirit." This commitment to the public sphere and public service inspired the dramatic growth in fin de siècle Russia of voluntary associations dedicated to an astonishing range of professional, scientific, and humanitarian interests. These voluntary associations (and late imperial Russia's Esperantist societies and clubs were among them) shared a general commitment to disseminating specialist knowledge for the benefit of the empire as a whole.[86] Moreover, the tsarist fin de siècle also witnessed the rapid expansion of what Mark Steinberg has termed the "proletarian intelligentsia"—plebeian literates who staked their claim to participation within, and a unique contribution to, Russia's intellectual life. This plebeian intelligentsia took advantage of people's education courses, lectures, and clubs; subscribed to and wrote for popular journals devoted to culture and enlightenment; and passionately ruminated and debated morality, justice, and their place in a rapidly changing Russian society and the wider world.[87]

Yet many within imperial Russia's educated society—including its upstart middle strata and plebeian intelligentsia—craved something still more than participation in ostensibly politically neutral voluntary associations. They craved citizenship, by which they meant belonging to a state that at the very least demanded of them participation in civic life and provided the adhesive mechanisms through which they were bonded and integrated into the civic whole.[88] The years between the 1905 Revolution and the outbreak of World War I were ones marked by widespread anxiety, raised expectations, and dashed hopes but, among Russia's struggling civil society, it was perhaps most characterized by a striving to participate actively in the shaping of political, social, and cultural life. It was at one and the same time a remarkable era of cultural and intellectual ferment in which wide-eyed and often radical visions for a progressive modernity and liberating future flourished. With his finger on the pulse of this aching civic spirit, Bitner argued that Russia's Esperantist leaders failed to understand that Esperantism was fated to remain a niche interest group and a lifeless movement if its advocates did not tie Esperanto's importance to the questions and ideas that were shaking Russian society and the globe.

Bitner's *Espero* had offered—in Russian and Esperanto—editorials and essays that provocatively explored political and philosophical debates about the role of workers, women, and experts in modern society. It also allowed a space for readers to publicly engage these debates. Reader responses to previous issues' contents were published, sometimes in lengthy essay form. Debate was avidly encouraged by a publisher and editor who believed that Esperantism could only succeed if Esperantists themselves made an ideological, rather than practical, case for their movement. In its short year of operation, Bitner's *Espero* also invited readers seeking pen pals with whom they could correspond in Esperanto to write in with short descriptions of their interests and their postal addresses. Many wrote in to express interest in corresponding about shared professional, scientific, or cultural interests—pedagogy, post and telegraph, chemistry, and literature, for example. The bulk, however, wanted to correspond with others in the international language so as to discuss and debate social and political issues or, as several of them put it: "figuring out [one's] worldview (*o vyrabotke mirosozertsaniia*)."

The postings of Esperantists seeking pen pals in the pages of "Espero" reveal the hunger on the part of ordinary people in the twilight of the Russian empire to use this international auxiliary language not just to satisfy a whim or to provide a pastime, but to serve as a conduit for exchanging ideas about the day's intensely political questions. "I want to correspond with Esperantists about social questions," wrote a teacher from a village in Tver' Province. A student in Vladikavkaz proposed to correspond with "Esperantists from all countries" on "the questions of internationalism and patriotism, federalism, centralism, and autonomy."[89] From Baku came a request to correspond with fellow Esperantists "on the most diverse questions of life," while from the village of Medvenka came a desire to discuss just one: "the question of women's equality."[90] An Esperantist in St. Petersburg sought pen pals with whom he could discuss "the question of workers and about progressive movements among them." From Baku came a request for Esperantists to engage in correspondence about "the Jewish question and Zionism." In Moscow, another wanted to engage in correspondence about the history of Russia's Old Believers.[91] From Saratov came a desire "to correspond about 'The New Art,' pessimism, the sex question, and life's other vexed questions."[92] These were men and women from throughout the great expanse of Russia who were invested and interested in an array of burning questions, of which the question of an international language was just one. As Bitner tried to point out to the conservative leaders of the Espero society, few could expect to recruit large numbers to Esperantism without exerting a simultaneous effort to tie the question of an international language to the broader political and social questions that were felt so urgently in late imperial Russian life. This was what Holly Case has called, "the age of questions"—and educated Russians wanted to take part in what were not only domestic, but also international debates.[93]

Yet old habits die hard. The leaders of late imperial Russia's Esperanto organizations and periodicals had, prior to the 1905 Revolution, learned in their struggles with the tsarist censors that their fight for survival depended in large measure on divorcing Esperanto from overt politics. They also took seriously the Esperantist conceit of political "neutrality"—one that, with the establishment of the Universal Esperanto

Association in 1908 as a transnational organization for all Esperantists, no matter their political persuasions, seemed to be reaffirmed as a global organizational principle.[94] Thus, when Esperantist leaders in St. Petersburg launched a new Russian League of Esperantists in 1909, they stipulated that "the discussion of political and religious questions is not permitted on the League's premises."[95] Local Esperantists throughout tsarist Russia often replicated this vision, as when the Tomsk Society of Esperantists likewise affirmed in its own statutes that "the discussion of questions of a political, religious, and national nature is not permitted on the premises of the Society."[96] Holding fast to a vision of righteous political neutrality, the leaders of Russia's Esperantist organizations committed to popularizing Esperanto as a language project that offered manifold utility to the modern, globalizing world. In the decade that followed the 1905 Revolution, Esperantists in Russia enjoyed more than they ever had before the opportunity to campaign on behalf of Esperantism. Fatefully, the most vocal among them hitched themselves to what they believed was a safely "neutral" vision of Esperanto as a utility to ease international relations, rather than as means of reimagining the world and the people, states, and ideas that decided its fate.

Campaigning for Modernity: Esperanto's Promises

In the decade prior to the outbreak of World War I, Russian Esperantists published a stream of brochures to campaign for Esperanto. Most were produced in the spirit of the ostensibly apolitical, so-called neutral Esperantism that promoted the language as a public utility rather than as a radical mode of reimagining the political and social future. Most were also framed by the conviction that in the post-1905 era, it was public skepticism, rather than governmental obstructionism, that was the greatest hindrance to Esperanto's growth in Russia. Imperial Russia's Esperantists sought to disabuse skeptics of the notion that Esperanto was the niche interest of wild-eyed dreamers. One bitingly commented, "Here, in Russia … the word 'Esperanto' is bandied about like some kind of symbol of foolishness, side by side with futurism, cubism, and the like."[97] Another lamented that in Russia, "the greater part of society regards Esperanto with contempt."[98]

Russia's Esperantists in the tsarist empire's last decade took every opportunity to explain in print why their detractors, in rejecting Esperanto as "foolishness," rejected modernity itself. They insisted that to be an Esperantist was to be a modern global citizen at the forefront of history and at home in a rapidly globalizing and interconnected world. In the uncompromising words of Moscow University linguistics professor R. F. Brandt, "Knowledge of Esperanto is necessary for every contemporary person of culture, for every campaigner for progress."[99] To reject Esperanto and its promises, Russia's Esperantists argued, was to ignore the forward march of history and, ultimately, to be left behind by it.

One of Esperanto's most basic and appealing selling points was the opportunities it made possible to correspond with foreigners in an international auxiliary language—to exchange ideas, expertise, colorful postcards, small gifts, and life stories. M. Mul'tanovskii, an Esperantist in Tomsk, wrote of the "true pleasure" to be gained from corresponding with foreign friends and colleagues. Moreover, he added, "It's not at all necessary to be a Rothschild to correspond with Africans or Japanese." For a reasonable cost of some fifty kopecks a month, an Esperantist could send letters abroad and, in turn, welcome the wonders of the world into his home.[100] This was the age of the postcard and of the pen pal—a time when the relatively small cost of a stamp and a postcard afforded literate men and women with an epistolary vehicle of adventure, globetrotting, and social networking. One Russian pen pal enthusiast described "the life of the postcard" in 1907, celebrating the escapism that this affordable means of long-distance communication offered. "Sitting in front of this postcard that you intend to send to one of your abstract friends," he wrote, "you cut yourself off from the real world for a while, letting go of all its petty troubles and worries, and shift to an idealized, otherworldly sphere."[101] Esperantist pen pal correspondence offered the fantasy of globetrotting in the inexpensive guise of paper and postage. It afforded participants technicolor daydreams as much as real, tangible epistolary friendships.

The opportunity to exchange ideas with a foreigner, to forge international friendships with pen pals, and to cement affective bonds with people they would likely never meet in real life entranced Russian Esperantists as much as it did their comrades abroad. In making the case for Esperantist correspondence, Mul'tanovskii explained that this inexpensive pen pal correspondence so warmed the hearts of all those who engaged in it that there could be no surprise in the tale of a young Russian Esperantist who, dying of tuberculosis, begged his mother to bury him with the Esperanto letters and postcards he had received from friends all over the world.[102] Likewise, A. A. Andreev boasted that he and his "distant Esperantist friend" whom he had only seen yet in a photograph regularly exchanged heartfelt letters exhausting "dozens of sheets of stationery."[103] Russia's Esperantists highly prized Esperanto's unprecedented success at linking people "from all nations, classes, ages, and professions" in a growing global community.[104] They invested their epistolary and transnational social networks with the power to expand their intellectual and emotional horizons and to make real Zamenhof's promise of Esperanto as a medium of human solidarity. To correspond with foreigners on a wide array of topics, both personal and professional, was to engage in the cultured work of elective global citizenship. Esperantists' correspondence was a status symbol of "cultured" global-mindedness. It was a means of fashioning new global subjectivities.

Yet most Esperantist advocacy literature was devoted to the broader, still more practical utilities Esperanto could provide in a world every day made smaller and more patently modern by revolutions in telecommunications, economic exchange, transportation, culture, and politics. In a brochure titled, *International Language and Contemporary Life* (1914), S. P. Rantov dismissed those skeptics who derided the Esperantists as utopians, arguing that those same condescending insults were once hurled at those who doubted the new world made possible by the steam engine. It could not be denied, Rantov argued, that "the history of our day is entirely saturated with the spirit of internationalism."[105] For Rantov, the internationality of modern life demanded not only new technologies like the telephone and automobile, but also a new international auxiliary language. In a world of international congresses, international education, international travel, international commerce, and international cooperation, he argued, Esperanto was a practical necessity.[106]

Russia's Esperantists eagerly enumerated the ways Esperanto could prove useful to a modern global citizenry. V. A. Kolosov predicted that Esperanto would provide the world markets with a "powerful, revitalizing jolt" once it had liberated entrepreneurs and merchants from Babel's constraints.[107] It also made travel easy and pleasant. One Russian Esperantist, Sorokin, wrote about how the language had helped him to enjoy his travels in England. Upon meeting local Esperantists, Sorokin claimed, they greeted him not with their typical "English coldness," but instead "with the tender heart of Esperantists."[108] One young Russian Esperantist described how Esperanto had helped him to acclimate to his new surroundings and make friends upon his arrival in France as a foreign student.[109] Elsewhere, the same young man made the case for Esperanto as the only choice for modern diplomacy. In an age of militant nationalism and increasingly hostile international competition, he explained, conflicts between states could only be solved or lessened through the neutral international auxiliary language of Esperanto. "No nation that has at least one drop of its own dignity and patriotism" would deny that diplomacy via Esperanto would be preferable and more productive than diplomacy carried out in another nation's native tongue.[110] In the pages of the popular journal *Priroda i liudi*, another argued that "Especially for us Russians, whose language is never used in international relations, it is important to possess knowledge of the international language given to humanity by a modest Russian doctor."[111]

N. Kabanov argued that "cultured countries" and their enterprising elites dominated the international pathways of science, scholarship, commerce, and diplomacy. Within these more advanced countries, Kabanov noted, robust civil societies had appeared in recent decades. Educated men and women had organized an array of independent institutions including temperance societies, pacifist groups, academic organizations, sporting leagues, tourist clubs, and educational advocacy groups. Given the global scope of these varied endeavors, Kabanov argued, civil society in the world's "cultured countries" realized with ever more urgency the need for an international language to facilitate communication and cooperation across borders.[112]

The argument that Esperanto was an indispensable tool of elite European culture and superior civilization was also regularly featured in editorials in *Ruslanda Esperantisto*. Zamenhof had given the modern world "one of the greatest weapons of cultural development" it had yet seen.[113] In Russia, the Esperanto movement represented a cross-section of educated society. Aristocrats, civil servants, academics, professionals, merchants, teachers, students, and other members of the growing bourgeoisie dominated the movement. In a lead article titled, "The Popular Masses and Esperanto," Vsevolod Loiko—a long-standing leader of St. Petersburg's Espero society—noted that of course Esperanto was a relatively elite enterprise. As yet, an international language was only of concern to "that part of humanity that is already identified with international cultural life." It was an educated person's pursuit, not an illiterate peasant's. "In the sphere of science, art, philosophy, as in the sphere of civilization understood in the narrow sense of the world," Loiko argued, "new, and the very greatest ideas are, in the first place and often for a very long time, understood and applied precisely among the most cultured segment of a people." Esperantists, he argued, had special duty to lead the simple folk into a global future whose achievement of progress was secured by forward-thinking educated elites on behalf of humanity as a whole.[114] For now, the wider world belonged to those who could afford to engage it. So, too, did Esperantoland.

Russian Travels to Esperantoland in the Tsarist Fin de Siècle

In the late tsarist empire, Russian Esperantists traveled often to Esperantoland—many without ever leaving their small towns. It was at the First World Congress of Esperantists in Boulogne-sur-Mer that Zamenhof anointed what he called "Esperantoland" (*Esperantujo*)—the international community of Esperantists that belonged to no one land or people; transcended national, linguistic, and cultural differences; and offered a flexible framework for enacting self-styled global citizenship. Esperantoland, Zamenhof insisted, existed wherever and whenever Esperantists came together to communicate in the international auxiliary language that had the power to unite humanity. Voyages to Esperantoland allowed Esperantists to enact their shared transnational culture and to assert their identity as citizens of the world, fluent in an international language and the values of global-mindedness. A clear precedent had been set at Boulogne, and thereafter making the pilgrimage to an Esperantist world congress was considered the pinnacle of lived Esperantism. The world Esperantist congresses typically convinced participants of Esperanto's ability to bring together people of diverse lands, languages, and cultures in a shared, living-and-breathing, community of human solidarity. "All who have actively participated in the congresses even but one time become forever passionate advocates of the idea of the international language," the Russian Esperantist A. Postnikov explained.[115]

Zamenhof was not the only Russian Esperantist to attend the First World Esperanto Congress in Boulogne, nor was he without his fellow countrymen at subsequent convocations of the annual world congress. Nearly two handfuls of prominent Russian Esperantists traveled from their homes in St. Petersburg, Tiflis, Odessa, Poltava, Yalta, and Warsaw to attend the first world congress. They were unanimous in their awe of the powerful feelings inspired by the event, which they hailed as having "enormous significance not only for Esperantists, but for the entire civilized world."[116] The joy of witnessing and participating in Zamenhof's dream come to life was like no other, they reported.[117]

Leo Belmont, one of imperial Russia's most prominent and wealthy Esperantists, published for his less fortunate peers an account of his travels from St. Petersburg to Boulogne.[118] Although one of Esperanto's earliest adopters, Belmont admitted that prior to his departure for the Boulogne congress, he feared that the event would prove Esperanto as a disappointment or worse, a failure. He worried that the Esperantists might not understand one another, that they would pronounce the Esperanto words differently. Upon arrival in Boulogne, he remained wary, but allowed himself to laugh at the "Zamenhof seltzer" and the "Esperanto wine" strategically marketed for sale in the cafes. Belmont was not emotionally prepared for the scene that awaited him at the congress venue: a huge, raucous crowd of Esperantists laughing and carrying on with shrieks of joy and happiness. He could scarcely believe his eyes as he watched these fellow Esperantists as they met face-to-face for the first time and embraced like old friends. Belmont recounted how, once the Congress began, attendees quickly abandoned their compatriots in search of interesting conversation with the foreigners all around them, foreigners with whom they could almost magically converse in Esperanto. Excitement radiated throughout the venue. Belmont explained, "there was something simply touching in that temporary evaporation of national difference."[119] There was pride, too, and a deep sense of satisfaction shared by the attendees. They had gambled on a vision of a future world harmony made possible by an international auxiliary language and, almost two decades after the experiment had begun, they discovered that it worked. In Boulogne, the atmosphere was euphoric.

Subsequent convocations of the World Esperanto Congress were thus greeted as singular events, special opportunities to experience the fullest realization of Esperantoland that money could buy. Russian Esperantists who bought tickets to these world congresses were promised a week of Esperanto immersion in an attractive foreign city, and all the delights of the programs offered: concerts, plays, sumptuous meals, champagne, dancing, lectures, tourist excursions, and nearly limitless Esperanto conversation. For those fated only to experience these annual convocations of Esperantoland vicariously, there were reports and travelogues printed in the Esperantist periodical press. *Ruslanda Esperantisto*, for example, printed a blow-by-blow account of the Second World Esperanto Congress that convened in Geneva in late August 1906. Armchair visitors to Esperantoland could thus imagine the hawkers of Esperanto souvenirs, the ovations inspired by Zamenhof's mere entrance into the conference hall, the thunderous applause that greeted Zamenhof's speech, the green stars pinned to the lapels and the green flags waving vigorously, and the sounds of Esperanto spoken by hundreds of devoted Esperantists from countries near and far.[120] Esperantist travelogues occupied a distinct niche within late imperial Russia's most popular genre of writing and reading—the travel accounts that literate Russians prized as much for their entertainment as for their information value, and upon which they relied for their armchair access to worldliness and globe-trotting imagination.[121]

Notably, the tsarist government also proved interested in the claims Esperantists made for the need for an international auxiliary language. In the late nineteenth and early twentieth centuries, governments around the world came to regard as essential their participation in the setting of "universal" and "uniform" norms of timekeeping, international commerce, telecommunications, and weights and measures. Great power status, or even just great power aspirations, required having a seat at the table when international conventions for standardizing and synchronizing the globe's increasingly international modes and mechanisms of moving people, goods, technology, expertise, currency, and telecommunications across borders (and time zones).[122] This fin de siècle "governmental internationalism" demanded that states send representatives to diplomatic conventions, but also to a wide range of "nongovernmental" conferences devoted to technological, scientific, economic, or intellectual questions of perceived global significance.[123]

As Esperanto gained in popularity, and especially in the first two decades of the twentieth century, governments around the world began to pay focused attention on the real possibility that, in time, the movement to unite the world with an international auxiliary language would succeed. In the event of Esperanto's global victory, the governments of the world's leading states would want to participate in establishing the conventions of adopting an international auxiliary language for trade, diplomacy, cultural exchange, and international law. In the meantime, they at least wanted a seat at the annual world congresses of Esperantists. In fin de siècle Europe, cultural internationalism developed apace with ever more militant nationalisms and emerged as a rapidly expanding arena of global power politics. Claimants to geopolitical leadership and "civilizational" status took seriously participation in international meetings of government representatives, experts, and public intellectuals committed to thinking about and cooperating in the administration of what were seen as "universal" questions in a self-consciously globalizing world.[124]

In 1910, Russia was one of twelve states to send an official representative to the Sixth World Esperanto Congress held in Washington, DC. On behalf of the Ministry of Trade and Industry, the tsarist government sent to Washington one of St. Petersburg's leading Esperantists, A. A. Postnikov, to deliver a brief speech congratulating the assembled Esperantists on having captured the attention of world leaders. On returning to St. Petersburg, Postnikov delivered a formal report to the Ministry of Trade and Industry in which he argued that the tsarist government should consider the question of international language an urgent one for any world power, but especially one, like Russia, whose national language was never considered as a potential lingua franca for diplomacy and trade. He also urged the tsarist government to look favorably upon the prospect of hosting a future World Esperanto Congress as a prime opportunity to acquaint foreigners with Russia's rich heritage and culture, no less than its growing economy.[125]

In 1911, the Ministry of Trade and Industry sent an employee, A. M. Nedoshivin, to serve as a delegate at the Eighth World Congress of Esperantists in Antwerp. Nedoshivin even enjoyed a private meeting with Zamenhof himself. Upon his return, Nedoshivin delivered a formal report to the Ministry of Trade and Industry that endorsed Esperanto as a language of a wide range of practical purposes for the tsarist bureaucracy in its wider European dealings. Nedoshivin also discounted what he described as the popular prejudices hurled against the Esperantist movement in general (namely, its rumored infiltration by Masons, pacifists, and other perceived ne'er-do-wells).[126] In that year, the Ministry of Trade and Industry again dispatched Nedoshivin to the World Esperanto Congress in Krakow and soon began to promote formal Esperanto coursework for that language's use in its potential civil service work. As Nedoshivin explained it, the ministry increasingly regarded Esperanto as a necessary aspect of conducting international business affairs.[127]

Esperantoland, however, extended beyond the annual world congresses of Esperantists and the governmental and corporate bodies who increasingly took interest in them. As one of imperial Russia's Esperantists rather improbably discovered on the eve of World War I, one did not even need to be Zamenhof to rise as a globe-trotting international Esperantist celebrity and trailblazer. The case of the blind poet Vasilii Eroshenko (1890–1952) demonstrates the sometimes surprising ways that Esperanto did open up the world to its adepts, allowing them to network creatively across borders and making it possible for them to assert themselves as global citizens and even international celebrities.

Born to peasants and blinded at age 4 as a side effect of illness, Eroshenko was "uplifted" by noble benefactors who enrolled him in a Moscow school for the blind, where he is said to have nurtured his talents for music, storytelling, and language-learning. At the age of 22, Eroshenko embarked on his first Esperantist adventure, traveling to London where he studied music, learned English, befriended fellow Esperantists, and met with Kropotkin and other anarchists before being expelled from school and sent packing back to Russia. Not content to sit still back at home, Eroshenko worked his Esperantist contacts again and this time found passage to Tokyo in 1912. At a time when Japan's educated public was swept up in a feverish craze for all things Esperanto, Eroshenko arrived on the scene and quickly immersed himself among Japanese intellectuals who shared his overlapping interests in Esperanto, anarchism, global transnational solidarity, and eventually, too, the Baha'i faith. Wearing a simple peasant's tunic, Eroshenko recited poetry, sang Russian folk songs, proselytized Esperanto, and gave lectures on cooperatist anarchism to crowds of Japanese admirers.[128]

As historian Sho Konishi has explained, after the Russo-Japanese war, many Japanese intellectuals were drawn to what they called "worldism"—a vision for a global moral community that rejected the national and racial hierarchies of Western modernity. Worldism sought to enable human connection across and beyond borders, irrespective of the cultural, racial, national, or religious differences that had divided humanity. Esperanto seemed tailor-made for this vision of a transnational, "translingual world order" and many "worldists" in early twentieth-century Japan embraced Zamenhof's language. With his charisma, enthusiastic Esperantism, and talents as a bard, Eroshenko found himself in the right place at the right time. A variety of Japanese intellectuals celebrated Eroshenko, welcomed him into their social networks, and embraced him as an icon of worldism and Esperanto alike. Eroshenko's popularity in Japanese society surged. Large, adoring crowds soon greeted him during his travels across the country as the celebrity Esperantist bard.[129] Eroshenko was so popular that in the aftermath of the Russian Revolution, the Japanese Foreign Ministry deported him on the pretext that he had the apparent power and influence to subversively import revolutionary Russia's disorder and chaos to Japan.[130]

Eroshenko proved an exceptional case of Esperantist globetrotting and international celebrity. Yet his was one of many life-altering Russian travels to Esperantoland in the twilight of the tsarist empire made by ordinary men and women seeking community and meaning in the wider world. Fatefully, late imperial Russia's Esperantists did not need to achieve celebrity or even to leave one's village to visit Esperantoland, make friends across the globe, and fashion themselves as world citizens. They could travel to and within Esperantoland for the mere cost of postage.

Epistolary Globe-Trotting

Most Esperantists in Russia (as elsewhere) could not afford the tremendous financial cost of traveling abroad for an Esperanto World Congress and its extensive itineraries of meals, lectures, theater, and ballroom dancing. The Esperanto World Congress was a luxury. Most rank-and-file Esperantists in late imperial Russia could not afford foreign travel at all. Esperantoland, however, could be found throughout the expanse of the tsarist empire and beyond it. In 1909, Peter Vasil'kovskii published in *Ruslanda Esperantisto* his diary of traveling from St. Petersburg to Saratov, where he found himself on the doorstep of a provincial Esperantist who greeted him with "youthful delight" and overwhelmed him with warmth and hospitality. "I am an Esperantist," Vasil'kovskii mused, "and that was more than enough for him to receive me as a welcome guest, as if I were close, as if I were kin." Soon, the two were discussing Esperanto and Vasil'kovskii asked his host, "You, obviously, quite seriously engage with Zamenhof's idea?" The young man responded feverishly, "I beg your pardon, but there's no other way!" He next shuffled across the room to his desk, retrieved a thick pile of letters, and began reciting the names of countries where he had Esperantist pen pals:

> From Germany, England, Spain, France, Italy … Turkey, China, Japan, India, yes from India…. Fourteen nationalities correspond with me, with me who doesn't know any other national language except Russian. And now I have so many friends, wonderful close friends, everywhere, from all over…. Look, here are their photographs. Read what kind, touching inscriptions. And it is Esperanto that has given me all of this!

This young man, Vasil'kovskii explained, was testimony to Esperanto's real ability to open the world to curious men and women who otherwise never had the chance to travel beyond their small corners of the world. This provincial Esperantist found in his correspondence with foreign pen pals a pathway to understanding the wider world without accruing the prohibitive costs of foreign travel, not to mention years of studying multiple foreign languages. "The world," the ardent Esperantist in Saratov told him earnestly, "has become intelligible and dear to me."[131]

Before the evening was through, Vasil'kovskii explained, the young man had invited Saratov's local Esperantists over to meet their guest from St. Petersburg. These were, Vasil'kovskii explained, "small, modest people of the type who do not have the resources or the time to visit Geneva or Cambridge or Barcelona to attend the Esperantist congresses." But Esperanto gave them the world. The post delivered into their hands foreign cultures, ideas, and friends from the exotic abroad. No matter how modest or provincial, these men and women were, by virtue of their Esperantism, emissaries of the future, of an interconnected world that was networked by means of an international language.[132]

Even if Vasil'kovskii's travelogue were an exaggerated account of voyaging into a provincial Russian outpost of Esperantoland, the archival record leaves no doubt that Esperantists throughout Russia and the world *did* delight in correspondence with their foreign pen pals and many *did* establish lifelong friendships through their epistolary exchanges. One of the language's greatest selling points was its promise of friendship, social connection, and intellectual stimulation. In 1908 the British Esperantist Margaret Jones promised that the language was a cure for boredom and loneliness. "If you are lonely and have no friends, if you long for intellectual sympathy, learn Esperanto," she urged. "You will find warm friends wherever you may seek them, at hand, or in the most distant corner of the earth."[133]

From the launch of the movement, Zamenhof had taken seriously the need to provide those "points of connection" that would enable Esperantists to correspond in the language, thereby infusing it with life. Using the modern means of post and telegraph first and foremost, Esperantists built a global community from the ground up. Most Esperantists in the late nineteenth and the twentieth century would never, as Vasil'kovskii noted, have the time or the money to attend the legendary world congresses. Most did, however, take pen to paper or postcard and send their thoughts and Esperantist sentiments across borders and into the hands of foreigners who, at the very least, shared their interest in an international language. It was not uncommon for an Esperantist of at least modest means to correspond with a dozen, or even dozens, of pen pals and to nurture these transnational friendships over the long term.

Once Esperantism began growing and taking on novel institutional forms in the early twentieth century, Zamenhof himself no longer shouldered sole responsibility for making sure that Esperantists could find one another via postal addresses. All manner of new Esperantist organizations—local, national, transnational—produced Esperantist directories and yearbooks. A mainstay of Esperantist publications were the "correspondence departments" that printed small classified ads of Esperantists seeking pen pals. Esperantists throughout Russia and the world were happy to pay nominal fees to list their addresses and their appeals for correspondents. While many of these featured nothing more than a correspondence-seeker's name and address, others revealed specific interests. Often enough, a correspondence seeker wanted nothing more than to exchange colorful postcards and stamps. Thus, one Russian Esperantist was quite specific in what he wanted from a foreign pen pal: "I would like to have views of foreign cities, and will be very diligent in sending in return illustrated postcards with views of the cities Nizhnii Novgorod, Kazan, Samara, Saratov, Astrakhan, and Viaznik."[134] Even if Russia's Esperantists never paid for their own listings, they were able to reply directly to the similar classified ads that foreign Esperantists regularly placed in Russian publications. In the pages of *La Ondo de Esperanto* (The Wave of Esperanto), a Russian Esperantist publication produced in the final decade of the tsarist empire, Russian Esperantists could regularly find the announcements of Esperantists abroad seeking pen pals. From Argentina, England, France, the Ottoman Empire, India, New Zealand, and Germany came requests for correspondence with their "fellow-thinkers."[135]

Thus, it was possible for a young man born in Rostov-on-Don in 1885 to make friends with Esperantist pen pals all over the world and to fashion himself an epistolary globe-trotter. Coming of age alongside the Esperanto movement itself, Genadii Ivanovich Tupitsyn studied in Moscow and Zurich before beginning his career as a geography teacher in Moscow not long after the 1905 Revolution. What began for Tupitsyn as a passing curiosity in Esperanto during his student days quickly became a passion that would last for the remainder of his life, following him into emigration twice: first, in 1919 to Latvia, and later, in the aftermath of World War II, to the United States. In this way, Tupitsyn's personal papers, the bulk of which comprised the Esperantist correspondence he pursued and so obviously prized throughout his life, came to be archived at the Hoover Institution Archives at Stanford University.[136]

Tupitsyn's personal papers contain literal stacks of colorful postcards he received in the final decade of the tsarist empire from Esperantists throughout Russia, but also from New York, Melbourne, London, and Kashmir. On April 19, 1912, the Albany, Oregon, post office stamped a postcard from George L. Howe and addressed to Tupitsyn in "Moskvo, Rusujo." Howe thanked Tupitsyn for his previous card and asked politely for a postcard with a photo of "Moscow's famous big bell." Howe then explained the import of the colorful postcard that he had chosen for Tupitsyn this time around, one that would impart some knowledge of an aspect of American life perhaps little understood in Russia. "This card," he wrote in neat cursive, "shows a group of children from the 'Pueblo tribe of Indians.' This tribe builds houses with sundried bricks. They are not savage. Note the donkeys."[137]

In this way, Tupitsyn collected hundreds of postcards from around the world featuring landscapes, peoples, and events that he would never see with his own eyes. He developed friendships with Esperantists all over the world who, like Tupitsyn himself, had been attracted to Esperanto precisely for its ability to connect curious "fellow-thinkers." The personal investment and existential meaning that Esperantists found in these friendships should not be underestimated or dismissed as the mere hyperbole of Esperantist propagandists. In April 1912, A. H. Johnson of Melbourne, Australia, sent Tupitsyn a special postcard he had printed, likely in the dozens, for use in his Esperantist correspondence. "My very dear friend," Johnson addressed Tupitsyn, before thanking him for the recent postcard featuring a view of Central Asia. Johnson wrote of life's recent stresses. His wife was ill and the anxieties of work were keeping him up at night. The whole family, he explained, was looking forward to the rest promised by an upcoming vacation in Adelaide. Johnson signed his note "from your Australian fellow-thinker and friend," and added, "Your cards and news are very interesting to me." On the postcard's obverse was Johnson's formal studio portrait, where he is shown in suit and tie, with an Esperantist green star affixed to his lapel. Johnson signed this side of the card too, inscribing it "Yours fraternally, A. H. Johnson, Melbourne, 1912."[138]

What is rare about Tupitsyn's avid correspondence with Esperantists abroad from his relatively humble corner of the world in Moscow is not the fact of the correspondence at all; it is that so much of it was preserved and made its way into an archive. One of the most widely advertised points of appeal made on Esperanto's behalf in late imperial Russia was the opportunity it provided educated men and women of even modest financial means to travel, even if in armchair and epistolary fashion, to Esperantoland—to make friends there, to exchange ideas, to collect postcards and trinkets that were tangible representations of a wide and colorful world beyond the borders of their own country and the narrow confines of their own individual lives. In Esperantist circles, one's Esperantist correspondence was a status symbol, a measure of

Figure 3 Postcard from A. H. Johnson of Melbourne, Australia to G. I. Tupitsyn, his Esperantist pen pal in late imperial Russia, 1912. *Source*: Hoover Institution Archives, Gennadii Ivanovich Tupitsyn Papers, Box 4, Folder 3.

one's worldliness and the reach of one's social network. Thus I. Ostrovskii, a prominent Esperantist physician from Yalta, was already bragging in the late 1890s "that he, not knowing a single foreign [national] language, corresponds by means of Esperanto with people from seventeen different nations, including: French, Germans, Englishmen,

Swedes, Norwegians, Italians, Spaniards, Portuguese, Americans, Africans, and others."[139] Epistolary globe-trotting was as much a means of self-fashioning as it was a source of entertainment and sociability.

When, in 1912, Esperanto celebrated its silver jubilee, one Russian Esperantist returned to the pages of *Vestnik znaniia* to appraise the movement's progress. Once a Warsaw eye doctor's obscure flight of fancy, Esperanto was now a "prominent feature of cultural life throughout all humanity." While obstacles remained, Esperanto was destined to triumph. If, in 1912, there remained skeptics of the benefits Esperanto promised future humanity, this was only so because some refused to acknowledge the supranational design of this international auxiliary language and therefore feared it as a threat to their national interests. The goal of Esperanto, however, had never been to destroy the world's national languages but rather to transcend them. Esperantists were patriotic cosmopolitans trailblazing a path toward shared human knowledge, technology, culture, wisdom, brotherhood, and peace.[140]

In this trailblazing, Esperantists like Eroshenko, Tupitsyn, Vasil'kovskii, Ostrovskii, and so many others in Russia and around the world found hope as well as joy in what was, for them, the very personal international relationships and expanded horizons that Esperanto had afforded them. It was still quite possible, many of them believed, for the world to choose unity over division, friendship over hatred, cooperation over conflict. Esperantists chose consciously to work toward a harmonious future, the fruits of which the whole world might one day enjoy. They modeled a new type of global citizenship, a new type of person networked into a shrinking world.

Collision Course

In 1914, some 3,739 Esperantists registered for the Tenth World Esperanto Congress that was to be held in early August of that fateful year in Paris.[141] Zamenhof never made it to Paris for the event, which was hastily canceled in response to the launch of World War I. Yet at least one of his compatriots, V. Zavialov, arrived in Paris several weeks in advance of the World Congress's scheduled opening, only to bear Esperantist witness to the start of the Great War—a scene he would late memorialize in a curious pamphlet titled *Guiding Star*. Published in 1915 during the humiliating chaos of imperial Russia's wartime experience, Zavialov's *Guiding Star* scarcely concerned itself with the horrors of the Great War. Instead, Zavialov ruminated on Esperanto's underestimated value and lamented a World Esperanto Congress interrupted by war's outbreak.[142]

Upon his eager arrival in Paris, Zavialov had found a café that advertised with a sign that read "We speak Esperanto here." Better yet, he soon found assembled on the street a small crowd of his fellow Esperantists—from Scotland, England, Spain, the United States, Brazil, Cuba, and Russia too. The crowd giddily erupted in lively conversation in Esperanto and began exchanging visiting cards. Each one, Zavialov noted, proudly wore a pinned green "guiding star" of Esperanto. "It was," Zavialov explained, "imperceptible that we had all arrived from different parts of the world and were representatives of different nationalities. The language united everyone."[143]

The euphoria felt by these early arrivals to the planned Tenth World Esperanto Congress, however, was soon cut short by the announcement of France's mobilization for war. The Esperantists, Zavialov recounted, huddled together to discuss the disconcerting news. The most optimistic among them predicted that "for the good of civilization, it was imperative to fittingly repulse [the Kaiser] Wilhelm. Then, the nations (*narody*) would still more closely ally (*sbliziatsia*) with one another and our language [Esperanto] would still more vigorously spread."[144] Within days, the hopeful Esperantists who had traveled to Paris dispersed. They rushed off to join their national armies, to volunteer for the Red Cross, or simply to navigate the sudden wartime circumstances that maddened their efforts to secure passage home.

The last pages of Zavialov's brief travelogue read as a requiem not for a world at war, but for a Tenth World Esperanto Congress that never officially convened. He fondly recalled those heady days in Paris when he saw Esperanto flags flying, conversed with fellow adepts from all over the world, and was introduced to the "city of lights" by means of excursions led by Esperanto-speaking guides. He marveled at Esperanto's unique ability to forge "a spiritual connection between people."[145] Zavialov's heart and mind remained in Esperantoland even after he returned home to Russia, his homeland now at war.

Blood, Ruins, and Hope for Regeneration

Historians have little appreciated the many varieties of internationalism that captivated the imagination of educated society in late imperial Russia. When considered at all, the grassroots internationalism of Esperantists in the tsarist fin de siècle has long been presumed a particularly tragic case of a movement strangled by a repressive and paranoid autocracy. This chapter has shed light instead on what appears upon closer investigation to be an energetic, if small Esperantist movement in late imperial Russia. This movement reflected the wider global conversations and communities that educated Russian society participated in during this self-conscious era of globalization and internationalism. It reflected, too, a yearning for a new kind of subjectivity—that of the global modern who was at one and the same time patriotic and cosmopolitan.

Ultimately, late imperial Russia's Esperantists represent a unique brand of grassroots internationalism born of educated Russians' as yet underappreciated craving for elective global citizenship in these years. Educated Russians' yearning to participate meaningfully and actively in their own society during the painful twilight of the tsarist empire extended well beyond Russia's borders as educated men and women self-consciously fashioned themselves as global actors with global concerns. They wanted a stake in global conversations—about science, literature, art, politics, and the novel ideological and technological changes that were rapidly transforming their local and global realities as "cultured" cosmopolitans. Imperial Russia's Esperantists embraced Esperanto for an array of reasons that overlapped and reflected a broader impulse to live and shape the internationality that they recognized as a fundamental condition of their globalizing era. Esperanto provided an outlet for epistolary and literal globetrotting, the transnational exchange of ideas and expertise, the forging of interpersonal relationships that defied linguistic, national, and cultural borders, and the fashioning of new global identities. Esperanto served its adepts as a readymade and even delightful vehicle for becoming a modern global citizen, at home and networked in the wider but rapidly shrinking world.

On the eve of World War I, imperial Russia's Esperantists were among those who every day felt more keenly "a new self-consciousness of the internationality of everyday life."[146] Arguably, Esperantists were among those both best and least prepared for the shocking devastation, violence, and revolutions wrought by the Great War. They had for several decades railed against the world's unnecessary fractures in an age of galloping globalization and proselytized the world harmony they believed Esperanto could help to achieve. In late imperial Russia as elsewhere in Europe, Esperanto had inspired an overwhelmingly upper- and middle-class constituency that delighted as much in internationalist hopes for a more humane future as they did the balls, concerts, and scholarly lectures hosted by their Esperantist organizations.

As the tsarist government bumbled its way through what quickly proved a humiliating and intractable global war, Russia's Esperantists did their best to persevere. As could be expected given the "difficult and dismal" circumstances of the war, membership to Russia's Esperanto societies declined, resources for programming and publications dried up, and hope for a better, more humane future increasingly seemed an illusion that few could afford.[147] Esperantists in Russia and throughout the world took advantage of the humanitarian services the "neutral" Universal Esperanto Association (UEA) offered from its headquarters in Geneva. The UEA transmitted private correspondence across the borders of warring countries, researched and provided information about soldiers presumed missing or dead, and distributed food and other scarce but necessary resources in wartime. From across the ideological spectrum, many Esperantists agitated for peace in the various names of religious pacifism, feminism, and Marxist internationalism.[148] Zamenhof's "An Appeal to the Diplomatists" was not the only Esperantist appeal during the war to anticipate peacetime diplomacy and argue for Esperanto's role in helping to heal the world. In early 1915, the Russian Esperantist Ia. Shapiro published his brochure, "The War among Peoples and Esperanto," in which he insisted that Esperanto's relevance was never more apparent than during the catastrophic global war whose end was not yet in sight. "Bravely, with faith in a new bright future that must arrive after the horrors of today's difficult time," Shapiro wrote, "Esperantists continue their work spreading a wonderful method of destroying the mutual incomprehensibility of nations that speak different languages."[149]

Esperantists were visionaries, always with an eye toward the future that they could not help but to see in global terms. The unprecedented global war launched in 1914 only reinforced their desire to see the world healed and remade by Esperanto. When the February Revolution of 1917 collapsed the monarchy, Russia's Esperantists joined their compatriots in imagining and pursuing a wide variety of futures for Russia and the world. Russia's revolutions in 1917 assured that not only Russia, but also Esperantoland, would never be the same again.

3

Bolshevik Tower of Babel

In memoirs of his coming of age as a British communist, Thomas Bell recalled arriving in Moscow in the spring of 1921 as a delegate to the upcoming Third World Congress of the Communist International (Comintern). "The Soviet capital—the headquarters of proletarian internationalism—seemed filled with a conglomeration of peoples from all over the world," Bell wrote. "For me, a worker from insular little England, the effect was tremendous. I had not realised before *how* insular we were. The babel of tongues; the characteristic types of peoples; the variety in manners and dress were overwhelming, as, indeed, they must be for the average British worker, who rarely goes abroad and knows no language but his own." The Comintern, Bell marveled, was "doing a great work in realising true international understanding and the unity of the workers of the world."[1]

Jack Murphy, another British Cominternarian, also recounted in his memoirs the transformative experience of serving the stunningly cosmopolitan Bolshevik headquarters of global communism. Yet Murphy also revisited a regret that in many ways came to define his time working toward the goals of proletarian internationalism in the early Soviet republic. Dispatched to revolutionary Russia as a representative of British socialism in 1920, Murphy time and again encountered the language barrier that stood in the way of his ability to fully participate in the Comintern's planning for what was then heralded by the Bolsheviks as the imminent "worldwide October." This formidable language barrier especially pained Murphy when, on the opening day of the Comintern's Second Congress, he sat helpless as his hero V. I. Lenin "rose amidst a storm of cheering" and then addressed the delegates about the world revolution that they had traveled to Soviet Russia to help ignite. "How I wished I had studied foreign languages," Murphy sighed. "Like many more I had to wait for the translation, for of course Lenin spoke in Russian."[2]

Murphy shared this frustration with many of his fellow socialists who traveled to revolutionary Russia intent on participating in the Comintern and its networks of proletarian internationalism. At the Comintern, engaging in the practical work of global communism immediately brought to the fore the inherent dilemmas and challenges of language diversity in an internationalist enterprise. For many proletarian internationalists who flocked to the Comintern, miscommunication and utter linguistic unintelligibility dominated their lived experience of this powerful node of interwar socialist internationalism. This chapter revisits their struggles and the wider, ultimately global politics of language in interwar revolutionary Russia. It examines, too, how Esperantists struggled to persuade the Bolsheviks that Esperanto was the best solution to the problem of language diversity among the global proletariat—especially as that problem presented itself within the Comintern.

In recent years, scholars have begun to rewrite the Comintern's history—now with a long overdue focus on the lived experience of the socialist revolutionaries from around the globe who endeavored to transform the Bolsheviks' October into a truly worldwide revolution. This scholarship has helped to reconstruct the vibrant life stories of these socialist internationalists and the cultures of global communism they helped to create both within the Comintern's institutional settings and far beyond them. This new historiography has focused on what it meant, and how it felt, to participate in the Comintern's transnational networks of socialist internationalism. It has helped to unpack but also to complicate what we know about how Comminternarians built a global community of border-crossing and code-switching revolutionaries.[3] In these exciting ways, the new Comintern historiography has pivotally helped to produce a more global and more intimate history of the Russian Revolution.[4]

This chapter joins in this historiographical mission to recapture the lived experience of interwar socialist internationalism and seeks also to better understand the culture of the Comintern in its early years especially. Upon the creation of the Comintern in 1919, Soviet Esperantists attempted to seize the moment and insisted that only an international auxiliary language made practical and ideological sense for a transnational organization plotting a worldwide October. The Bolsheviks opted instead, however, for more traditional language politics. The Comintern made do, more or less, with a small handful of working national languages and a growing army of translators and interpreters. Given the Bolsheviks' primary preoccupation with the West, and with Europe in particular, the early Comintern privileged German, but also Russian, French, and English as the working languages of socialist internationalism.[5] As the prospects for imminent world revolution faded, especially after the failure of German October in 1923, the Bolsheviks changed course. The Bolsheviks' first priority would be building socialism in one country. Ultimately, it was the Russian language—not German, and not Esperanto either—that the Bolsheviks would promote as the lingua franca of a new socialist internationalism unquestionably under their lead.

Revolutionary Possibilities

"The great Russian revolution, so quickly, so unexpectedly, like oxygen to a dying man, came to save the Russian people at the very moment when those in authority did not expect it."[6] So gushed an editorial in the *Daily Kopeck Gazette* in March 1917. Its author articulated the hopeful feelings of many when he referred to Russia's revolutionary present as "the springtime of freedom."[7] Freedom was a watchword of the first months of Russia's 1917 revolution. Few freedoms inspired as much revolutionary talk in the spring of 1917 as the freedom of speech—the freedom to agitate and proselytize all possible futures for Russia and the world. Times were no doubt uncertain, chaotic, and disorienting, but many voices once on the periphery and in the underground of late imperial Russian life found in 1917's "springtime of freedom" the opportunity to grab a bullhorn and advocate for one's ideological vision within the rowdy revolutionary public sphere.

In the early months of the Russian Revolution, new Esperantist organizations—most of them shoestring operations—sprouted overnight throughout the country. Until the Bolsheviks seized power in October, the Esperantist movement in revolutionary Russia operated as an ideological big tent. All were invited to participate and to agitate on behalf of Esperanto and any other political vision. What united Russia's Esperantists in these days was first and foremost a commitment to Esperanto. Admittedly, the relatively conservative pre-revolutionary intelligentsia still dominated Esperantist circles.[8] Yet new organizations of young "socialist Esperantists" were already making efforts to direct Russia and the world into a bold and radical Esperantist future.

In agitating for Esperanto's essential role in the revolution, these young Esperantists joined their fellow citizens in deploying the key words and slogans of the evolving revolutionary discourse. In February's wake, they spoke of liberty, equality, and fraternity. They also framed their arguments about Esperanto's revolutionary role within the broad moral claims of the revolution—its seeming promise of long overdue political and economic justice for the so-called common people. They embedded their arguments in favor of Esperanto in larger discussions of democracy, class, and socialism. They rarely explicated what they meant by these terms; the point was instead to imagine and work toward a more humane and morally just future. In this embrace of an early revolutionary discourse whose vocabulary was ubiquitous but whose meanings were not yet fixed, the Esperantists were joined by millions of their compatriots who were learning the political language of Russia's revolution in real time, as it evolved.[9]

One relatively radical approach to pursuing a role for Esperanto in Russia's revolution between February and October 1917 was Richard Tsyvinskii and Timofei Sikora's *Manifesto of the Union of Socialist Esperantists*.[10] Although nothing is known of Sikora, Tsyvinskii had organized the All-Russian Esperanto Student Society shortly before the outbreak of World War I. An architect, Tsyvinskii in 1917 was then still operating in loose association with the pre-revolutionary "Espero" society in Petrograd and with the Moscow Society of Esperantists. Yet the *Manifesto* he coauthored with Sikora was part of Tsyvinskii's larger effort to launch what he envisioned as a "Universal League of Socialist Esperantists."[11] The *Manifesto* sought to explain in clear terms why Russia's revolution needed Esperanto and why Russia's Esperantists needed to embrace revolutionary socialism (as yet broadly defined). They anticipated, in an unspecified future, an international democracy enshrined in a confederation of the world's peoples and made possible by the international auxiliary language of Esperanto.

"We, socialist Esperantists," Tsyvinskii and Sikora explained, "are the representatives of a new political worldview today freshly born from the smoke and ashes of the world war." In all its devastating violence, the Great War had revealed the "absurdity" of relying on Europe's proletarians to work on their own accord toward global proletarian solidarity.[12] So long as the world was patterned along national-chauvinist lines and fated to disunity owing to linguistic incomprehensibility among nations, the global proletariat would never unite in revolution. Marx's socialist vision, they argued, could not be historically realized without its marriage to Zamenhof's international language of Esperanto. It was high time to recognize that "the authors of *The Communist Manifesto* and all contemporary socialist parties had not accounted and do not take into account to the necessary degree the magnitude of the negative effect" of linguistic difference under the conditions of modern capitalism and nationalism.[13] It was time to appreciate that "language links people"—it makes them kin. Language allows not only for mutual understanding, but also for affection and loyalty between its speakers. An international auxiliary language was a prerequisite of international socialist revolution because, without it, common workers would feel a stronger psychological bond with their conationals even of the enemy classes than they would with foreigners of their same proletarian class. Without an international auxiliary language (Esperanto, namely), there could be no unified international proletariat and no international proletarian revolution.[14]

Tsyvinskii and Sikora insisted that they were not utopians, but instead patriots, realists, socialists, Esperantists. Esperanto required no human being to abandon his or her native language. Rather, on the international stage, all would communicate and come to understand one another better in a shared international auxiliary language. Thereby, the "friction" born of national and linguistic difference would lessen and fade away. Gradually, the world's countries would be transformed into "modern, non-national provinces (*sovremennye, vnenatsional'nye gubernii*)" of what, in time, would organically evolve into "the true reign of the Brotherhood of Peoples and a true International."[15] It was time now to begin the process of building a new world—"not with stone and clay, but with Love and Reason!"[16]

Tsyvinskii and Sikora's *Manifesto of Socialist Esperantists* captures well the breathless hopefulness in Russia's early revolutionary days—a time when exuberant revolutionary visions flourished and competed with one another. Yet Russia's "springtime of freedom" soon passed. For the socialist Esperantists and for so many other eager voices of the revolution, October meant a smaller and more exclusionary "cultural ecosystem."[17] After October, Russia's Esperantists would quickly realize the need to exchange Esperanto's "inner idea" for Bolshevism.

Lean Years, Big Dreams

Russia's Civil War demanded of most who endured it a commitment to the future if for no other reason than the present was so miserable. Esperantists were by definition future-oriented thinkers. Esperanto's so-called inner idea demanded fealty to a future that would bring harmonious human relations that transcended the borders that had for too long divided humanity. Esperanto's "inner idea" did not, however, demand commitment to any specific political program or ideological affiliation—a fact that soon garnered for Esperanto an unfounded reputation as a "neutral" arena immunized from the fractiousness of modern politics. This was a reputation that Esperantists in the early twentieth century did much themselves to promote. Yet as Esther Schor has argued, "Esperanto is essentially political" and was designed to be expressly political in the sense that "it was created to enable diverse peoples to talk not only past their differences but about them."[18]

For revolutionary Russia's Esperantists, the Bolshevik seizure of power and, in time, the Bolsheviks' successes in the civil war made even the conceit of political neutrality unviable. Their only hope in the emerging Soviet republic was Esperanto's political marriage to Bolshevism. Esperantism's former status in tsarist times as a largely "bourgeois" affair and, in the wake of the February Revolution, as an ideological big tent was no longer tenable. It soon became clear that under the Bolsheviks, the Esperantists would need to take an uncompromising stance against "neutral" ("bourgeois") Esperantism. They needed to embrace Esperanto *as politics*—namely as revolutionary, communist politics. In an emerging political culture that was everywhere "imbued with the notion of worldwide struggle," they needed to convince skeptics that Esperanto was an essential weapon of international proletarian revolution.[19]

Still, the ideological transition was for many Esperantists (as for many of their fellow citizens) neither easy nor graceful. One surviving text that Esperantists managed to produce in the extraordinarily lean year of 1918 exemplified the discomfiting, uncertain liminality of the authors' social position and ideological commitment in early civil war Petrograd. V. A. Dmitriev and P. D. Medem's *The International Auxiliary Language Esperanto* in many ways mirrored the standard type of Esperantist brochure that had been produced in the dozens during the last decade of the tsarist empire. It promised that Esperanto would "open the whole world" to all those who adopted this easy-to-learn international auxiliary language.[20] It described Esperanto's undeniable utility for those who traveled abroad, participated in international professional and scientific congresses, consumed foreign literature in translation, and who nurtured coin and stamp collections. Crudely grafted onto this otherwise exceedingly "bourgeois" brochure, however, was one section—titled "Esperanto and Democracy"—that had clearly been drafted in the wake of Russia's revolutionary upheavals in 1917. Offering a confused mishmash of revolutionary catchphrases, it attempted to harmonize Esperanto with the vaguely defined needs of a new era of democracy and workers' ascendancy. The word socialism was conspicuous in its absence.

"Democracies all over the world," Dmitriev and Medem blandly intoned, "must strive toward unification, and a valuable means of unification is an international language." From here, the authors waded awkwardly into a strained class analysis that betrayed their lack of fluency in the new revolutionary discourse, let alone a socialist worldview. They emphasized that Esperanto democratized international relations by virtue of the ease with which anyone, even workers, could ostensibly learn it. Esperanto would diminish the "inordinate influence of the luckiest people who, thanks to the happenstance of their birth, have enjoyed the means to acquire knowledge of foreign languages." Esperanto was, they argued, the natural ally of the worker, who could master the language by studying it for a mere one hour per day for three months. Worker-Esperantists could look forward to availing themselves of the novel ability "to correspond and speak with their comrades from every country in the world." Invoking Marx, albeit not by name, Dmitriev and Medem advised readers: "One ought to remember that "workers of the world unite" is a futile slogan so long as the proletariat lacks a single common language for mutual understanding, without which the unity of the peoples of different countries is impossible." Only Esperanto, they claimed, could guarantee "unity among the democracies of all peoples."[21] Their pamphlet concluded with an encomium to Esperanto's so-called inner idea and neutral foundation for human communication—an ideological premise that could not be reconciled with militant class struggle. Anachronistic at the time of its publication in 1918, it exemplified the awkwardness faced by a generation of Esperantists reared on "bourgeois" and "neutral" talking points.

Like Dmitriev and Medem's pamphlet, Boris Breslau's *The International Language and the Proletariat* attempted to synthesize prerevolutionary Esperantist talking points with vaguely defined revolutionary ideals of democracy, socialism, and proletarian internationalism. Breslau's pamphlet betrayed an incomplete understanding of Marxist dogma, yet it was a concerted attempt to bridge the gap, to weld Esperantism with proletarian internationalism. Everywhere, Breslau wrote, one heard invoked the slogan, "workers of the world, unite!" Yet, he explained, the workers of the world needed a common language in order to unite in socialist revolution.[22] Knowledge of other national languages did not solve the proletariat's language dilemmas. Whereas "the bourgeoisie" enjoyed the luxury of foreign language learning, workers did not and never had enjoyed the time, money, and education that effective foreign language study demanded. Esperanto was easy even for workers to learn, and the cost of an Esperanto textbook and dictionary was not prohibitive. Esperanto was the language of the future—a future shaped by "the international proletariat, united in one close family."[23]

Breslau's *The International Language and the Proletariat* takes on still more significance when considered alongside other of Breslau's revolutionary-era texts. In September 1917, Breslau had applied to Moscow's Institute for Esperanto seeking formal certification of his Esperanto language skills and had paid the necessary ten-ruble fee in pursuit of the same. He signed his application with his birth name, Khaim-Boruch Movshevich Breslav, included a brief autobiography, and, in a separate examination essay explained why he had become "a fervent adept of Esperanto."

Breslau was born into a Jewish family in 1891 in a small town in the Pale of Settlement. His father, he wrote, was "a very enlightened and progressive Jew" who instilled in him a love of learning. After working for several years as a clerk in his hometown, Breslau was mobilized to serve in the tsar's army during the First World War, but he was eventually discharged for medical reasons. Most recently, he had been working for a Swedish engineer's office in Moscow, putting his foreign language skills to professional use. This job was made possible by his knowledge of Esperanto, for he had seen the position advertised in *La Ondo de Esperanto*, one of Russia's pre-revolutionary Esperantist periodicals. An Esperantist since 1909, Breslau was attracted to the language and the movement it inspired not so much for the practical utilities an international language promised the modern world, but more so for the existential meaning it promised. Esperanto provided him "moral satisfaction." It nourished his "spirit" and helped satisfy his "interest in global life, art, and culture." Zamenhof's "inner idea" was, in his mind, a beautiful ideal and one worth striving for on behalf of humanity as a whole. "Speaking with an Esperantist," Breslau explained, "I forget that he is from a different nation, class, office, or rank; I speak with a fellow-thinker, with a confrère (*kunfrato*)."[24]

Taking these texts of Breslau's together—one written some six weeks before the Bolshevik seizure of power in 1917 and the other published in 1918—we gain a personalized glimpse into how one Esperantist was adapting to the revolutionary currents in which he and his country were swept up. Breslau was actively attempting to syncretize his Esperantist worldview born in the prerevolutionary period to the new revolutionary discourses as they rapidly evolved in 1917 and 1918. In the process, Breslau began exchanging Esperanto's inner idea—Zamenhof's so-called neutral vision of a human unity that could transcend ethnic, national, class, and even ideological divisions—for a vision of Esperanto as a weapon of militant class struggle in the novice workers' state. Whatever his personal or political motivations, in 1918 he was trying to find his feet on the shifting grounds of the revolution. Sometime in that same year, he joined the Bolshevik Party.[25]

Educating the Next Generation in the Language of the Future

In April 1918, another young Muscovite named R. N. Bakushinskii also applied to Moscow's Institute of Esperanto for a certifying exam. Born in 1892, Bakushinskii was a self-described working-class striver. He first became acquainted with Esperanto in 1913, when he was a student. In his examination essay, Bakushinskii expressed pride that it was Russia that had birthed Esperanto. Now, he argued, in the revolution's wake, it was time to teach the Russian people Esperanto. It was time for Russia's Esperantists to work ever more energetically toward "our ultimate goal: the brotherhood of peoples and global citizenship. Let's go!"[26]

Bakushinskii was not alone among Russia's Esperantists in seeing the Revolution as a prime opportunity to grow their movement, even under the bleak conditions of the civil war. Esperantists continued throughout the civil war to organize Esperanto clubs, lectures, and courses in cities and towns both big and small. In Moscow, they plastered the cityscape with austere posters exhorting fellow citizens to study Esperanto and insisting that the future of Russia's revolution and a worldwide October depended on it.[27] They managed to recruit new, young Esperantists into their circles. While the ideological tenor of Esperantist rhetoric shifted during the civil war, so too did the sociological profile of Russia's Esperantists. In the pre-revolutionary period, the Esperantist movement in Russia was led by a wealthy, educated elite that did not apologize for its distance from the "masses." Now, young Esperantists welcomed into their ranks fresh working-class recruits to help advance the cause of an international language that they argued was essential for the global proletarian revolution.

In Nizhnii Novgorod, I. L. Bazhenov, a 17-year old from a family of relatively modest means, stumbled in 1918 upon a public lecture delivered by a young woman about Esperanto. Bazhenov found the lecture and the very logic of Esperanto fascinating and so signed on to join a local "Young Esperantists' Circle." Even decades later, Bazhenov recalled with pride how, in the winter of 1918–19, he and his comrades performed a Chekhov play in Esperanto translation for an appreciative public.

Despite it being a "hungry time," Bazhenov recalled, he and his fellow Esperantists found meaningful community during the civil war. They studied, conversed, danced, and typed Esperantist texts on the group's prized Latin typewriter (purchased abroad by the leading member of the circle). When Bazhenov was mobilized for the Red Army in 1920, he left his Young Esperantists' Circle behind, but only temporarily. It was during the lean years of the civil war, Bazhenov insisted later in life, that his Esperantist dreams were nourished, sparking a lifelong commitment to the international language.[28]

As this new generation of revolutionary Esperantists began to assert itself, the older generation of unrepentant "bourgeois Esperantists" receded from view. Increasingly, Esperantists of counter-revolutionary persuasions with their anachronistic "pacifist slogans" were sidelined from Esperantist organizations that quickly learned to redefine themselves as Bolshevik in spirit.[29] From Moscow, Petrograd, and a variety of provincial towns came appeals to the various emerging People's Commissariats that the Soviet authorities "use us [the Esperantists] … in the matter of Soviet propaganda" both at home and abroad.[30] The restyled "communist Esperantists" offered up a variety of services to the Bolsheviks throughout the civil war years: the translation of Soviet and classic Marxist-Leninist literature into Esperanto; the design of "a proletarian textbook about the proletarian international language Esperanto for adults who don't know Russian grammar"; and the organization and teaching of Esperanto courses for children as well as adults.[31] Hitching their cause to that of the Bolsheviks, these youthful Esperantists campaigned for the people of Russia to be taught Esperanto, which they framed as the language of the global socialist future.

Logically, they directed many of their early appeals to the People's Commissariat of Enlightenment (Narkompros). They urged Narkompros to adopt Esperanto as a mandatory subject in Soviet schools, arguing that Esperanto would help the proletariat to unseat the "caste of privileged intelligentsia" who had dominated prerevolutionary life. Esperanto, they emphasized, was "the proletarian international language." The children of the revolution need not study the foreign languages of capitalist nations as the bourgeoisie greedily did in the days of old. Instead, the pioneers of the international socialist future needed to learn to read and write in their native language first, and in the "proletarian international language Esperanto" second.[32]

In early 1919, Narkompros organized an investigatory committee to explore "the question of international language" so as to determine the perceived need to incorporate international language education in Russian schools. The commission was also tasked with exploring which, if any, international language was suitable to the tasks of communist education, let alone international proletarian revolution. Staffed by professors, pedagogues, bureaucrats, and even a few Esperantists, the commission debated the international language question throughout 1919 and devoted much of its efforts to determining the viability of Esperanto as a language that could live up to all the claims its advocates made for it.[33] As one of the commission's non-Esperantist members argued during its proceedings, it was clear in the wake of the devastating world war and the "revolutionary wave" that had washed over Europe since that "despite polyglottism, people are members of one family—humanity—and that they now more than ever need an international language to facilitate mutual understanding."[34]

Figure 4 Registration for Esperanto courses in revolutionary Petrograd, 1919. *Source*: Alamy.

The commission's conclusions resulted, however, only in a partial and slight victory for the Esperantists. In February 1919, the commission concluded that of all the competing international languages "only Esperanto" had proven itself as viable, with a global track record of adoption, use, functionality, and publication.[35] Yet Narkompros washed its hands of the matter of decreeing an international language for use in Soviet schools, let alone in the Bolsheviks' international relations. The commission encouraged the Bolsheviks to take seriously the issue of "the international language question," but ultimately concluded that the answer to that question would be decided as a result of practical "agreements between governments representing individual nations."[36]

Russia's "communist Esperantists" who strained during the civil war years to identify and merge with the Bolshevik regime were thus greeted with a strikingly conservative answer to their plea to have Esperanto taught in all Soviet schools. As far as Narkompros was concerned, Esperanto was not a priority. Rather, the commission insisted that the "question of international language" would essentially sort itself out (or not at all). Either way, it was a matter, Narkompros insisted, for representatives of "governments" and "nations" to decide.

When, just a few weeks after the Narkompros commission met, a new Third International (Comintern) was established in Moscow in March 1919, Esperantists saw a fresh opportunity to lobby on behalf of Esperanto. They recast Esperanto as the international language of global proletarian revolution, essential to the work of the new Comintern. What, after all, could a Communist International achieve without an international language for the global proletariat?

A New International

"Comrades, I deeply regret that I speak neither German, which Comrade Zinoviev yesterday called the 'language of international socialism,' nor Russian, which will be the language of international communism tomorrow." One can imagine the sigh with which Jacques Sadoul, a self-declared representative of French Communists, began his speech to the so-called International Communist Conference that the Bolsheviks hastily convened in Moscow in early March 1919. Sadoul bowed to the inescapable reality of his own linguistic limits. Apologetically, he explained: "I must address you in French, the only language in which I am reasonably fluent, a language that for now, at least, can unfortunately be referred to only as the language of a revolution of long ago."[37]

Sadoul was one of several dozen foreign comrades who answered the Bolsheviks' call to serve as delegates to the International Communist Conference, soon to be re-branded as the First Congress of the Communist International. A few months prior, in late December 1918, the Bolsheviks had attempted to address "communists of all countries" via radio, hoping the electromagnetic waves would effectively transmit around the world their appeal that true communists "must rally around the Third International which, for all intents and purposes, has already been launched."[38] Desperate and eager for the international proletarian revolution that would help secure Russia's underdog revolution and transform the world, the Bolsheviks next began making plans for the founding congress of the Third International.

Constrained by the blockade imposed by capitalist-imperialist enemies, preoccupied by the demands of successfully prosecuting the Red Army effort in a devastating civil war, and facing the stark realities of trying to secure revolutionary victory in the dire circumstances of widespread hunger, trauma, and chaos across Russia's vast territory, the Bolsheviks realized that the founding of the Third International would need to be accomplished in creative yet ragtag fashion. With so many practical barriers impeding their ability to communicate with foreign communists abroad, no less than the literal roadblocks that prevented their foreign comrades' entry into revolutionary Russia to attend such an historic international congress, the Bolsheviks had to make do with a modest assembly of delegates who claimed to represent communist organizations based in twenty-two (mostly European) countries abroad. Many of the foreign delegates had already been residing in Russia at the time the Bolsheviks attempted to issue invitations. Some of them had lived in Russia since long before the Revolution. Nearly all of the invitations that the Bolsheviks sent to communist parties and organizations abroad never reached their destinations, and most of the intended recipients would only learn of the congress sometime after it had convened.[39] That the Bolsheviks managed at all to assemble this modest internationalist crowd in Moscow in March 1919, one historian has noted, "was no small achievement."[40] Others have been less generous in their appraisals, noting that at this disorganized congress, improvisation and practiced Leninist subterfuge provided little cover for the fact that most of the foreign delegates who participated in the founding congress of the Third International "had received no authorization whatever to represent the movements whose delegates they purported to be."[41] In the words of Duncan Hallas, "It was not a particularly weighty or representative gathering."[42]

If, however, one thing united all the delegates, it was the shared faith that socialist revolution abroad, most notably in Germany, was imminent. Several of Europe's creaky old empires—the Russian, German, and Austro-Hungarian—had shattered, collapsing under the weight of the Great War and the structural failures and social fissures it had laid bare. The proletariat had been awakened to the real possibilities of their power. Russia was the beleaguered forerunner of revolutions soon to ignite elsewhere. Global proletarian revolution was on the horizon.

Hosted in the Kremlin, the founding congress of the Third International reflected both the Bolsheviks' grand internationalist ambitions and the stark material impoverishment of revolutionary Russia, still dogged by war. The British journalist Arthur Ransome arrived on the second day of the congress and was immediately struck by how the small conference hall had been lavishly decorated with red carpets and drapes—red everywhere. Banners, he claimed, were strung all over the room "with 'Long Live the Third International' inscribed upon them in many languages."[43] Sadoul, too, was impressed by the banners, the blood red of the drapes, and the reverential portraits of Marx and Engels. Yet he was pained by the memory of the physical discomfort he and his fellow delegates endured as they sat through hour upon hour of proceedings. "The delegates took their seats on flimsy chairs on rickety tables obviously borrowed from some café," he recalled. "It was cold, very cold in that hall," Sadoul explained. "The carpets strove, though in vain, to make up for the heaters that blew terrible gusts of frigid air at the delegates."[44]

There were other inconveniences as well, prominent among them dilemmas of language diversity. At the preliminary meeting of the conference, held on March 1, it was decided that the official language of the conference would be German, although Russian would also be permitted. This decision was in keeping with German's decades-long standing as the unofficial lingua franca of the international Left. As Sadoul's apology for his French-language speech attests, the congress proceedings themselves were both a test of the delegates' language skills and, at times, a revolutionary incarnation of the Tower of Babel. Ransome reported that "business was conducted and speeches were made in all languages, though where possible German was used, because more of the foreigners knew German than knew French." Betraying his own linguistic limits, the Brit added: "This was unlucky for me."[45]

Ransome and Sadoul were not the only "unlucky" ones in attendance for the founding meeting of the Communist International. Multiple national languages were spoken throughout the proceedings. Translation services—although provided by the Bolshevik organizers for much of the event—were not always available or on offer. Ransome recalled, "When I got there people were making reports about the situation in the different countries. Finberg spoke in English, Rakovsky in French, Sadoul also. Skripnik, who, being asked, refused to talk German and said he would speak in

92 *Esperanto and Languages of Internationalism in Revolutionary Russia*

Figure 5 First Congress of the Third International (Comintern). Moscow, 1919. *Source*: Getty Images.

either Ukrainian or Russian, and to most people's relief chose the latter."⁴⁶ Claiming to represent the Chinese Socialist Workers Party, Liu Shaozhou [Liu Zerong] began his remarks in Chinese, but this was a performative gesture.⁴⁷ The son of a Cantonese tea magnate who had successfully pursued business in late imperial Russia, Liu Shaozhou had lived in Russia since childhood, had graduated from St. Petersburg University, and was known to his Russian friends and colleagues as Sergei Ivanovich.⁴⁸ For the sake of being understood by his fellow delegates, he delivered his report in fluent Russian.

The official transcripts of the congress proceedings reflected the linguistic divides, occasional code-switching, and various logistical problems of translation encountered by the delegates who participated in the Comintern's founding. As John Riddell has explained, "A German-language stenographic transcript was taken, which frequently failed to record remarks made in Russian. A separate transcript was made of the Russian-language contributions."⁴⁹ One is left to wonder how many words spoken in French, English, or any other national language but German and Russian never made it into the transcripts at all. Translators on hand did their best to render reports made in French or English into German and Russian. Yet the pace of the events often meant that those who needed translated drafts of resolutions would need to wait. Thus, when introducing draft theses on the question of "Bourgeois Democracy and the Dictatorship of the Proletariat," Lenin demanded his comrades' patience and forbearance—especially those who did not speak or read the working languages of the congress. "Theses have been drafted on this question," Lenin announced. "Everyone present has copies of them in German and Russian, and the English and French comrades will receive English and French translations later on. Consequently, I consider it unnecessary to read the theses aloud again." For the time being, some comrades were to remain—even if just for a short while—lost without the translations.[50] On the fourth afternoon of the congress, it was suddenly announced that the remainder of that day's business would need be put off until the next day. The problem? Lack of translation staff. "Comrades," Fritz Platten announced, "we must cut the session short. No translation is available from Russian to German. We have no choice but to propose ending the session at this point."[51]

The translator-interpreters who served at the Comintern's founding congress were recruited from its very audience: they were themselves participating delegates or else leading Bolsheviks in attendance for the meetings. There was nothing particularly exceptional in this arrangement. One of the delegates who tirelessly provided translation and interpretation services at the founding Comintern Congress, Anzhelika Balabanova, had made a name for herself in previous decades as a one-woman "living incarnation of the International"—so nicknamed precisely because of her devoted application of her linguistic skills to translating and interpreting at meetings of the international Left.[52]

Moreover, the Bolshevik leaders' multilingualism was something that they themselves generally took for granted. Many of the leading Bolsheviks were fluent in at least one, if not multiple European languages in addition to Russian. Some of them were particularly talented when it came to foreign languages, and were known for their highly useful ability to fluently deploy multiple foreign languages in conversation and in formal writing. These linguistic talents owed in some small measure to the circumstances of some of the Bolsheviks' elite birth and top-notch educations. Aleksandra Kollontai, who provided essential translation services at the first Comintern congress, was the skilled linguist of aristocratic birth so often conjured in the class analyses that Esperantists put forward in defense of Esperanto as a truly *proletarian* international language. Born into a wealthy landowning family in late imperial Russia, Kollontai had been tended to as a child by a small army of foreign-born governesses whose job it was to teach her, among other prized skill sets, native fluency in English, French, and German. She had also, like so many of her leading Bolshevik comrades, spent many of her years prior to the Revolution living, studying, and agitating in Western Europe, where her elite education in foreign languages was put to considerable use.

Unlike Kollontai, Trotsky did not have a British nanny to teach him English grammar and colloquialisms. Yet he and Kollontai did share—as they did with so many of their old comrades—the experience of living abroad in revolutionary exile from the tsarist regime. In Zurich, Geneva, Paris, Berlin, Vienna, London, Rome, and New York, the Bolsheviks had had their language abilities tested and, in many cases, forged throughout their years of living, agitating, and conspiring abroad. Their lived internationalism as radical émigrés required them to speak, read, and agitate in foreign languages in their adopted homes. In the decades prior to the October Revolution, no Russian Marxist could hope to prove himself (or herself) as a leading thinker and agitator without confronting the need to study foreign languages. Several Old Bolsheviks gained reputations for their fluent mastery of multiple foreign tongues—Litvinov, Radek, and Kollontai stood out for their agile multilingualism. Lenin was known to confess to a failure to master any foreign tongue.[53] Yet he, Trotsky, and Bukharin succeeded in gaining what was seen as the necessary fluency in German and even French, although they suffered a much more limited command of English. Sometimes, they even memorized a smattering of Italian and Spanish vocabulary for potential use.

For Russian Marxists living in exile in the two decades prior to the Russian Revolution, foreign language learning was both a practical and a revolutionary requirement. Gesture and pantomime, the Russian Marxists in exile quickly learned, only got them so far. Their native Russian was a devalued currency and rarely useful except when they were talking among themselves. Preparing for revolution meant foreign language study as much as theoretical debate or gun-running and money-laundering. Most took foreign language learning quite seriously, considering it a badge of revolutionary honor as much as a practical necessity. Some, like Stalin, were ultimately embarrassed not only by their lack of experience abroad, but also by their lack of foreign language fluency.[54] While training for revolution, Stalin had attempted to engage in some self-study of English, German, and French. While in tsarist prison, he famously studied Esperanto, telling a cellmate that he believed it was "the language of the future."[55] Nothing much came of these endeavors. Even after he cemented his leadership of the Bolsheviks, Stalin would never quite live down the personal shame of not mastering German, the prerevolutionary lingua franca of the European Left.[56] In the 1930s, Stalin still hoped to improve his German through self-study with textbooks.[57]

In the prerevolutionary years, Old Bolsheviks found a variety of ways to improve their foreign language skills beyond the requirements of making do in a Parisian shop or on a London tram. A native Yiddish speaker from the tsarist Pale of Settlement, Maksim Litvinov proved one of few to thoroughly master English. His marriage to a British writer, Ivy Low Litvinov, no doubt helped his English language acquisition to proceed at galloping pace in the years prior to the monarchy's collapse. Fleeing Russia after the 1905 Revolution, Mikhail Gruzenberg reinvented himself in the United States, mastered English, and ultimately opened a school in Chicago where he taught English to other Russian immigrants. In the summer of 1918, Gruzenberg returned to revolutionary Russia and reinvented himself again, this time as Mikhail Borodin. With his mastery of at least five languages, Borodin prominently served the Comintern—crossing borders and code-switching in the name of world revolution.[58]

Known internationally for his charismatic oratory, Trotsky dedicated his various stints in tsarist prison to concentrated foreign language study. During his first incarceration, he arranged for his sister to bring him "four copies of the Bible in different languages." The results, he claimed, were astonishing even if ultimately insufficient. "I read the Gospels, verse by verse, with the help of the little knowledge of German and French that I had acquired in school, and side by side with this a parallel reading in English and Italian," Trotsky explained. "In a few months, I made excellent progress in this way." Yet, most foreign language learners could sympathize with Trotsky's frustrations with the daunting challenges of mastering a foreign tongue. In his autobiography, he confessed: "I must admit ... that my linguistic talents are very mediocre. Even now I do not know a single foreign language well, although I stayed for some time in various European countries."[59] This, though, was a rare moment of Trotsky being modest, and, given his legendary ability to speak at length and at ease in Russian, German, and French at the Comintern's meetings, it was false modesty at that. At the first Comintern Congress in March 1919, he served as one of the translators.[60] In this and subsequent Comintern meetings he would also often serve as his own translator, awing the audience as he deftly delivered his lengthy speeches in German, French, and Russian—a task that at least once famously exceeded six hours.[61]

Thus relying on multilingual comrades whose knowledge of languages owed to elite educations, foreign exile, and even transnational family ties forged in the decades prior to the revolution, the attendees at the First Comintern Congress were not terribly impeded by the challenges of language diversity at their so-declared international congress. Adopted lingua francas—of international socialism (German) and of the global communist future (Russian)—more or less worked to get the business of the modest-sized congress accomplished. Comrades who had the ability to translate from German or Russian into French, Italian, or English helped to bridge the linguistic gaps.

At the celebrations that concluded the founding Comintern Congress, the Bolsheviks' confidence in the imminence of world revolution was on festive display. So, too, was their confidence in their ability to make do with their revolutionary lingua francas. In a rousing speech, Lenin waved in his hands a copy of *Avanti!*—the newspaper of the Italian Socialist Party. Lenin himself could not fluently read the Italian text that filled its pages, but he could look at it nonetheless and find reassurance of a global proletarian revolution to come. Pointing to the text, Lenin explained that a news story had appeared about how workers in an Italian village had declared their support of the German Spartacists. "Then," Lenin explained, "there follow the words '*Sovietisti russi*' which, even though they are in Italian, can be understood all over the world."[62] To thunderous applause, Lenin concluded: "Now that the meaning of the word 'soviet' is understood by everybody, the victory of the communist revolution is assured."[63] He was confident that the proletarians of the world could speak in their different national tongues and yet effectively express a shared communist meaning. When all else failed, there were always translators who could be put to work in the service of the global proletariat.

An International Language for the Global Proletariat?

Born in 1890 to Russian radicals living in exile in Belgium, Victor Serge was an anarchist who traveled to his parents' native land in the wake of the October Revolution. He arrived in 1919 to a country ravaged by war, chaos, and hunger. In his memoir, Serge described his arrival in Petrograd:

At a reception center we were issued with basic rations of black bread and dried fish. Never until now had any of us known such a horrid diet. Girls with red headbands joined with young bespectacled agitators to give us a summary of the state of affairs: "Famine, typhus and counterrevolution everywhere. But the world revolution is bound to save us." They were surer of it than we were, and our doubts made them momentarily suspicious of us.[64]

Despite his skepticism about the impending outbreak of world revolution in 1919, Serge had traveled to the Soviet Republic with optimism and hope for the revolution's success in Russia and abroad. He immediately immersed himself in the business of Bolshevism and of fomenting global proletarian revolution in particular. Serge was fluent in five languages and these credentials recommended him for work in the newly established Comintern. Its chairman, G. Zinoviev, set Serge to work in the Comintern's makeshift Petrograd office. What actual work he was meant to do, however, was at first not terribly clear. In 1919, he later recalled, he and a comrade were astonished to find themselves tasked with designing Comintern insignia to celebrate the coming world revolution. "We decided," he wrote, "that the globe would be the emblem on it."[65] Soon enough, Serge and his comrade were racing around town to build the Comintern. "We spent our lives among telephones," he remembered, "trailing around the huge dead city in wheezy motorcars, commandeering printshops; selecting staff; correcting proofs even in the trams; bargaining with the Board of Trade for string and with the State Bank's printers for paper."[66]

The March 1919 Congress had established a Communist International that at first existed more on deficit paper than in a global institutional reality. Yet the Bolsheviks and their foreign allies wasted no time in propagandizing the new International at home and abroad, trumpeting it as the "Communist Party of the international proletariat."[67] The Comintern's founding came as welcome news to young Esperantists in Soviet Russia.[68] While maneuvering for a secure place in the cultural ecosystem of Bolshevism during the civil war, these Esperantists looked to the Comintern as a still more natural ally for their cause than Narkompros. In their eyes, it was only logical that a Communist International would need an international language. But pragmatism was not the only argument on Esperanto's side. Esperanto, they would claim, was the only language available to the Comintern that would free it, and the world's workers, from the chains of linguistic chauvinism that were symptomatic of "bourgeois" international relations and global language politics in the past. Soon after the Comintern's founding in 1919, Esperantists throughout revolutionary Russia launched a loosely coordinated campaign to persuade the Comintern to adopt Esperanto as its official international auxiliary language.

In a pamphlet published in 1919 in the name of a "Petersburg group of Esperantist-propagandists," V. P. Artiushkin-Kormilitsyn offered a rousing defense of Esperanto as a necessary weapon for achieving international proletarian revolution. He insisted that Esperanto *must become* the language of the Communist International. Capitalism was dying and the workers were busy digging the bourgeoisie's grave. The old bourgeois ways—including the bourgeoisie's reliance on French as a diplomatic lingua franca—had to go. French was the language of global capitalist exploitation and so in tsarist

Russia, as elsewhere in the world's imperialist centers, the bourgeois elites and aristocrats had mastered French, and sometimes spoke it even more fluently than their own national tongue. Esperanto provided a means for the international proletariat to conquer the chauvinism of using a national language as their shared language of communication. "Any literate worker or peasant could learn it, and in the shortest possible time."[69] Without Esperanto, Artiushkin-Kormilitsyn argued, "'Workers of the world, unite' is and will remain an empty phrase, a futile appeal."[70]

In late 1919, another group of self-described communist Esperantists established what they called the Organizing Committee of "ESKI"—the Esperantist Section of the Third Communist International. From the start, they struggled to gain the attention of Comintern officials who never authorized the presumptuous Esperantist group's name.[71] Yet ESKI nonetheless energetically campaigned for the arguable marriage of interests between Esperanto and Bolshevism, and Esperanto and international revolution in particular. Few at the Comintern cared to listen.

Given its anational quality as an international *auxiliary* language, they argued, Esperanto was inherently anti-imperialist and anti-chauvinist. Esperanto was also inherently democratic and "proletarian" in a way that the national languages could never be. The revolution demanded an international language that would "destroy the masses' dependency on translators and the handfuls of patented intellectuals who … could otherwise lay claim to leadership" of what was rightfully the *workers'* international revolution.[72] To conduct international relations in any of the existing national languages was to cave to "imperialist traditional polyglottism" when what was demanded was "proletarian revolutionary internationalism."[73] To reject Esperanto or to ignore it was thus a counter-revolutionary act. The dilemma of international language, the Soviet Esperantists argued, presented a test case for the Bolsheviks' and the Comintern's revolutionary credentials. It was time for the Bolsheviks to serve as the vanguard on the international language front.

Looking ahead to the Comintern's planned Second Congress in summer 1920, the Esperantists stressed the simple fact that the delegates who were slated to arrive in Moscow to advance the cause of international proletarian revolution spoke dozens of different national languages. Even with translators in place, they argued, precious time and energy that could be better spent would be wasted. Without Esperanto, an organization of youthful Esperantists from outside Saratov urged, the Comintern simply would not be able to reach out to the "workers of England, France, and Germany" and effectively translate for them the insights that the "Russian working class, the avant-garde of the global proletarian revolution" had gleaned in their heroic struggles for October. "The Russian working class," they argued, "must be the initiator, the first destroyer of the iron barrier of linguistic difference" now standing in the way of the global proletariat's victory.[74]

Throughout the spring and early summer of 1920, Esperantist groups throughout Russia sent their pleas to the Comintern's Executive Committee asking that Esperanto be deployed at the upcoming Second World Comintern Congress. One group even offered to produce an Esperanto edition of the Comintern's journal, *Kommunisticheskii Internatsional*, which the Bolsheviks were already producing in Russian, German, French, and English for circulation throughout the world.[75] All these appeals that

Esperantists sent to the Comintern Executive Committee—including a few received from Esperantists in England and France—in the lead-up to its Second Congress in 1920 were filed away, but generally ignored.[76]

Language Politics as Usual at the Comintern

When the Second Congress of the Comintern met at sessions held in both Petrograd and Moscow between July 19 and August 7, 1920, much had changed since the convocation of the founding Congress in March 1919. The short life of the Hungarian Soviet Republic had come and gone, vanquished by the forces of reaction. A worldwide October had not yet ignited, but there was still hope for the impending collapse of capitalism. The Bolsheviks had achieved key victories in the ongoing Russian civil war, but the Red Army was still battling White forces and struggling in its military contest with independent Poland. Against all odds, the Soviet Republic still stood, even if its people were ravaged and hungry. From Moscow, the red star still shone its light, reaching toward comrades all over the world. This time, the Comintern hosted foreign delegates hailing from North and South America, Europe, the Middle East, Central and East Asia. At the First Comintern Congress, delegates had shivered in the cold. At the Second Congress, 218 delegates representing workers' parties in 37 countries enjoyed summertime weather, delighted in concerts and other cultural activities organized for them, and played spirited games of football. This time, the Comintern opened its Congress having resolved upon three working languages for its proceedings: German, Russian, and French. By the time it closed on August 7, English also would be added to the list—but only after a measure of controversy stirred by English-speaking delegates.[77]

The Second Congress's expanded list of working languages did not represent a shift from the traditional politics of language to which the Comintern had reconciled itself at its first world congress. Nor did it solve the problem of language diversity as it impacted delegates' ability to fully participate in and understand the proceedings. As at the founding congress, apologies were frequently offered as when Nikolai Bukharin modestly begged his comrades to "please excuse my German. It will by no means be the German language but a substitute for it."[78] Stenographic reports reveal that much of the discussion was conducted in German or French, but Russian, English, Turkish, and other languages were spoken throughout the event. Translators did their best to keep up and make the words of their comrades intelligible to all, yet the imperfect system left gaps of understanding.

Moreover, the need for translation slowed the pace of the often vituperative proceedings. The Comintern's system of consecutive interpretation meant that after every speech, the congress delegates who required translation would reconvene in their various "language groups" to meet with appointed interpreters. An American delegate described the inequities and tiring dynamics of this system. "While separate interpreters were repeating long speeches in different languages (with varying fidelity to the original)," he explained, "half the congress drifted into an adjoining room to smoke, to confer, and, when snacks were available, to eat."[79] Given the time this consecutive interpretation required, some sessions extended well into the early morning hours. The participants' nerves quickly began to fray.

John Reed, the famous American communist, was exasperated. In the first three sessions, Reed three times put forward a motion to have English added to the Congress's working languages and three times the motion failed. "The number of English-speaking delegates in this hall exceeds the number of those using French," Reed complained on July 24. "We have been promised an English translator, but we have not got him yet." Giacinto Serrati of the Italian Socialist Party and a member of the Congress's Presiding Committee formally addressed Reed's concerns without satisfying them: "We will try to accommodate Comrade Reed regarding an interpreter. But as he has already repeatedly been informed, the Bureau cannot accept Reed's motion to permit the use of English as an official language."[80]

Reed was not the only English-speaking delegate aggrieved by the Congress's language politics. On July 28, the Brit Jack Murphy addressed his fellow delegates, complaining that "It is one of the ironies of this congress that the delegates most vitally interested in the most important questions before the congress are hindered from following the discussions by the exclusion of the English language."[81] Although it was not recorded in the official Congress proceedings, the American and British delegates ultimately staged a boycott and refused to attend a whole day of sessions. According to one of the British delegates, the English speakers were fed up with having to hope for the occasional "garbled translation" offered them by a sympathetic and ostensibly polyglot attendee.[82] What was the point in participating in the Comintern Congress if they could not understand most of what was being said in hour upon hour of speeches and debate?

Despite the Anglophone delegates' repeated efforts to lobby for the inclusion of English, it was not until August 2 that Zinoviev announced the adoption of English as a working language for the Congress. He did so, however, at the expense of the French speakers. "I move that the English language be used now instead of French for the following reasons: Six or seven more comrades have arrived who do not understand French," Zinoviev said at the start of the Congress's ninth session. "We have conducted half of the congress in French. Now we must save time, and particularly since the questions of the trade unions and parliamentarism will be discussed next, we must speak English."[83] It was a belated concession to Anglophone delegates for whom so much of the proceedings had already been lost in translation (or never translated at all). It also did not solve the problem of linguistic diversity at this congress of internationalists. On August 3, Eadmon MacAlpine of the Communist Party of America complained, "Radek's speech, which lasted two hours, was given to us in a twenty-minute translation. It strikes me as rather strange that time is being valued so highly here, because on the whole it is hard in Russia to notice any such economizing of time."[84]

The greatest controversy to emerge at the Second Comintern Congress centered on the so-called Twenty-One Conditions, not on the working languages or faulty system for providing translation and interpretation services. The Twenty-One Conditions were the prerequisites for Comintern affiliation that the Bolsheviks pushed through in a bid to mandate a uniformity in practices among communist parties throughout the world.

They also underscored the Bolsheviks' leadership role in this emerging international organization. The Twenty-One Conditions dictated that the Bolsheviks' version of how a communist party should behave, organize, propagandize, and regulate and discipline its membership must be replicated in the communist parties throughout the world.[85] Foremost among the Bolsheviks' priorities in devising this notable list of Twenty-One Conditions was the requirement that Comintern member parties formally name themselves as "Communist" and divorce themselves from Social Democrats and any other socialists whom the Bolsheviks deemed insufficiently dedicated to the overthrow of capitalism and the pursuit of global socialist revolution. Although a sizable number of delegates expressed bitter opposition to the Twenty-One Conditions (in whole or in part), the Second Comintern Congress adopted them.[86] Lenin insisted, however, that all—including the Bolsheviks themselves—could expect that the Bolsheviks' singular authority would soon enough be reduced and likely replaced. "Soon after the victory of the proletarian revolution in at least one of the advanced countries, a sharp change will probably come about: Russia will cease to be the model and will once again become a backward country (in the 'soviet' and socialist sense)," he wrote.[87] There was still hope for an impending worldwide proletarian revolution.

Although the debate over the Twenty-One Conditions and other theoretical and organizational issues took priority over the language problems that had afflicted this and the previous Comintern congresses, it was becoming clear that the Bolsheviks' improvised style of providing for translation and interpretation at these international events was untenable. Just as the Esperantists had anticipated, planning and preparing for global communism entailed the practical challenges of linguistic diversity. The Comintern brought together comrades from all over the world and they proceeded, for better or worse, to speak in their various proletarian tongues. Consecutive translation of speeches into the other working languages of the Comintern was exhausting for all concerned. Angel Pestana, a syndicalist delegate from Spain, recalled how the problems of language diversity drained the participants' energy and enthusiasm. "The sessions began to lose their appeal. The number of translations required made the discussions endless ... the whole thing was immensely time wasting," he wrote.[88] The Indian communist M. N. Roy similarly painted a portrait of inefficiency and revolutionary boredom. "A lot of time was wasted," he recalled. "Batches of delegates wandered all over the palace" as the Comintern's language problems seemingly multiplied without remedy.[89] No matter their native language, all the Comintern delegates could agree that consecutive interpretation was necessary, but a drag on the world revolution. "The plight of the Congress was becoming desperate," Pestana explained, "it was losing impetus, and unless Lenin or Trotsky were speaking the discussions took place in the midst of general indifference." In response to the delegates' flagging morale and the ticking clock, the interpreters began to take drastic measures. Pestana explained, "The translations were shortened more and more until there scarcely remained anything of what the speaker had actually said."[90]

On the penultimate day of the Second Congress, Pestana proposed a different strategy for dealing with the confusion of Babel that prevailed at the Comintern congresses. Why, he asked, should the Congress delegates resign themselves to the babble of their communist glossolalia when there already existed a ready-made solution to their linguistic woes? Why not adopt Esperanto—at the very least as the single working language of translation? "Whereas," he argued,

> the work of world congresses such as the present one is made much more difficult by the translation of everything said into several languages, I propose that in the future every speaker use whatever language they find easiest, and that translation take place into the auxiliary language Esperanto. This language is readily learned and quite appropriate to our needs. We can save much time and labor by using it for translation.[91]

Zinoviev summarily sent Pestana's suggestion for consideration by a new committee, named the Advisory Commission for the Introduction of an International Auxiliary Language in the Third International.

When Esperantists throughout revolutionary Russia received news of Pestana's endorsement of Esperanto and the Comintern's decision to charge a special committee with the task of considering an international auxiliary language, many of them no doubt celebrated what must have seemed, at least at first, a hard-won victory and cause for newfound hope.[92] Yet, such hopefulness did not last long. It quickly became clear to them that the Comintern's commission to consider "the question of an international language" was a likely dead end for Esperanto's proposed role in Comintern affairs. Headed by the Hungarian communist Jozsef Pogany, the Advisory Commission was staffed with at least one ardent advocate of Ido—a rival international language whose adherents touted it as a perfected Esperanto.[93] Moreover, the "communist Esperantists" who had appealed to the Comintern's Executive Committee since its founding were not invited to participate in the Advisory Commission's work. The self-declared "communist Esperantists" were well aware, as one memorandum drafted in the spring of 1920 made clear, that "the center"—that is, the Bolshevik leadership and emerging Soviet state—was "indifferent" or at the very least full of doubts about Esperanto and the idea of an auxiliary international language.[94] Pestana's had proven a lonely voice from within a Comintern that continued to rebuff the Soviet Esperantists who were so eager to offer it their services.

The Esperantists' skepticism about the Comintern Advisory Commission appeared more than justified once plans proceeded apace for the convocation of the Third Comintern Congress in June 1921. Despite pleas from the Esperantists, the question of an international language was not placed on the agenda.[95] Although now there were 509 delegates hailing from 48 countries to attend its Third World Congress, the Comintern clung to its traditional, Eurocentric language politics. Again, German, French, Russian, and English were selected as the congress's working languages. Again, the Comintern hired translators and interpreters to provide, to the best of their ability, their services to the foreign delegates during the formal proceedings.[96]

This privileging and reliance on European national languages reflected the Bolsheviks' Eurocentrism but also increasingly strained their working relationship with the so-called Eastern comrades whom they recruited from among the colonial peoples of Asia, the Middle East, and Africa. For the increasing number of "Eastern" comrades sojourning to Moscow, joining the work of the Comintern, and attending its congresses, the Bolsheviks' traditional and unapologetically Eurocentric language politics was an especial burden. These comrades were known to complain about the "difficult position" they were in linguistically—most especially for those who did not know a single European language.[97] Soviet Esperantists, too, dared to suggest the Eurocentric chauvinism at the heart of the Comintern's language politics. I. Izgur critiqued the Comintern's reliance on European languages in his treatise *International Language in the Service of the Proletariat*:

> Can it be that the revolutionization (*revoliutsionizirovanie*) of the proletariat of Persia, Turkey, and India is less important than the revolutionization of the proletariat of Romania, Switzerland, and Norway? Can it be that the awakening of the class consciousness of China's proletariat ... is less important than the awakening of the class consciousness of Holland's proletariat?[98]

Yet such complaints were frequently sidelined—to be resolved at a more opportune time, presumably once more cadres of interpreters and translators could be recruited to the Comintern's mission.[99] There was also the growing expectation, soon to be more prominent in Bolshevik strategy toward training its "Eastern" comrades, that knowledge of the Russian language should be a prerequisite of communist internationalism.

For now, the Comintern proceeded as usual with its exhausting and exclusionary system of consecutive interpretation. As in the previous Comintern congresses, corners were cut and compromises made as the delegates coped with the inescapable obstacles that linguistic diversity imposed upon their proceedings. In other words, it was international language politics as usual at the Third Comintern Congress.

Going It Alone: The Union of Soviet Esperantists

Even before the Third Comintern Congress met, it had become clear to most of revolutionary Russia's self-declared communist Esperantists that they needed to forge a place for Esperanto in the Soviet Republic that did not depend on the disinterested officials at the Comintern or Narkompros. They decided to forge their own "all-Russian" organization—one that would be, if necessary, "independent from the government and the Party."[100] They needed an organizational foothold from which they could centralize their efforts to make Esperanto an indispensable weapon of international proletarian revolution. In time, they would be better prepared to coordinate efforts with the Comintern, Narkompros, and other Soviet and international organizations.

The decision to establish an independent organization to unite, direct, and finance the efforts of all Soviet Esperantists coincided with the conclusion of the Russian Civil War. The convocation of representatives of the scattered Esperantist organizations had been a documented priority of the various Esperantist groups in Russia throughout the civil war.[101] An organizing committee for a conceived "All-Russian Federation of Esperantists" predated the October Revolution by several months.[102] Yet such an all-union organization remained a dream beyond reach so long as war communism ensured the "chaotic condition" of Esperantist and most other grassroots affairs in Soviet Russia.¹⁰³ The result, as one sympathetic government memorandum reported in 1920, was that throughout Soviet Russia, "there are groups of Esperantists here and there, but not a mass that could serve as stronghold (*opornyi sil*) of the language."¹⁰⁴

Organized to convene just weeks in advance of the Comintern's Third World Congress (where the question of Esperanto would not be broached even once), the so-called Third All-Russian Congress of Esperantists met in Petrograd in early June 1921. At the center of its agenda was Esperanto's role in Soviet Russia and global revolution.¹⁰⁵ Delegates representing Esperantist groups from throughout Soviet Russia arrived from Siberia, the Far East, Ukraine, and the Caucasus. According to the organizers, 163 delegates from seventy-three different Soviet cities participated in the congress. Only 21 percent of the attendees were professed communists. Congress statistics also revealed that of the 163 delegates, only 4 could be termed "Old Esperantists" who studied the language prior to 1900. Many had been inspired by the revolution to undertake study of this international auxiliary language. As one triumphant account of the proceedings declared, "Russian Esperantists have made their choice. Henceforth, they are embarking on a new path in their work." This new path was the path of Bolshevism, of Bolshevik Esperantism.¹⁰⁶

The congress was hailed as a "turning point in the history of the Esperantist movement in Russia" marked by the establishment of the Union of Soviet Esperantists (SEU)—a new organization under firm communist leadership. During the congress's actual proceedings, a minority of attendees *did* protest Bolshevik leadership and the marriage of Esperantism to Bolshevism, but they were outnumbered and outvoted. The Bolshevik victors at the congress derided their minority detractors as the "pathetic" remainders of a starry-eyed "neutralism" characteristic of the bourgeois Esperantist movement that was now "doomed to death" by the revolution. The leaders of the new Union of Soviet Esperantists declared that the "essential task of the Russian Esperantist movement is to support, by means of Esperanto, the Soviet Government and to help it in the matter of fulfilling its international agenda." Under the SEU's leadership, there would be no room for the "intelligentsia and petit-bourgeois circles" of Esperantists that had proliferated prior to the revolution. The SEU was not to serve as an ideological big tent, but instead as a disciplined communist organization whose primary purpose was to popularize and use the international language of Esperanto in the interests of proletarian revolution at home and abroad.¹⁰⁷

To promote the new SEU, the self-styled communist Esperantists attempted to take full advantage of a public relations coup that had recently been won in the form of a letter of support from Maxim Gorky. In the famed proletarian writer's letter—a letter that the SEU circulated widely—Gorky stridently discounted the "conservative" opinion of Esperanto as nothing more than a "utopian escapade." Gorky defended Esperanto as a tool that all committed revolutionaries should eagerly take into their hands so that they could make real the fought-for "utopia" of "establishing social justice in the world." Esperanto would admirably serve the worldwide proletariat in desperate need of an international language with which to communicate and unite under the banner of revolution. It was impossible "to deny that a language, one for use by all people, will give a powerful jolt to the process of cultural development" in these urgent times. All revolutionaries, Gorky argued, must at the very least commit to the *idea* of Esperanto.[108] Tellingly, this appears to have been the extent of Gorky's own actual commitment to Esperanto. Yet even if Gorky never learned a word of Esperanto, the significance of his endorsement for the international language should not be underestimated. In Soviet Russia, at least until he departed in anguish for Sicily in late 1921, Gorky was one of the most important patrons of Soviet intellectuals, and artists—the "great interceder" who lobbied recalcitrant Bolshevik officials in support of a wide range of cultural projects. In offering his vocal support of Esperanto, Gorky bestowed upon the early Soviet Esperantists moral support, legitimacy, and revolutionary credentials at a time when they needed any well-positioned help they could get.[109]

Yet, Gorky could not work miracles. The Esperantists remained on the far periphery of the Party's attention and much further removed in the minds of Russian society in general. Esperantists in the early Soviet Union battled the same dilemmas that dogged the Bolsheviks: the overwhelming poverty of the devastated and traumatized country they were in; a population that was overwhelmingly illiterate in their own native tongue; and a sorely needed proletarian revolution abroad that never seemed to arrive. To name just a few.

Shifting Horizons

The summer of 1921 was a decisive one for reframing the Bolshevik imaginary of how and when international proletarian revolution would ignite. Although the Comintern delegates were not willing to concede defeat in the face of a resurgent capitalism, they did acknowledge at the Third Congress that, contrary to expectations, world revolution had not immediately followed upon the Great War. The working class of central and western Europe had suffered a series of defeats at the hands of the tenacious bourgeoisie, thus halting the progress of the revolutionary proletariat outside of Soviet Russia. It was undeniable that the international proletarian revolution was developing at a slower tempo than anticipated. Capitalism's downfall was assured but the timetable for global revolution was uncertain.[110]

For now, Trotsky reminded the Cominternarians, Soviet Russia remained the sole "bulwark of world revolution" despite all the historic improbabilities of its position. "Our country is still very backward," Trotsky thundered. "It unfolds before you a panorama of unheard-of-poverty. But we are defending this bulwark of the world revolution since at the given moment there is no other in the world." The Bolsheviks, he insisted, were still waiting for revolution abroad, at whatever tempo it might come. "When another stronghold is erected in France or Germany, then the one in Russia will lose nine-tenths of its significance; and we shall then go to you in Europe to defend this other and more important stronghold," he argued. In the meantime, however, Soviet Russia was "the stronghold of the revolution" and would remain so until such time as socialist revolution succeeded abroad.[111]

Despite the bravado of their rhetoric, the Bolsheviks were changing course in terms of their revolutionary tactics at home and abroad. The adoption of the New Economic Policy in March had inaugurated the Bolsheviks' controversial tactical retreat at home.

The theses adopted at the Third Comintern Congress in the summer of 1921 signaled their new "defensive" approach to world revolution—an adaptation to "an obviously receding revolutionary wave." Soviet Russia was the embattled headquarters of world revolution and it was unlikely to be relieved of this singular leadership position in the near future. Therefore, Soviet Russia would lead international communism and do so with its interests foremost in mind.[112]

The summer of 1921 was a decisive one as well for the Soviet Esperantists who had committed, despite repeated rebuffs by the early Soviet state, to deploy Esperanto in the service of establishing the global dictatorship of the proletariat. As the Bolsheviks began in the summer of 1921 to revise their own and the Comintern's timeline of worldwide October, the Soviet Esperantists' horizons began to shift as well. In late August, a gathering of leftist Esperantists in Prague established the Sennacieca Asocio Tutmonda (SAT)—the Worldwide Anational Association. Led by Eugene Lanti (born Eugene Adam), an Esperantist and member of the French Communist Party who had learned Esperanto while serving as an ambulance driver in World War I, SAT was a transnational organization of Esperantists who aligned politically on the broadly defined Left. Its mission was to unite the global proletariat in wielding the weapon of Esperanto in their efforts to defeat capitalism and to create a new socialist and decidedly nonnational world.

SAT was in many ways designed to function in an opposite organizational manner than the Comintern, and not just in its use of Esperanto as an instrument of advancing the international proletarian revolution. For Lanti, equally at home among anarchists and socialists, the key organizing principles of SAT were to be ecumenical Leftism, decentralization, and the uncompromising rejection of nationalism and the nation-state. Lanti explained the logic of SAT's ecumenical Leftism as follows:

> The working-class movement is disjointedly organized. There are sundry parties, trade unions, co-operatives, sports associations or other similar organizations. Each of them endeavors to attract the entire working class to itself, and in pursuit of that object controversies, disputes, sometimes even fights occur between these competing tendencies. SAT does not meddle in such disputes. All the parties in these controversies are equally in need of Esperanto.[113]

Anarchists, syndicalists, social democrats, communists—all had a seat at SAT's table.

SAT's so-called anationality was likewise simple and straightforward, at least in principle. SAT was founded on "the conviction that the working class can free itself completely, and establish peace on earth, only if it becomes solidly organized on a worldwide scale and strives to form an indivisible unit."[114] In Lanti's vision of radical anti-nationalism, Esperanto would serve as "a kind of spiritual hygiene against the nationalist miasma that we inhale constantly in the chauvinist atmosphere created by governments."[115] In his perhaps most radical expression of this view, Lanti would ultimately claim in 1930 that "The anti-nationalists are against everything national: against the national languages, cultures, traditions, and cultures. For them, Esperanto is the most important language, and their national languages only are auxiliary languages."[116]

At the time of SAT's founding in 1921, however, Lanti emphasized that the global proletariat could succeed only if its individual members fundamentally defined themselves and recognized one another as human beings, not as members of individual nations. They needed to destroy the class differences as well as the national differences that divided humanity. In the future, national differences and divisions would be dissolved as a consequence of capitalism's destruction and the global proletariat would unite in refashioning human relations in a universal socialism. Using Esperanto, Lanti explained, "we will incorporate in our beings characteristics suitable for making us true citizens of the world."[117] As SAT worked to advance this goal of universal socialism, global citizenship, and transformed humanity, it had no organizational need for national Esperantist organizations whose perceived usefulness was limited to lobbying local governments and educational authorities to embrace Esperanto. Membership to SAT was open only to individuals.

In founding SAT in August 1921, Lanti's primary motivation was not to define the proletarian Esperantist movement against or in competition with the Comintern, but rather to define it in opposition to the sham "neutrality" of the bourgeois Esperantist movement that had, at least since 1905, been predicated on the "inner idea" that Zamenhof had enshrined in the Boulogne Declaration. Whereas many bourgeois Esperantists had interpreted Zamenhof's "inner idea" of Esperanto as a mandate for political neutrality within the movement, Lanti rejected their premise of political neutrality as false consciousness as well as simple-minded folly. The proletarian Esperantism of SAT, Lanti insisted proudly, was essentially about struggle—the righteous and militant struggle of the working class to overthrow the capitalist order and the national forms it used to exploit the masses. Lanti embraced Esperanto not as a mediating force that could bring together men and women of the most diverse ideological persuasions, class positions, and nationalities, and allow them to understand one another and accept and appreciate their differences. Rather, he embraced Esperanto as a weapon that would help to obliterate class and national divisions and vanquish the capitalists and their sick bourgeois mentality. For Lanti, Esperanto's value was not its potential as a "neutral" healer and mild-mannered unifier of humanity but rather its radical potential as a weapon for achieving the defeat of capitalism and the achievement of universal socialism.[118] At the time of SAT's founding, its organizers declared, "Down with neutralist hypocrisy, down with capitalism, long live SAT!"[119]

Not a single Soviet Esperantist was present in Prague when SAT was established. Yet when news of its founding reached the leaders of the nascent SEU in Moscow, they no doubt saw much in Lanti's new organization to both excite and worry them. A global and transnational organization that prioritized Esperanto as essential— indeed, central—to the effort to advance the cause of international proletarian revolution was what the Soviet Esperantists had hoped for when they had first set their sights on the Comintern in 1919. Yet SAT also gave pause to the SEU leaders who had developed a keen understanding of the Bolsheviks' emerging approach to leading the international communist movement in its role as the as-yet only stronghold of the revolution in Europe. SAT's umbrella Leftism and principled anational policy of individual membership was clearly at odds with the Bolsheviks' more militant approach to regulating membership in the Comintern; after the adoption of the Twenty-One Conditions at the Second Comintern Congress, membership was open only to national Communist parties that followed the revolutionary Bolshevik example in their work. Still, it remained to be seen if SAT could provide a workable and desirable outlet for the SEU to exert its influence—a necessarily Soviet influence that faithfully represented Bolshevik mandates. As will be explored in subsequent chapters, this is precisely what the SEU would attempt to do throughout the years of the New Economic Policy and the Comintern's "united front" policy. The Soviet Esperantists would exert influence over SAT with varying degrees of success and, in so doing, would set in motion long-term, ultimately fatal implications for themselves and their movement that no one could have anticipated at the time.

What the Soviet Esperantists could and did reasonably anticipate in the early years of NEP was that the Comintern was unlikely to adopt Esperanto or any other international auxiliary language for its work, at least in the near future. In June 1921, the Advisory Commission for the Introduction of an International Auxiliary Language in the Third International issued its first formal communication to the Comintern. It argued that while the idea of using an international auxiliary language for the Comintern's work was attractive in theory, the actual application of the idea would require a great deal of time and effort to persuade Comintern delegates and workers to learn and use such a language. With an undisguised measure of doubt, the Advisory Commission acknowledged that its "first task" was "to investigate as to whether such an expenditure of energy would be worthwhile."[120] Yet Boris Souvarine, a French Comintern delegate, confirmed the Esperantists' worst fears when he confided in a letter to a comrade, "That Commission has practically done nothing."[121]

Already in 1922, the Advisory Commission was dissolved without fanfare, and its business declared accomplished.[122] The question of an international auxiliary language had arguably been considered, but was discarded in the end as a fruitless distraction, an expenditure of energy that would prove a greater folly than an advantage. For the Bolsheviks, Esperanto was at best a "utopian luxury" that they and the global proletariat simply could not afford.[123] Having considered the commission's findings, the Comintern Executive Committee ultimately refused to side with the Esperantists or any other group advocating for the adoption of an international language in Comintern work. The Comintern stipulated that "no language organization has the right to claim for itself the authority of the Comintern."[124]

At its Fourth Congress held in November 1922, the Comintern persisted with its imperfect system of relying on translators and interpreters. It insisted that its delegates make do with German, Russian, French, and English as working languages. Zinoviev made sure to go on record in offering thanks to the Comintern's staff of translators and interpreters for their "diligent and efficient work." He also joked at the Congress's end, "The Presidium has decided that at this moment all delegates are obliged to understand all languages, and there will be no translators." The stenographic record notes that Zinoviev's joke was greeted with laughter, but it remains unclear how many delegates were laughing along to a joke delivered in a language they simply could not understand.[125]

Bolshevization and the Language of Lenin

After the decisive failure of the German Revolution in 1923, the Comintern began its aggressive pursuit of unapologetic "Bolshevization" within its ranks and, between 1924 and 1926, the CPSU debated and ultimately adopted "socialism in one country" as the party line. International proletarian revolution remained a long-term Bolshevik goal, but—given the geopolitical circumstances of the absence of socialist revolution anywhere but in devastated Russia—the Bolsheviks' first priority needed to be building socialism within the Soviet Union and defending it from its capitalist enemies.[126] In practice, this soon meant that the Comintern oriented itself primarily toward supporting and advancing Soviet foreign policy goals in its work. Fomenting revolution abroad was subsidiary to building and protecting socialism at home.

These tactical and ideological shifts within the Comintern and the CPSU as a whole were soon reflected in the Bolsheviks' approach to the global politics of language and the apparently long-haul struggle for world revolution. At the Fifth Comintern Congress in July 1924—the first held since Lenin's death and the defeat of so-called German October—German, Russian, French, and English remained the working languages. Yet, a major linguistic shift took place that mirrored the geopolitical shift that had taken place since the last Comintern congress. At the Fifth Comintern Congress, for the first time, the Russian language eclipsed German as the primary language used in the proceedings. Bolshevik leaders who had at previous congresses typically given their speeches in German now did so in Russian. According to historian Warren Lerner, "The change in language, insignificant as it may have seemed at the time, actually reflected the change that was taking place in the Comintern leadership. Lenin was dead, Zinoviev and Stalin were in ascendance, and Trotsky and Radek were on their way out."[127]

These shifting politics of language testified not only to the political shake-ups within the Comintern and the CPSU, but also to the monumental shift in how socialists within and without the Soviet Union imagined the prospects of global proletarian revolution and who would lead. It was not German that was to be the language of international proletarian revolution, and certainly not Esperanto. Russian—the language of Lenin—was to be the language of socialist internationalism. This shift in the language politics of global communism was expressed neatly in the mid-1920s by the rector of the Communist University for the Toilers of the East (KUTV), a Soviet training ground for the international revolutionaries who were to bow to Moscow's lead and follow Comintern orders in pursuing revolution in their own countries. "It's impossible to study Leninism without knowledge of the Russian language," KUTV's rector explained. "It's just as necessary as the study of German was, in its time, for Russian Marxists."[128] At KUTV and other Comintern schools for foreigners, students engaged in intensive Russian language coursework in the 1920s and 1930s.[129] Mastery of Russian—while not required of foreign students—was expected of those who aspired for leadership roles within the Comintern schools and the Comintern itself.[130] Recast as the language of global communism, Russian was seen not only as an essential requirement for deep study of Marxist-Leninism, but also as loyal preparation for meaningful participation in

Soviet-led world revolution.[131] In the mid-1930s, Comintern leaders Georgi Dimitrov and Osip Piatnitskii would even tie foreign comrades' commitment to Russian language learning (or lack thereof) to the question of their political reliability.[132]

Elevating Russian to the first among equals on the Comintern's list of working languages did not solve the problems of polyglottism that the Esperantists had diagnosed in revolutionary Russia. So long as the Comintern functioned, language diversity bedeviled its operations and left a significant portion of its affairs lost in translation. To alleviate these problems, the Comintern ultimately chose to welcome not Esperanto but instead technological innovations that soon revolutionized the way interpretation services were provided at its meetings. At the Sixth Comintern Congress convened in Moscow in July 1928, the meeting hall was for the first time equipped with the telephone technology that made simultaneous interpretation possible.[133] Henri Barbusse recalled how cables and wires, linking listeners' headsets to interpreters' microphone boxes, slithered prominently across the floor and were strung up in the air too. The cables, wires, and headsets, he suggested, lent a sci-fi aura to the Comintern's Sixth Congress.[134] One of the interpreters hired for the event later described how this new technology of simultaneous interpretation worked. "On each Comintern delegate's seat was an earphone with five buttons marked Russian, French, German, Chinese, English," Markoosha Fischer recalled. "As the speaker talked, the translators, in low voice, translated his words into microphones connected with the earphones." Though impressed by what this technology had made possible, Fischer nonetheless added, "The strain of working constantly in four languages prevented me from following all the proceedings of the Congress."[135]

Comintern delegates could not plug into buttons that would provide them with telephonically delivered translations of the proceedings in Esperanto or in countless national languages spoken natively by attendees. In Moscow, the undisputed headquarters of international proletarian revolution, Russian was the language of Bolshevism and so of the Comintern's "new" socialist internationalism. At the Comintern, Esperanto did not upend traditional international language politics. Instead, traditional language politics were retrofitted with electronic headsets and put to the service of international proletarian revolution.

The Prohibitive Costs of Utopia

The February Revolution seemingly burst the door into an alternative Russian future wide open, inviting Russians across the political and socioeconomic spectrum to imagine new possibilities for their homeland and the world. For Russia's Esperantists, it presented an unparalleled opportunity to advocate for Esperanto as essential for resurrecting Russia and transforming the globe, uniting all into a global citizenry dedicated to a shared liberty, fraternity, and equality. After the October Revolution, Esperantists adapted and learned to make the case for Esperanto on a Marxist basis. They insisted that Marxism begged for an essential correction—an accounting for the fact that workers of the world could not and would never be able to unite without an international auxiliary language that enabled their communication, collaboration, and camaraderie. Only an international auxiliary language could serve the global proletariat in the fashion their revolution demanded. It was incredibly easy to learn, they optimistically claimed, even for un- or undereducated workers and peasants. Esperanto did not belong to any singular nation or people and therefore acquitted itself of the chauvinism and imperialism of using a national language for international relations. It was an essential weapon in the militant struggle to defeat capitalism and refashion human beings under the banner of socialism.

With the establishment of the Comintern in March 1919, the Esperantists shifted their focus to advocating for Esperanto as the logical and necessary choice as a working language—if not *the* working language—of the Comintern and its growing transnational network of international proletarian revolutionaries. In making their case, the Esperantists had an undeniable point, or rather a few, in their favor. On a sheer practical level, the reliance on communist polyglots to serve as translators and interpreters at the Comintern gatherings impeded efficiency, disrupted work, exhausted the attendees, and inspired feelings of resentment and exasperation among those who were not well served by the Comintern's system of translating from a mere handful of national languages. At times, the early Comintern's proceedings resembled a theater of the absurd owing to the insults, interruptions, infelicities, and incomprehensibility that resulted from the Bolsheviks' often improvised system of providing translation services to its foreign comrades. At one point, Bukharin was moved to satirize the Comintern's glossolalia from the rostrum. "People, O People," he regaled the foreign delegates, "I have to apologize to you that you should have today to endure four and twenty addresses of welcome. But remember that the sacred of the World Revolution calls for sacrifice."[136]

The Bolsheviks recognized the limits and problems imposed by the conditions of linguistic diversity among the Comintern's agents of proletarian internationalism. Yet they reconciled themselves to traditional, unabashedly Eurocentric methods of dealing, or attempting to deal, with the global politics of language in pursuit of international proletarian revolution. Instead of adopting an international auxiliary language, the Comintern dealt in a mere handful of dominant national languages, hired a growing legion of translators and interpreters, sought technological solutions to the challenges of translation and interpretation, and demanded that participants make do as best they could under the often frustrating and exhausting conditions of the Bolsheviks' Tower of Babel. On matters of culture, Lenin and his fellow Bolshevik leaders often revealed themselves to be strikingly conservative. In the context of the Russian Civil War and the monumental challenges that faced them in building the new socialist society even after the war was won, the Bolsheviks time and again proved themselves intolerant of "utopian luxuries" like Esperanto.[137] They focused instead on what they regarded as the sober need for pragmatism, cost-saving, and revolutionary discipline. With the shifting of priorities and revolutionary timelines after the failure of German October in 1923, the Bolsheviks elevated the Russian language above all others as the lingua franca of a new twentieth-century socialist internationalism led, without question, from Comintern headquarters in Moscow. Foreigners working in the service of Soviet internationalism would need to master Russian, not Esperanto.

Sidelined to the periphery of Bolshevik culture and rebuffed in their early efforts to aid the Bolsheviks' internationalist agenda, Esperantists did not give up hope that Esperanto could be put to use in the service of the global proletariat and the Soviet state. In 1921, the leaders of the Soviet Esperanto Union laid the foundation for what would serve as the singular organizational center for all Esperantist activities in the Soviet Union and announced themselves as ready footservants of the Bolsheviks' domestic and international agendas. The SEU soon gained its own institutional strength, even while Narkompros and Comintern officials remained largely content to keep this "independent organization" at arm's length. Soviet Esperantists never managed to recover from the failure, in the chaotic years of revolution and civil war, to convince the Bolsheviks, no less than the wider public, of the urgent need of an international auxiliary language for the purposes of refashioning life on earth. In an era of highly anticipated international revolution, Esperanto and its characteristically zealous adepts remained on the margins of Soviet politics and culture.

Yet as will be explored in the next chapters, in the 1920s and 1930s the SEU continued to promote Soviet interests at home and abroad via the international language of Esperanto. In the early Soviet Union, the Bolshevik leadership tolerated Esperanto as a revolutionary dream that might still offer them some small practical uses in advancing their revolution at home and abroad. It remained to be seen, however, if the early Soviet state would tolerate Soviet citizens' participation in building a radical proletarian Esperantoland that operated well outside of Party control, radically transgressed the Soviet Union's own borders, and was built on transnational relationships forged through communication in Esperanto rather than in Russian—the language of Lenin and emerging lingua franca of global communism.

4

Comrades with(out) Borders

In Innokentii Zhukov's *Voyage of the Red Star Pioneer Troop to Wonderland* (1924), eight young Soviet boys and their dog Sharik travel to the future—to the year 1957, to be precise. In their accidental detour from summer camp, the pioneers stumble into a Soviet future in which men and women all over the world enjoy communist plenty, technological mastery, good health, gender equality, a shared world culture, and international harmony. In this global future, men and women from all the world's many Soviet republics travel freely using their "radioplanes," dispatch messages using their "radiophones," and video chat using their "radioscopes." They communicate with ease in their shared international auxiliary language of Esperanto.[1]

Awestruck and shamefaced at not yet knowing Esperanto, the pioneers beg to know how the global Soviet future of 1957—so unlike their Soviet origins in 1924—had come to be. They learn that in 1924 the Soviet Union led the international proletariat in defeating global capital. The red banner of Soviet socialism enveloped the globe and all the world's peoples eagerly incorporated into a global Union of Soviet Socialist Republics—a modern paradise populated by new, modern people. Every day brought new achievements. Quite recently, the boys are told, workers had built a gigantic Lenin monument in the Himalayas in a successful project overseen by the "Central Bureau for Global Improvement."[2]

Zhukov's short story of the coming utopia ends with the Red Star pioneer troop waking up at daybreak in their forest campsite. Their travels to 1957 had been but a dream. Their dog Sharik is still biting at his fleas—stark evidence that the glorious future is in the distance. Yet the boys are ready to begin the hard work of building the socialist future of their dreams. Zhukov's *Voyage of the Red Star Pioneer Troop to Wonderland* was but one fictional representation of the Soviet "culture of anticipation" that flourished in the NEP era as visions of the coming utopia made by Soviet hands gave meaning to the miseries of the present.[3] It was one of several popular science fiction works produced in the early years of the Bolshevik Revolution that anticipated a future made possible by an international language.[4] As "road maps" to the socialist future and the modern people who would inhabit it, such works of science fiction insisted that an international language was essential for the creation of a distinctly socialist world.[5]

Coupled with this fixation on the perfected future was the conviction that the Soviet Union in the imperfect present was—despite the persistent backwardness of its socioeconomic, culture, and infrastructural realities in the 1920s—a revolutionary model to be emulated abroad. During the steep climb to socialism, therefore, Soviet citizens and foreign visitors to the USSR alike were instructed to judge the Soviet present—in the words of American journalist Louis Fischer—against "Russia's ugly past and her plans for the beautiful future."[6] In the demanding here and now, Soviet men and women needed to lead the way as heralds of that beautiful future. Among their tasks was to engage foreign comrades abroad so as to testify to Soviet achievements as well as to persuade them that a glorious socialist future could be theirs, too. Crucially, this was a future that foreign comrades could help Soviet pioneers to build and to finance. As citizen diplomats conversing with potential comrades abroad, Soviet men and women could aid the Soviet regime in its creative efforts in these years to court foreign allies even in the face of formal diplomatic nonrecognition. Michael David-Fox has described the Bolsheviks' early embrace of citizen diplomacy as a strategic effort to "bypass conventional diplomacy and appeal directly to public opinion" abroad.[7]

Embracing this mission, Soviet Esperantists presented themselves as best suited to the task of facilitating Soviet cultural diplomacy from below in the NEP era. "The use of the international language Esperanto," SEU leaders argued, "results in the maximum strengthening of relations between the working masses of the whole world irrespective of nationality."[8] Throughout the 1920s and early 1930s, Soviet Esperantists claimed that they were uniquely capable of unmediated conversation with foreign comrades. They argued that Esperanto allowed for international communication—by post, in the press, and in person—without the mediating and potentially distorting influence of translators and interpreters. This chapter will explore how they deployed radio technology, the transnational Esperantist press, international postal services, and the opportunity to host delegations of foreign Esperantist visitors in their Esperantist citizen diplomacy on behalf of the Soviet state. Ultimately, the Esperantists' promises to collapse language barriers and transgress borders strained against the Bolsheviks' increasingly hardened insistence on strategically and practically confronting the imperfect present—a time of Soviet singularity and threats from the capitalist West. Whereas the Esperantists promised unmediated conversation between Soviet citizens and foreign comrades, Soviet officials increasingly feared dangerous intimacies and alternative solidarities made possible by an international language whose adepts were rooted in a world of very real borders—ideological, linguistic, and national—that the Soviet state was invested in policing.

In the 1920s and early 1930s, Esperantism in the Soviet Union enjoyed license, but never robust state investment. In the early Stalinist era, what was already limited state support and tolerance for Esperantism quickly began to decline. By the launch of Stalin's First Five-Year Plan, Esperanto was increasingly regarded as a language of subversion—dangerous precisely because of its ability to subvert borders as well as evade state micromanagement of Soviet cultural diplomacy. In the Stalinist era, it was highly mediated conversations that the architects of Soviet international relations and citizen diplomacy wanted. These conversations were entrusted less and less to Esperantists than to trained cadres of Soviet guides and interpreters, fluent in the ever more standardized scripts of Soviet cultural diplomacy and techniques of surveillance. Global communism's ostensible need for an international language was shunted to an ever-distant Soviet future and Esperanto's celebrated borderlessness was increasingly regarded as out of sync—or worse, at odds—with the needs of the Stalinist present.

Negotiating an Uneasy Relationship with SAT

The Union of Soviet Esperantists emerged from the Russian Civil War era much like the Soviet Republic itself: embattled, lean, hungry, but alive. Its failure to persuade the Comintern to pursue Esperanto as the international language of communism left the SEU uncertain of its role in the early Soviet Republic. In the early NEP years, the SEU was self-consciously halted on the timeline of historic development, spinning its wheels and searching for a workable plan to persuade the Soviet public and the Bolshevik regime of Esperanto's essential viability for worldwide proletarian revolution.

Throughout 1923, the SEU's member *Bulletin* kept insisting that its primary mission was to assist, by means of using Esperanto, in helping the Bolsheviks to realize "the ideals of Soviet construction."[9] Yet, the SEU's leaders puzzled over how to provide that assistance, especially under the conditions of their organization's miserably small budget.[10] They printed cheap leaflets—"Does the Proletariat Need an International Language?" and "What is the International Auxiliary Language Esperanto?"—to advertise their mission. These leaflets demanded that Soviet citizens appreciate that "life has become excessively international" and that "not a single country, not a single government can exist in isolation." A globalizing world—one moving toward global proletarian revolution, no less—required an international auxiliary language.[11] In April, the SEU chairman Drezen debuted on Soviet radio, giving a lecture in Russian and Esperanto about the global proletariat's need of Esperanto. Broadcast from Moscow's Comintern radio station, Drezen's lecture traveled airwaves that reached cities throughout the Soviet Union and, it was hoped, Europe as well.[12] Otherwise, the organization of public lectures, poetry readings, and study circles was generally the extent of the SEU's practical agitprop work in the early 1920s.

By 1924, the SEU began to more energetically pursue collaboration with foreign Esperantist comrades and with SAT, in particular. In previous years, the SEU had publicly embraced SAT, urged its members to subscribe to its periodicals, and kept its members apprised of SAT's activities and growth abroad. Yet, the SEU leadership had also guarded itself, keeping some distance between itself and the transnational proletarian Esperantist organization whose leader and whose core activities and membership resided well outside the Soviet Union.

Some of this distance no doubt owed to the strained relationship between Lanti, SAT's founder and leader, and Drezen, the SEU chairman. Lanti was skeptical that global proletarian revolution should be entrusted to the Bolsheviks at all. Lanti regarded the Soviet government, the SEU, and the SEU's leaders with intense suspicion and no small degree of hostility. The roots of these ill feelings were planted in 1922 when, not long after SAT's founding in Prague in August 1921, Lanti traveled to Moscow in order to meet with the Soviet Esperantists, to acquaint himself with Bolshevism firsthand, and also to encourage the use of Esperanto within the Comintern. In his telling, his travels to the capital of the world's first workers' state produced one disappointment after another. He was profoundly disillusioned by Soviet realities.

In Moscow, Lanti took up residence at the Lux Hotel—a hotel (in)famous in the memories of many of the foreign leftists and Comintern delegates who took up residence there during their hopeful sojourns to the early Soviet Republic. One later described the Lux Hotel as akin to "an overcrowded tenement" filled with men and women "of all nations, colors, and tongues, few of them able to understand one another, all of them awed by the grandeur and the might of the enthroned revolution."[13] Here at the Lux, Lanti chatted with a French Comintern delegate who urged him to rush to Comintern headquarters, where he found "a tall building on whose façade can be read in four languages the famous phrase: 'workers of all countries unite.'" Once inside, he was tossed from one functionary to the next. Eventually, Lanti recalled, "a German-speaking woman made it understood that I should return at 2:00."[14] When Lanti finally sat down to a meeting with Rakosi, secretary of the Comintern's Executive Committee, it proved a disastrous encounter.

In Lanti's account of the conversation, Rakosi made clear his lack of interest in SAT. "Is it communist?" Rakosi queried with undisguised condescension. "We can't be bothered with Esperanto," Rakosi reportedly said. "We have other, more pressing tasks." The insult, however, did not end there. "I don't understand why you've come here from Paris for this," Rakosi continued, before adding, "The Comintern can't pay for tourists." At this point, Lanti recalled, his "blood was beginning to boil." He was, after all, visiting the USSR at his own expense and *his* version of proletarian internationalism took seriously the question of an international language for world revolution. "After conversing for twenty minutes," Lanti explained, "Rakosi confessed that it was possible that our activity could be useful for communism but ended by saying that the Comintern could not at this time take up the matter."[15]

Lanti, by all accounts, was an undiscriminating iconoclast, always ready to smash any idol he regarded as false.[16] He had already shown his independent approach to proletarian internationalism before stepping foot in Moscow. It had been a point of worry for Soviet Esperantists from the start that Lanti's SAT had been founded on rigid principles of *party* neutrality and anationality. Lanti himself was a communist, but his meeting with Rakosi convinced him that there was something altogether rotten about communism as the Bolsheviks practiced it. Lanti's discovery that both the Comintern and Narkompros had dismissed the question of an international language further confirmed his suspicion that the Bolsheviks were not as revolutionary or as internationalist as they claimed to be. The dirty streets of Moscow only further deepened his misery and disenchantment. The capital of the USSR, he noted with sorrow, was teeming with bureaucrats, prostitutes, and hungry workers.[17]

Lanti was further dismayed upon his meeting with the SEU's leaders, and in particular with the SEU's chairman, Drezen. Born in 1892, Ernest Karlovich Drezen was a Latvian by nationality and a member of the Bolshevik Party since 1918. He described himself in personnel files as the son of a father who descended from the peasantry and who had worked in the merchant marine. An active participant in student Esperantist groups, Drezen had attended a modest secondary school in Kronshtadt before advancing to the Petrograd Technological Institute and serving the imperial army during World War I. An exemplary model of the October Revolution's new crop of self-made men, Drezen next served in the civil war as a Red Army commissar. In 1921, he gained employment in the Kremlin as an assistant to the Central Executive Committee.[18] In that same year, he served as a founding member and chairman of the SEU. Upon meeting him in Moscow, Lanti was convinced that Drezen was a showboater, a Bolshevik lackey, and an Esperantist ashamed of defending Esperantism to his Communist Party superiors. Lanti concluded that his three weeks in the Soviet Union, and those spent with representatives of the Comintern and the SEU, in particular, had proven "the ruin of [his] beliefs."[19] Lanti remained a communist, but one whose allegiance would never be to the Bolsheviks or to the Soviet Esperantists who had already, in his view, failed the global proletariat.

Despite Lanti's resentments toward Drezen, the Comintern, and the Bolsheviks generally, the SEU ultimately established a working relationship with SAT that would last through the NEP and nearly the duration of the First Five-Year Plan. Yet strains continued to plague the relationship. The SEU balked at SAT's umbrella membership policy and its stalwart refusal to be remade into a Soviet, or even Sovietized institution. SAT's bylaws officially encouraged its members to commit to tolerant, open-mindedness

Figure 6 Ernest Karlovich Drezen (1892–1937). *Source*: Wikimedia Commons.

regarding one another's party affiliations, while Drezen scarcely disguised his desire to transform SAT into a Bolshevized Esperantist Comintern in miniature.[20] Mutual resentments between the leaders of SAT and the SEU were occasionally emblazoned onto the pages of the transnational leftist Esperantist press. Overall, however, there were broad currents of agreement between the SAT and SEU leaders. Most fundamentally, there was a shared commitment to using Esperanto as a weapon of class struggle and a joint rejection of the "neutralism" that characterized bourgeois Esperantism. The Comintern's adoption of its "united front" policy in 1922 cleared the path for the SEU to put aside their complaints that SAT was an insufficiently communist organization that brought anarchists, Social Democrats, and others under its umbrella.[21]

In early 1923, Drezen informed the SEU's members that SAT was the only foreign Esperantist organization that Soviet Esperantists should engage. It was the only one that shared the SEU's goals and ideology, its commitment to proletarian revolution. The rest were bourgeois organizations mired in the capitalist world. Drezen urged SEU members to join SAT's ranks, thereby joining "the fraternal family of Esperantist revolutionaries worldwide."[22] The SEU promoted subscriptions to SAT periodicals as a practical means of participating in the workers' Esperanto movement and helping in its "struggle against bourgeois Esperantists."[23] By 1924, the SEU leadership instructed its membership to regard the two as complementary organizations working in partnership toward the same worldwide goals. "Esperanto is our weapon," an editorial appearing in the SEU's *Bulletin* announced. "We don't need Esperanto to be our plaything, satisfying our personal needs and whims; it's as a weapon that Esperanto is valuable to us." To effectively deploy that weapon, it was time to start using the channels made available to Soviet Esperantists by SAT and its transnational publishing for effective citizen diplomacy. It was time to tell foreign Esperantists what life was like for Soviet citizens. Foreign comrades wanted and needed to know about the pace of building socialism in the USSR and about the everyday life of Soviet workers at their factories and in their homes.[24] They needed to converse with the future—the future then being built in the imperfect Soviet present. To facilitate these conversations, Soviet Esperantists first turned to radio, international correspondence, and transnational publishing.

On the Radio Waves of the Future

In 1921, the Russian Futurist Velimir Khlebnikov predicted that radio would "unite all mankind" as it washed over the globe as a "spiritual wave" and a "silver shower of sound." In the future, he predicted, radio's "metal trumpet mouth" would transmit "the news of the day, the activities of the government, weather information, events from the exciting life of the capital cities." Lectures would be transmitted into even the most distant of schoolrooms, spreading enlightenment to all. Radio, Khlebnikov insisted, would also "transmit images in color" and one day, he promised, "we will have learned to transmit the sense of taste." Khlebnikov imagined a future landscape of radio clubs that would "annihilate distance" and link men and women worldwide. He imagined "majestic skyscrapers wrapped in clouds, a game of chess between two people located at opposite ends of Planet Earth, an animated conversation between someone in America and someone in Europe." In all of these ways, Khlebnikov anticipated, radio will "forge continuous links in the universal soul and mold mankind into a single entity."[25]

Many of Khlebnikov's contemporaries shared his wide-eyed vision for radio's revolutionary potential. In the 1920s, radio enthusiasts worldwide were eagerly anticipating a "future, when, ensconced in a comfortable armchair at home, one will see and hear what is taking place on the other side of the world."[26] As historian Steven Lovell has noted, radio arrived on the world scene as a "big bang" whose explosion reverberated nationally and globally and seemed to offer a revolutionary upending of political, cultural, social, economic, and military norms.[27] For the Bolsheviks, radio's propaganda potential at home and abroad was as heartening as was its promise for aiding in the coherent governance of the Soviet Union's enormous territory.

In addition to radio's revolutionary promises, however, there always lurked threat and danger too. Radio heralded a future in which, potentially at least, borders would be rendered meaningless, impossible to police. In the 1920s, it was not merely the Bolsheviks who worked simultaneously to build their country's radio infrastructure and to protect their state's borders from radio's subversive, border-crossing potential. In the 1920s, governments worldwide scrambled to both make use of wireless broadcasting and protect themselves from its transgressive possibilities.[28] As World War I had shown, telecommunications were a matter of national security in the age of global warfare. Radio, with its wireless, border-transgressing capacity could be used as a tool of espionage and warfare.[29] The discovery, in 1924, that shortwave could transmit radio signals around the world at incredible speed and astonishingly affordable cost further stimulated government efforts at regulation and control over this revolutionary media technology.[30] For the first time, the prospect of the "electric word" traveling easily across the world's newly "ethereally linked continents" became a realistic and potentially harrowing proposition.[31] Regulation, surveillance, and censorship of radio became urgent state priorities throughout the world.

Yet for everyday radio enthusiasts, no less than for champions of world citizenship and internationalism of all manner of ideological stripes, radio's potential to cross and collapse borders was cause for celebration. For Esperantists, in particular, radio seemed to herald a technological means capable of linking Esperanto speakers worldwide. Many Esperantists ultimately argued that without Esperanto, radio was fated to remain a replicated Babel in the air. Yet Esperanto could liberate radio from its linguistic constraints and transcend and defy earthly borders.

In the early Soviet Union, Esperantists marshaled such claims as a bid to advertise their, and Esperanto's, distinctive and valuable contribution to Soviet cultural diplomacy. The SEU's leaders were insistent that they could uniquely harness the modern power of radio technology to transmit good news about the Soviet future in an international auxiliary language that foreign workers could understand without need of translation. Once in the ionosphere, Esperantist speech subverted and traveled across otherwise regulated borders and could not be corrupted by interpreters. In this way, Esperanto penetrated the defenses of enemy capitalist states and managed, too, to break through the "lies" they tried to feed their populations about the Soviet Union.

In 1923, Soviet Esperantists launched regular transnational radio transmissions via Moscow's Comintern radio station with a lecture delivered in Russian and in

Esperanto, "Does the proletariat need an international language?"[32] By 1926, they were broadcasting bimonthly addresses in Esperanto for foreign listeners and hosting weekly radio lessons in Esperanto itself. In 1927, they began broadcasting Esperanto news programs that transmitted abroad the good news from the Soviet press.[33] The Esperantist S. Podkaminer declared in 1926: "There is not the slightest doubt that in the near future Esperanto will become so widespread that 'the millions of rallies' that Lenin dreamed about will become a reality, and only then will radio really become a global agitator of worldwide revolution." He noted with satisfaction that it was not just Moscow, but also radio stations in Vienna, Berlin, Paris, New York, Madrid, Rome, and other cities abroad that were broadcasting in Esperanto.[34]

Yet this meant that Esperantists in capitalist countries were also capable of spreading their own messages—and potentially messages counter to Soviet interests—to radio receivers in Soviet hands. In 1924, the International Radio Association was founded as an explicitly transnational organization dedicated most broadly to "facilitate relations between radio users in all parts of the world by means of Esperanto." With offices based in more than twenty nations by the following year, the International Radio Association was then a largely Western European and North American affair that offered membership to anyone, anywhere, who supported "the adoption of Esperanto as the International Radio language."[35] It advertised Esperanto programs broadcast throughout North America, Australia, and across Europe—including the Soviet Union.[36] By 1926, as many as one hundred radio stations in twenty-eight different countries were said to broadcast programs in Esperanto.[37] In the 1920s, Esperantist radio enthusiasts throughout the world embraced the slogan that "wireless waves know no frontiers, the international language has become indispensable."[38] From a statist perspective, however, if wireless waves knew no frontiers, then the international language potentially threatened national and ideological borders.

Yet the rhetoric about radio and Esperanto far outpaced the reality. In the 1920s and 1930s, Soviet radio broadcasting's potential reach and impact was far more limited than its enthusiasts claimed. Although a much-hyped and mythologized new technology, radio in the USSR remained an expensive and unreliable means of reaching out to audiences both domestic and international.[39] For all the Esperantists' hopes that foreigners were avidly consuming the lectures and literary "radio concerts" they were broadcasting from the Comintern radio station, confirmation that their signal was received by foreign Esperantists in Europe, especially in the 1920s, was rare.[40] Meanwhile, radio sets and broadcasting equipment were expensive luxuries in the industrializing Soviet Union. When undertaken in the 1930s, wired radiofication was an urban phenomenon that primarily allowed Soviet apartment dwellers to tune in and imbibe Soviet cultural norms.

Nonetheless, the Soviet state moved quickly to establish bureaucratic control over Soviet radio broadcasting and shaped the industry in these early years into an outlet of public agitation oriented toward collective "organized listening," rather than individual, self-directed listening. Bureaucrats, engineers, and leaders within Soviet arts helped to harness radio, organize and expand its infrastructure, and to direct its potential toward the Soviet mission to civilize, first and foremost, its own citizenry. While Esperanto programming was a common feature of Soviet radio in the 1920s and early 1930s, the hopeful vision of linking Esperantists worldwide over the airwaves remained as yet a dream beyond reach for Soviet enthusiasts. Esperanto radio broadcasting in the Soviet Union in the 1920s and 1930s was most successful in reaching a domestic audience. Regularly broadcast Esperanto lessons and radio concerts helped to recruit new Esperantists and aid them with their language study. But uniting the world in Esperanto airwaves would have to wait. The state's insistent priority in the 1920s and 1930s was to utilize radio for the domestic purposes of uniting the Soviet people in shared culture and a commitment to the task of building socialism in their embattled country.[41]

Traveling the World in an Envelope, Heralding the Socialist Future

S. Rublev's popular textbook *Esperanto Study Group* was printed eight times between 1928 and 1936. Rublev's textbook promised that its users would gain sufficient fluency in the language to enable their "practical application" of Esperanto—international correspondence first of all.[42] The primer instructed users to begin their correspondence with foreigners at the earliest opportunity, while still completing their beginner's course in Esperanto.[43] As one of Rublev's practice texts emphasized, exchanging ideas with foreigners was the whole point of Esperanto:

> We want to correspond with our comrades—with English, French, Italian, American, and German workers. The working class has an international language and we can understand our comrades—proletarian Esperantists in Europe, Asia, Africa, Australia, and in America. They can't speak Russian; they can't understand the Russian language. They are learning the international language and they correspond with us in Esperanto. We must learn the international language well and correspond with proletarian Esperantists.[44]

To this end, Rublev's *Esperanto Study Group* was as much a textbook for learning Esperanto as it was an instruction manual for engaging in patriotic correspondence with foreign comrades in Esperanto. It contained insights into how to find foreign pen pals and how to write an interesting letter to a worker friend abroad. Rublev taught readers that Esperantist correspondence with foreign workers was and must always be a patriotic act, meant to uphold and defend the interests of the Soviet state.

Early Soviet Esperanto textbooks and promotional materials typically placed correspondence with foreigners above all other possible motivations to learn the language. They titillated possible converts to Esperanto with the prospects of reaching out to men and women in a wider world that was largely unknown to the average Soviet worker. Europe, the Americas, Africa, Asia, and Australia were invoked as virtual tourist destinations for Soviet citizens for whom foreign leisure travel was inconceivable. Soviet citizens might find it impossible to travel abroad to stare up at the Eiffel Tower, stroll down Broadway, or climb the Himalayas, but a postcard or a letter could travel the world at relatively low cost. Yet even while appealing to Soviet citizens' curiosity about the world and promising a salve for their stunted wanderlust, the Soviet Esperantists never failed to emphasize that correspondence with foreigners was a means to a higher end—that is, effective cultural diplomacy from below.

Throughout the 1920s and early 1930s, the Union of Soviet Esperantists sought to oversee and regulate correspondence with foreigners abroad as a specific brand of citizen diplomacy that they and their fellow Esperanto adepts could uniquely offer in the service of the broad goals of Soviet internationalism. During these years, the SEU oversaw the exchange of tens of thousands of letters and postcards between Soviet citizens and foreigners abroad. Esperantist correspondence with foreigners abroad was branded as a specialty outgrowth of the larger early Soviet cultural program known as worker correspondence. In the early 1920s, the worker correspondence movement began as a journalistic and literary training ground for the Soviet proletariat.[45] Literate and semiliterate workers were exhorted to contemplate their material, political, and cultural conditions and to write accounts of their everyday life for the Soviet press. Soviet newspapers and journals could then use the worker correspondents' accounts—prized for their presumed authenticity and folksy ground-level reporting—in their publications so that Soviet and potentially foreign audiences could learn about everyday life in the world's first workers' state.[46]

Worker correspondence was likewise intended to be a "form of civic activism" (and thus Soviet self-fashioning) for its participants.[47] Worker (and peasant) correspondents learned how to narrate their experience within distinctly Soviet frameworks for understanding the past, present, and future and how the individual citizen fit into the larger collective. As Trotsky explained the movement in 1924, "Worker correspondents are the closest, most direct instruments of the newly awakened working class at the grass roots level."[48] In pursuing worker correspondence, he argued, Soviet citizens not only enlightened themselves, but also contributed to the cultural advancement of the Soviet population as a whole. "The worker correspondents use their pens like levers," Trotsky explained. "It is a small lever, but there are many worker correspondents, and that means there are many little levers for elevating the culture of the working masses."[49]

Although the worker correspondence movement began at the start of NEP as a somewhat chaotic and undisciplined initiative to incorporate the Soviet proletariat in the journalistic and literary modes of teaching socialist values, Soviet cultural authorities soon brought it to heel. As Jeremy Hicks has explained, the worker correspondence movement soon became so regulated as to all but ensure that "information from below was fed into a template enforced from above, so that no unwelcome information could actually penetrate the pages of the press."[50] This embrace of template contributions and journalistic clichés reinforced the didactic function of the project as a whole. Worker correspondents quickly learned from both explicit templates given them, no less from repeated rejection of any material of theirs that deviated from mandated norms, what types of worker self-expression were allowable. In this way, worker correspondence was a means for state authorities to discipline and "organize" public opinion.[51]

It was also a mechanism for shaping public opinion about the Soviet Union abroad. Worker correspondence was deployed to communicate Soviet achievements to foreign publications and their working-class readers. A brochure written by Maria Ulianova in 1928, *The Workers' Correspondence Movement Abroad and International*

Communication, listed a series of questions and topics deemed "important and interesting for workers in foreign countries" who needed to be acquainted with the conditions of Soviet life.[52] Worker correspondents, Ulianova instructed, should write about the seven-hour workday; pay and material benefits in the Soviet workplace; health-care provisions for Soviet workers; the Soviet emancipation of national minorities; questions of marriage, family life, and legal abortion; and workers' living conditions and everyday life. Worker correspondents, Ulianova advised, should not sugarcoat the realities of Soviet life, but instead honestly acknowledge the difficulties of the Soviet effort to build socialism. Deficiencies needed to be discussed alongside achievements. "The fewer generalities, hackneyed agitation, and superficial cries there are in this correspondence," Ulianova advised, "the greater impression it will make on the foreign worker."[53]

Esperanto was, to borrow Trotksy's phrasing, one "little lever" in the broader worker correspondence movement. Soviet Esperantists adapted the methods of worker correspondence, committing themselves to flooding foreign news outlets, workers' associations, foreign proletarian Esperantist societies, and even individual Esperantist pen pals abroad with template-based missives. They adopted the acronym "Esperkor" to describe their work. As one Komsomol circular insisted in 1926, Esperantist correspondence with foreigners must advance the "goals of international propaganda."[54] It was also to have an edifying effect on the Soviet citizens who participated in these campaigns. Thinking globally was, in the early Soviet Union, part of becoming and being "cultured." The Soviet state might have been building socialism in one country, but the pretext of building socialism in one country was the Soviet Union's situatedness in a wider world full of perils and potential opportunities. The Soviet state insisted that its citizens appreciate their country's straitened geopolitical circumstances, no less than their great fortune of laboring for the world's first socialist state.

Soviet citizens were also expected to nurture their global consciousness as New Soviet Men and Women. Backward, illiterate people were those who could not find other countries on a map. Becoming modern, cultured, and Soviet required being aware of the world and fluent in knowledge about the geographies, histories, and cultures of foreign countries and their people. In a speech to library workers in 1924, Trotsky emphasized that it was not enough for peasants and workers to sing the *Internationale*. "It is necessary that," he lectured, "when they read or hear a news story, they visualize to which living part of our planet it is referring."[55] New Soviet Men and Women needed to learn how "to orient themselves in the international situation so that they can consciously have an effect on it, if necessary, perhaps even with gun in hand."[56]

Because Soviet Esperantists were still developing their appropriate global sensibilities, Esperkor was subject to the same heavy-handed disciplining that was applied to the wider worker correspondence movement in these years. Esperantist publications issued by the SEU thus offered letter-writing templates that Soviet workers were encouraged to adopt even if, as one model instructed, they need not be "copied verbatim."[57] As could be expected, these letter templates read like singsong recitations of generic talking points issued from a bureaucratic office. By design, they were devoid of personality, individual experience, and diversions from the reporting of Soviet achievements. Thus, one lesson in a popular Esperanto textbook gave the following sample letter for students to translate into Esperanto:

> Comrades! We wish to write to you today about the lives of workers in Soviet Russia. In Soviet Russia there are no capitalists. The working day is seven hours long. Write to us about your life. We await your response. Esperanto unites the workers of the world.[58]

The generic template shows how the SEU's leaders were increasingly conscious of the Soviet ideal of a highly micromanaged approach to Soviet citizen diplomacy. As one circular instructed Esperantist youth, "correspondence about trifles is not needed."[59]

In the 1920s, the SEU's worker correspondence found its most reliable outlets in transnationally circulating Esperantist periodicals published abroad by SAT, especially its journal *Sennaciulo* (*Nationless One*). The SEU frequently placed in *Sennaciulo*'s pages reports about the SEU's work and about Soviet everyday life. By design, much of the Esperkor product placed in *Sennaciulo*'s pages were straightforward news articles and essays meant to convey information and statistics about such diverse topics as abortion, foreign delegations, urban living, and the "emancipation" of women in the Soviet Union.[60]

More personalized content could be found in *Sennaciulo*'s "A Day in My Life" feature. "A Day in My Life" was the Soviet Esperantists' opportunity in the transnational Esperanto press to put a name and a face to the millions of Soviet citizens building socialism. These human-interest pieces were often written by Soviet Esperanto-learners making their first attempt at worker correspondence. "A Day in My Life" often included a personal photo and at least several paragraphs in which a Soviet Esperantist wrote about his or her daily life. Thus, the Soviet Esperantist Nikolai Usov wrote about his daily life as "a 28-year-old bachelor and a village teacher." Usov described his living quarters, meals, leisure activities, and efforts to raise the cultural level of his "backward village." Usov became an Esperantist, he explained, because the international language provided a means for him to connect with the whole world. After only two years as an Esperantist, he proudly explained, "I have friends in Germany, France, Czechoslovakia, Italy, Canada, Argentina, and the United States with whom I correspond on a variety of issues." Alongside his photograph, Usov included a painting of his village in winter.[61]

Soviet contributions to "A Day in My Life" did not always present daily life in the Soviet Union in rosy hues. V. Fedorovski wrote about his struggles, hopes, and dreams as a 21-year-old living in a small town well outside Kiev. Fedorovski described the challenges he faced as an unemployed young man who scraped to get by while also constrained by the responsibility of caring for his young brother. While his parents' circumstances are never explained, Fedorovski wrote about how he tried, every day, to profitably instruct his 8-year-old brother in the study of both the Russian and Esperanto languages. For three hours each afternoon, he studied foreign languages, including German, French, and English, because it was his professional goal to become a linguist. Fedorovski's life was not easy, but his life in the Soviet Union at least afforded him the leisure time to read the works of Lenin, to write articles about philately, and to engage in correspondence with his Esperantist friends around the world. Unfortunately, he lamented, there were few in his local community who shared his interest in Esperanto.[62]

Fire in the Envelopes!

In the 1920s and early 1930s, Esperantist worker correspondence was considered a useful tool of international agitprop that helped foreign comrades to "know" the Soviet Union and to combat the "lies" the bourgeois press tried to feed them about Soviet life. The Komsomol, VOKS, the Society for the Friends of Radio, International Red Aid (MOPR), and other Soviet organizations regularly urged Soviet citizens to take up Esperanto as a means of engaging in this civic and patriotic act of citizen diplomacy, of "international propaganda."[63] Combined with pen, paper, and postage, Esperanto provided a unique opportunity to alchemize one's Soviet patriotism, to send the fire of revolution around the world in the seemingly innocuous vehicle of an envelope.[64] Yet the question of private, individual correspondence between Soviet Esperantists and foreigners was less certain of its answers.

Private correspondence between Soviet Esperantists and their comrades abroad was a phenomenon with all the potential to be radically different from the worker correspondence the SEU helped to sponsor and oversee in the 1920s. Explaining the mechanics of international Esperantist correspondence in a report for CPSU and government officials in 1926, the SEU boasted of the excellent opportunities for Soviet Esperantists to engage in pen pal exchanges with foreign comrades who were interested in exchanging letters on the themes of communism, the labor union movement, women's emancipation, everyday life, and technical expertise. The SEU explained that Esperantist pen pals often exchanged more than their thoughts on such weighty topics—they also exchanged "journals, newspapers, books, drawings, various objects, and even clothes."[65] Pen pal exchanges with workers abroad, the SEU argued, was a uniquely effective and highly popular way for Soviet citizens to embody socialist internationalism. One report noted that of the nearly 3,600 addresses listed in SAT's 1926 directory, approximately 1,100 belonged to Soviet citizens.[66]

Yet individual Esperanto correspondence, Soviet officials presumed, always presented the threat of subversion—counterrevolution transmitted in an international language and contained in an otherwise innocuous-seeming envelope. A confidential, though largely positive, report on the Soviet Esperantist movement and prepared in 1926 for Stalin stated bluntly: "Of course, it is impossible to control Esperanto correspondence between individual persons."[67] As early as 1928, CPSU Control Commission member Maria Ulianova argued that Esperanto was not a useful tool of proletarian internationalism when instead it was used "by anti-Soviet elements for their own purposes."[68] Esperanto—especially in private hands—could be weaponized just as easily against the Soviet Union as against its enemies. Esperantists, *Pravda* warned during NEP, occupied "a dark corner of the cultural front."[69] Even the most ardent Soviet defenders of Esperanto's potential as a weapon of international class struggle could not deny that it was the petit bourgeoisie that had most invested in Esperanto abroad.[70] It was not always clear how or to what ends this unusual linguistic weapon of class struggle was being used. As one critic charged in 1928, Esperantist correspondence "is conducted without any supervision, systemic planning, and without preliminary study and it is almost exclusively of a personal character." It was no wonder, then, that "enemies of the working class" had already succeeded in deploying Esperanto as a means of spreading lies about the Soviet Union abroad.[71] The leaders of the SEU admitted in a 1926 report, "The majority of comrades write to their foreign correspondents (*pishut zagranitsu*) whatever comes to their mind." Without proper surveillance and guidance on the part of Esperantist leaders, "mistakes" were often made in this individual correspondence.[72]

Yet for much of the 1920s and even into the 1930s, the possibilities for private Esperantist correspondence were wide open—dependent largely on Soviet citizens' ability to afford the stamps, paper, and energy such correspondence required. As before the revolution, Esperantists in the Soviet Union could still rely on the pen pal classifieds that regularly appeared in the transnational Esperantist press to find correspondents. Active members of the SEU typically had access to SAT's regular periodicals, *Sennacieca Revuo* and *Sennaciulo* either via individual or collective subscriptions. In them, they could find the postings of their like-minded "proletarian Esperantists" in Europe and around the world who were in search of new pen pals. Likewise, they could for a nominal fee place their own classified ad. Thus, in *Sennaciulo* one could find, for example, the request of N. Kondratenko, a teacher from Moscow who sought pen pals interested in "scientific, political, and pedagogical themes." A. I. Serdiukov, an Esperantist from Astrakhan, wanted to exchange ideas about painting. While some Soviet Esperantists sought pen pals explicitly to discuss the international workers' movement, others had far more diverse interests. A. V. Moiseev in Moscow wanted to discuss vegetarianism and pacifism, while S. Sarichev in Astrakhan wanted to discuss "bookkeeping, politics, and hypnosis." Anna Kalinin, also of Astrakhan, sought pen pals interested in discussing any and all topics.[73]

Foreign Esperantists were hungry for insights into Soviet life and they wanted to hear about it directly from their Soviet comrades—their pen pals and, in some cases, their close friends with whom they shared intimate details about their lives, dreams, and hopes. As the Smolensk outlet of the SEU reported in 1926, letters in the hundreds were flowing in from comrades in Germany, the United States, China, France, and other countries. They were written by leftists of all manner of ideological stripes— sympathizers with the Bolshevik regime, but also "social democrats, Christian socialists, anarchists." These foreign pen pals craved details about their Soviet comrades' private and public lives. "They ask about everything … even about marriage, love, and death," the Smolensk SEU outpost reported. "Most often they ask about the new everyday life, the dissemination of Esperanto, and personal questions."[74]

Ordinary Soviet citizens attracted to Esperanto in the 1920s were, like their foreign pen pals, eager to discover what life was like on other shores and beyond borders they would never cross in real life. In the absence of the ability to travel abroad, exchanging letters with foreign pen pals seemed a rich opportunity to visit other lands vicariously, to get to know their peoples and cultures by means of epistolary exchange in a language designed to link comrades across otherwise impassable borders. Among communist youth in the Soviet 1920s, there was a well-documented passion to live revolutionary internationalism and forge emotional bonds with comrades abroad.[75] Esperanto appeared as an ideal opportunity to meaningful pursue their commitment to internationalism and satisfy their curiosity about foreign cultures. In 1926, one Soviet Esperantist invoked the electrifying thrill of correspondence with foreign comrades, describing Esperanto as the "valve through which bursts forth the electric charge of internationality."[76]

Lev Kopelev later recalled how, as an adolescent schoolboy in the 1920s, he had been introduced to the "beautiful sacrament" of Esperanto by an otherwise dreadful teacher who introduced him to the international language and the pen pal exchanges it afforded him. Kopelev recalled how the teacher "came to life" as "he spoke about the international brotherhood which recognized no borders, about the fact that the people of the whole world, all nations and races, should join together in the name of goodness, justice, and enlightenment."[77] Young Kopelev sat thunderstruck as his teacher carefully pulled from an "old satchel" his prized possessions—letters, postcards, and envelopes received from abroad. Kopelev was mesmerized; these souvenirs of a distant and wide world were "so bright they seemed lacquered, with rare and wondrous stamps. You could hold them in your hands, sniff them—inhale the air of London, Paris, San Francisco, Tokyo."[78] Kopelev admired his schoolteacher's postcards from South America, Australia, Europe, and Asia and envied the small library of Esperantist and other foreign publications he had accumulated. After much begging, he gained his teacher's permission to explore this small library. "I confidently picked through the newspapers and letters," Kopelev recalled, "sought out the special announcements in the Esperanto magazines which gave the addresses of people who wanted to correspond with Esperantists of other countries, exchange illustrated publications with texts translated into Esperanto."[79]

Yet, this intoxication with the fascinating abroad which drew Kopelev and so many others to Esperantism as pen pal seekers was also a liability for the Soviet Esperantist movement. In 1927, the SEU warned its membership of the danger of "thoughtless letters" being sent to foreign comrades abroad that were filled with errors, inflated statistics, and untruths about everyday life in the Soviet Union.[80] By the late 1920s, the SEU was attempting as best it could to encourage what it called the "transition from individual to collective correspondence." As one critic of the Esperantists' dangerous tradition of individual correspondence put it, "It is better to send one fully developed and well thought-out collective letter than dozens of personal letters."[81] The SEU instructed that Esperantist correspondents should, in composing their letters, "consult their local party committee, factory committee, wall newspaper, and Komsomol."[82] In this way, they would be sending the necessary and appropriate information to their pen pals and contributing to a collective citizen diplomacy campaign in ideal fashion. Individual pen pal correspondence was derided as "apolitical chatter" that distracted from Soviet Esperantists' duty of engaging in foreign correspondence for the purpose of aiding international class struggle. Esperantists who hoarded foreign correspondence, selfishly hiding "private" letters in their pockets, disengaged themselves from the comradely work of international education and cultural diplomacy. Patriotic duty required that all Soviet Esperantists transition from individual to collective correspondence.[83]

To aid in this work, the SEU regularly published in its journals "useful facts and statistics" that Soviet Esperantists were encouraged to include in the letters they sent abroad.[84] They also regularly printed "sample questions" that Soviet Esperantists were likely to field from correspondents abroad and were provided lengthy texts that were approved responses to those questions. Relying on templates for collective correspondence would guard against untrained Soviet Esperantists unintentionally sending "misinformation" about Soviet life to their foreign correspondents. It would also reduce the possibility that the correspondence would degenerate into egotistical intimacy and petit bourgeois navel-gazing.

"International correspondence," the SEU's leaders insisted, "was a politically sensitive and important matter and it must be approached very seriously. We must ensure that every sentence in our letter will be in the hands of our foreign friends a powerful weapon of agitating for the Soviet Union."[85] Collective correspondence was to be pursued under the guidance of trusted party leaders at the club or the workplace. Local SEU cells were obliged to reach out to "loner" Esperantists who tended to operate independently and thus outside the purview of SEU surveillance and guidance. They needed to be integrated into collective correspondence and educated on the proper use of communicating about Soviet life to their pen pals abroad.[86] As a 1929 Komsomol resolution on "internationalist education" emphasized, Esperantist correspondence was valuable but the "petit bourgeois" tendencies of individual Esperantists needed to be policed and curtailed.[87] A 1931 study of SEU cells in Leningrad conducted by city authorities worried that the SEU exerted "insufficient control" over the "ideological orientation of the correspondence."[88]

Leaders at the SEU's own local "cells" were instructed to screen letters received from abroad.[89] At club meetings, study circles, and regular meetings of the SEU, leaders were to select appropriate material from the letters received from abroad and use them as a prompt for studying and discussing the political, social, economic, and cultural life in the countries from which they were received. These methods were as much about devising a thoughtful international education as they were clearly methods of surveillance. Each SEU cell was to diligently "take inventory of its members' individual correspondence with foreigners (*s zagranitsei*)" and guide its transformation into collective, party-approved and monitored correspondence.[90]

The problem with the Soviet Esperantists' collective correspondence, at least from the perspective of the foreign workers who received it, was that it was impersonal, repetitive, predictable, and therefore boring. Letters devised at an Esperantist club meeting read like templates because they were drawn from templates. Recipients opened their envelopes from the USSR with excitement and expectation, but increasingly found within them nothing but singsong recitations of party-approved talking points and statistics meant to produce a generic but positive portrait of Soviet life. The foreign recipients of these crowdsourced letters began to recoil at the idea that they were expected to exchange ideas and thoughts not with a real comrade, but instead with a faceless composite beneficiary of the October Revolution.

It did not take long for foreigners to complain that these letters lacked the human touch of the Soviet citizens who ostensibly wrote them. The Soviet Esperantist Ida Lisichnik conceded that foreign comrades were understandably annoyed by the "soulless, formal boilerplate letters" that the SEU produced under the banner of collective correspondence.[91] A group of communist Esperantists in Germany forswore their correspondence with Soviet comrades, insisting that they wanted to read letters, not newspaper clippings repackaged as correspondence. Another German comrade pleaded with the Soviets to write fresh letters illuminating their real lives. He instructed: "Write your letters not in the language of newspapers, but in the language of workers."[92] Intimacy and affective bonding could not be achieved by means of depersonalized content. Esperantists wanted to hear about the lives of real Soviet citizens, to correspond with individuals who had personalities, families, worries, dreams, ideas, and insights. As a group of Esperantists in France complained, Soviet letter writers never wrote about what Soviet industrialization meant in "their personal lives."[93]

Soviet Esperantists, too, wanted to correspond with individuals abroad, learn about their personal lives, and nurture epistolary friendships with them. In a 1929 article in *Mezhdunarodnyi iazyk*, Pavel Kiriushin—otherwise a staunch advocate of collective correspondence—admitted that he regularly corresponded with a Bolshevik skeptic in Chicago, an unemployed young woman in the Parisian suburbs, and a semiliterate farmer struggling to make ends meet outside of Barcelona. This individual correspondence, he said, offered a "special freshness and sincerity" that could not be achieved otherwise.[94] Try as they might to discourage individual Esperantist correspondence in favor of party-approved, depersonalized collective correspondence, the SEU's leaders could not regulate Soviet Esperantists' ability, as individuals, to exchange letters with foreign comrades abroad. As with Esperantist radio, Esperantist correspondence represented exciting possibilities for citizen diplomacy, but also the worrying potential for subversion and selfish intimacy.

After all, intimate Esperantist correspondence exchanged between Soviet citizens and foreign friends abroad could masquerade as patriotic citizen diplomacy linking comrades. The concern was that Esperanto veiled petit bourgeois friendship that defied both Soviet ideals of living publicly and Soviet borders that were to protect from bourgeois contamination from abroad. As historian Juliane Fürst explains, the Soviets distinguished early on between comradeship and friendship, idealizing the former and regarding the latter with suspicion and at times contempt. Because interpersonal relationships were to serve as sites of ideological mobilization, Soviet citizens were to invest themselves in comradeship—understood broadly as Soviet ideological unity and affective bonding over shared socialist values. By comparison, friendship carried the taint of bourgeois values and egotistical selfishness. As Fürst explains, "Comrades were all part of the large Soviet cause. Friends were made for a variety of reasons, some of which had very little to do or even went against Soviet values and morals."[95] If Esperanto were to acquit itself of its unique claims to Soviet citizen diplomacy, it needed to service global comradeship and socialist internationalism, not individual friendships between far-flung pen pals and their petty, egoist concerns. To be acceptable let alone desirable, Esperantist encounters needed to mobilize Soviet ideology. They needed to be public, surveillable, and driven by the needs of socialist internationalism. In such a frame, the "loner" Soviet Esperantists who narrowly prized their foreign friendships, obsessively collected their foreign postcards, and cataloged trinkets and postage stamps received from abroad were not good comrades. It was possible, rather, that they were enemies of the most dangerous sort.

Meeting Face-to-Face in the Land of the Future

For Soviet Esperantists, pen pal exchanges, workers correspondence, and radio broadcasting were so important precisely because the opportunity to travel abroad or meet foreign comrades in person was so fantastical as to be otherworldly. Yet such travel and meetings did take place, though on rare occasions. In the 1920s, several SEU leaders—Drezen, most prominently—were authorized to travel abroad to international meetings of proletarian Esperantists.[96] This opportunity remained, however, well beyond the reach of most Soviet Esperantists. Yet during NEP, the Soviet Union embraced foreign tourism to the USSR as an opportunity to display Soviet achievements, to court prominent Westerners as "friends of the Soviet Union," and to raise valuable hard currency.[97] Soviet Esperantists quickly proved eager to offer their unique services to facilitate foreign comrades' pilgrimage to the Soviet promised land.

In 1925, the SEU's leaders began lobbying Soviet officials for permission to host SAT's annual international convention.[98] In their appeals, they claimed that recent experience had overwhelmingly shown that the Esperantists among prior foreign delegations to the Soviet Union had gained more from their visit than non-Esperantists, and perhaps had committed themselves more energetically to the task of championing the Soviet Union once returned to their home countries.[99] The Esperantists invoked one of the key benefits of the Soviet practice of hosting foreign delegations—sympathetic visitors' ability to propagandize the Soviet future in their native lands and to counter capitalist "lies" about socialist construction in the USSR in the foreign press.[100]

By 1925, the hosting of foreign delegations was quickly becoming a norm of Soviet cultural diplomacy. In April of that year, the All-Union Society for Cultural Ties Abroad (VOKS) was established to oversee and manage many of the logistic and didactic functions of Soviet cultural diplomacy. VOKS oversaw managing and achieving the goals of hosting foreign celebrities and delegations in the USSR and, to a lesser extent, organizing domestic programs to cultivate Soviet citizens' "international education."[101] As one of VOKS's tour guide-interpreters later described its work, "We were trying to establish contact between good people here and good people there. To help them understand one another."[102]

Shortly after its creation, VOKS incorporated a small "Esperanto department" and its bureaucratic interactions with the SEU were not uncommon. The leaders of the SEU were eager to demonstrate how Esperanto could make for a more direct and pleasant encounter between the Soviet Union and its foreign guests. The Esperantist Podkaminer argued that foreigners travel to the Soviet Union "with a burning desire to closely familiarize themselves with the life of the Russian worker, with Soviet construction, and with the development of our industry. On the other side, the Russian worker wants to shower our guests with questions about life and working conditions abroad." The inability of these workers to communicate in a shared language, Podkaminer argued, divided and alienated them, frustrating and souring the entire encounter.¹⁰³ Esperanto would allow for an unfiltered, unmediated conversation between foreign delegates and Soviet citizens. In fact, the SEU leadership argued in 1925, the Esperantists who had traveled to the USSR as members of larger workers' delegations had already shown that they "received significantly greater opportunity to get to know in detail the Soviet Union's everyday life and situation than did those comrades not fluent in Esperanto."¹⁰⁴

The SEU's greatest coup came when it won its bid to host SAT's Sixth International Congress of Proletarian Esperantists in Leningrad in August 1926. For the SEU, this was an enormous opportunity to display the value of Esperanto to proletarian internationalism. The SEU sought to persuade Soviet officials and ordinary citizens alike that Esperanto provided the ideal means by which Soviet citizens could interact with foreigners and achieve authentic mutual understanding. They wanted to demonstrate how Esperanto uniquely enabled unmediated communication, independent of interpreters and translators. The SEU considered the Leningrad Congress such a make-it-or-break-it opportunity that, in the months leading up to the SAT convocation in Leningrad, Drezen warned members that the entire fate of the Esperantist movement in the Soviet Union depended on the successful execution of this SAT Congress—the first of any Esperantist congress to be held on Soviet, let alone Russian, soil.¹⁰⁵

In the months leading up to the congress, the pages of *Mezhdunarodnyi iazyk* spilled forth with announcements both big and small concerning preparations. "Exert yourselves!" the SEU instructed its members, prodding them to practice their Esperanto skills and recruit new adepts of the language.¹⁰⁶ The journal advertised a range of products designed to help make the congress a success. In addition to a new textbook and Russian–Esperanto dictionary, Soviet Esperantists could also avail themselves of a freshly produced brochure-guidebook, *Around the Soviet Union with the Help of Esperanto*. The People's Commissariat of Post and Telegraph issued a special international postage stamp dedicated to the upcoming world congress of proletarian Esperantists in Leningrad. The SEU celebrated the stamp as tangible state recognition of Esperanto as a vital and unique means of connecting the world's workers and giving them the opportunity to communicate freely.¹⁰⁷

The SEU hyped news of organized caravans of Esperantists—foreign and Soviet—traveling to Leningrad for the world congress.¹⁰⁸ In late June, Pavel Kiriushin, an Esperantist in Minsk, reported excitedly of the recent arrival of two delegates from Austria, the Michalicskas. According to Kiriushin, Minsk's Esperantists rushed about, guiding their foreign comrades through the city, showing them the sights and arranging meetings with local workers. Kiriushin described how the Michalicskas refused to speak German and would only converse and lecture in Esperanto. They testified to how their visit had swiftly disproven what they called the capitalists' false "rumors of the Bolsheviks' cruel barbarism." In sum, Kiriushin wrote, "We have fully 100% made use of SAT delegates' visit from abroad."¹⁰⁹ It had already been proven, he insisted, that foreign comrades who spoke Esperanto were ideal foreign guests because they could appreciate Soviet successes and communicate with Soviet citizens without a mediating voice to interpret their experiences for them. Foreign Esperantist comrades were, in this way, equipped with a linguistic skill that would more effectively combat class enemies' disinformation campaigns abroad.

The opportunity to "prove" this claim on a wider scale arrived on August 6, 1926, when the SEU opened SAT's Sixth World Congress in Leningrad. In total, 240 foreign delegates participated in the event; these were "representatives of 37 peoples and languages arriving from 27 countries."[110] They arrived by boat and by train, and hailed from as far away as Uruguay and Colombia. One young communist from Vienna reportedly led a small group of mostly unemployed Esperantists on a trek by foot from Vienna to Szczecin so as to economize under the circumstances of not being able to afford the price of a full railway trip to Leningrad.[111] According to the SEU's statistics, 41 percent of the foreign delegates were communists; 15 percent were Social Democrats; 4 percent were anarchists; and the remainder did not subscribe to any specific party affiliation. The majority identified as workers.[112] As many as 150 Soviet Esperantists joined them in Leningrad for the event.[113]

Congress attendees kicked off their historic meeting by marching through the streets of Leningrad to the Tauride Palace, where the proceedings began. Drezen, serving as Congress Chairman, ascended the rostrum and, in Esperanto, welcomed the foreign guests to the land of the socialist future. He invoked the past, too, noting that "the first Esperantists were Russians."[114] The opening ceremony was broadcast over radio for comrades near and far. Delegates sang the *Internationale* and recited the salutations and greetings the Congress had received from around the world. Elected honorary chair of the congress, A. Lunacharskii of Nakompros sent along a message to

Figure 7 Attendees of the 1926 SAT Congress held in Leningrad. *Source*: Wikimedia Commons.

the delegates in which he expressed his doubts about international language projects, but nonetheless conceded that "facts are a stubborn thing, and the facts speak for Esperanto."[115]

In accord with the goals of Soviet cultural diplomacy, the Leningrad Congress was intended to acquaint foreign Esperantists with Soviet economic and cultural achievements as well as with Soviet workers who would testify to the benefits of working in a socialist state. The foreign Esperantists visited the Academy of Sciences, the Hermitage Museum, the Museum of the Revolution, Peterhof, local factories, orphanages, sanatoria, and other "model" Leningrad sites.[116] The conference hall at the Tauride Palace was outfitted with temporary kiosks for the sale of Esperantist literature and the celebratory Soviet Esperantist stamps with which they could send postcards and letters abroad via an on-premises post-and-telegraph station. The foreign guests need not wait to return home to begin spreading the good news about the Soviet Union; they could begin testifying to Soviet greatness by post.[117] In a report submitted to the Central Committee of the Communist Party after the congress, Drezen affirmed the logic of Soviet tourism: "All of this was done to mold (*sozdavat'*) the foreign delegates into friends of the Soviet Union and to strengthen them in the service of the cause of a united proletarian front."[118]

In the months following the congress, the SEU also publicized how the foreign delegates positively reported back to their home countries about their experiences as visitors to the Soviet Union.[119] According to the Esperantist historian Ulrich Lins, "The brotherly atmosphere during the days of the congress put the participants in a state bordering on euphoria, which had a positive influence on their general judgment of the Soviet Union."[120] Lins highlights in particular the published reminiscences of Norbert Barthelmess that appeared in SAT's periodical, *Sennaciulo*, following the 1926 congress. A German delegate, Barthelmess waxed poetic about the Leningrad experience, claiming he had found there "a paradise for Esperantists and people with free ideas."[121] He characterized the Soviet Union as a land of liberty and a workers' state worthy of the name. Einar Adamson, a Swedish delegate, hurried home to publish a "voluminous book" about his travels in the Soviet Union during and after the congress. Other foreign delegates returned to their homes and hosted what the SEU claimed were "hundreds of meetings" in which they shared their positive experiences of the Soviet Union.[122]

Even twenty years after the Leningrad congress, the American Esperantist Mark Starr would recall, "In 1926, I stayed for a month in Russia, spoke Esperanto continually, and almost forgot how to talk English."[123] In 1926, he published in *Sennaciulo* some of his impressions of the Soviet Union—both good and bad. Among the bad impressions were the homeless children Starr saw on Leningrad's streets, the unforgettably terrible smell of the toilets, and the workers without boots on their feet. Yet there were many more good impressions than bad, Starr wrote, and these included "The brightly colored posters. The publication of educational books. The new art and the life in the workers' clubs. The pride and happiness of the Red Army soldier." Starr delighted in the ubiquitous Lenin portraits and was reassured by "the hope and certain belief" of the Soviet workers that the Bolshevik regime would lead them to socialism.[124]

These Esperantist guests experienced *en Esperanto* what many other sympathetic foreign visitors to the Soviet Union described in their travel accounts. The Austrian novelist Stefan Zweig recalled feeling a "warm haze of spiritual intoxication" as he was guided and instructed by his guide-interpreters throughout his visit to the Soviet 1920s.[125] "One saw, one heard, one admired, one was repelled, fascinated, annoyed, the current always alternating between hot and cold," Zweig explained.[126] The exhilaration of feeling one's self a witness to a socialist future-in-the-making had a powerful effect. Zweig admitted, "I must admit that I myself in many a moment in Russia came near to crying hosanna and to becoming exalted from the exaltation."[127]

As Michael David-Fox has argued, "Soviet methodologies of receiving foreign visitors were all about ranking and evaluating; the Holy Grail of Soviet cultural diplomacy was to secure a formal foreign recognition of superiority."[128] According to this calculus of success, the 1926 World Congress of Proletarian Esperantists in Leningrad had been a success. It had brought Esperantists from around the world face-to-face and allowed them to converse with one another in a language of mutual understanding and camaraderie. It had inspired foreign Esperantists guests to return home and sing the Soviet Union's praises—in Esperanto and in their national tongues. For the SEU, it appeared as good a time as any to start organizing the next international meeting of proletarian Esperantists in the USSR.

Celebrating October En Esperanto

The SEU's next opportunity to host a delegation of foreign Esperantists arrived in November 1927. As part of the spectacular Tenth Anniversary Celebration of the October Revolution, a small delegation of foreign Esperantists was invited to travel to the Soviet Union to join in the event's massive festivities, as well as to participate in the Congress of Friends of the Soviet Union. According to Frederick Corney, the Tenth Anniversary Celebration of the October Revolution in 1927 was designed to impress foreigners as "a kind of World's Fair of socialism."[129] It was also regarded by Soviet officials as a test of Soviet cultural diplomacy—an opportunity to evaluate the methods and personnel involved in guiding foreign tourists through the headquarters and model sites of the socialist future.[130]

Bolshevik leaders considered the tenth anniversary jubilee well worth the exorbitant cost of the spectacular celebration of the October Revolution that they designed for Soviet citizens and foreigners alike. They oversaw the lavish decoration of Moscow, the intricate choreography of parades, and the commission of films, poetry, and memoirs. Instruments were tuned in preparation for a triumphant, revolutionary soundtrack to the celebration's events. Oppositionists were arrested, heckled, and variously demonized.[131] Homeless children and beggars were forcibly removed from the streets of Moscow.[132] Throughout the country, Soviet authorities opened bathhouses, cinemas, reading huts, and health clinics in honor of the anniversary.[133] And nearly a year in advance of the November celebrations, VOKS began training courses for guide-interpreters who would help narrate and mediate foreign visitors' experience of the grand spectacle. VOKS trained guide-interpreters in English, French,

German, Spanish, Italian, Persian, Esperanto, and still other languages. The guide-interpreters also took dedicated coursework in the history of the October Revolution and were taught a litany of talking points about the political, economic, and cultural achievements of the Soviet Union.[134]

The Soviet Union invited hundreds of foreign guests to join in the Tenth Anniversary celebrations.[135] In addition to foreign labor delegations, VOKS invited an array of renowned foreign artists, journalists, and scientists, but also ordinary people too. Yet the foreigners invited to the anniversary celebrations in 1927 were not selected at random. Most foreign delegates were participants, in their home countries, in a variety of organizations that sought to better understand the Soviet Union. Among the invitations extended to foreign guests, twelve were offered to Esperantists, eleven of whom signed on to join in the anniversary festivities in Moscow in November 1927.[136]

These eleven Esperantists hailed from Austria, England, Estonia, Finland, France, Germany, Latvia, Norway, and Sweden. All were members of SAT.[137] Only four of the delegates were professed communists. Four identified as Social Democrats, and the remaining three did not affiliate with any party. Among the eleven, there was one student, five workers, and five white-collar professionals. One of the delegates, Frederik Sons from England, had previously visited Leningrad in 1926 to attend the SAT World Congress. As a result of this venture, he had been fired from his job upon his return to England and had spent half a year without work.[138] The SEU described all of the Esperantist delegates as "true friends" of the Soviet Union.[139]

Upon arrival in the USSR, the foreign Esperantists were greeted immediately by the Soviet Union's already well-established "techniques of hospitality"—techniques for micromanaging and surveilling foreign tourists' experiences.[140] Through VOKS (and, after its establishment in 1929, Intourist), early Soviet cultural diplomacy was designed to provide visitors with a carefully curated and monitored entrée into the inspiring land of the socialist future. Thus, the foreign Esperantists' itineraries were filled to the brim with excursions to notable sites of socialist construction and Soviet culture. As was typical with foreign delegations to the Soviet Union in the 1920s and 1930s, these foreign guests were relentlessly guided through model factories, schools, museums, clubs, and lectures. Soviet authorities chose to feature many of these sites because of their "cutting-edge" and future-facing quality.[141] As one skeptical American visitor scoffed upon his return from a visit to the USSR, the Soviets "seem to have acquired the American method of salesmanship so far as selling the idea that communism or state socialism, whichever it is, is a success."[142]

As Shawn Salmon has argued, these relentless Soviet guided itineraries were designed to provide, in a metaphoric sense at least, "a common language for the world to engage with Soviet socialism."[143] With the anniversary celebrations in 1927 as with its broader approach to tourism generally, the Soviet Union was exhibiting its strengths for its foreign guests so as not only to impress them, but also to supply them with positive talking points about Soviet life when they returned to their home countries. In the words of the *VOKS Weekly News Bulletin*, "Now it will be a good deal more difficult for the venomous capitalist press to pour out its habitual torrents of fabricated stories concerning the Soviet Union. The powerful voice of hundreds of eyewitnesses will prove a serious antidote."[144] The foreign guests were expected to hold up their end of the bargain. Their expected duty was to return home and publicly testify to Soviet achievements they had seen with their own eyes.

Yet the Esperantist guests also proved that there already was a literal common international language through which workers of the world could unite and converse. The Soviet Esperantist Kiriushin described how among the Esperantist guests there "were Germans, French, English, Swedes, Japanese, and others, but anyone who saw them sitting together and conversing among themselves would never have believed (if that person had never heard of Esperantists) that these were delegates of such distant from one another nationalities."[145] Esperanto, Kiriushin insisted, enabled these foreign guests not only to converse among themselves without issue, but also to interact freely with the Soviet Esperantists who served as citizen diplomats. Among Esperantists, there was no need of "any outside mediators and translators who often garble the translations."[146]

The centerpiece of the anniversary celebrations was the November 7 holiday itself. In the Soviet capital, Muscovites streamed into the streets and squares of the metropolis which "seemed to be painted red."[147] As Malte Rolf has explained, the 1927 anniversary celebrations were designed to create an irresistible "narrative of joy."[148] The *Internationale* played repeatedly to stir the celebrants' hearts. Choreographed parades of Soviet youth, soldiers, gymnasts, and workers streamed past the foreign delegates ensconced in the Red Square tribunes that provided a privileged view of the carefully orchestrated processions. Many foreign delegates were said to have spontaneously decided to alight from their viewing posts and join in the processions themselves, to fuse with this stunning "October symphony."[149]

While taking part in the anniversary celebrations, the foreign Esperantists were tasked on four occasions to broadcast from Moscow's "Comintern" radio station their impressions of Soviet life. Delivered in Esperanto to listeners in potentially seventy countries, the SEU claimed, their speeches were "full of revolutionary enthusiasm."[150] One German Esperantist excitedly rallied listeners, insisting that "with our combined strength, we will succeed in establishing a global USSR."[151] The SEU chose the most celebratory snippets of the foreign delegates' radio broadcasts in Esperanto, translated them into Russian, and submitted the texts to VOKS with evident pride.[152]

As it attempted to do with all foreign guests to the early Soviet Union, VOKS worked in determined fashion to monitor and report the reactions of the foreign Esperantist delegates to their experiences in the Soviet Union. VOKS's information-gathering practices were designed to evaluate foreigners' reactions and level of sympathy toward the USSR. VOKS reports were also designed to provide evaluative summaries of foreign visitors' character, personality, and perceived level of culture. Written most often by the VOKS guide-interpreters who managed the foreigners' visits, these reports were used internally by VOKS, but also shared with other agencies involved in Soviet cultural diplomacy and—no doubt—with the Party and its organs of state security, including the secret police.[153] As Michael David-Fox has argued, the surveillance functions of VOKS and its guide-interpreters was never merely about information gathering, but also about molding the "mental outlook of those observed" and shaping foreign guests' positive impressions of the Soviet future-in-the-making.[154]

Thus, VOKS commissioned the foreign Esperantist guests to write down their impressions of the USSR prior to their departure. VOKS and the SEU also interviewed the foreign delegates, recording their answers in detailed post-trip reports that emphasized the success of their efforts to court these visiting foreign Esperantists.[155] The SEU publicized their Esperantist guests' positive responses to what they had seen in the Soviet Union "with their own eyes" in *Sennaciulo* as well as in reports intended for the approving eyes of the Central Committee and an array of Soviet officials.[156] Lidin, an SEU members and a worker in VOKS's special Esperanto department reported that the Esperantist guests "relate to the Soviet Union with such love and even tenderness." They had expressed "the sincere desire to promote rapprochement between the USSR and abroad, and vice versa."[157]

One Esperantist guest, Martin Klein from Austria, offered particularly noteworthy testimony. Klein was a Social Democrat and a white-collar professional.[158] The SEU described him as "elderly, practical."[159] He was a man who openly admitted that he had arrived in the Soviet Union skeptical of its grandiose claims. After spending ten days in Moscow for the anniversary celebrations, however, Klein announced that his prejudices had been wiped away, replaced by admiration for all that he had seen with his own eyes. Klein described how, while crossing the border from Poland into the USSR, his heart started pounding, and pounded every more strongly as he touched down, for the first time, on the "sacred earth of the Soviets." Greeted by workers and soldiers, Klein emotionally joined his fellow foreign delegates at the Soviet border in singing the *Internationale*. In his telling, this was a profound moment of conversion. Klein claims to have realized that in the Soviet Union, truly, the dreams of the worldwide proletariat were being realized. As Klein explained, "My joy grew with every moment, to the point that I don't have the words to describe it."

Klein described his entire visit to the Soviet Union as a revelation—an eye-opening view into a new type of society and a liberating future. "I realized," he wrote, "that this was a state that one must love from the very depths of one's heart." Klein described how he had, on November 7, stood for twelve hours on Red Square, watching Soviet workers and soldiers parade by him. The effect of these "twelve long, but at the same time very short hours" was the realization that Soviet citizens would never again tolerate or suffer "the chains of capitalism or imperialism," nor would they submit to fascism.[160]

The SEU giddily reported how, before his departure, Klein had informed them of his plans upon returning to Austria. He explained that he would use his platform to propagandize the Soviet Union among fellow Social Democrats. These, after all, were men and women like himself who had their doubts about the USSR. "Let the party kick me out," Klein exclaimed, "But while I remain in its ranks, I will conduct my own business." He promised to give lectures on all that he had seen in Moscow. He asked the Soviet Esperantists for photographs and film clips to aid him in his propaganda work at home. As for themselves, the Soviet Esperantists were overjoyed by the vision of Klein at Red Square on November 7. The elderly Social Democrat had boisterously participated in the celebration, shouting "Hurrah" and exuberantly singing the *Internationale*.[161]

Klein's fellow foreign Esperantist delegates to the 1927 celebrations also expressed their enthusiasm for what they had seen during their visit to the Soviet Union. Richard Lerchner, a German delegate without party affiliation, was wowed by the festivities on

November 7. After watching "more than a million" workers parade triumphantly past him on Red Square, Lerchner argued, it was impossible to doubt that the Soviet people would succeed in building communism. Give the Soviet Union another ten years, he claimed, and it would prove the most developed country in the world.[162] Reporting on meetings with Soviet workers, Lerchner insisted, they "are very happy."[163] Hugo Hempel, a fellow German, was similarly impressed by Soviet workers and vowed to devote his energies to mobilizing German workers to work side by side with the Soviets in establishing worldwide communism.[164]

Another German Esperantist, Otto Bässler explained: "My participation in the October celebrations gave me new strength, new enthusiasm, new fervor to actively work in my homeland in the spirit of Leninism." Everywhere in the Soviet Union, he claimed, he had seen the glories of a socialist future-in-the-making. Sure, he had seen some weaknesses too—in particular, the Soviet Union's deficiency in terms of equipment and up-to-date technology. But these weaknesses owed not to Soviet failure, but to the vampiric selfishness of the Soviet Union's capitalist enemies. Technological backwardness aside, Bässler argued, cultural work in the Soviet Union far exceeded that which was pursued in capitalist countries that exploited workers, rather than uplift them.[165]

Even the foreign Esperantist delegates whose public praise was described by the Union of Soviet Esperantists as "faint-hearted" celebrated Soviet achievements.[166] A Swedish delegate praised the Soviet Union for teaching its citizens about hygiene and providing them with well-lit, spacious quarters for living and working. Such efforts were not seen in his home country, he noted.[167] A Social Democrat from Latvia acknowledged that workers in the Soviet Union lived far better than they had under the tsars. The Soviet Union was undergoing a "grand metamorphosis." The Soviet people were enthusiastic and strong, he argued, and "the foundation of the USSR is unshakeable."[168] If, the SEU claimed, these comrades were less effusive in their praise for the Soviet Union than their fellow foreign Esperantist delegates, this was only so because they feared punishment in their home countries.[169] All of the delegates vowed, upon return to their home countries, "to tell our working class the full truth about the Soviet Union." Their words would travel across the globe, they promised, "with the help of Esperanto."[170]

Once their foreign guests departed in November 1927, the SEU's leaders celebrated that the foreign Esperantist guests were particularly overcome with enthusiasm for the Soviet Union as a result of the powerful, unmediated experiences that they were able to enjoy *as Esperantists* while visiting the Soviet Union. In advancing this claim, the Soviet Esperantists invoked the testimony of their foreign guests. In one of the speeches broadcast internationally over the radio during the foreigners' visit, Rosa Marthinsen of Norway explained how Norwegian Esperantists had been exchanging letters, in Esperanto, with Soviet Esperantists for some time. Marthinsen remarked on the "comfort" this had provided her and her fellow compatriots who sought to know more about life in the USSR. "From the Soviet Esperantists," she claimed, "we derive experiences that are necessary in our struggle against the yoke of capitalism."[171]

In a report to VOKS, the SEU emphasized how it came to be that Marthinsen and her fellow foreign Esperantist guests came "to feel at home in the USSR" before even arriving on Soviet territory. Foreigners, the SEU argued, had long been "getting to know the USSR" through their pen pal letter exchanges with Soviet Esperantists. The foreign Esperantists' visit to the Soviet Union in 1927 enabled some of them to meet with their Soviet pen pals face-to-face, allowing them to cement affective no less than ideological bonds. As the Union of Soviet Esperantists explained, "The general comradely spirit, the love for the idea of a single international language of workers" results in the fact that when Esperantists from different nations meet for the first time, they meet already as friends. They are comfortable with one another; nothing stands in the way of them understanding one another. For an Esperantist, the SEU claimed, it was impossible to regard another country as "alien." It was impossible for an Esperantist to meet another Esperantist and feel the alienation born of foreignness.[172]

Esperanto was a crucial tool of forging international proletarian solidarity because, the SEU argued, this international auxiliary language worked precisely as it was designed to do. "The foreign Esperantist guests," the SEU reported, "were better able to get to know the USSR because they carried out conversations without interpreters." They were able to converse "directly with Soviet Esperantists" from all walks of life—"workers, white-collar workers, intellectuals, communists, and those without party affiliation." These conversations were not mediated, truncated, or lost in translation. As a result, the foreign Esperantists gained much more from their experience in the Soviet Union than did other foreign guests who had to rely on interpreters. The foreign Esperantists engaged Soviet citizens and Soviet life directly, without the filters of translation. In this way, the SEU claimed, the foreign Esperantists gained "richer impressions of the USSR" that they would be better able to popularize, both locally and globally, upon their return home.[173] However, from the vantage point of Soviet officials at the close of NEP, this unmediated access to Soviet citizens and Soviet life was precisely the problem with Esperanto.

The Eyes, Ears, and Mouths of the Party

In the 1920s and 1930s, approximately one hundred thousand foreign visitors traveled to the Soviet Union to see and experience Soviet life firsthand. The overwhelming majority of those who made their way to the Land of Lenin in these years knew not a word of the Russian language. Yet as the American leftist journal the *Nation* reassured readers in 1933, "Travel in Soviet Russia is not difficult, it is not dangerous, it is more than reasonably comfortable, it is always completely engrossing and different, and it is probably the most friendly sort of trip you could undertake." This owed in no small part, the *Nation* explained, to the Soviet state's micromanaging approach to cultural diplomacy—its insistence on organized itineraries for foreign visitors who were led and guided by knowledgeable guide-interpreters. These were guide-interpreters who were trained in foreign languages as much as in Soviet hospitality. Most of them, the *Nation* noted, were "young women without hats."[174]

The nature and meaning of Soviet cultural diplomacy in the 1920s and 1930s has been hotly debated ever since foreign visitors first began sojourning to the socialist future at the start of NEP. Michael David-Fox has described "the interwar 'pilgrimage to Russia'" as "one of the most notorious events in the political and intellectual history of the twentieth century."[175] An earlier historiography focused on interwar Soviet cultural diplomacy as the sordid history of Soviet officials pampering foreign guests, parading them through carefully managed model sites of socialism, and deliberately misleading them at every step. The Soviet Union, these scholars insisted, was often successful in manipulating, flattering, and otherwise "duping" foreign visitors into believing the hype of Soviet achievements.[176] This veritable seduction, it has been argued, met with little resistance on the part of leftist foreign visitors who arrived in the USSR as "political pilgrims" intent on seeing with their own believing eyes the vindication of Soviet socialism.[177]

More recently, however, historians have reconsidered foreign tourism in the early USSR so as to better understand the contours of Soviet internationalism and to better appreciate the agency of all parties—foreigners and hosts—engaged in the dynamic encounter of early Soviet cultural diplomacy. This frame of reexamination has illuminated the overwhelming complexity that marked these interactions between foreigners and the Soviet citizens they encountered.[178] What remains largely taken for granted, though, was how central were the language barriers that defined so many foreign visitors' sojourns to the Soviet future. These same language barriers were in many ways essential to the effective operation of Soviet cultural diplomacy as pursued by VOKS, Intourist, and other Soviet agencies. Whereas Soviet Esperantists vowed to serve the Soviet Union by collapsing the language barriers that many foreign visitors unavoidably encountered on their tours of the Soviet future-in-the-making, the officials tasked with carrying out Soviet cultural diplomacy on the ground often *depended* on those barriers as essential nuts and bolts of the micromanagement of foreigners' interactions with Soviet realities and Soviet citizens.

Upon their return home, many Western visitors to the early Soviet Union published travelogues reporting what they had seen and what their experiences foretold for the fate of the USSR and the world. Many of these accounts give insight into the tactics of VOKS guide-interpreters who were assigned to curate foreign guests' experiences and, notably, to translate and mediate their attempts at conversation with Soviet citizens. Repeated plotlines and mainstay characters of these Western visitors' travelogues were the hapless, disheveled, ill-dressed, but otherwise relentless guide-interpreters who, with dogged determination, carried out their undisguised duties of surveillance and cultural and linguistic mediation. The travelogues highlight not only the language barriers that shaped Soviet cultural diplomacy in these years, but also the Soviet state's commitment to a largely mediated experience for foreign guests. They underscore how mismatched the Soviet Esperantists' designs for Soviet cultural diplomacy were with the emerging techniques, tactics, and goals adopted by VOKS, Intourist, and other Soviet agencies in catering to foreign visitors of all manner of ideological stripes.

In his account of his visit to the early Soviet Union, the Irish novelist Liam O'Flaherty noted approvingly that VOKS assigned to foreign visitors "very charming girl guides and instructors in the Russian language." Yet, he insisted, "the Russians carry espionage and police surveillance to such an extent as to make it ridiculous. They certainly succeed in antagonizing foreigners who might otherwise be sympathetic. Nobody likes to be followed about and watched continually."[179] When Theodore

Dreiser arrived in the USSR as an important guest, he haughtily insisted on hiring his own guide-interpreter—a young American woman fluent in Russian. This renegade act was met with the outrage of the head of VOKS, who sputtered in objection, "She is not at all a Soviet woman"—that is to say, not politically reliable. In the end, Dreiser was permitted to hire his own guide, but he could not escape having a "reliable" VOKS guide assigned to him all the same.[180]

P. L. Travers, more well known for writing the *Mary Poppins* books, wrote an account of her own tour of the Soviet Union in the early 1930s in which she insisted that, "Properly to see Russia one must not be a tourist. One must know the language, move about alone and dispense with the questionable blessing of State guides."[181] Inescapably, she claimed, the tourist is beholden to the "iron-sinewed guides" and their cheerless march through the carefully selected sites of the socialist future.[182] "This *prison*!" Travers exhaled sharply in a particularly agitated moment in her travelogue—her outrage owed to finding that Soviet security agents had perlustrated her incoming mail.[183] It was terribly "demoralizing."[184] She concluded that the constant Soviet surveillance of foreign tourists "seemed unnecessarily dramatic."[185]

Other foreign visitors were able to spin Soviet surveillance more positively, or else to dismiss their peers' claims as exaggerations. Hubert Griffith, a British journalist and playwright who traveled to the USSR during the First Five-Year Plan, showed considerable affection for the Soviet guides who did their "worried best."[186] He was particularly fond of one spunky Soviet guide who "had learnt her English in America, and from whose lips poured a flood of the purest Chicago." All of the Soviet guides, he nonetheless conceded, were "propagandists."[187] Yet in his account of the trip, Griffith insisted that notions of constant Soviet surveillance over foreign visitors were much exaggerated by the Western press. "Unless a man is watched *all* the time he might as well not be watched at all," Griffith opined.[188] He insisted that foreigners enjoyed ready opportunity to "wander on our own, or merely to sit about and talk." He claimed that he was not compelled to stay hitched to the Soviet guides whose "enthusiasm" he described as "insatiable."[189]

Yet Griffith typically joined the itinerary laid out to him by his guide, he explained, for fear of missing out on something spectacular. The result was, however, that he soon "became so sick of factories."[190] The problem was that these encounters left too little opportunity to engage in real conversation with Soviet citizens. Griffith explained:

> One could always talk to and cross-examine any Russians that one met through the interpretership of our guides. There were discussions arranged in most of the factories, clubs, etc, that we went to, for this purpose. We could ask questions, and would have questions in turn fired at us. But the medium of an interpreter meant that conversation was always second-hand, and often unsatisfactory.

For this reason, he sought every possibility to interact with Soviet citizens without the need of an interpreter. He looked for people with whom he could communicate in German or French—languages, he claimed, that he was "reasonably" fluent in. He prized these interactions above all others, insisting they were not rare—at least among Soviet engineers. It was only when he encountered Soviet citizens who spoke German or French that the guide-interpreters' mediating—and distorting—power diminished and authenticity prevailed.[191]

Yet Griffith overstated his case and underestimated the class dynamics at work in his purported access to "unmediated" conversations with Soviet citizens in foreign tongues. Griffith could speak freely in German, perhaps, with a highly educated Soviet engineer, but he could scarcely mingle with workers and expect to engage them directly—in German, French, or his native English—so as to freely talk about their lives. As an American visitor to the early USSR noted, one could easily stumble upon Soviet "officials, army officers, factory managers, and the like, nearly half of whom are able to speak some German or English."[192] Yet unmediated conversation with Soviet workers was extremely difficult if not impossible for most foreign visitors who toured the USSR without recourse to the Russian language. They relied upon guide-interpreters to transact dialogue with ordinary Soviets whom they encountered throughout their journey. In fact, it was in part because of Soviet authorities' desire to prevent the very possibility of foreign guests engaging in unmediated conversation with Soviet citizens who knew foreign languages that Soviet officials accepted what by the late 1920s were the growing costs of having a reputation abroad for subjecting foreign visitors to relentless itineraries jam-packed with tightly micromanaged visits to Potemkin villages.[193]

According to Michael David-Fox, Soviet officials' unwillingness to risk the possibilities of unguided foreign tourism (and thus potential for unmediated conversation) in the land of the socialist future resulted in their reliance on a tactic of "planned spontaneity."[194] Pre-arranged meetings with "average" Soviet citizens was a mainstay feature of Soviet cultural diplomacy in the 1920s and 1930s. Foreign guests met with groups of workers, students, and others in carefully orchestrated meetings at factories, schools, museums, prisons, and clubs. According to Sophia Margulies, Soviet citizens who attended these meetings "were instructed to remain quiet or were told what to say during the visits of foreign guests or delegations." Moreover, she explains, most Soviet citizens who participated in such meetings with foreign guests were knowingly wary of saying anything out of turn or controversial in the presence of the guide-interpreters.[195]

The American cultural critic Waldo Frank described one of his Soviet guide-interpreters as "a brainy fellow from an academy of languages wearing an Esperanto button" who answered foreigners' questions during a factory visit in strikingly rote fashion. According to Frank, the conscientious guide recited "figures and details, soberly, in a monotone that sounded almost like a prayer."[196] Foreign visitors, even those who sympathized with Soviet ideals, often expressed skepticism during these encounters, and frequently asked painful questions about Soviet realities.[197] Guide-interpreters were instructed to hew closely to the scripts of Soviet cultural diplomacy. By the early 1930s, they received explicit training on how to reply to foreigners' prickly questions.[198]

Spontaneous, unplanned encounters between foreign visitors and Soviet citizens were cause for alarm, especially if Soviet citizens attempted to speak in unflattering fashion about Soviet realities. VOKS guides were instructed to creatively maneuver around troublesome utterances in Russian—that is, to purposefully mistranslate for the sake of political correctness.¹⁹⁹ In her émigré account of her time as a guide-interpreter for foreign delegations to the early USSR, Tamara Solonevich described the improvised art of translating unsanctioned Soviet speech into acceptable talking points for foreign guests whose lack of fluency in Russian thus immunized them from the damning "truths" that aggrieved Soviet workers attempted to reveal to them.²⁰⁰

Soviet guide-interpreters were understood to be the very "backbone" of Soviet management of foreign tourism and their multifaceted jobs were undoubtedly stressful and demanding.²⁰¹ In addition to the pressures of interpreting, the VOKS staff endured the varied stresses of managing foreign guests' idiosyncrasies and not infrequent bad behavior. The VOKS guides also had to maneuver the guests' insistent questioning on politically sensitive topics. Their express job was to make sure the foreign guests returned home with positive impressions of the Soviet Union.²⁰² The nerve-wracking reality for these guide-interpreters was that conversations between Soviet citizens and foreign guests could always stray from the hoped-for and oft-rehearsed scripts, leading to all kinds of unpredictable problems—not least for themselves.

Moreover, the Soviet secret police kept a close watch not only on the activities and attitudes of the foreign guests, but also on the guide-interpreters who managed visitors' encounter with Soviet life. VOKS workers were variously implicated in police surveillance of foreign guests.²⁰³ Recalling her work as a VOKS guide-interpreter in the second half of the 1930s, Natalia Semper recounted worrying about being seen as too friendly with the "class enemies" she guided through the USSR. She worried too about colleagues who began disappearing in 1937. The job became too much to bear, she recalled, once she was summoned by the NKVD as an informant—to answer questions not only about foreign visitors, but also about her VOKS colleagues.²⁰⁴

It's no wonder that one Australian visitor to the USSR in the late 1930s remembered her Soviet guides as being notably nervous in their roles.²⁰⁵ The Brit Alexander Wicksteed quipped that he would rather be doomed to a "life on the dole" than suffer the stress and anxiety of a Soviet guide to foreign tourists.²⁰⁶ Soviet authorities in the 1930s stepped up efforts to train the guides and verify their political reliability in open recognition of how central these cultural mediators were to achieving the goals of Soviet cultural diplomacy.²⁰⁷ Underscoring the significance but also the stress of the guide-interpreters' work, Alexander Arosev—VOKS's head in the 1930s—described them as "barrage units leading the army."²⁰⁸ Foreign guests, Arosev insisted, formulated their very first impressions of the USSR on the basis of their encounter with their guide-interpreters. "Our comrade interpreters are very important people," he explained, while reminding VOKS staff of the need for careful, meticulous work in mediating foreigners' experiences in the USSR.²⁰⁹

Understandably, the VOKS guide-interpreters were especially anxious when their foreign charges were capable of speaking Russian; they were still more guarded when Russian-speaking guests pretended not to know Russian. Russian-speaking foreign visitors were able to discern what others were not: they knew when their guide-interpreters were deliberately mistranslating and otherwise "correcting" speech considered politically incorrect or insufficiently fulsome in its praise of Soviet achievements.²¹⁰ The guide-interpreters were no less annoyed and anxious when their foreign charges engaged in unplanned conversations with Soviet citizens in French,

English, or German. On both sides of these encounters, the question of language fluency or lack thereof was an ever-present source of potential anxiety, confusion, subterfuge, danger, misunderstanding, and mistrust. The "techniques" and modes of micromanaged Soviet cultural diplomacy were in large measure premised on the convenient—at least from the Soviets' perspective—language barrier that stood in the way of the average foreign visitor and the average Soviet citizen.

Esperantist visitors to the Soviet Union represented a different kind of possibility for Soviet cultural diplomacy—or a different kind of threat, depending on one's view in the early USSR. While Esperantist visitors did not visit the USSR in great numbers in the 1920s and the 1930s, they did travel to the socialist future as members of delegations and as individual tourists. It was not unheard of for them to arrive with the names and addresses of Soviet pen pals whom they were desperate to meet and converse with in person. Others provided letters of introduction for Soviet Esperantist pen pals to friends or acquaintances who would be visiting the USSR.[211] For the SEU, these foreign Esperantist guests were pioneers of a global socialist future, of comradeship without borders. Theoretically, they were linguistically equipped to experience Soviet reality more authentically and to converse with Soviet citizens more meaningfully than other foreign guests who were limited by language barriers. Yet for the curators of foreign tourism to the USSR, Esperantists disrupted the normal order of business—which was unabashedly oriented toward mediation and surveillance. Esperantists promised to obliterate language barriers imposing distance and opaqueness between Soviet citizens and foreign guests. Yet Soviet officials responsible for cultural diplomacy in many ways *relied* on those language barriers for the successful carrying out of their duties and overall mission.

The Boundaries of Cultural Diplomacy from Below

In the 1920s and 1930s, the stakes of cultural diplomacy and transnational exchange were high and Soviet officials were, by the close of NEP, increasingly aware of the significance of the cultural mediators who made the Soviet experience comprehensible to foreigners who knew not a lick of the Russian language. So much depended on these cultural mediators—the guide-interpreters, the translators, the radio programmers, and even the Soviet pen pal correspondents who interacted with foreigners on a basis that ranged from the generic to the remarkably intimate. As a 1931 Soviet treatise on foreign language learning remarked of the need for the USSR to train guide-interpreters who were as politically reliable as they were fluent in foreign tongues, the business of interpreting Soviet realities for foreigners "opens a much too wide margin for wrecking activity."[212] Soviet cultural mediators *did* exert tremendous powers of influence over how foreigners perceived and understood Soviet realities. It was not for nothing, as Michael David-Fox has argued, that, especially after the launch of the First Five-Year Plan, "Soviet cultural diplomacy assigned these figures an outsized role."[213]

Soviet Esperantists may have been few in number and culturally peripheral in the larger scheme of the Soviet Union's expanding cultural diplomacy efforts in the late 1920s, but it was their ability to engage foreigners using an international language largely unchecked by Soviet bureaucratic oversight that made them so potentially dangerous. As a confidential report on the Soviet Esperanto movement that was prepared for the Central Committee in 1926 conceded, "It is of course impossible to regulate the correspondence in Esperanto of individuals."[214] Yet, the report urged, the Party needed to find some way of better supervising and exerting control over the Esperantists and their transnational exchanges. As the same report noted, the Foreign Intelligence Division of the OGPU had warned that even within the ranks of the SEU there remained a stark contrast between the "revolutionary minded Esperantists" and those of the "old breed" (*esperantistov starogo zakala*). There was also the issue of old anarchist hangers-on within the movement too.[215] Workers comprised a mere 30 percent of the SEU's membership.[216] The Soviet Esperantist movement was small, Party and police officials were quick to point out, but potentially plagued by ideological contaminants that were difficult to control. As early as 1926, A. K. Abolin, Deputy Directory of the CPSU's agitprop department, urged a strengthening of party control over the Esperantist movement. The sensitive matter of Esperantist correspondence with foreigners demanded special attention and more energetic oversight, Abolin argued.[217]

The leaders of the Soviet Esperantist movement were nothing if not self-conscious of state and Party officials' growing wariness of their ability to transgress borders and disrupt routine methods of surveillance, no less than of the potentially subversive possibilities of the individual correspondence that Soviet Esperantists continued to engage in with friends and comrades abroad. They repeatedly appealed to CPSU and Comintern officials for guidance, direction, and oversight of their work.[218]

In the context of Stalin's First Five-Year Plan, however, the Soviet Esperantists adapted to the USSR's radically shifting ideological, economic, and technological priorities. By the launch of the Second Five-Year Plan, the leaders of the Soviet Esperantist movement no longer emphasized in first order the value of Esperanto's radical transparency for Soviet cultural diplomacy. Instead, they appealed to a more explicit technocratic logic. Soviet industrialization, the Soviet Esperantists claimed, demanded that Soviet citizens be able to access and comprehend blueprints, manuals, and scientific expertise that was largely unavailable to them in the Russian language. Joining a larger conversation in the early 1930s about the need for the Soviet masses to learn foreign languages, the Esperantists competed for Esperanto to be declared the most useful and most appropriate—in a Marxist-Leninist sense—foreign language to teach a Soviet citizenry in need of Western technical expertise. As the next chapter will explore, this new campaign introduced new opportunities for the Esperantists, but also new challenges. Meanwhile, the Esperantists' long-standing challenges—growing suspicion, lack of substantive state support, and general skepticism about Esperanto's ability to meet the demands of the modern age—not only remained but also worsened.

5

Language Revolutions and Their Discontents

Should Soviet workers study German, English, or French or should they study Esperanto? In late 1928, Maria Ulianova—CPSU higher-up and Lenin's sister—posed precisely this question in a fiery article appearing in the Soviet journal *Worker-Peasant Correspondent*. "Language diversity," Ulianova wrote, "seriously hinders international relations between workers of the different countries and the strengthening of international solidarity between them." Given the needs of industrialization especially, Soviet citizens needed to be able to communicate and exchange expertise on an international basis. However, Ulianova argued, the solution to the dilemmas of Babel was not to study Esperanto, but instead to study "living foreign languages." Esperanto, in her view, offered Soviet workers only a limited, "narrowly practical" utility in its capacity to facilitate communication with comrades abroad. It was a language, she insisted, "that does not have a future"—and one that Lenin had dismissed as "too artificial, simplistic, dead." Esperanto might be an easy language to learn, she argued, but it was a deficient one: oversimplified, undersubscribed, and lacking a full-fledged literature in all realms of science and technology. Soviet citizens needed to study the foreign languages of the capitalist West in order to access the "bourgeois science and technology" needed to build socialism in one country. They needed, Ulianova argued, to study not Esperanto but instead "the most commonly used foreign languages"—that is, English, German, and French.[1]

Ulianova's article posed questions that would in many ways define the Esperantists' struggles during Stalin's first two five-year plans. What were the languages necessary to achieve *Stalin's* revolution? Which languages would be essential for the Soviet Union to navigate the hostility of the capitalist world and to gain access to the foreign capitalist expertise that was necessary to build socialism in one country? Looking ahead to the distant future, what language would the global proletariat speak once they had arrived at the higher phase of communism? In the meantime, was Esperanto a language of subversion, a dangerous tool in the hands of class enemies?

Unfortunately for the Esperantists, Ulianova's insistence that it was time for the Soviet Union to energetically teach its citizens foreign languages—and, in particular, the so-called living languages of the capitalist West rather than an international auxiliary language—was the emerging Party line in 1928. More than a decade after Soviet Esperantists had predicted that the future of Russia's revolution depended on the proletariat's adoption of an international auxiliary language, the Soviet Union took up the question of language and international communication as fundamental to socialist construction. Now that the Soviet Union was transitioning fully to a socialist economy and industrializing at breakneck speed, it desperately needed to be able to exchange expertise with the capitalist West. Even more to the point, the Soviet Union needed to be able to access the manuals, blueprints, plans, and techniques developed in advanced industrial societies so that they could be put to work in advancing the goals of socialist industrialization in the USSR. The launch of Stalin's First Five-Year plan thus included a little-studied Stalinist campaign to bring "foreign languages to the masses." Soviet success, as envisioned in Stalin's revolution from above, demanded—at least in theory—a heroic campaign for the Soviet Union to master the living languages of advanced industrial societies. Stalin's revolution demanded Soviet mastery of the English and German languages most of all.[2]

This chapter explores the Stalinist endeavor to master not only advanced industry, but also foreign language learning and practical international communication. In the late 1920s and 1930s, the Soviet Union was engaged in wide-ranging and probing considerations of socialist internationalism's methods of communication and relationship with language. Stalin's Great Break imposed an urgency on those engaged in Soviet cultural diplomacy—an urgency for their endeavors to offer immediate, cost-effective, and practical contributions to the USSR's ambitious industrialization program.[3] Considerations of language and international communication revolved first and foremost around the practical needs of Stalin's five-year plans and the need for technical expertise from abroad in particular. At the same time, Soviet linguists, officials, language enthusiasts, and even Stalin himself engaged in a robust theoretical discussion about Marxism-Leninism's prediction of a coming international language under the conditions of fully developed communism.

Esperantists were often implicated in these wider discussions—ever more so even as Esperanto was increasingly rejected as useful for the Soviet present let alone the global communist future. By the time the CPSU and Soviet society caught up to the Esperantists in insisting on the urgency of deciding the Soviet Union's relationship to foreign language learning and questions of international language, the Esperantists were already on the defense, struggling to find a respectable even if small place for Esperanto in the Soviet march toward communism in an increasingly hostile and dangerous geopolitical climate. As the Nazi threat gained in its intensity during the 1930s, the Soviet Union was also increasingly on the defense. Domestic and international concerns not only shaped Soviet approaches to foreign language study in the Stalinist 1930s, but also dictated the shifting terms of patriotic international communication. By the late 1930s, as Stalinist xenophobia suffused Soviet daily life, Esperanto came to be regarded as a language of espionage and treason.

Foreign Languages to the Masses!

In 1928, Maria Ulianova was not alone in her demand that the USSR revolutionize its approach to foreign language learning. Soviet workers, Ulianova argued, urgently needed to study German, English, and French as these "living" languages were the key to accessing essential technical and scientific expertise developed abroad.[4] At the close of NEP, a chorus of voices joined Ulianova in urging Soviet officials to take seriously the question of foreign language learning as essential to socialist construction and, in particular, to the education of new cadres of Soviet technical specialists. The prominent linguist L. V. Shcherba insisted that foreign languages must be taught in Soviet schools. A professor at Leningrad State University who published widely on the pedagogy of foreign language instruction, Shcherba argued that the USSR could not achieve any of its economic or diplomatic goals without training cadres of specialists fluent in foreign languages. Invoking the immediate needs of Stalin's industrial revolution, Shcherba argued in one of his characteristic treatises on the need to teach foreign languages in Soviet schools, that "every specialist must be able to read the necessary specialist literature not only in his native language, but also in at least one European language." More broadly, a cultured citizenry need be one that prized knowledge of foreign languages. Shcherba argued that foreign language study trained students' critical thinking skills, deepened their understanding of their own native language, and broadened their intellectual and cultural horizons.[5]

Ultimately, the first push to inaugurate a five-year plan for foreign language instruction came from VOKS, the USSR's civic headquarters of cultural diplomacy. In the 1920s and 1930s, VOKS saw its purpose as not only educating foreigners about the Soviet Union, but also providing for "the international education of Soviet citizens." This included—even if modestly at first—the assumed responsibility for promoting foreign language study in the USSR. In its first years of existence, VOKS's work in this arena was limited, but already in 1926 it was instrumental in organizing courses in German and in Esperanto.[6] It also trained dozens of guide-interpreters for their mission to narrate foreign tourists' experience in the appropriate ideological light. In 1928, VOKS began to take a more proactive role in stimulating public interest and providing opportunity for Soviet citizens to study foreign languages. It was on the eve of the First Five-Year Plan that Soviet education and party officials took up the perceived urgent issue of teaching foreign languages to the Soviet citizenry.[7]

In 1928, the Central Committee adopted a resolution "On the Strengthening of the International Education of the Working Masses" that prompted VOKS to launch a new initiative known by its slogan, "Foreign Languages to the Masses!" Unveiling the campaign in the journal *Revolution and Culture*, VOKS's Olga Kameneva explained how foreign language study was essential to both international solidarity and Soviet economic and scientific advancement. Whereas in the prerevolutionary past, knowledge of foreign languages was the exclusive preserve of the aristocracy, she argued, today's builders of socialism needed foreign language skills so as to unite the worldwide proletariat and enable them to communicate technical expertise. "We must," Kameneva argued, "teach the European languages to significant cadres of proletarian-builders." The practical demands of industrialization demanded it, she explained, "because technical progress in the West continues, and the West's achievements are very vital for us." Every day, Kameneva wrote, pioneering new works were published abroad and in all the key branches of industry and knowledge. "It is impossible to translate them all into Russian," she explained. Foreign Languages to the Masses was thus a five-year plan for teaching Soviet citizens the European languages deemed essential to the success of Stalin's five-year plan in industry.⁸ It was a program explicitly oriented toward the practical need to train Soviet cadres capable of accessing from abroad the technical and scientific knowledge needed to grow Soviet industry, modernize the country, and guarantee national security.⁹

Launched in the summer of 1928, Foreign Languages to the Masses began modestly at first, with VOKS hosting evening events meant to inspire public interest in foreign language study. Yet, as the campaign's organizers soon discovered, the Soviet masses were enormously eager to study foreign languages. VOKS was unprepared for the urban public's enthusiastic response to this campaign. The stunning popularity of Foreign Languages to the Masses in Soviet cities underscored how quickly it was becoming "common knowledge" among Soviet workers, and among technical specialists in particular, that foreign language study was seen as a prerequisite for professional advancement.¹⁰ To cope with the overwhelming demand, VOKS quickly joined forces with Narkompros to expand the initiative. Soon, activists from Moscow State University, the Komsomol, and a range of workers' organizations were participating in an ever-more coordinated campaign to propagandize the merits of studying foreign languages and to organize language courses for urban workers.¹¹

Despite their limitations, the Foreign Languages to the Masses courses represented a serious effort to develop workers' functional abilities to read, write, and speak in prioritized foreign languages. VOKS also distributed foreign language textbooks in workers' clubs and factory libraries and developed a program of conversation hours that brought together Soviet foreign language learners with native speakers who were living and working in the Soviet Union. By the close of 1928, several thousand workers and engineers had been enrolled in foreign language study circles organized in Moscow, Leningrad, and other Soviet cities. VOKS soon confronted the reality that it did not have enough qualified teachers of German, English, or French to satisfy popular demand. Foreign Languages to the Masses dramatically highlighted the Soviet Union's need to train cadres of foreign language instructors. Already in 1928, VOKS began working with Moscow State University to organize teacher-training courses for the cadres of foreign language instructors that Soviet officials were suddenly realizing that they desperately needed.¹² Despite the lack of trained specialists, the number of foreign language study circles in Moscow, Leningrad, and other Soviet cities continued to grow in the campaign's second year. Yet the deficit of trained personnel shortchanged the enthusiasm that the campaign had inspired. Kameneva was forced to admit that many of the language study circles first formed after the launch of the campaign "quickly disintegrated, despite the workers' extraordinary thirst to master foreign languages."¹³

Despite the myriad practical challenges of staffing and equipping foreign language courses and study circles for Soviet adults, Soviet officials more vigorously promoted the Foreign Languages to the Masses campaign as the country pursued Stalin's First Five-Year Plan with feverish pace. In 1929, the CPSU Central Committee issued a directive on "Foreign Language Study by Party Activists" calling on a range of Soviet institutions to organize German and English language courses and study circles. It instructed its party members to regard foreign language study as a fundamental duty—a demonstration of patriotic loyalty and understanding of the urgent needs of socialist construction.¹⁴ Study of German and English was prioritized above all else given the obvious need for Soviet engineers, architects, scientists, and even average workers to be able to access the scientific and technical knowledge produced in Western Europe and the United States.

Conspicuous in its absence from the Foreign Languages to the Masses campaign, however, was Esperanto. During the First Five-Year Plan, it was only the rare advocate of reforming the Soviet Union's approach to teaching foreign languages who suggested that Esperanto be taught in Soviet schools rather than the European national languages prioritized by the Foreign Languages to the Masses campaign.¹⁵ If they thought about Esperanto at all in these years, Soviet policymakers tended to agree with Nadezhda Krupskaia's withering description of it as a language that had been "invented in an office rather than grown from the conditions of life"—a language, she said, that "will always be impoverished, will always be dead, cold, poor, and pathetic."¹⁶ In the initial rush to revolutionize foreign language study in the industrializing USSR, Esperanto was either overlooked entirely or else dismissed as irrelevant and even harmful to the urgent mission to train Soviet cadres of fluent German, English, and French speakers. For Soviet Esperantists, it was agonizing to see Esperanto excluded from the Foreign Languages to the Masses campaign. They, after all, had long been arguing that the

Figure 8 Detail from the front cover of the SEU's journal *Mezhdunarodnyi iazyk*, 1926.

success of the Bolsheviks' revolution depended on international communication and a thoughtful approach to the dilemmas of language diversity.

From the outset, some within the SEU's ranks regarded VOKS's Foreign Languages to the Masses as a threat as well as sheer misguided folly. In the pages of the SEU's various publications came fiery challenges to the campaign. Effective mastery of German, English, French, and other national languages could not be achieved in a study circle or an after-work conversation hour, Soviet Esperantists argued. It required extensive formal education. To learn but one foreign language required many years of concentrated study and intensive practice in reading, writing, and conversation. Besides, one could never truly learn a language by means of books. Language learners needed to incorporate the foreign languages into their real life—they at the very least needed to correspond with foreign native speakers of the languages they were studying.[17] The Esperantists also hinted at the campaign's unabashed Eurocentrism, contrasting it to what they portrayed as Esperanto's inherent internationalism. "An Esperantist," one lectured, is "an internationalist in the most deep and true meaning of the word."[18] The Irkutsk chapter of the SEU angrily published a leaflet in which they charged that the insistence on teaching the foreign languages of the West was itself rooted in a "bourgeois utopia."[19] Most frequently, they argued that the Soviet Union was simply not prepared to undertake such an educational campaign owing to the lack of qualified foreign language instructors. Though well-intentioned, Pavel Kiriushin argued, Foreign Languages to the Masses had already cratered against Soviet realities of resource scarcity. It would be most profitable and efficient, Kiriushin argued, for Soviet workers to study Esperanto—not the labor-intensive languages of German, English, and French. Esperanto was astonishingly easy for workers to master quickly. Moreover, Kiriushin claimed, Esperanto would allow Soviet workers to engage the whole wide world—not just those portions of it that were home to native speakers of German, English, or French.[20]

Yet as the Esperantist G. M. Filippov argued, it would be foolish for the SEU to adopt a stubborn position of "Esperantist imperialism." Filippov agreed with the fundamental premise of Foreign Languages to the Masses—Soviet citizens needed to study foreign languages. He argued that his fellow Esperantists must support the campaign and "come to the aid of the working masses in their striving to master foreign languages!" In particular, they needed to promote Esperanto as preparation for more profitable study of the much more difficult foreign languages of the West.[21] Soviet Esperantists thus emphasized Esperanto as a gateway to a more effective study of the "living languages" of the capitalist West. As early as 1928, SEU leaders were urging Soviet officials to widen investment in Esperanto as a helpmate of the larger Foreign Languages to the Masses campaign.[22]

Yet at the start of the First Five-Year Plan, it could not be denied that the Foreign Language to the Masses campaign represented an existential threat to the Soviet Esperantist movement. Esperanto had been cast aside as irrelevant and lifeless. The SEU was in trouble. For at least some of the SEU's leaders, it was already clear in 1928 that the Esperantists needed to change course in identifying the key benefits Esperanto could bring to the pursuit of Soviet policy goals at home and abroad. In particular, they needed to prove their usefulness in translating foreign technical journals, manuals, and other literature essential to the First Five-Year Plan.

Translating Expertise for Stalin's Revolution

Prior to Stalin's First Five-Year Plan, Soviet Esperantists typically did not prioritize technocratic arguments in Esperanto's favor. Switching course in 1928, they declared the goal of aiding Soviet mastery of technical and scientific expertise by means of Esperanto to be the SEU's first priority. "Technology decides everything," SEU leader N. Intsertov wrote, invoking Stalin's slogan. "And SEU organizations must decisively turn their face to industry, to technology. Esperanto must be put in the service of technology."[23] This meant, in practical terms, that Esperantist correspondence conducted in Soviet factories would now be oriented not only toward propagandizing the gains of Soviet socialism, but also to soliciting technical "support, help, and advice" from foreign experts and workers.[24] Questions of science, technology, and rational workplace organization were to be the central focus of Esperantists' correspondence with foreign comrades. During the First Five-Year Plan, it was not enough to simply communicate with foreign comrades. Esperantist correspondence needed to be reframed as consultation with foreign experts and a means of importing technical knowledge from abroad.[25]

The SEU sought every opportunity to advertise the ostensible usefulness of corresponding with foreign comrades in pursuit of technical expertise. For Esperanto language learners, they published stories like E. Ivnitskii's short story, "Esperantist Tractor"—a hopeful tale of how a young Komsomol member named Andrei wrote to his Esperantist pen pal in Dresden about his village's desperate need of a second tractor to maximize productivity on their collective farm. With its strained budget, the Soviet state could only supply the collective farm with one tractor. In this Esperantist fairy-tale packaged as socialist realism, Andrei's German pen pal raises funds from workers in Dresden to buy a second tractor for Andrei's kolkhoz.[26] The SEU even encouraged members to send copies of "Esperantist Tractor" to their foreign correspondents.[27]

Foreign recipients of Soviet pen pal letters asking for specialized technical expertise were often befuddled and annoyed by this new turn in Soviet correspondence.[28] Yet Soviet Esperantists were dogged in their pursuit of foreign technocratic expertise. In the industrializing Donbass, Esperantist miners in Stalino conducted what the SEU called a "shockwork" pen pal campaign in which they inundated foreign comrades with technical questions whose answers could help them in their work.[29] In one exemplary letter, Soviet Esperantists pled with their foreign comrades for advice on the mechanization of mines and for information on "new methods of uninterrupted coal extraction in the pits." How best were pneumatic drills and conveyer belts put to the task? And what of the "latest methods of air compression?" They requested "detailed descriptions of this work, inventions, improvements, and also articles, books, brochures, and newspapers that discuss them." They asked for "calculations, graphs, drafts, sketches, drawings, photographs—everything that can help to better understand

and practically apply these methods in the Donbass." More broadly, they asked for their pen pals to "describe the methods of all the work in the mines from the moment when a worker receives his assignment, takes his lamp, and up until that moment when he returns home from work." All of this material would help "to transform the old Donbass into a new, Bolshevik, socialist Donbass."[30]

Although the SEU celebrated the bits of expertise that its members received from comrades abroad, it remained to be seen how successful such a campaign could possibly be.[31] In late 1931, representatives of the CPSU's Moscow Committee undertook an evaluation of the SEU's work. Their report praised the SEU for its efforts to solicit technical expertise from abroad and to provide Soviet citizens with an international education at home. Yet the report suggested that perhaps Esperanto's greatest contribution to socialist construction was its capacity to aid Soviet citizens in preparing them for "further study of the fundamental European languages."[32] A similar evaluation conducted by Leningrad city officials, however, questioned the political reliability of using Esperanto for international correspondence, which was, after all, a matter of "great social and political importance." Soviet officials—and party organs in particular—needed to pay more attention to the Esperantists' activities, the Leningrad evaluation urged. As it was, the Esperantists worked without any direction or oversight—a fact deemed in the evaluation as "absolutely abnormal." While it was admirable that Esperantists were engaged in international correspondence that offered potential value to socialist construction, the evaluators concluded that there was as yet "insufficient control" exerted over the "ideological orientation of the correspondence."[33]

Despite their efforts to reorient their work to focus on translating expertise for Stalin's revolution, Soviet skepticism toward Esperanto prevailed. One advocate of the Foreign Languages to the Masses campaign conceded in 1931 that Esperanto courses served narrow purposes but insisted that "it is clear to everyone that the fundamental languages, the ones we need to study, are English and German."[34] In their 1931 text, *Study Foreign Languages*, authors Matiushkin-Gerke and Rozenblit likewise urged Soviet citizens to devote their time to studying English and German—the languages of Western technology—rather than to waste precious effort on learning Esperanto. "Esperanto is not a living language," they wrote. "No one speaks it in their everyday life." Few books containing precious technological and scientific expertise were produced in Esperanto translation, they claimed.[35] "The study of languages is a monumental political task," they argued, and Esperanto simply wasn't up to the task.[36] This attitude was formally enshrined in Soviet educational policy in August 1932, when the Central Committee declared that all students must be taught at least one foreign language in secondary school—German, English, or French.[37]

By the close of the First Five-Year Plan, the SEU's challenges and frustrations were multiplying rapidly. The Soviet Esperantists were regarded with suspicion and at times outright contempt by some Party leaders and powerbrokers in the realm of Soviet cultural diplomacy who considered Esperanto as either a language of subversion or else one of pitiable irrelevance. The Soviet Esperantists' long-standing struggle to find a respectable niche within the USSR's formal state structure had produced nothing but a decade of disappointments. Pleas to Soviet officials for support of the SEU's work went unanswered.[38] The Culture and Propaganda Department of the Central Committee admitted in 1931 that the "party organs ignored Esperantist work" and routinely brushed aside the SEU's requests for support. The SEU's entire operations were headquartered in an uninviting basement where the Esperantists worked determinedly without even a telephone or a typewriter.[39]

On March 10, 1931, the SEU's leaders wrote a desperate appeal to Stalin himself. "Comrade Stalin," they began, "we turn to you because we have already exhausted all other routes without result." They were not the starry-eyed utopians of Zamenhof's day, they explained. They were pragmatists seeking to use Esperanto as a "tool of international communication" and "in the interests of informing the workers of the West, America, and Japan about the building of socialism in the USSR." For years, the SEU had desperately sought out not only financial support, but also clear directives from the Party leadership so that they could best fulfill their special role in the service of the Soviet Union's domestic and international goals. All their pleas for support and guidance were ignored, they wrote. What they needed most of all, they told Stalin, was guidance from the Party.

In their letter, the Soviet Esperantist leaders also alerted Stalin to a crisis that now faced them from outside the Soviet Union. "Among foreign workers' Esperantist organizations that count among them greater than 20,000 members," they wrote, "there is taking place a secession of the revolutionary, class-conscious elements from the opportunists. We in Moscow are organizing this struggle against rightist-leftists." In this vague and tortured way, the SEU leaders were not only begging Stalin for help, but also calling his attention to a growing schism within SAT—the transnational organization of proletarian Esperantists with whom the SEU had cooperated for nearly a decade.[40] The SEU was, as they intimated in their letter to Stalin, at the center of this movement for "uncorrupted" proletarian Esperantists to break away from SAT, which the Soviet Esperantists now decried as a headquarters of Trotskyite degenerates. The SEU needed Stalin's help because it was an organization attempting to do more than translate foreign expertise for Soviet industrialization. The SEU was also struggling to lead the worldwide movement of socialist Esperantists. The Soviet Esperantists were waging a battle that transcended Soviet borders—a battle, as the SEU's chairman Drezen described it, between "communists and opportunists."[41]

Schism and Singularity: Proletarian Esperantists Divided

By the time of the SEU leadership's letter to Stalin in March 1931, their battle with SAT was in its third year and the transnational world of proletarian Esperantists was, it seemed, already irremediably divided. The roots of the SAT schism, however, could be traced back to the organization's very origins and organizing principles. Since SAT's founding in Prague in 1921, the Soviet Esperantists' relationship to this transnational organization of proletarian Esperantists had always been uneasy. On the surface, it had appeared for much of the 1920s that the SEU had a strong working relationship with SAT. As discussed in the previous chapters, rank-and-file Soviet Esperantists were encouraged to join SAT, subscribe and contribute to *Sennaciulo*, and otherwise participate—even if just in epistolary fashion—in SAT's transnational culture and community. Yet SAT's founding principles as an umbrella organization of leftist Esperantists of all manner of ideological stripes had always posed a threat to the SEU—an organization defined and judged at home by its usefulness to the construction of socialism in the Soviet Union and under the Bolsheviks' lead. For the SEU, Soviet needs and goals would always be the first priority in its participation in SAT. Yet SAT's bylaws stood in stark opposition to the SEU's single-minded fealty to the Bolsheviks. "Not being a political, but an enlightening, educational and cultural organization," the SAT bylaws read, "it endeavors to make its members tolerant and broadminded regarding the different political and philosophical schools or systems [of the working-class movement]. By the exchange of facts and ideas and free discussion, it strives to counteract the dogmatization of the teachings instilled by their respective schools."[42]

The SEU's leaders could not abide SAT's so-called open-mindedness and tolerance. Throughout the 1920s, the SEU had worked actively to stack SAT's membership with communists.[43] The SEU reported to the Comintern Executive Committee that it was able to exploit its relationship with SAT as a means of actively funneling abroad "propaganda about the ideals of Sovietism" and reliable information about life in the Soviet Union.[44] While SAT's founder Lanti strove to maintain the organization's ecumenical character, Drezen worked to build Soviet influence over the organization and its journal *Sennaciulo*. By 1925, this Soviet influence was starting to bear fruit. It became *Sennaciulo*'s de facto editorial policy to reject stories critical of the Soviet Union and instead to frequently feature stories that portrayed the Soviet Union and the SEU in a positive light.[45] This growing Soviet influence was also reflected in SAT's membership rolls. According to SAT's own statistics for 1929, of the transnational organization's 6,329 members worldwide, 1,987 lived in the Soviet Union. No one, meanwhile, could deny that Soviet participation in the organization in the previous years had significantly helped to grow SAT's ranks.[46] Soviet attempts at dominance in the 1920s had also chased some members *out* of SAT—most notably, a constituency of aggrieved anarchists who ditched SAT in 1924 to create their own World League of Stateless Esperantists.[47]

Meanwhile, Lanti—whose disillusionment with the Bolsheviks and personal dislike of Drezen dated at least back to his ill-fated visit to Moscow in 1922—stopped paying dues to the French Communist Party in 1927. Worse still, by 1928 Lanti had begun to promote anti-Soviet content in the pages of *Sennaciulo*.[48] From Drezen's perspective, Lanti's "revisionism" began to threaten "to explode from the inside the revolutionary unity" that animated SAT's work. According to the SEU's version of events, until Lanti began engaging in Trotskyite heresy, SAT had been a reliably revolutionary organization that was, in a practical sense, led by its most active communist members.[49] Increasingly, the SEU defined "revolutionary unity" in SAT as being measured by communist dominance within the organization and uncompromising allegiance to the Soviet Union in the pages of its publications.

In 1929, however, Drezen took a still more aggressive approach to attempting to discipline SAT into folding into a Soviet-dominated communist organization. This change in tactics was informed by the recent change in how the CPSU conceptualized the pursuit of revolution at home and abroad. As Stalin's First Five-Year Plan was launched, the Comintern entered in 1928 what would come to be known as its Third Period (1928–34). As initially articulated by Bukharin in late 1926, this third period followed upon the recent contraction of a brief interlude of "relative capitalist stabilization" that had followed the first period of revolutionary struggle inspired by the Bolsheviks' revolution. This new third period, Bukharin anticipated, would soon bring still sharper class struggle and a more emboldened working class abroad. To take full advantage of this emerging revolutionary moment, communist parties throughout the world needed to be vigilant and disciplined in leading the working class without deviation from Marxist-Leninism. The time for a "united front" with the noncommunist left was deemed over. In newly updated Soviet parlance, social democrats were rebranded as "social fascists." While the Bolsheviks' marked contempt for social democracy predated the October Revolution, the third period inaugurated a vigorous rejection of any further collaboration with social democrats who were maligned as dangerous lackeys of the bourgeoisie. "Social fascists" needed to be "unmasked" and disarmed. Their threat to communist leadership of the working class needed to be neutralized.[50]

Drezen first imported the Comintern's Third Period approach to SAT at its international meeting in August 1929 in Leipzig. Here, under Drezen's lead, a self-declared "left wing" of communist members urged a change in SAT's leadership. Lanti, Drezen claimed, was threatening the entire movement with his "revisionist" betrayal of SAT's revolutionary purpose.[51] Clearly, Drezen was attempting to wrest the leadership of SAT from Lanti's hands so as to exert not just communist, but Soviet authority over the organization. In so doing, he launched what snowballed into a protracted SEU campaign against Lanti and, ultimately, against SAT itself.[52] The SEU leadership soon denounced SAT as an enemy organization led by double-dealing class enemies whose "ideology may be characterized in brief as counter-revolutionary Trotskyism, developing from social-fascism."[53] By 1931, the SEU had definitively broken from SAT, which the Soviet Esperantists now described as "antiproletarian, counter-revolutionary, anti-Soviet."[54] At the annual SAT world congress held in Amsterdam in August 1931, the schism was cemented. No Soviet Esperantists were in attendance, but some of their European comrades served as voluble oppositionists at the fateful congress. During Lanti's concluding speech, these SEU-aligned schismatics interrupted him with barbs and insults. They accused him of being a "fascist," "bourgeois," "charlatan," and "social fascist." At one point, Lanti objected in vain, "I am a communist." He was shouted down by an oppositionist: "Liar!"[55]

The SEU leadership treated the Amsterdam congress as a definitive, irreversible break from SAT and Lanti. Yet it could not be denied that many rank-and-file Soviet Esperantists were bewildered by the schism and unprepared to condemn Lanti and abandon SAT. It would take some work for the SEU to persuade many ordinary Soviet Esperantists to adopt the new party line condemning SAT, Lanti, and *Sennaciulo*. It would require, the SEU leadership insisted, vigilance and discipline. Soviet Esperantists were encouraged to "unmask" Lanti's defenders within the SEU's ranks and to persuade them of their grave political error before it was too late. Those who could not be persuaded were to be purged from the SEU.[56] As the 1931 SEU membership booklet reminded the rank and file, Lanti had corrupted SAT and allowed Trotskyites to take over the organization and transform *Sennaciulo* into an anti-Soviet publication. The SEU and its communist allies abroad had no choice but to battle SAT.[57]

Having broken with SAT, the SEU and its foreign allies agreed that it was imperative to create a "new international of revolutionary proletarian Esperantists standing on the platform of the Comintern."[58] In 1932, the SEU allied with communist Esperantists groups in France, Germany, Japan, China, Bulgaria, and elsewhere to organize the so-called International of Proletarian Esperantists (IPE)—a transnational organization that at the time of its establishment claimed some 12,000 members worldwide. The IPE would serve the global proletariat in a fashion that SAT had not. In its founding charter, the IPE committed itself first and foremost to deploying Esperanto "in the service of the class struggle of the international proletariat and socialist construction in the USSR."[59] To that end, the IPE published transnational Esperantist literature—journals, press bulletins, and translations of the works of Stalin, Lenin, and Marx in Esperanto translation. It also facilitated international correspondence with a focus on "the exchange of technical expertise" for the benefit of Soviet industry. With an international bureau in Berlin and in partnership with a communist Esperantist publishing house (EKRELO) in Leipzig, the IPE was led by the Soviet Esperantists and its publishing program prioritized the worldwide circulation of Soviet texts in Esperanto translation.[60] It was a transnational organization, yet there was to be no doubt that it would take its direction from Moscow and position itself "under the banner of the Comintern."[61]

In early 1932, *Mezhdunarodnyi iazyk* crowed that "the best workers' Esperanto organizations are withdrawing from SAT" and branded SAT as the "vanguard of the global bourgeoisie" and a den of "social-Esperantist-fascists."[62] The SEU celebrated the fact that SAT's membership was "catastrophically falling."[63] And indeed the schism spelled disaster for Lanti's organization and very nearly destroyed it. In 1933 Lanti resigned his post as the head of SAT, now much diminished in its size and influence among Esperantists on the Left.[64] Lanti also soon took to proudly adopting one of the barbed monikers Drezen had thrown his way: Herezulo, the Heretic. This bravado could not hide the physical markers of a man shaken to his core. "The ordeals of the past decade had aged Lanti," Esther Schor writes. "At fifty-five, he looked about seventy-five. For years, disillusionment had been his daily bread."[65] In the late 1930s, as the world careered toward war, Lanti left France and began traveling the globe. By the time World War II began, Lanti—the self-proclaimed "nationless one"—was in South America. He explored the continent peripatetically as the world shuddered in apocalyptic violence and his own health declined. In 1946, he hung himself in Mexico, leaving a suicide note in Esperanto.[66]

The SEU also suffered dramatically as a result of the schism, and in critical ways that would only reveal themselves in subsequent years. In waging this battle against SAT, the SEU had cast a negative light over itself and its own members—Soviet citizens who in the 1920s had actively participated in this transnational organization now "unmasked" as a hotbed of Trotskyites and social fascists. In 1932, the SEU decried Lanti and his supposed minions abroad as still trying to sneakily "confuse the brains of proletarian Esperantists"—not least, they claimed, by slandering the USSR in *Sennaciulo* and continuing to send Trotskyite propaganda in the mail.[67] In a secret memorandum addressed to the Comintern's agitprop department in 1931, Drezen suggested that at least one double-dealing French communist was attempting to spy on the SEU's activities on behalf of Lanti.[68] In the pages of their own journal, the SEU leadership conceded that there were still some Soviet Esperantists who sided with the enemy Lanti.[69] In decrying Lanti and his so-called agents, the SEU leadership inescapably implicated the Soviet Esperantist movement in the dealings of an organization now condemned as a Trotskyite-social fascist battalion operating stealthily in the service of the worldwide bourgeoisie. Even if not immediately, this would have fateful—and in some cases fatal—consequences for the SEU and its members.

The Language of Communism's Higher Phase

As the SEU was battling Lanti for control of SAT, its leaders were also struggling at home to emerge victorious in Soviet debates over the nature of a truly Marxist linguistics and Esperanto's role in building socialism and achieving communism. Stalin's revolution appeared to give Soviet Esperantists the opportunity to contribute uniquely to Marxist linguistics, especially as it was oriented toward a theorization of global language "hybridization" and the human potential to accelerate the process of achieving a unified human language. Leading Soviet Esperantists—Drezen most prominently—participated in wider theoretical debates about Marxist linguistics and Esperanto's role in accelerating humanity's approach to global communism and its inevitable achievement of a new unifying world language. In the 1920s and 1930s, Drezen published a series of works that advocated Esperanto as essential to the scientific management of labor and, much more broadly, to the achievement of communism and its linguistic crown: a universal language for the triumphant global proletariat. He endeavored to lead the Soviet Esperantists to the frontlines of revolutionary linguistics in Stalin's industrializing USSR.

For revolutionary linguists, the Soviet 1920s had been an exciting time as an ostensibly Marxist linguistics took shape under the academic celebrity leadership of N. Ia. Marr (1864–1934). Marr, whose career in comparative linguistics took off in the late imperial era, became interested as a child in questions of interethnic and international communication. The son of a Scottish father who spoke English and French and a Georgian mother who spoke only Georgian, the young Marr was first drawn to the study of linguistics by the fact of his parents' lack of a common language.[70] In 1908, Marr published his study of Georgian and Semitic languages, thereby launching what he would in subsequent years further develop into his Japhetic theory—his evolutionary theory of all human language. In 1911, Marr assumed the deanship of the Department of Oriental Languages at St. Petersburg University and was elected a full member of the Russian Academy of Sciences in the following year. After the October Revolution, however, Marr's career skyrocketed. Marr's Japhetic theory, once revised in the 1920s to sync with Marxism, would ultimately dominate Soviet linguistics until Stalin later refuted it (and Marr) in 1950.[71] Until then, Marr's revolutionary linguistics would inspire nearly three decades of Soviet panegyrics.

Marr proved an eager ally of the Bolsheviks and his scholarship offered what appeared a "new" linguistics perfectly suited to Marxism-Leninism.[72] Marr stridently dismissed the "bourgeois" Indo-Europeanists of Western linguistics and announced the ascendency of a new Marxist (indeed, Marrist) linguistic science. In 1925, he somewhat revised his Japhetic theory, rebranding it as his "new theory of language"—one that was fully consonant with historical materialism. Marr's linguistic theory was realigned with what he called "the clear aim" to which humanity was heading—that is, toward "the unity of future humanity in language, as in economy, as in society."[73]

Language, Marr argued, belonged to the superstructure, not the base, and therefore evolved historically. Marr's theory of evolutionary linguistic development mirrored Marx's timeline of historical development. The epochal shifts from feudalism to capitalism to communism produced epochal shifts in language and human communication. On the path to communism, he argued, the world's many so-called national languages would organically blend and hybridize apace with the class struggle's unfolding toward communism. Upon the achievement of global communism, a unified humanity would speak a new universal language. This truly global and universal language was conceivable *only* under the conditions of the Marxist "end of history," he argued. It was the ultimate dialectical fruit of humankind's linguistic evolution. Eventually Marr even hailed this future universal language in ecstatic tones, describing it as "a new unified language based on the final accomplishments of both manual and sound languages—a language wherein supreme beauty will merge with the highest development of the mind." This would be possible, he emphasized, "only in a classless, communist society."[74]

Despite the vagueness of his vision of this future unified language and how it would come to be, Marr was clear on a few key points. First, it was impossible, he said, that any of the existing national languages could serve as the world language under communism. The language of the future would be the product of human history as a whole, not the history of one national group. The "hybridization" (*skreshchenie*) of *all* the world's languages was a creative, dialectical process, he argued, that would gradually, organically produce an altogether new world language. Marr also acknowledged that throughout human history there had been attempts at constructing an international language and that these had enjoyed various degrees of success in their time. Yet these constructed international languages like Esperanto were also not fated to become the unified language of the communist future. "The path of human speech," Marr wrote, "moves from multilingualism to the unity of language. The emergence of auxiliary, artificial languages like Esperanto ... is in principle, of course, an anticipation of the future, but in their execution and design (*tekhnika*), they are naturally a surrogate of that unity of language that will inevitably come about along the paths of the natural process of the social life of nations (*narodov*)."[75] Lastly, Marr shared with the Bolsheviks what Katerina Clark has called a defining "evolutionary impatience." Marr, she explains, "urged a 'creative' approach to linguistic evolution, guiding it and helping it to accelerate."[76] Just as the Bolsheviks were ostensibly guiding the Soviet Union's own "backward peoples" along an expertly accelerated path to socialist modernity, so too could Soviet linguists quicken the process whereby the world's languages mixed and merged on the inevitable path toward global linguistic unity. Indeed, Marr insisted that "a more developed society can and must accelerate" the evolutionary process that would result naturally in the linguistic unity of mankind.[77]

Influenced by Marr's Japhetic theory, many Soviet scholars and students of linguistics in the 1920s sought to revolutionize language in the socialist here and now in the service of accelerating humanity's arrival at the higher phase of communism. Early Soviet linguists writing in the Marrist vein looked ahead to the global proletariat's fusing of national languages into a new universal language and theorized how best they might help to accelerate the process under the conditions of building socialism in the Soviet Union. Among Marr's acolytes, there was consensus early on that language could be rationalized as part and parcel of the larger Bolshevik mission to scientifically manage not only labor and production, but also society as a whole.[78] Early Soviet linguists hypothesized a Taylorist approach to language reform. As historian Michael G. Smith explains, "They referred to language as a machine, an 'industrialization' process, and to linguists as engineers of a kind. They looked at the ways in which engineers applied the principles of the 'scientific organization of labor'... to the means of production as a model for their own project to apply the structural method to language reform."[79]

Drezen was among these revolutionary linguists who embraced early Soviet theories of the scientific organization of labor. In the mid-1920s, Drezen had even published a treatise "on the science of office record keeping and office management" as well as a study of how best to rationalize the USSR's "state apparatus." Overshadowed by his career in (inter-)linguistics, these texts were lauded in their time as valuable contributions to socialist scientific management.[80] Yet Drezen's interest in the scientific management of labor was not divorced from his life's passion—the study and promotion of Esperanto. In the 1920s, Drezen viewed Esperanto, Marrism, and Taylorism as a productive combination and he anticipated another way that Esperantists could contribute linguistically to the task of accelerating progress along the evolutionary timeline leading to the communist society of the future. He was not alone among early Soviet linguists who could appreciate Esperanto for its variously perceived potential as a tool of socialist construction and/or bridge to the universal language of the future under the conditions of communism's higher phase.[81]

Linguistics appeared to Drezen in the 1920s as a rare scholarly arena in which Esperanto and the broader question of international language was treated with seriousness. For his entire career, Drezen braced himself against those who refused to recognize Esperanto as a subject worthy of discussion at all. His evident frustration with Esperanto's many skeptics could be seen in a 1926 report "On the question of the practical application of an international language" that the SEU dispatched to a laundry list of party and state authorities. Many refused to even discuss the question of an international language from the perspective of Marxism-Leninism. Yet, Drezen explained, only those comrades without a truly Marxist understanding of linguistics could insist upon such willful ignorance in denying the historic significance of the question of an international language for humankind's past, present, and inevitably communist future.[82] In the 1920s, Marr's celebrity advancement of a so-called new theory of language that both insisted upon the possibility of an international language under communism and on the informed acceleration of humankind's linguistic evolution was welcome relief for Drezen. Marr's theories provided Drezen and his fellow Esperantists not only hospitable scholarly room within which to maneuver, but also a seeming cover of legitimacy in the face of comrades who otherwise laughed in their faces. Thus, Drezen wrote in response to one bitter critic in 1926, "For a Marxist, the arrival of the era of a universal language ... is as inevitable and undoubted as the arrival in the future at a unified global system of socialist economy."[83] Throughout the 1920s, Drezen endeavored to make ample use of the legitimacy and scholarly relevance that Marrism seemingly afforded him and Esperanto.

In 1925, Drezen published a study titled *In Search of a Universal Language* that examined humankind's centuries-long struggle with the "international language problem." In it, he provided an overview of dozens of historical attempts at this dilemma's solution. Yet Drezen, writing under the obvious influence of Marr, also looked ahead to the future—to the higher phase of communism—and the prospect of the universal language that would be spoken by a humanity united and liberated by its own hands. That future language would neither be any of the existing national languages, nor would it be Esperanto. And yet, Drezen argued, Esperanto needed to be utilized by the proletariat in the present as a means of accelerating humankind's transition from capitalism to socialism and eventually to communism.

In the present day, Drezen argued, the world's languages were already in the productive and natural process of "assimilation" and gradual transformation. At the current stage of human evolution, this natural process of linguistic assimilation was marked by a notable "internationalization" of languages—the incorporation of so-called international terminology into the world's languages. By way of example, Drezen pointed to the words "automobile" and "bicycle"—these were terms already "known by all Europeans" and would inevitably need to be assimilated by "colonial and Asiatic peoples" too.[84] Drezen maintained that this technical "internationalization" of the world's languages under the current conditions of industrial modernity was a mere foretaste—a blanched one at that—of the distant emergence of the universal human language to come under communism.

It was also, Drezen claimed, a sobering reminder of the urgent need for humans still in the present to use an international auxiliary language to ease their transition to global proletarian unity, the construction of socialism worldwide, and the eventual transition of humanity to communism. In order to one day arrive at communism's higher phase, humanity needed now to master and use an appropriate international auxiliary language that belonged equally to all—a second language for every one of the world's peoples. To get to the higher phase of communism, and to get there more quickly and humanely, humanity still needed Esperanto in the imperfect here and now. The alternative, he claimed, was for humanity to needlessly prolong the "natural birth of a common language." The truly revolutionary, Marxist approach would be to help quicken the pace on the path to humankind's communist liberation by means of adopting Esperanto as a rational tool of international communication. "The application of an artificial international language," Drezen argued, "hastens the moment of the drawing together (*sblizhenie*) of the workers of all countries, represents a necessary, intermediate stage in the cultures of the world's many peoples, and accelerates the assimilation process that has been dictated by the course of history."[85]

In 1928, Drezen published a much expanded and somewhat revised version of his earlier treatise under the new title *For a Universal Language*. In what could only be considered a coup for the Esperantists, Marr wrote the preface to this new edition under the heading "On the Question of a Unified Language." Marr's preface was in many ways perfunctory. Laden with oversized block quotes bluntly extracted from Marr's own writings on his Japhetic theory, the preface served to applaud Marr's own ideas and publications rather than to say much about Drezen's text or its claims. And yet even in its limited and self-serving way, the preface nonetheless gave Marr's imprimatur to Drezen and his ideas. This was no small thing for the Soviet Esperantist movement, as it put Drezen on the map of serious linguistic scholarship. It also seemed to offer at least tacit support to the idea that Esperanto could prove both instructive and useful in the scholarly endeavor to accelerate humanity's approach to communism and the evolution of that future epoch's unified language.[86]

For a Universal Language was not much of a substantive departure from the version of the treatise Drezen had published three years previously. Yet, in subtle ways it showed that Drezen was learning to adapt to the shifting vocabulary and emphases of Soviet rhetoric in the era of Stalin's First Five-Year Plan. Drezen refined his articulation of Esperanto's role in the evolutionary process as understood by "revolutionary Marxism," writing:

> Under our conditions, an international auxiliary language is a language of a transitional period: the collapse and breaking of the old capitalist world and old capitalist relations, when the old still has not completely withered away, when the various national languages still preserve their strength and their significance, but when simultaneously with these there arises and builds a new culture, new economic relations and a new universal language, that in the last instance leads to the establishment of socialism and communism in all the countries of the world.[87]

Yet Drezen's *For a Universal Language* did not chart in any specific way *how* Esperanto would prove essential to the "conscious linguistic construction" that he hailed as an urgent revolutionary task. He ended his study on an optimistic but altogether vague note, exclaiming "The future opens wide horizons before Esperantism and offers absolute assurance of the final triumph of the idea of a universal language."[88]

For Drezen, it was clear that among the "tasks facing Esperantists in the period of proletarian dictatorship" the most pressing was "to find their place in the ranks of the fighters for the liberation of humanity." Namely, the SEU needed to determine what *exact* role Esperanto was to play in helping to move humanity along the Marxist timeline of human development and the Marrist timeline of language evolution. Drezen struggled to figure out that role but he touted the Esperantists' wealth of "technical experience" in using, teaching, and expanding an international language as inherently useful for the "future merging of existing languages into one common language."[89] By 1930, however, it was becoming increasingly clear that Drezen was struggling to emerge out from under Marr's heavy overcoat with a clear plan for integrating Esperanto as essential to humankind's achievement of communism and a new universal language.

Out from Under Marr's Overcoat

At the Sixteenth Party Congress of the Communist Party held in 1930, Stalin affirmed Marr's ostensibly Marxist vision of the linguistic revolutions that would unfold as humankind approached the final triumph of global communism. The merging and mixing of national languages would gradually and organically proceed on the path toward an as-yet-unknown universal human language. But, Stalin insisted, this would only take place at a more advanced stage of building socialism worldwide.[90] He reiterated a stance that he had asserted in the previous year in a treatise titled, "The National Question and Leninism." Those who anticipated that the disappearance of national languages would and must begin under the Soviet Union's current conditions, Stalin wrote, had confused the fundamental principles of Marxist-Leninism and mistaken the enormous differences that would and must separate the realities of building socialism in one country with those of achieving communism worldwide. Naturally, Stalin explained, under the conditions of building socialism in the USSR, national languages were not disappearing. Instead, they were proliferating. This was the natural product of the Bolsheviks' emancipatory nationality policy that enabled the previously oppressed national minorities of the Soviet Union to advance their national languages and cultures. It was also an appropriate reflection of the Soviet Union's current position on the Marxist timeline of human development. Yet Stalin affirmed that the "merging of the nations and the national languages of the world into one integral whole" was on the distant horizon of a global socialist future.[91] Humanity would arrive at communism eventually and speak in a new universal language of communism when it did. This new universal language would, Stalin emphasized, not be the Russian language or any other national language. The future universal language was unknowable in the present and would only be possible under the higher phase of communism—that is, Stalin, noted, when "the proletariat is victorious all over the world and when socialism becomes the way of life."[92]

Shortly after the Sixteenth Party Congress, Marr formally joined the CPSU. His career had already become—in the words of one biographer—a "triumphal procession."[93] Yet, as Craig Brandist notes, Marr's colleagues tended to regard him "as either a genius or a madman."[94] By the close of 1930 a strident challenge to Marr began to cohere in the halls of Soviet academia, and in particular among Soviet scholars of linguistics who banded together under the banner of "Iazykfront"—the Language Front. The brash Iazykfrontists criticized the theoretical contributions of nearly all their scholarly forbears, yet what proved most controversial was their attack on Marr himself. The Iazykfrontists attempted an unsparing iconoclasm and accused Marr of having retrofitted his Japhetic theory to conform to Marxism in slapdash and absurdly simplistic fashion. They imagined themselves the true architects of a revolutionary, Marxist-Leninist linguistics and called upon the Soviet masses to participate in revolutionary acts of language reform.[95] In late 1930, the SEU printed in *Mezhdunarodnyi iazyk* a Iazykfront statement of principles whose signatories included none other than Drezen himself. An editorial note explained that the SEU "expresses its full solidarity" with the Iazykfront's commitment to pursuing a Marxist linguistics that would be attentive to the revolutionary needs of socialist construction.[96]

It was no coincidence that in 1931, the SEU prioritized "scientific research work in the realms of Marxist linguistics" and especially of "Marxist theory of international language."[97] The emergence of the Iazykfront seemed to open new windows of opportunity for Soviet Esperantists who wanted desperately to imagine a different role for Esperanto than the relatively narrow one that Marr's theory of linguistic evolution allowed. Some Soviet Esperantists had already harbored doubts that Marr's ostensibly Marxist linguistics had decided the question of an international language once and for all. Well before Iazykfront emerged, Efim Spiridovich, a seeming polymath among the Soviet Esperantists, had published essays on linguistics and the question of international language that were at least mildly critical of Marr in the pages of *Mezhdunarodnyi iazyk*. In his view, Marr had left the question of international language under-analyzed and under-theorized.[98] With the rise of Iazykfront, Spiridovich embarked upon a much more explicit and aggressive criticism of Marr's Japhetic theory.

In 1931, Spiridovich published his lengthy treatise *Linguistics and International Language* under the auspices of the SEU. It was time for a truly Marxist linguistics to emerge, Spiridovich argued—one that would place Esperanto at its very center.[99] Spiridovich praised Marr as a "genius" but claimed his Japhetic theory begged for refinement.[100] In particular, Spiridovich maintained, a truly Marxist linguistics needed to better account for how humanity would evolve toward the universal language of the global communist future. As it was, Marr's Japhetic theory promised only a vaguely defined future universal language arrived at by means of an "enormous leap."[101] Marr dismissed Esperanto and thus failed to recognize its revolutionary potential as the international auxiliary language of the transitional epoch of socialism. Whereas Marr had been focused almost exclusively on theorizing the origins of language, Spiridovich argued, Marxist linguistics needed primarily to be concerned with the "construction of the language of the future."[102] Spiridovich went so far as to contend that Zamenhof was "the greatest linguist of all times"—a genius who had laid all the essential foundations for the "Marxist revision of linguistics as a whole" despite the fact that he was not a Marxist.[103]

According to Spiridovich, the petit-bourgeois Zamenhof had demonstrated how the masses could be engaged productively in "linguistic engineering (*lingvotekhnika*)."[104] When he launched the language in 1887, Spiridovich noted, Zamenhof gave the world 16 grammar rules and 800 root words that were the basis of an international auxiliary language that was easy to learn because it was simply designed. Crucially, he had urged adepts of the new language to contribute new words to the language. Those adepts heeded Zamenhof's call and enriched Esperanto year after year in an act of collective linguistic construction. Likewise, in the transitional epoch of socialism, Spiridovich concluded, Esperantists would work as the linguistic engineers who would help to rationally accelerate humankind on its inevitable path to the "creation of the unified universal language of the nation-less society of communism's epoch."[105] The language revolution ahead, he insisted, was a "technical revolution" that could best be executed by Zamenhof's heirs.[106]

Drezen took a markedly different approach to searching for a more prominent role for Esperanto in revolutionary linguistics and avoided Spiridovich's bombast. In his published writings in these years, Drezen did not criticize Marr or his Japhetic theory outright. He openly criticized Spiridovich for exaggerating the purported Marxism of Zamenhof and inflating his contributions to linguistics as a science.[107] Drezen did, however, join Spiridovich in pushing for a language revolution that called upon the Soviet masses to contribute to the process of revolutionizing Esperanto so as to prime it for its role in humanity's transition to communism's higher phase and the universal language of the future. As the head of the SEU, Drezen—not Spiridovich—voiced the "authorized" account of the movement's vision of Esperanto's role in paving the way to the higher phase of communism and the attendant universal language of the future.

In 1931, Drezen drafted an emblematic report titled, "Esperanto—Language—National, International, and Universal" that he submitted to Soviet officialdom and also published in the pages of *Mezhdunarodnyi iazyk*.[108] Drezen invoked Stalin's words at the Sixteenth Party Congress explicitly—the universal language of communism's higher phase, Stalin had said "will be neither Great Russian nor German, but something new."[109] Soviet Esperantists therefore needed to define their contribution to the cultural revolution already underway in Stalin's Soviet Union. "Having accepted the thesis that today's Esperanto is not to be the universal global language of the future," Drezen wrote, "we must try to find the correct determination for Esperanto in our current epoch."[110] Esperanto was still "necessary for the future cultural and linguistic progress of humanity," Drezen argued, because it would "assist in the design of the foundation on which the future common international language will grow." In order to achieve this, however, Esperantists would need to embark upon a "genuine linguistic revolution."[111] They would need to accelerate the evolution of Esperanto in order to help accelerate humankind's ascent to global communism.

Drezen explained that Esperanto—like all other languages—was a dynamic, living organism and an altogether human creation. Its refinement could be achieved no less than accelerated by conscious human effort. In a word, Drezen argued, Esperanto could be rationalized. It was time for Esperantists to engage in a revolutionary reconstruction of Esperanto so as to accelerate the path by which the future international language of global communism would sprout from the "nucleus of today's Esperanto."[112] In the first place, Drezen argued that Esperantists needed to collectively grow Esperanto's technical vocabulary and transform this present-day international language into a language of socialist industrialization. Practically speaking, such a role required that Esperantists stock the language with "social and technological terminology needed by the proletariat."[113] To some extent, they had already done just that to accommodate the new Soviet way of life by integrating such words as *kolkhozo*, *serpo*, and *soskonkurado* into the language.[114] Yet much critical work still needed to be done. They also needed to prepare dictionaries of technical terms in Esperanto that Soviet specialists could use on the frontlines of the First Five-Year Plan.[115]

For a short while, the Soviet Esperantists seemed to have carved out a productive niche for themselves within the wider Iazykfront movement. In early 1932, the scholars based at Iazykfront's institutional headquarters, the Scientific Research Institute for Linguistics (NIIaz) in Moscow, adopted ten "Theses on International Language" that the SEU recognized as a turning point for Soviet Esperantism and Marxist linguistics alike.[116] NIIaz's theses acknowledged Esperanto as a robust international auxiliary language that enabled communication and helped to strengthen relations among the global proletariat. The theses highlighted Esperanto's Eurocentric design, Zamenhof's "petit-bourgeois illusions," and the early Esperanto movement's origins in bourgeois Europe, but affirmed Esperanto's currency among proletarian revolutionaries worldwide.[117] Spiridovich was criticized by name for his wrong-headed insistence that a truly Marxist linguistics would be one concerned most of all with the question of an international auxiliary language in the transitional epoch of socialism and with the construction of the future universal language of communism's higher phase. In general NIIaz encouraged Soviet Esperantists to temper their "aggressiveness" and focus more productively on how to reconstruct Esperanto to suit not only the practical, but also the ideological needs of building socialism. "Esperanto must be an auxiliary language that is international, but not interclass," the theses warned the SEU.[118] Even while accounting for the critiques embedded within NIIaz's theses, the SEU's leaders welcomed this Iazykfront acknowledgment of Esperanto's place in Marxist linguistics and the construction of Soviet socialism as an instructive and landmark victory.[119] Even Spiridovich was moved to celebrate the theses and to admit that he was guilty in his prior writings of having committed a "series of rude mistakes."[120]

Unfortunately for the SEU, within weeks of NIIaz's adoption of its "Theses on International Language," the Iazykfront movement came under the assault of party authorities who moved swiftly to shut down this cohort of renegade linguistics scholars and unmask them as "agents of the class enemy."[121] Drezen himself was called before the Communist Academy to confess his mistakes and he was discredited by one critic of Iazykfront as an "illiterate Indo-Europeanist."[122] In May 1932, the CPSU forced Iazykfront to disband and put NIIaz on probation (only to shutter the institute in 1933). Marrism was to reign supreme as *the* Marxist linguistics—unthreatened and unrivalled by upstart language revolutionaries.[123] If they were to find their way in the realm of Soviet linguistic theory, the Soviet Esperantists would have to do so by toeing the Marrist line.

As Iazykfront came under fire, Drezen found new inspiration in a quieter corner of language study. Drezen abandoned the frontlines of radical language revolution and began to direct his scholarly energy toward the Esperanto-friendly ideas of Eugen Wüster (1898–1977), a "bourgeois" Austrian engineer who would in time come to be regarded as the founder of the modern discipline of terminology science. In 1931, Wüster published his German-language dissertation, *International Language Standardization in Engineering with Special Reference to Electrical Engineering*, as an ambitious attempt to establish the international standards for technical language standardization. In a modern industrializing and interconnected world, Wüster maintained, technical nomenclature needed to be governed by clear and precise international standards so as to make possible efficient and effective international communication in a multilingual world. An ardent Esperantist, Wüster believed that the principles that governed Zamenhof's international auxiliary language could be productively applied to technical language standardization.[124]

In late 1932, Drezen published a lengthy review essay of Wüster's dissertation in *Mezhdunarodnyi iazyk* in which he praised the book for addressing concretely—in the manner of an engineer, rather than a theoretical linguist—the "question of the tying together the problem of language, the problem of technical development, and the problem of the mastery of technology."¹²⁵ Wüster, Drezen conceded, was neither a Marxist nor a linguist, but instead a bourgeois European intellectual. However, Wüster had addressed perhaps better than anyone else the industrializing Soviet Union's urgent need of a standardized international technical and scientific technology.¹²⁶ Notable throughout this essay was Drezen's insistence that Wüster's vision comported well with Marr's Japhetic theory. Drezen went to great pains to point out that Wüster had—even if unwittingly—incorporated into his vision a core principle of Japhetic theory: the inevitable human linguistic evolution "from a multitude to unity." Moreover, Drezen suggested, Wüster's unwitting Marrism led logically to Esperantism. In Wüster's mind, Esperanto was the best of all possible choices for an international auxiliary language to communicate expertise across borders. The effort to connect Wüster's work to Marr's Japhetic theory was by no means an accident on Drezen's part. Instead, it reflected the rapid decline of Iazykfront over the course of 1932–3 and the Esperantists' need to realign with the party line—Marrism—in Soviet linguistics.

By the close of the First Five-Year Plan, the SEU's horizons were narrowing and their opportunities to make grand claims for Esperanto were dwindling rapidly. With the shuttering of Iazykfront, the SEU called for members to embrace a singular Marxist linguistics, and thus follow the lead of the CPSU and comrade Stalin. The question of the international language of the global communist future was, the SEU conceded, "a question far more political than strictly linguistic" in nature.¹²⁷ While some Soviet Esperantists continued to protest Marr's inattention to Esperanto in 1933, the SEU no longer prioritized entering the fray over Marxist linguistic theory.¹²⁸

For his own part, Drezen was searching for a respectable, if small, corner of linguistics to which he could retreat. After 1932, his ventures into linguistics did not stray far beyond his investment in transforming Esperanto into a language with a large technical vocabulary—an international language for the modern technocratic age. He corresponded with Wüster, prepared a Russian translation of Wüster's dissertation, and promoted the Austrian engineer's work in Soviet circles. In 1934, Drezen joined the work of the All-Union Committee on Standardization of the Soviet Council of Labor and Defense. More and more, Drezen self-admittedly buried his nose in "the matter of researching methods of the possible unification of the scientific-technical terminology of the various languages."¹²⁹ In the wake of Iazykfront's demise, the burgeoning field of terminology science was seemingly the only safe space left within which Drezen could pursue his long-standing passions for both Esperanto and rationalization.

The Battle with Basic English

In early 1934, as the SEU continued its struggle to assert the legitimacy of their enterprise, a perceived threat arrived from an unexpected source: Ivy Litvinov, internationally known as the British-born wife of Maksim Litvinov, the Soviet Commissar of Foreign Affairs. Comrades from the British Esperanto Association informed the SEU of Ivy Litvinov's perceived treachery. Her name had appeared as a signatory to a manifesto that advocated Basic English as the only suitable option for an international auxiliary language. From the Soviet Esperantists' perspective, the scandal arose from the fact that Litvinov, the wife of a prominent commissar, had publicly affixed her name in support of a rival international language project designed to aid and abet bourgeois imperialism. This minor scandal—and scandal is how both sides regarded the otherwise obscure encounter between these advocates of rival international language projects—reveals much about the Soviet Esperantists' increasingly dismal situation in the Stalinist 1930s.

Born Ivy Low in London in 1889, the woman who would come to be known internationally in the 1930s as "Madame Litvinoff" came of age in Europe's revolutionary fin de siècle as a "modern woman" who bridled against bourgeois British convention. While pursuing a career as a fiction writer, Ivy Low was fatefully introduced to a shabbily dressed Bolshevik living in London in exile from the tsarist regime. She and Maksim fell in love and married in 1916. As Ivy would later tell the tale, neither expected that the Russian revolution to which Maksim had devoted himself would happen in their lifetimes. In the aftermath of the October Revolution, Ivy's vision of her future shattered and her fate was tethered to that of the Bolsheviks. In 1918, Maksim returned to Moscow and assumed various duties within the Commissariat of Foreign Affairs. Ivy and their two children arrived in Moscow in 1922. Thus began what was for Ivy a decades-long struggle to adapt to her new Soviet life—a task made all the more difficult by her nagging lack of fluency in the Russian language.[130]

Ivy Litvinov's struggles as an Anglophone in the Soviet Union no doubt helped to inspire her campaign in the 1930s to promote the teaching of English—or at least a simplified version of it—to Soviet citizens. This campaign originated in her visit home to London in 1932, when Litvinov met Charles Kay Ogden, the founder of Cambridge's Orthological Institute and inventor of Basic English—a radically simplified version of the English language that he proposed as the world's sorely needed international language. Ogden had recently begun popularizing Basic English as "a system in which 850 words do all the work of over 20,000, and so give everyone a second or international language which will take as little of the learner's time as possible."[131] In promoting Basic English as his solution for "Debabelization," Ogden had explicitly rejected its primary contender, Esperanto, as an unworthy rival whose proponents were sickly obsessed with "linguistic minutiae."[132] Ogden was no outlier in his view that the contemporary world appeared headed toward "the inevitable universalization of English."[133] It was not Esperanto, Ogden argued, but English—at the very least a "basic" and easily mastered version of it—that would emerge as the "international language of the future."[134] Everyone needed to prepare for the triumph of what he called "World English."[135]

Litvinov returned to Moscow inspired to promote Basic English in the Soviet Union. Ogden transferred to her copyright authority to produce Basic English texts and textbooks in the Soviet Union.[136] In their avid correspondence, they discussed Basic English pedagogy and began planning for Litvinov's adaptation of Ogden's Basic English primer into Russian. Already in 1933, Litvinov was teaching Basic English to small groups of Red Army officers, doctors, and officials at the Foreign Trade Academy. In February 1933, she wrote to Ogden that she was advocating Basic English in conversation with every conceivably important Soviet higher-up she came across.[137]

For their own part, the Soviet Esperantists first devoted attention to Basic English at the start of 1934. In an article for *Mezhdunarodnyi iazyk*, Drezen explained the folly of the bourgeois "Basicists." He dutifully invoked Lenin—who denied that any one nation or any one language could be privileged above all others under socialism. Drezen likewise quoted Stalin's claim that "the future common language will be neither Great Russian, nor German, but something new." Drezen acknowledged that the English language superficially appeared a good choice for an international language, given its relatively simple grammar and its contemporary use throughout much of the modern world. Yet, Drezen argued, advocates of global English overlooked its primary "defect"—its "non-neutrality." As a proposed international language, English—even a radically simplified version of it—would privilege its native speakers and oppress all other peoples. Despite this obvious deficiency, Drezen noted, advocates of Ogden's Basic English had recently amassed an "impressive army of propagandists" to spread their reactionary and imperialist message even in the USSR. The only thing Basic English could possibly be good for, Drezen argued, was as a tool to help teach non-native speakers the English language at a beginner's level. All other claims made for it, however, were "saturated through and through with the spirit of imperialism, the spirit of the glorification of the English, the English language, and the English race."[138]

For Ivy Litvinov, the trouble began in March, when she received an indignant missive from W. G. Keable of the British Labour Esperanto Association expressing shock at Litvinov's advocacy of Basic English. It was unacceptable, Keable argued, for a Marxist to embrace Ogden's "imperialist" Basic English. Ogden, he explained, justified Basic English by invoking the reality that millions of people all over the world knew English if not as their "natural" language, then as their "governmental" one. "There speaks your true imperialist," Keable declared. "The majority of these 500 millions cannot speak English; it is the language in which they are suppressed." Keable argued that Basic English, in contrast to Esperanto, was not only crudely imperialist, but also entirely ineffective for international communication. "As a self-sufficient international language," Keable railed, "it is simply a swindle; and its teaching is only directed to the admitted hope of its leader—the complete obliteration of all other languages by English." In conclusion, Keable demanded that Litvinov "justify" her support of Basic English "from the point of view of Leninism."[139]

Drezen also wrote to Litvinov, explaining that Keable had requested that his inflammatory letter to Litvinov be published in *Mezhdunarodnyi iazyk*. Yet Drezen adopted a much more even-handed tone than had Keable. He conceded that Basic English was an "interesting proposition" for helping to teach foreigners the English language, but insisted it was an unsuitable candidate for an international auxiliary language. Drezen also emphasized the grotesque politics embedded in Ogden's "imperialist" system. Ogden's Basic English dictionary, after all, had defined socialism as "a system of government control over trade" and the proletariat as "the lowest members of society." In closing, he invited Litvinov to reply with a letter that the Soviet Esperantists could publish in the pages of their journal.[140]

Ivy Litvinov forwarded to Ogden the letters from Keable and Drezen, as well as angry drafts of letters she had conceived as replies. Her pique over the whole affair was apparent in the sarcastic marginalia she scrawled onto her copy of Keable's letter.

In a flurry of follow-up correspondence with Ogden, Litvinov agonized over how to respond to Drezen and Keable. She also succeeded in having her name scrubbed from the list of signatories to the original Basic English Manifesto that had prompted the hullabaloo from the start.[141] Her commissar husband was annoyed with her over the whole affair, and Litvinov was forced to admit that she had carelessly stumbled into a controversy over the Marxist politics of international languages.[142] Reassuring herself, Litvinov wrote to Ogden that "surely rows with Esperantists don't matter."[143]

In the end, the SEU published the letters exchanged between Keable, Litvinov, and Drezen in *Mezhdunarodnyi iazyk*.[144] Litvinov disavowed any sympathy for Ogden's claims for Basic English as the logical choice for an international language and underscored that the very question of an international language was of no interest to her. She reaffirmed her commitment to Basic English as promising pedagogical tool for teaching English to non-native speakers of the language. She explained to Keable that the CPSU had prioritized the teaching of English, French, and German in Soviet schools. She suggested sharply that if Keable wanted an answer to the question of why English was taught in Soviet schools and not Esperanto, he should address those concerns not to her, but instead to Soviet education officials. As for Ogden's political views, she claimed not to identify with them "and therefore the question of imperialism does not arise." Perhaps most curious of all was Litvinov's claim, in her published letter to Drezen, that "I intend this summer to study Esperanto and would be very grateful for any help you could provide." She added in a postscript, however, that she was only interested in Esperanto's "theoretical and linguistic" aspects, not in the question of its possible value as an international language.[145]

With these conciliatory letters, Litvinov managed to shut down further public debate with the Esperantists. Privately, she underscored that she had absolutely no intention of learning Esperanto or having anything at all to do with the Esperantists whose cause, she insisted, was entirely irrelevant to Soviet society or its needs.[146] "Esperanto matters ONLY to Esperantists!" she wrote in exasperation to Ogden. "You have to be one of the faithful, or it doesn't exist."[147] Litvinov claimed the Esperantists to be so irrelevant, "that if I ever think about Esperanto at all, it is to marvel at the irrationalness of man." What the poor Soviet Esperantists failed to realize, she explained to Ogden, was that the Soviet Union was never going to be interested in the question of an international language. In the Soviet Union, she claimed, "the very idea of an international language is considered the mark of a Utopian and almost counter-revolutionary mind."[148]

What Litvinov's correspondence with Ogden throughout the remainder of the 1930s reveals, however, is that she could scarcely afford to be smug. In 1935, Litvinov published her *Basic Step by Step* textbook for use in Soviet classrooms.[149] Decades later, she would exaggerate its success, claiming that the textbook "sold out in no time" and resulted in her being "invited to give experimental classes in Basic English to the Red Army and at the Ministry for Foreign Affairs."[150] Yet Litvinov's Basic English courses in Moscow were short-lived and small-scale ventures. She never succeeded in obtaining anything more than tepid Party support for her Basic English project and was harassed by claims that Basic was tainted by an inherent bourgeois imperialism. However, she was still writing to Ogden in early 1936 that Soviet officials continued to consult with her on matters of what remained a Soviet priority—effectively teaching the English language to Soviet cadres of military and technical specialists.[151] By September 1936, Litvinov had moved away from her family in Moscow for a small gig teaching English at an industrial institute in Sverdlovsk.[152] A few months later, on January 23, 1937, she wrote despairingly to Ogden, suggesting that Soviet officials and Soviet society considered Basic English to be no more urgent for their needs than Esperanto. "All I feel is that I have a sort of grudging permission to teach it in out-of-the-way places."[153] In March she wrote to Ogden to say that "As far as Basic goes everything is pretty rotten." Throughout the entire Soviet Union, there were maybe one or two organized Basic English classes that had not yet been shuttered. "There is no support anywhere—at best a very little vague, slippery tolerance," Litvinov confessed.[154]

Like its rival Esperanto, Basic English had failed to garner anything more than marginal state support in the Soviet 1930s—a "vague, slippery tolerance" in Ivy Litvinov's apt phrasing. By 1937, scarcely any such support remained. Fortunately for Litvinov, she—unlike most leading Soviet Esperantists—would survive the year 1937 without being arrested by the NKVD on charges of espionage and Trotskyite conspiracy conducted in a foreign language.

Tongue-Tied

In a report prepared in honor of the Seventeenth Party Congress—the infamous "Congress of the Victors"—that was held in early 1934, the SEU touted what it framed as its recent successes. "The SEU," the report boasted, "has aided the mastery of new technology with dozens of technical devices, rationalization proposals, and hundreds of copies of technical literature. With its connections abroad, the SEU has served hundreds of factories and industrial plants and a score of social and scientific-technical organizations."[155] The Esperantists also claimed to have imported from their contacts abroad essential technological insights useful for Soviet industrial development in the arenas of telecommunications, chemicals, electronics, aviation, railways, engine manufacturing, and textiles production.[156] Soviet Esperantists were focused on "the import of technology and the export of the ideas of Leninism."[157] Communist Esperantists abroad continued to look hopefully to the Soviet Union as "the stronghold of Esperanto."[158]

Throughout 1934 and 1935, the SEU's leaders also attempted to champion the Comintern's emerging Popular Front strategy. Hitler's ascent in 1933 and his swift and brutal suppression of German communists had led to a rethinking of the Comintern's disastrous "Third Period" attempt to alienate and destroy noncommunist socialist parties. In 1934, the Comintern shifted into the Popular Front strategy and it was formally confirmed at the Comintern's Seventh (and last) World Congress held in the summer of 1935. This strategy called for cooperation across the Left in pursuit of broad-based socialist unity in the battle to defeat fascism. One of its first tangible successes was the election of a Popular Front government in France in 1936.[159]

Soviet Esperantists lobbied the Comintern to formally incorporate into its organizational structure the IPE—the Soviet-led transnational organization of proletarian Esperantists founded in the wake of the SAT schism. Already in late 1933,

Drezen wrote to Comintern officials explaining that the IPE had been much harmed by the rise of Hitler in Germany and the Nazis' subsequent persecution of communists and communist Esperantists in particular. The IPE's Berlin headquarters had been raided and its publishing operation in Leipzig was effectively shuttered.[160] In *Mein Kampf*, Hitler had spat on Esperanto as a Jewish plot designed to facilitate what he hatefully described as the larger Jewish conspiracy toward world domination. Joseph Goebbels shared his Fuhrer's opinion of Esperanto when he called it the "language of Jews and communists."[161] The Nazi government effectively shut down the German workers' Esperantist movement well before it formally outlawed Esperantist organizations in 1936.[162] Despite the IPE's setbacks in Nazi Germany and elsewhere, the SEU remained committed to this transnational union of communist Esperantists and to deploying it in the service of the Popular Front.

The SEU's leaders urged the Comintern to invest in the IPE because of its potential as a weapon against fascism abroad. It was not for nothing, the Soviet Esperantists argued, that fascist governments abroad were criminalizing and otherwise curtailing Esperantism. Fascists suppressed the Esperanto movement at least in part because they wanted to cut off workers' links with their Soviet comrades and to prevent the spread of Bolshevism.[163] The IPE needed to continue its important work, they claimed—and especially its "legal, semi-legal, and illegal" ventures to publish and distribute anti-fascist, anti-war, and pro-Soviet literature abroad.[164] The IPE's very own general secretary, G. I. Muravkin, knew firsthand how essential this work was—he himself was a foreign-born political refugee. A native of Berlin and member of the German Communist Party, Muravkin had fled Nazi Germany for the USSR in April 1933.

By mid-decade, however, the Soviet Esperantists' hyperbole and IPE boosterism could not cover up the fact that the SEU had not even been allotted enough paper on which they could print Esperantist literature for either domestic or foreign consumption. In 1935, the SEU barely managed to publish but a few early issues of *Mezhdunarodnyi iazyk* for its Esperantist subscribers.[165] Drezen had been reporting to Party officials since at least 1933 that the SEU's finances were "catastrophic."[166] Without access even to paper, the SEU's practical and financial situation in 1935 was altogether dire. An SEU report to the IPE in 1935 confessed that the Soviet state neither supported nor expressed interest in the Esperantists' work, hence the SEU's allotment of "paper only in extremely small quantities."[167]

As for the efforts to lobby the Comintern on the IPE's behalf, these had also failed. At meetings hosted by the Comintern's Executive Committee in May 1934, Comintern leaders expressed their disinterest in taking any responsibility for the IPE or its work. One, comrade Bronkovskii, argued forcefully against the Comintern's involvement in the IPE's affairs. The Comintern, he warned, "cannot answer for the ideology of the proletarian Esperanto movement in so far as no one understands the language."[168] Muravkin's claims that Esperanto would prove useful for Comintern work as a tool of camouflaged communication across borders perhaps generated more suspicion than enthusiasm on the part of Comintern officials.[169]

The SEU's work, and that of the IPE, had been brought to an effective standstill. In late 1935, Muravkin wrote to Stalin, repeating the SEU leaders' long-standing complaint that Party leaders had failed to provide the Esperantists with the necessary support to engage in their work and, most recently, had sharply cut off their access to paper supplies. This had resulted in foreign communists abandoning the IPE. With the Soviet Union appearing to have failed the proletarian Esperanto movement, Muravkin explained, the result was "an international scandal."[170] He pleaded with Stalin as "the great proletarian leader, theoretician, and practical man of action" to set things right—to put an end to the indifference, negligence, and narrow-mindedness the Soviet Esperantists had faced in their efforts to coordinate with Party and Comintern officials.[171] In February 1936, Muravkin wrote to Dimitrov, urging the Comintern to more meaningfully support the Soviet Esperantists and their foreign comrades in their valuable efforts to deploy Esperanto in the service of "international anti-fascist communication." Proletarian Esperantists were a "united front" dedicated to waging a shared "battle for peace and culture and against fascism." They needed resources— namely, rubles and paper—so that they could, via the IPE, publish and distribute anti-fascist Esperantist literature throughout Europe.[172] This letter, too, failed to produce the desired results.

In May, Drezen and Muravkin cosigned a letter they addressed to Stalin as well as to the NKVD's Yezhov and the Comintern leaders Dimitrov, Manuilsky, and Moskvin. It was a desperate, angry plea. Drezen and Muravkin begged the Party's leaders to clarify the SEU's position and to decide if its work should continue. Among the many thousands of Esperantists all over the world, they explained, there were many who were "friends of the Soviet Union" and who had long looked to the SEU as the headquarters of proletarian Esperantism and, more recently, as leaders in the struggle against fascism. Yet, in the current moment, as Esperantists in Nazi Germany suffered special persecution, Soviet Esperantists were facing a new challenge. In a paragraph underlined with what appears to have been Stalin's infamous blue pencil, Drezen and Muravkin argued that "our enemies abroad are beginning to draw parallels between the situation of Esperantist work in the Soviet Union and that of fascist Germany. In the current moment, the Soviet organization of Esperantists has become the disgrace of the Esperanto movement and a source of disappointment for the Esperanto movement in general." Since its inception, they argued, the SEU had worked faithfully to advance Soviet interests abroad, as well as to contribute meaningfully to the international education of the Soviet masses. Yet, the SEU had never been adequately supported in its work and had been left "suspended in air" by the Party's recent refusal to even release critical paper supplies to the SEU for its work. The result was that the SEU and the Soviet Union as a whole had been "discredited" abroad and to the full advantage of all manner of "anti-Soviet and Trotskyite elements" in the global Esperantist movement.

In a foolhardy move, Drezen and Muravkin questioned the wisdom of allowing an unsupported and unsupervised organization such as the SEU to engage in international communication on the Soviet Union's behalf. In another paragraph underlined in blue pencil, they insisted: "We consider it from a political standpoint to be entirely inadmissible for officially there to be an organization communicating with foreigners that is at the same time in some kind of semi-legal status (*polozhenie*)." Drezen and Muravkin begged for a resolution to the SEU's demoralizing and precarious state of affairs after having been treated for years by Party officials with "callousness, inattention, and a lack of sympathy." No doubt, they conceded, Esperanto was but a "small question" when compared with that of the enormous concerns of socialist construction. And yet, they begged in closing, it was a question that demanded a Bolshevik resolution given its significance as a matter of international proletarian solidarity and communication.[173]

In July 1936, the Cominternarian A. I. Zholdak scrawled a handwritten note at the end of another pleading letter sent to Dimitrov from Muravkin. The SEU and the IPE might still exist on paper, Zholdak wrote, but the institutions were lifeless. Drezen and Muravkin, he claimed, had been reduced to doing nothing more than writing letters begging Party leaders for support.[174] The following month, the SEU leadership convened to discuss their organization's state of affairs. A representative of the CPSU's Agitprop Department was on hand to observe the meeting. Here, Drezen resigned from his long-standing post as the SEU's General Secretary—a leadership position he had occupied since the SEU's founding. Those in attendance adopted a resolution that demanded that the SEU immediately reform its ways. It was noted that some of the SEU's members and even some of its leaders had failed to "always carry with the requisite honor the high rank of a worker of international communication and a Soviet Esperantist." Irregular, un-Soviet behavior had gone unchecked owing to "a lack of necessary vigilance that is especially needed in the ranks of an organization that counts among its primary tasks the organization and facilitation of international communication." It was time for the SEU to "conduct a careful review of the SEU's ranks and work methods."[175]

In that same month, the British Labor Association sent a petition to the Comintern urging it to adopt Esperanto in its work and encourage its use for international communication between communists all over the world.[176] By the time this petition—with pages of signatures collected from among the UK's Leftists—reached Moscow, however, the SEU and its leaders were effectively paralyzed. What the Soviet Esperantists' British comrades did not yet appreciate or understand was that 1936 had already proven an utterly calamitous year not only for the SEU and its leaders, but still more broadly for Soviet citizens with foreign origins, foreign accents, and foreign ties. And it would only get worse.

The Beginning of the End

In March 1936, a highly classified CPSU report on the SEU painted a portrait of a dangerous organization that operated wildly outside of the Party's control and without even the slightest supervision. Esperantists in the Soviet Union, the report noted, were engaged in frequent, unregulated correspondence with Esperantists abroad. More worrying still was the fact that unsupervised Esperantist correspondence with foreigners was actively pursued by SEU cells organized within several large factories in Moscow and Leningrad that were key to Soviet armaments and military defense production. Most alarming, however, was the suspect leadership of the SEU itself. The SEU's chairman Drezen, the report noted, had only joined the Bolshevik Party in 1918—that is, only after time spent in the first year of Russia's revolution as a member of the Socialist Revolutionary (SR) Party. There were other reasons, too, the report intimated, to be suspicious of Drezen. While attending an international congress of Esperantists in Leipzig in 1929, the report noted, Drezen had told his audience in a speech: "For twelve years I have been a bad communist, but a very good Esperantist."[177]

According to this confidential report, all manner of unreliable and suspect individuals staffed the SEU's leadership. Drezen's comrade N. Ia. Intsertov was described as "the son of a priest, an officer in the tsar's army, who belonged to the VKP(b) from 1920 through 1925 but was expelled from the Party for concealing a stint in Denikin's army." Intsertov was presented as a classic case of a counterrevolutionary already known for wearing a mask of Bolshevik loyalty—an enemy operating devilishly, yet in plain sight. Around Drezen and Intsertov, the report noted, circled other nonparty individuals who were entrusted with the sensitive task of overseeing SEU members' international correspondence.[178] The report portrayed the SEU as an unsupervised den of suspect individuals who had for years corresponded freely with foreigners.

These were increasingly dark and worrisome times for Soviet citizens who had extensive contacts abroad and for foreign leftists living in the Soviet Union. Already by 1936, xenophobia was swiftly becoming a new norm of Soviet life and official attitudes and practices. This xenophobia awkwardly coexisted alongside a still official commitment to internationalism as a fundamental principle of Soviet ideology.[179] With the Trial of the Sixteen in August 1936, the spectacle of Old Bolsheviks as Trotskyite conspirators—including the former head of the Comintern, Zinoviev—was loosed upon the Soviet imagination. It helped to cement a frightening vision of double-dealing comrades engaged in vast international conspiracy to take down not just Stalin but also the entire Soviet state. The impact was felt almost immediately at Soviet organizations whose purpose was international relations and cultural diplomacy abroad. In 1936, Michael David-Fox writes, "waves of suspicion beat down on Soviet cultural officials for their contacts with foreigners, and truckloads of books received from abroad were carted out of the VOKS library and burned."[180] VOKS's head, the cosmopolitan intellectual Arosev, would be arrested in July 1937 and executed in February 1938. Arosev was, David-Fox grimly concludes, a perfect target of the xenophobic wave of purges and arrests that had begun in 1936. He was multilingual, carried himself in a self-proud European style, and was married to a Czech ballerina. His social networks had spanned Europe for decades. Arosev's arrest in 1937 and the wider deadly era of purges and terror of which it was part, David-Fox has argued, signaled "the end of Soviet interwar cultural diplomacy"—at least in its most robust and expansive guise.[181]

The Comintern was an especially vulnerable target during the Purges and Terror, as it was staffed by revolutionaries from all over the world—revolutionaries whose jobs often required international travel, international communication (in a variety of languages and ciphers, no less), ties to foreign organizations, the assumption of aliases, and training in cryptography. Comintern headquarters in Moscow employed comrades of widely diverse ethnicities and origin stories. It was home to Soviet citizens as well as to a significant number of political émigrés from abroad who came under suspicion in the mid-1930s as threats to Soviet national security. Cast as a "nest of spies" by Nikolai Yezhov, head of the NKVD in 1936–8, the Comintern was decimated during these terrible years. Foreign-born and Soviet Comintern employees were arrested and repressed in large numbers. Those who deployed their foreign language and ciphered communication skills in the service of Comintern work were frequently targeted during this xenophobic campaign to unmask and neutralize the spies presumed to have overtaken the Bolshevik headquarters of global communism.[182] The Comintern's Communications Service—the Moscow office that housed and trained many of the Comintern's foreign-born translators, cryptographers, and other technical experts who were tasked with the organization's international communications— was soon presumed to be "saturated" with spies. The NKVD ruthlessly purged the Communications Service and at least several dozen of its employees were arrested as traitorous enemies of the Soviet people.[183]

Markoosha Fischer, who had served as a Comintern interpreter in the 1920s and was married to an American journalist, remembered 1936 as a bleak turning point in Soviet life. She became deathly afraid to speak German in public. A German friend in Moscow tearfully warned her, "Every one of us is suspected of being a Gestapo spy."[184] Russian friends soon cut off ties with the Fischers, whose foreignness and ties abroad made them socially and politically radioactive.[185] In May 1936, Ivy Litvinov wrote cryptically to Charles Ogden in London about an ominous turn at the academy where she was then teaching small Basic English courses. "Because of recent events we are without an enormous per cent of our v[ery] best German teachers, some of whom have been ill-advised to teach 'Fascist phonetics.'" She added, "(Make what you can of that!)."[186] Alexander Barmine, who worked in the Soviet foreign service during these years, later recalled how fears of espionage and international conspiracy suffused the daily life of Soviet citizens. The Soviet press demanded its readers be vigilant. "There was a distinct tendency to regard all foreigners, even Communists and revolutionary refugees who had been living in in the USSR for fifteen years, as spies," Barmine wrote after defecting from the USSR. "People grew afraid to know foreigners, to receive postcards from abroad."[187]

One NKVD official later recalled how he and his colleagues were instructed to visit the City of Moscow Housing Department and scrutinize its directories and files for "foreign-sounding" surnames. They dutifully compiled lists of these presumed foreigners so that warrants could be issued in their unfortunate "foreign-sounding" names.[188] Under these conditions of "hysteria, spy mania, and xenophobia," the historian J. Arch Getty writes, NKVD employees "combed old records of tsarist-era foreign firms working in Russia and arrested their surviving employees." Any connection to life abroad was suspect—even stamp collectors were branded as spies and traitors.[189] As this xenophobia worsened, entire ethnicities within the Soviet Union were deemed "suspect," anti-Soviet, and loyal to homelands abroad. The NKVD rounded up representatives of diaspora nationalities living in border regions and deported them en masse to locations elsewhere in the Soviet Union. Poles, Germans, Koreans, Iranians, Finns, and other suspect diaspora nationalities were swept up in these mass operations of prewar Soviet ethnic cleansing.[190]

Under these conditions of Stalinist xenophobia, the Soviet Esperantists were sitting ducks, soon to be overtaken by the NKVD's growing tidal wave of arrests and purging. In 1936, Lev Kopelev—who had learned Esperanto as a boy—was a student in Moscow's Institute of Foreign Languages. Tapped as an informer by the NKVD, he was instructed "to join an Esperanto study group and find out who its members were and what mail it received from abroad."¹⁹¹ Desperate to demonstrate their loyalty, the SEU reviewed its membership rolls. It was time "to bring order to the Soviet Esperantists' house" and cast out the disorderly and unfaithful. Individual correspondence with Esperantists abroad was recategorized as unacceptable, and the SEU committed to taking a meticulous inventory of the SEU members' activity, the nature of their foreign correspondence, and the characteristics of their contacts abroad.¹⁹² In September, Intsertov wrote a stern letter to an Esperantist in the city of Kirov, rebuking him for inquiring about where to find addresses that could be used in individual pen pal correspondence. Intsertov wrote:

> The international situation today is such (do remember the trial of the Trotskyite-Zinovievite gang), that international correspondence is a much more sensitive matter (*otvetstvennym delom*) than it was earlier. Is it really possible that you don't understand this? We do not recommend engaging in individual correspondence, and our committees must organize *only* collective correspondence.

Intsertov further insisted that SEU organizers should "never allude to individual correspondence in their conversations."¹⁹³

On November 21, 1936, the NKVD arrested Muravkin, the foreign-born general secretary of the IPE. Accused of being a German spy, Muravkin "confessed" to his NKVD interrogators that the SEU leadership was a nest of counterrevolutionary Trotskyite sabotage. Muravkin claimed that Drezen and other SEU leaders were operating an Esperantist terrorist organization devoted to undoing the Soviet regime. For his alleged role in this ostensible international conspiracy, Muravkin would be executed the following year, on December 11, 1937.¹⁹⁴

The situation of the Soviet Esperantists worsened further on January 1, 1937, when the NKVD arrested a Hungarian political refugee to the USSR named Iosif Bata, charging him with espionage. Bata, the NKVD insisted, had been sent to the Soviet Union as an "emissary of a foreign Trotskyite center." That ostensible foreign Trotskyite center was none other than SAT. According to the NKVD's version of events, "The German spy Lanti [sic] recruited Bata for espionage work against the USSR." Bata also confessed to recruiting other SEU members to join in this widening international anti-Soviet conspiracy. Subject to the NKVD's methods of interrogation and torture, Bata implicated a number of his SEU comrades in an ostensible international conspiracy to bring down the Soviet regime with the aid of Esperanto.¹⁹⁵ Prior to his execution in 1938, Bata told his interrogators that it was Drezen, in his capacity as chairman of the SEU, who helped him to first secure his visa to the Soviet Union. He had first met Drezen in 1929, Bata explained, at the annual SAT world congress held in Leipzig. He affirmed what was no doubt the NKVD's scripted version of events: that several hundred Soviet Esperantists were agents of this international spy ring. They worked in the Soviet defense industry, telecommunications agencies, for its railways, and even served in the Red Army. Subversive international correspondence in Esperanto was but one of the spy ring's methods of recruiting more Esperantist agents and otherwise undermining the USSR. Drezen, Bata said in interrogations, led the SEU as cover for what was, in actuality, a fascist headquarters in the Soviet Union for training Esperantists as "terrorist cadres" who would help topple the Soviet regime.[196]

Drezen's Austrian colleague and friend Wüster received one last letter from Drezen on March 9, 1937. Wüster attempted to write his Soviet comrade two more times, but never received further response.[197] On April 17, 1937, the NKVD arrested Drezen. He was accused of treason, espionage, and Trotskyite scheming to bring down the Soviet government. Under the cover of the SEU, the NKVD charged, Drezen had led a "counter-revolutionary Trotskyite organization."[198] In the NKVD's framing, the SEU had not deployed Esperanto in the service of international proletarian revolution and in pursuit of Soviet ideological and technological supremacy. Instead, the SEU had served as a front for what was an international spy ring dedicated to the overthrow of the Soviet government.[199] In this deadly reframing, Esperanto was a language of Trotskyite treason, espionage, and betrayal—and its Soviet adepts were traitors, spies, wreckers, and terrorists networked into an international anti-Soviet conspiracy.

Epilogue: The Death of Esperanto

In the early morning hours of March 22, 1938, NKVD officers showed up at Nikolai Rytkov's front door and demanded that he put his hands in the air. A young actor in his prime, Rytkov was doomed in 1938 by his Esperantism. When the NKVD muscled their way into his apartment on that fateful morning, they immediately began searching his apartment for evidence of Rytkov's alleged espionage. They rifled through a trunk that archived Rytkov's collection of Esperantist correspondence received from abroad. They collected letters and envelopes as evidence of Rytkov's perfidy. Rytkov was taken to the Lubyanka prison where he was tortured under interrogation. In an interview given in 1968, Rytkov recalled the merciless beatings he suffered at the hands of the NKVD officers who demanded that he confess to his participation in a grand international Esperantist conspiracy to undermine the USSR. Rytkov refused to admit to the crimes of espionage of which he was accused. He refused to name his fellow Esperantists as ostensible coconspirators in what the NKVD insisted was an anti-Soviet Esperantist conspiracy orchestrated by the SEU and its foreign collaborators.[1] For "counter-revolutionary activity" specified as "participation in 'the fascist espionage organization of Esperantists" and spreading "slanderous falsehoods about the situation in the USSR,'" Rytkov was sentenced to eight years in the Gulag. He survived those eight years in the camps in Kolyma and was rehabilitated in 1955.[2]

Rytkov was one of many Esperantists who were caught up in the deadly webs of a supposed international conspiracy headquartered at the SEU and manufactured in the deadly interrogation rooms of the NKVD during Stalin's Great Purge and Terror. Richard Tsyvinskii, whose 1917 *Manifesto of the Union of Socialist Esperantists* was discussed in Chapter 3, was arrested in Leningrad on January 28, 1936, on charges of espionage. Sentenced to ten years of hard labor, Tsyvinskii was sent to the Ukhta-Pechora Camp in the Komi ASSR.[3] The Esperantist R. N. Bakushinskii had in his youthful days in revolutionary Russia enthused about Esperanto's promise to achieve "the brotherhood of peoples and global citizenship."[4] In March 1938, Bakushinskii was arrested for participating as a spy and a terrorist in the SEU's alleged anti-Soviet conspiracy. Sentenced in July 1938 to eight years in the Gulag, Bakushinskii died some five months later in a Kolyma labor camp.[5] Like Bakushinskii, Boris Breslau had, in the wake of the October Revolution, energetically adapted his prerevolutionary Esperantism to Bolshevism. Even in 1934, Breslau was moved to celebrate Zamenhof as a "friend of humanity" who had selflessly given the world Esperanto, his "immortal legacy."⁶ On January 16, 1937, Breslau was arrested. The NKVD claimed in their arrest report that they had confiscated from Breslau's home "a large quantity of counter-revolutionary Trotskyite literature" and an illegal firearm. In June of that same year, Breslau was sentenced as a "socially dangerous element" to a three-year term in the Gulag.⁷ Breslau was never heard from again.

Drezen was the most prominent of the Soviet Esperantists to be arrested during the Great Terror. As head of the SEU for some fifteen years, Drezen had been the face of Soviet Esperantism. He often traveled abroad to represent the USSR at international meetings of Leftist Esperantists in the 1920s and 1930s and was known internationally, too, as a specialist on interlinguistics and the history of Esperanto. Yet the prominence Drezen had enjoyed in previous years was alchemized during the Purges into a stained biography of masked counterrevolution.

In 1918, Drezen joined the Bolshevik Party and dedicated himself to the triumph of the October Revolution. After serving in the Red Army, he launched an energetic career in the new Soviet state. In the 1920s, Drezen worked as a deputy within the All-Russian Central Executive Committee, while also moonlighting as a lecturer at Moscow State University and other institutes of higher education, an advisor to VOKS, and a departmental director within the All-Union Committee for a New Alphabet within the Soviet of Nationalities.⁸ During these years, he also led the Union of Soviet Esperantists and published widely on the theoretical question of an international language from an ostensibly Marxist-Leninist perspective.

Reframed by the NKVD agents who arrested him on April 17, 1937, Drezen's biography was a galling record of anti-Soviet machinations and Trotskyite counterrevolution pursued by a cunning wolf in sheep's clothing. A Latvian, former officer in the tsarist army, former SR, and a globe-trotting, Esperanto-speaking cosmopolitan, Drezen was accused of being the mastermind behind the establishment on Soviet territory of a fascist-terrorist-spy organization committed to counterrevolution.⁹ On the same day of Drezen's arrest, the NKVD also arrested the SEU's executive secretary, N. Ia. Intsertov, for his alleged role in helping to operate the Esperantists' "counter-revolutionary Trotskyite terrorist organization, whose aim was to prepare terrorist acts against the VKP(b)'s leaders and the Soviet government."¹⁰ Under interrogation, Drezen "confessed" to having recruited Intsertov to this fascist spy ring and to directing him in the secretive distribution of Trotskyite literature and other counterrevolutionary crimes. In vain, Intsertov protested these claims, insisting on his innocence. On October 27, 1937, both Drezen and Intsertov were sentenced to death and summarily executed.¹¹ On November 3, 1937, Elena Sazonova—an active Esperantist and Drezen's wife—was also executed for her alleged crimes of espionage and counterrevolutionary agitation.¹² Drezen's successor to the chairmanship of the SEU, P. N. Shumilov, was arrested in February 1938 and ultimately "survived some eighteen years of hard labor" in the Gulag.¹³

It was not merely the SEU's leaders who were dragged by the undertow of the NKVD's claims that hundreds of Soviet Esperantists had been recruited into an international fascist Trotskyite spy conspiracy to overthrow the Soviet government. In March 1938, Antonina Sergeevna Smirnova was arrested for her alleged role in the Esperantist-Trotskyite-spy conspiracy. A telegraph sorter in the People's

Commissariat of Transportation, Smirnova was an Esperantist who had joined both SAT and the SEU in 1926. Her NKVD file noted that Smirnova had corresponded with Esperantists throughout Europe and had led an Esperanto study club—in addition to her alleged activities as an Esperantist spy who took advantage of her connections to the Soviet railways. For her alleged crimes, Smirnova was sentenced to eight years in the Gulag.[14] Under interrogation a few weeks prior to Smirnova's arrest, one of her Soviet Esperantist comrades had told the NKVD that Smirnova had smuggled photographs of Soviet locomotives and information about Soviet telegraph operations to her contacts abroad.[15] Thus the gyre widened. Smirnova's denouncer, P. A. Gavrilov, "confessed" under torture to serving as a courier for the "counter-revolutionary spy organization of Esperantists" under Drezen's lead. He confessed to recruiting workers to study Esperanto so that he could conduct anti-Soviet propaganda among them. In September 1938, Gavrilov was sentenced to eight years in the Gulag. In June 1939, Gavrilov unsuccessfully appealed to the Soviet Procuracy and recanted his testimony as having been coerced under physical pressure from his interrogators.[16]

In the NKVD records of the Soviet Esperantists' arrests that have been made publicly available, no less than in the retrospective testimonies that surviving Soviet Esperantists have given about their struggles during this deadly and dangerous time of Stalin's Purges and Terror, repeated reference is made to the NKVD's confiscation of the Esperantists' international correspondence at the time of their arrest. In 1937, the NKVD arrested Sergei Mastepanov, a young and provincial German-language teacher whose precocious love of studying languages resembled that of Zamenhof. Accused of espionage like so many of his SEU comrades, Mastepanov survived ten years in the Gulag. Looking back on his Esperantist youth, Mastepanov in 1990 recalled the delights of corresponding with foreigners. He remembered exchanging letters with correspondents in Tokyo, New York, and France—and even with a British woman who claimed to be "some kind of English princess." Upon his arrest, however, the NKVD confiscated all of his Esperantist correspondence as well as his SEU membership card. Looking back on the horrors he endured, Mastepanov was quick to note that he ceased to be an Esperantist after his arrest on December 25, 1937. He never resumed his prior hobby, even after he was rehabilitated in 1957. "One can with absolute certainty say that [my] Esperantist activity was the cause of this entire tragedy," he said of the arrest and Gulag term that destroyed and defined so much of his life.[17]

On March 18, 1937, the NKVD arrested Dmitrii Viktorov-Chekhovich in Kiev and seized from his home an array of "Trotskyite literature" bearing SAT's imprint. He was accused of having received this Trotskyite propaganda from abroad in order to distribute it among Soviet citizens and recruit them to the Esperantists' Trotskyite spy ring. Viktorov-Chekhovich was executed on September 2, 1937.[18] Under interrogation, Boris Eggers confessed that he and his Esperantist friends (including Viktorov-Chekhovich) regularly gathered in Kiev to read Trotskyite literature in Esperanto received from abroad. It was through this Trotskyite Esperanto collective, Eggers conceded, that he had been recruited into a terrorist group that conspired against the CPSU and Soviet government. Eggers was executed on October 3, 1937.[19] In Odessa, Veniamin Vozdvizhenskii was arrested on June 13, 1937, for heading up a Trotskyite terror group that received its orders from SAT. At the time of his arrest, the NKVD seized from Vozdvizhenskii an ostensible cache of "counter-revolutionary literature received from abroad." He was executed on November 24, 1937.[20]

The Hungarian Fyodor Robichek was executed on October 19, 1938. He was sentenced to death for his alleged role in the SEU's spy ring and accused, in particular, of funneling state secrets about the Soviet aviation industry to the USSR's enemies abroad.[21] V. M. Zykov was also accused of transmitting sensitive information about Soviet aeronautics by means of international Esperantist correspondence. Arrested on March 10, 1938, Zykov was sentenced in July of the same year to eight years in the Gulag. Less than five months later, he died in a Kolyma labor camp.[22] Upon his arrest and interrogation in March 1938, A. K. Timofeevskii "confessed" to the NKVD that he had used his Esperantist correspondence with foreigners in England, Sweden, France, and Holland as a cover for his nefarious spy work. Timofeevskii later tried to recant this ostensible confession but could not deny that he had corresponded with foreign Esperantists. In May 1939, Timofeevskii was sentenced to three years hard labor in the Gulag.[23] Under interrogation following his arrest in February 1928, A. T. Samoilenko told the NKVD that the SEU had carried out its espionage by means not only of foreign Esperantist correspondence, but also by smuggling secrets out of the USSR in the hands of visiting Esperantist tourists to the USSR. Samoilenko was sentenced and executed on October 4, 1938.[24] In an interrogation conducted by the NKVD on March 12, 1938, A. A. Novozhilov "confessed" that from the moment of his recruitment into the SEU's spy ring, he was instructed to correspond with Esperantists abroad. He was guilty, he affirmed, of using Esperanto to funnel classified information about Soviet industry to foreign contacts abroad.[25] On March 27, 1938, N. N. Temerin "confessed" to his NKVD interrogators that he followed the orders of his handlers within the SEU and, using Esperanto, wrote to contacts in Australia to share "slanderous information about the Soviet Union." A few months later, Temerin was sentenced to eight years in the Gulag for counterrevolutionary activity.[26] On March 17, 1938, F. A. Filippov "confessed" to the NKVD that in 1927, he was recruited as a spy by a German Esperantist whom he never met in person but with whom he exchanged correspondence. Filippov was sentenced to eight years in the Gulag for his alleged counterrevolutionary crimes.[27] N. P. Usov, a schoolteacher in the Kyrgyz SSSR, was arrested on February 8, 1938. His correspondence with individuals in the United States, Canada, Japan, Austria, the UK, and elsewhere was put forward as evidence of his alleged espionage. Usov was executed on October 4, 1938.[28] In NKVD records documenting the arrest of A. N. Nevolin on March 10, 1938, it was noted that "Nevolin was fanatically devoted to Esperanto" and often complained in his letters to fellow Esperantists about the CPSU's attitude toward Esperanto. On July 2, 1938, Nevolin was sentenced to eight years in the Gulag.[29]

On May 29, 1937, the NKVD arrested a young Esperantist activist named A.P. Eriukhin in Arkhangelsk. Left behind in the devastating wake of his arrest was Eriukhin's wife, Liudmila, and their two small sons Viktor and Valentin, aged 2 and 6. A decade earlier, Eriukhin had led an Esperanto study circle at Arkhangelsk's central telegraph office and it was here that he had met his future wife. The two young Esperantists wed in 1929. When Eriukhin returned to Arkhangelsk after serving a reduced term in the Gulag, he boldly organized local Esperanto study circles anew.[30]

Valentin Luk'ianin was in his mother's womb at the time of his father's arrest in August 1937. Valentin never met his father, Pyotr Matveevich, as the elder Luk'ianin was executed on October 12, 1937, for the alleged crime of espionage and "counterrevolutionary terrorist agitation." At the time of his arrest, Pyotr Luk'ianin was the head of an elementary school in the village of Pisarevka in the Soviet Union's western borderlands. In his spare time, he enjoyed writing poetry in his native Russian and Polish. In addition to the child they were expecting, Luk'ianin and his wife were parents to a 6-year-old son at the time of his arrest. Only after the fall of the Soviet Union, however, did Valentin and his brother discover their father's true fate and the NKVD's reason for arresting their father in August 1937. After making some inquiries, Valentin ultimately visited a regional FSB office to review his father's archived case file. Here, he learned of his father's Esperantist correspondence that had served as the NKVD's pretext for his arrest and subsequent execution in 1937. The elder Luk'ianin was accused of espionage by means of Esperantist correspondence with contacts in Sweden, Spain, and France. Under interrogation, Luk'ianin "confessed" that he undertook study of Esperanto in 1930 because he was intrigued by the prospect of corresponding with foreigners abroad. He quickly learned the language, joined the SEU, and began exchanging letters with pen pals in Sweden, Spain, and France in 1931. He was guilty, he said, of writing on occasion to his Esperantist correspondents about the "difficult— in my opinion—life of the peasants" in the USSR. This nefarious activity, the NKVD charged, was an international extension of Luk'ianin's counterrevolutionary agitation against collectivization that he was said to have conducted among the local peasantry. According to the NKVD's narrative of events, Pyotr Luk'ianin was an enemy of the people, through and through. The son, Valentin Luk'ianin, noted that not once did the NKVD interrogator correctly spell the word "Esperanto" in the entire file recording his father's unhappy and unjust end.[31]

G. P. Demidiuk learned Esperanto in 1909, when he was just 14 years old. In his youth he participated actively in prerevolutionary Moscow Esperanto circles—a pastime interrupted by World War I and then the Russian Civil War. After demobilization, Demidiuk returned to Moscow and fatefully saw one of the SEU's early posters plastered on a building. Demidiuk joined the SEU and immersed himself in its work, focusing on its publishing program in particular. In the 1920s, he traveled abroad with Drezen to international SAT congresses and was present at the fateful Leipzig congress where Drezen challenged Lanti and quipped that he was a better Esperantist than communist. In addition to his work within the SEU, Demidiuk served socialist construction as a mining engineer. He would later recall that in the 1930s, he spent less of his time at the SEU and more time studying industrial mining techniques. In 1938, Demidiuk successfully defended his dissertation. Shortly thereafter, he was arrested and charged with participating in counterrevolutionary activity under the mask of Esperantism. Sent to the Gulag, Demidiuk spent nearly eighteen years in the camps. He was rehabilitated in 1955. The following year, he returned to Moscow and took up a position at the Mining Institute of the Soviet Academy of Sciences, where he worked until his retirement in 1980.[32]

The prominent Leningrad Esperantist S. N. Podkaminer managed to escape arrest, but later recalled how his world crashed spectacularly and terrifyingly all around him during the Purges and Terror. As his friends and colleagues were arrested, he remembered, he was left to sit at home "trembling" as he waited for what increasingly seemed to be the inevitable dreaded knock on his own door.[33] While that knock on the door never came for Podkaminer, it came for hundreds of Esperantists throughout the Soviet Union. The precise number of arrests and executions of the Soviet Esperantists may never be known with certainty, but what was clear to those Esperantists who remained relatively unscathed by the wave of repression that violently washed over the Soviet Esperantist movement in 1936–8 was that their specific brand of internationalism had been deemed treasonous and dangerously un-Soviet. Esperantists throughout Europe and the world who had been in regular or semi-regular contact with Soviet comrades in the years (if not decades) prior to the wave of arrests of Esperantists that began in 1936 noted a stunning silence as they looked in vain for letters to arrive via post from the Soviet Union. Esperanto radio broadcasts from the Soviet Union conspicuously disappeared from the airwaves.[34] Rumors of the Soviet Esperantists' demise began to circulate among their comrades abroad as early as 1936, according to Ulrich Lins. Only during Khrushchev's Thaw, Lins writes, did details about the fate of the Soviet Esperantists repressed during the Purges and Terror begin to trickle across Soviet borders.[35]

Other stories took much longer to cross Soviet borders. Varlam Shalamov wrote his *Kolyma Tales* in the years following his own release from the Gulag in 1951. Shalamov's bracing autofictional portraits of the relentless suffering of everyday life in the Gulag featured vignettes of several encounters with Esperantists—prisoners who, alongside Shalamov, struggled to survive their terms in the camps. In Shalamov's short story "Esperanto," a fellow prisoner sputters bitterly: "I'm an Esperantist. Got it? The universal language. Not some 'Basic English' rubbish. And I got sentenced because of Esperanto." In the Soviet Union, Shalamov's *Kolyma Tales* were published only posthumously in 1989.[36]

In 1959, Ida Lisichnik reflected on her life of Esperantism from the vantage point of her nearly sixty-six years and of her own fortunate survival of the very worst of Stalin's Terror. Born in 1893, Lisichnik was a 19-year-old student in Kiev when she first learned of Esperanto from a friend. "I still remember," she recalled, "how the very idea of an international language astonished me." Lisichnik was dazzled and inspired by the idea of a language that had been created with the express purpose of giving a world divided into nations "a unified language for communication, a language of goodwill and friendship." Esperanto, she believed, would heal the world's divisions, would deliver humanity from the scourge of language diversity. "I was literally burning with enthusiasm," she recalled.

Lisichnik's enthusiasm for Esperanto only grew after the revolutionary events of 1917. A young woman at the time of the October Revolution, Lisichnik enrolled in an institute of international relations in Kiev and honed her skills in German, French, and English while also pursuing her Esperanto activism on the side. In 1927, Lisichnik moved to Sevastopol where she single-handedly kickstarted a culture of Esperantism in this provincial city. She established an Esperanto department at the local newspaper and organized Esperanto courses, clubs, pen pal campaigns, and workers' circles. Lisichnik recruited more than 1,500 workers in Sevastopol to join the SEU. Lisichnik would later recall with pride that in the early 1930s Party officials in Crimea as well as in Moscow regularly celebrated her exemplary internationalist activism. Yet in composing her autobiography as a Soviet Esperantist in 1959, Lisichnik recounted proud and happy memories of a Soviet Esperantist youth that conspicuously dated only to the mid-1930s. She mentioned nothing of the repression that her Soviet Esperantist comrades suffered, let alone her own suffering during Stalin's Terror. In closing her brief reminiscences, she wished only to acknowledge her fellow tireless Esperantists all over the world who still remained committed to the international solidarity that the language helped them to achieve.[37]

Visiting Lisichnik at her home in Kutaisi in 1967 to write a profile on this aging pensioner, a Soviet journalist found evidence everywhere of the Esperantist dreams that continued to inspire her: bookshelves of Esperantist (and English) texts and a desk littered with envelopes containing letters received from correspondents in dozens of foreign countries. It was clear, the journalist wrote, that the ten years that Lisichnik spent actively engaged in distinctly Esperantist Soviet internationalism in Sevastopol— that is, from 1927 until 1937—was the "very brightest page in her biography."[38] Lisichnik disclosed nothing of her personal experience of the Terror—the repression that followed once one of her comrades in Kiev named her under interrogation as a participant in the vast Trotskyite conspiracy of Esperantist spies that the NKVD was so insistent on "unmasking" in 1937-8.[39] As late as 1973, Lisichnik still insisted that Esperanto had given her the "happiest days of my life."[40]

* * *

The happiest days of Ida Lisichnik's life represent an era of great hope and great anxiety— an era of globalization that opened up new possibilities for ordinary people like Lisichnik to fashion themselves into global citizens and to network into transnational communities that defied linguistic and political borders. In the late nineteenth and early twentieth centuries, ordinary women and men across the globe contemplated the rapid shrinking of their world and sought new identities for themselves within it. They embraced revolutionary new technologies and novel social networks that allowed them to communicate effectively with others across vast physical and cultural distances. Among them were those, like Ida Lisichnik, who seriously grappled with the persistent question of an international language and who sought a solution to the dilemmas of language diversity that was at once—at least in their minds—both practical and revolutionary.

For Esperantists like Lisichnik and tens of thousands of others—in Russia and around the world—Zamenhof's international auxiliary language promised not only effective international communication, but also an attractive, meaningful mode of self-transformation. In sharing their thoughts and ideas with fellow Esperantists all over the world, they networked themselves into a global community that transcended linguistic and geographic borders and offered them both a sense of universal purpose and real, meaningful relationships with comrades and friends, near and far. Esperanto, they believed, was the ideal and most modern mechanism for uniting the world without flattening it or obliterating human differences. By means of a shared international auxiliary language, Esperantists believed, humanity could realize itself in the truest sense and in the most humane of ways.

Moreover, Esperanto did not nullify or demean their locally rooted sense of self. Esperantism did not demand sublimation in the global at the expense of the local. On the contrary, it encouraged a global consciousness and a practical internationalism that was not only informed by, but also rooted in individual Esperantists' local community as much as by the hoped-for unity of humankind. From the start, Zamenhof's vision of Esperanto insisted that humankind's unity could only be achieved through the fostering of mutual respect and empathic, respectful communication between diverse peoples. Esperanto was designed not to trounce the world's diverse linguistic, ethnic, and religious cultures or to set them into conflict with one another. Rather, it was designed to enable harmonious communication and real solidarity among people who could, Zamenhof believed, be taught to understand and respect each others' differences by means of an international auxiliary language that transcended those differences—that encouraged solidarity rather than sowed discord. Zamenhof's Esperanto was a utopian vision in an era of competing utopian schemes for humanity liberated by its own hand. In an "age of questions," Zamenhof offered Esperanto as a solution not only to the dilemma of international communication, but also to the challenge of seeing in our fellow human beings—so different as they often are from ourselves—their fundamental, inviolable humanity.[41] A shared international language, he promised, would give humankind not only the linguistic vehicle, but also the emotional vocabulary of shared humanity that was needed to achieve a truly humane global consciousness. It would give its speakers the psychology necessary for humanity to become one. The Esperantists who embraced Zamenhof's language challenged themselves but also the world to move purposefully toward a more just and moral human universe where all, theoretically, would be welcome to belong, to connect, to converse, and to become global citizens.

Those who dismiss Esperanto as a spectacular failure and who brush aside the Esperantists as quirky historical nobodies fail to see what Esperanto and Esperantists can help us to better understand about globalization in the fin de siècle. This was a revolutionary era that transformed how people traveled and communicated with one another. It upended how people thought about time, space, and their relationship to both. The late nineteenth and early twentieth centuries witnessed ordinary people's drawing in to a world's fair of new imagined communities, social networks, and circuits of exchange. These were national and transnational, local and global, planetary, and even intergalactic. As the world shrunk and the universe of possibilities expanded during this era, ordinary people reached out to the world and across borders. They sought not only global consciousness or a worldly identity, but also meaning and membership in global communities committed to humankind's transformation. Esperantists were not outliers. Rather, they were exemplars of the era that produced them. They were exemplars of the lived, ordinary internationalism that they pursued in the most creative and mundane of ways using the tools of their era's defining, all too self-conscious "cosmoplastic modernity."[42] They were self-styled, self-made global citizens empowered by a language that afforded them the opportunity to communicate above and beyond borders, as well as to fashion themselves as modern cosmopolitans. Esperanto offered people like Ida Lisichnik and many others like her an avenue toward feeling at home and consciously situated in the world—even if they never traveled beyond the borders of their hometowns, nations, or empires.

World War I betrayed the hopes of Esperantists and so many other ordinary internationalists who came of age in this era and who had hoped for a world healed of its worst divisions and united by expertise, science, commerce, and a bold vision of universal humanity. The Great War devastated a generation, collapsed European empires, enabled the spread of a global pandemic, inspired the creation of new national borders, and helped to harden and further entrench interethnic and international animosities across the globe. In all its widespread devastation, World War I also helped to unleash visions of a radical, liberating future and to inspire hope of a better future. In Russia, exasperated women and men protested in the streets and the monarchy swiftly crumbled under the weight of decades of imperial crisis. When the Bolsheviks seized power in late 1917, they moved—against all odds—to bring their socialist revolution to the farthest corners of what remained of the tsars' enormous empire and to ignite a truly global proletarian revolution.

In revolutionary Russia, young Esperantists hinged Esperanto to the fate of the Bolsheviks' vision of a worldwide October. They raised the same question that Esperantists had been posing for decades, only now they framed it as an urgent matter of proletarian internationalism, of global communism. Without an international auxiliary language, they argued, the world's workers could neither communicate nor unite. In order for the global proletariat to achieve the shared goal of socialism worldwide, they required a shared, nonnational—indeed supranational—universal and auxiliary language. Adopting Esperanto as the international auxiliary language of the global proletariat was the only revolutionary way to defy the chauvinism that inhered in prerevolutionary international relations, they claimed. Eager young Esperantists hailed Zamenhof's language as the only true worker's international language—one that did not require extensive schooling to master. In their vision of the global communist future, Esperanto was fated to become the lingua franca of proletarian internationalism.

As this book has shown, Esperanto's fate in the early Soviet Union proved lackluster at its very best. Esperanto was all but doomed by an overriding Bolshevik disinterest from the start. Despite all the obstacles they faced, however, the eager Esperantists of the SEU pushed forward with dogged determination. Even while the Comintern repeatedly rebuffed their efforts to make Esperanto the international auxiliary language of the Comintern and its transnational networks of global revolution, they remained intent on deploying Zamenhof's creation as a useful language of Soviet cultural diplomacy and international communication in the patriotic Soviet interest. The leaders as well as the rank and file of the SEU served as Esperantist guides to the Soviet Union and the triumphant future that the Bolsheviks foretold. They attempted to live revolution as globally conscious Soviet patriots. As Esperantists, they deployed their niche language skills toward serving the Bolsheviks' domestic and foreign policy goals. They assumed the roles of pen pals, worker-correspondents, radio enthusiasts, language teachers, tour guides, translators, interpreters, transmitters of technical expertise, revolutionary linguists, theorists of the higher phase of communism, and anti-fascists. Perhaps most successfully of all, they kept alive the question of international language and international communication. They pressed for answers to the question of how best the global proletariat might communicate and collaborate in the era of building socialism. They demanded thoughtful anticipation and sober imagining of the global language of the communist future. They also demonstrated the relative ease with which men and women all over the world could effectively communicate in an international auxiliary language—a moral and righteous endeavor, they insisted, that required a mere modicum of effort and investment on the part of the proletariat and its defenders.

By the mid-1930s, the Soviet Esperantists' ardent global-mindedness no less than their investment in transnational Esperantist networks came under increasing scrutiny and suspicion. In a Stalinist culture that ever more ominously embraced xenophobia, isolationist retreat into both real and reasonable fears of external threats, and outsized conspiracy theories of subversion from within, Esperantists were swiftly demonized as enemies fluent in anti-Soviet conspiracy and international espionage. Although Soviet internationalism was not obliterated during the Purges and Terror of the late 1930s, the dream of grassroots proletarian internationalism powered by an international auxiliary language promising hope and unfiltered transnational conversations was foreclosed. The death of Esperanto in the Soviet Union may not have signaled the death of Soviet internationalism writ large, but it did spell the death of a vision of proletarian internationalism in the early Soviet Union that was premised on socialist liberation by means of a willing disavowal of traditional language power politics—and its attendant inequities—on the global stage. Stalin's Purges and Terror obliterated a unique vision of grassroots citizen diplomacy and cross-border solidarity that relied on Esperanto as an international auxiliary language with the power to transcend not only borders, but also state authority to micromanage cross-cultural exchange between ordinary people.

The death of Esperanto in Stalin's Soviet Union captures in stark and devastating fashion how foreign languages fit awkwardly in the Soviet internationalist imagination as practical necessities of profitable cross-border exchanges and yet as dangerous linguistic weapons of potential subversion, subterfuge, and espionage. As Eleonory Gilburd has noted, "The precarious balance between openness and security concerns, between internationalism and fear of foreigners remained a structural feature of the Soviet system until nearly the end."[43] The history of Esperanto in revolutionary Russia and its death in Stalin's Soviet Union reminds us not only of the practical dilemmas of international communication in a globalizing and fractured world or of the agency of a variety of actors who sought the best solutions to those dilemmas. It also highlights how ideologically fraught the internationalist politics of language were in the Soviet Union of Lenin, Stalin, and their successors.

The dream of socialist internationalism powered by Esperanto may have indeed died in gruesome fashion in the 1930s—in Stalin's Soviet Union no less than in Hitler's Germany.[44] Yet the death of Esperanto in the Soviet Union did not obviate the need for effective languages of socialist internationalism, nor did it by any means foretell an intended death of socialist internationalism under the guiding Soviet star.[45] Instead, Stalin's Soviet Union would—after surviving the apocalypse of World War II—strive to make real a linguistic priority seen in the Comintern in the interwar period: the elevation of Russian as the undisputed lingua franca of global communism. Against the backdrop of the early Cold War's hardening fractures, Stalin's Soviet Union sought energetically to make Russian *the* international language of socialism, the language of socialist superpower. The postwar Soviet Union invested Russian—the language of Lenin—with the power to transform a fractured globe and to unite the peoples of the socialist world, if not the world as a whole. As a language of global superpower rather than as an international auxiliary language, Russian deployed as a world language was not intended to transcend borders so much as to confidently cross and make effective use of those borders in the Soviet state's micromanaged interest. Recast as a world language, Russian was invested with the power not only to facilitate unequal partnerships between the Soviet Union and the socialist world, but also to transparently transact long-distance friendships between trusted Soviet citizens and foreigners abroad. Deployed as a world language, Russian would embody Soviet civilization, transmit Soviet culture and its values, and articulate the Soviet Union's superpower status.[46] Instead of languages of internationalism or a universal language, the Soviet Union opted instead for Russian as a world language, a language of superpower, a language of civilizational supremacy, a language of Cold War might and authority.

Amidst the babel of Cold War contests and clashes, Zamenhof's dream of humanity united in a shared international auxiliary language—in conversation among equals—scarcely registered a whisper. By then, Zamenhof's dream emitted but a faint echo in the global consciousness of this new Cold War era of competing worlds and worldviews. Except by those who remained among its erstwhile adepts, Esperanto was laid aside as a curious souvenir of an earlier—seemingly more hopeful—era of global entanglement, competing voices, transnational loyalties, and worlds colliding.

Notes

Introduction

1. C. A. Bayly, *The Birth of the Modern World, 1780–1914: Global Connections and Comparisons* (Oxford: Blackwell, 2004), chapter 13.
2. The best portrait of Esperantist culture from Zamenhof's launch of the language to the present day is Esther Schor, *Bridge of Words: Esperanto and the Dream of a Universal Language* (New York: Metropolitan Books, 2016). See also Young S. Kim, "Constructing a Global Identity: The Role of Esperanto," in *Constructing World Culture: International Nongovernmental Organizations Since 1875*, ed. John Boli and George M. Thomas (Stanford, CA: Stanford University Press, 1999), 127–48.
3. As Jessica Reinisch has so eloquently argued, a broad understanding of internationalism as encompassing "the complex social, cultural, political and economic connections between individuals from different states, regions, and locales" allows us to better appreciate the full variety of historical actors who have acted meaningfully in the past as "agents of internationalism." See her "Introduction: Agents of Internationalism," *Contemporary European History* 25, no. 2 (2016): 195–205 (quote on 200).
4. See, for example, the special section on the Russian Revolution's global impact in the *Journal of Contemporary History* as introduced in Mary Neuberger, "The 100th Anniversary of the Russian Revolution: Introduction," *Journal of Contemporary History* 52, no. 4 (2017): 807–15; Choi Chatterjee, Steven G. Marks, Mary Neuberger, and Steven Sabol, eds., *The Global Impact of Russia's Great War and Revolution, Book 2: The Wider Arc of the Russian Revolution*, 2 vols. (Bloomington, IN: Slavica, 2019).
5. See, for example, Jürgen Osterhammel, *The Transformation of the World: A Global History of the Nineteenth Century* (Princeton, NJ: Princeton University Press, 2014); Emily S. Rosenberg, *Transnational Currents in a Shrinking World 1870–1945* (Cambridge, MA: Harvard University Press, 2012); Glenda Sluga, *Internationalism in the Age of Nationalism* (Philadelphia: University of Pennsylvania Press, 2015); Peter N. Stearns, *Globalization in World History*, 2nd ed. (New York: Routledge, 2016), chapter 5.
6. Vanessa Ogle, *The Global Transformation of Time 1870–1950* (Cambridge, MA: Harvard University Press, 2015), 4.
7. Holly Case, *The Age of Questions: Or, a First Attempt at an Aggregate History of the Eastern, Social, Woman, American, Jewish, Polish, Bullion, Tuberculosis, and Many Other Questions Over the Nineteenth Century, and Beyond* (Princeton, NJ: Princeton University Press, 2018)
8. A notable and welcome exception is T. N. Harper, "Empire, Diaspora, and the Languages of Globalism, 1850–1914," in *Globalization in World History*, ed. A. G. Hopkins (New York: Norton, 2002), 141–66.
9. Roberto Garvia, *Esperanto and Its Rivals: The Struggle for an International Language* (Philadelphia: University of Pennsylvania Press, 2015); Michael D. Gordin, *Scientific*

Babel: How Science Was Done Before and After Global English (Chicago: University of Chicago Press, 2015). A valuable popular history of constructed languages is Akira Orent, *In the Land of Invented Languages: Esperanto Rock Stars, Klingon Poets, Loglan Lovers, and the Mad Dreamers Who Tried to Build a Perfect Language* (New York: Spiegel & Grau, 2009).

10. Garvia, *Esperanto and its Rivals*, chapters 2–6.
11. Sluga, *Internationalism*. See also Akira Iriye, *Cultural Internationalism and World Order* (Baltimore, MD: John Hopkins University Press, 1997).
12. Gordin, *Scientific Babel*, 110–1.
13. Dr. Esperanto [Zamenhof], *Mezhdunarodnyi iazyk: Predislovie i polnyi uchebnik [por Rusoj]* (Warsaw: Tipo-Litografiia Kh. Khel'tera, 1887 [reprinted in facsimile, Moscow: Moskva Gazeto, 1992]), 19.
14. Rossiiskii gosudarstvennyi istoricheskii arkhiv (RGIA) f. 776 o. 12 d. 56 l. 6ob.
15. Ogle, *Global Transformation*, 13.
16. Rosenberg, *Transnational Currents*, 86.
17. A recent exception is Edyta Bojanowska's compelling portrait of the nineteenth-century explosion of global consciousness and investment in imperial rivalry among tsarist Russia's educated elites. See her *A World of Empires: The Russian Voyage of the Frigate Pallada* (Cambridge, MA: Harvard University Press, 2018).
18. Gosudarstvennyi arkhiv Rossiiskoi Federatsii (GARF) f. 9550 o. 14 d. 19 l. 1.
19. Lisa Kirschenbaum, *International Communism and the Spanish Civil War: Solidarity and Suspicion* (Cambridge: Cambridge University Press, 2015), quote on 244.
20. Karl Qualls, *Stalin's Niños: Educating Spanish Civil War Refugee Children in the Soviet Union, 1937–1951* (Toronto: University of Toronto Press, 2020).
21. See, for example, Rachel Applebaum, *Empire of Friends: Soviet Power and Socialist Internationalism* (Ithaca, NY: Cornell University Press, 2019); Elidor Mëhilli, *From Stalin to Mao: Albania in the Socialist World* (Ithaca, NY: Cornell University Press, 2017).
22. Ana Antic, Johanna Conterio, and Dora Vargha, "Conclusion: Beyond Liberal Internationalism," *Contemporary European History* 25, no. 2 (2016): 359–71.
23. Katerina Clark, *Moscow The Fourth Rome: Stalinism, Cosmopolitanism, and the Evolution of Soviet Culture, 1931–1941* (Cambridge, MA: Harvard University Press, 2011); Michael David-Fox, *Crossing Borders: Modernity, Ideology, and Culture in Russia and the Soviet Union* (Pittsburgh, PA: Pittsburgh University Press, 2015), esp. chapters 6 and 7; Eleonory Gilburd, *To See Paris and Die: The Soviet Lives of Western Culture* (Cambridge, MA: Harvard University Press, 2018).
24. Michael David-Fox, *Showcasing the Great Experiment: Cultural Diplomacy and Western Visitors to the Soviet Union, 1921–1941* (New York: Oxford University Press, 2012); Michael David-Fox, "The Fellow Travelers Revisited: The 'Cultured' West through Soviet Eyes," *The Journal of Modern History* 75, no. 2 (2003): 300–35; and Sheila Fitzpatrick, "Foreigners Observed: Moscow Visitors in the 1930s Under the Gaze of their Soviet Guides," *Russian History/Histoire Russe* 35, nos. 1–2 (2008): 215–234.
25. See, for example, Kirschenbaum, *International Communism*; Julia L. Mickenberg, *American Girls in Red Russia: Chasing the Soviet Dream* (Chicago: University of Chicago Press, 2017); Choi Chatterjee, "Imperial Subjects in the Soviet Union: M.N. Roy, Rabindranath Tagore, and Re-Thinking Freedom and Authoritarianism," *Journal of Contemporary History* 52, no. 4 (2017): 913–34; Elizabeth McGuire, *Red at Heart: How Chinese Communists Fell in Love with the Russian Revolution*

(Oxford: Oxford University Press, 2017); Brigitte Studer, *The Transnational World of the Cominternarians*, trans. Dafydd Rees Roberts (London: Palgrave Macmillan, 2015); and Glennys Young, *The Communist Experience in the Twentieth Century: A Global History through Sources* (New York: Oxford University Press, 2012).

26. Notable exceptions are Rachel Applebaum, "The Rise of Russian in the Cold War: How Three Worlds Made a World Language," *Kritika: Explorations in Russian and Eurasian History* 21, no. 2 (2020): 347–70; Gilburd, *To See Paris and Die*; Kirschenbaum, *International Communism*, especially chapter 3; McGuire, *Red at Heart*; and McGuire, "Sino-Soviet Every Day: Chinese Revolutionaries in Moscow Military Schools," in *Everyday Life in Russia Past and Present*, ed. Choi Chatterjee, David L. Ransel, Mary Cavender, and Karen Petrone (Bloomington: Indiana University Press, 2014), 329–49.
27. On these contests, see especially Applebaum, "The Rise of Russian," and Michael D. Gordin, "The Forgetting and Rediscovery of Soviet Machine Translation," *Critical Inquiry* 46 (Summer 2020): 835–66.

1 A Universal Language for a Globalizing World

1. Zamenhof, *Mezhdunarodnyi iazyk*, 3–4.
2. Ibid., 9. Italics and emphasis as in original.
3. Garvia, *Esperanto and Its Rivals*; Gordin, *Scientific Babel*.
4. Sluga, *Internationalism*.
5. Zamenhof, *Mezhdunarodnyi iazyk*, 5. Italics as in the original.
6. Edmond Privat, *The Life of Zamenhof*, trans. Ralph Elliot (London: George Allen & Unwin, 1931); Marjorie Boulton, *Zamenhof: Creator of Esperanto* (London: Routledge and Paul, 1960).
7. Schor, *Bridge of Words*; Aleksandr Korzhenkov, *Zamenhof: The Life, Works and Ideas of the Author of Esperanto*, trans. Ian M. Richmond (New York: Mondial, 2009); Roberto Garvia, "Religion and Artificial Languages at the Turn of the Twentieth Century: Ostwald and Zamenhof," *Language Problems and Language Planning* 37, no. 1 (2013): 47–70; and Ulrich Lins, *Dangerous Language: Esperanto under Hitler and Stalin*, trans. Humphrey Tonkin (London: Palgrave Macmillan) 1: chapter 1. See also Norman Berdichevsky, "Zamenhof and Esperanto," *Ariel* 64 (1986): 58–71; Liora R. Halperin, "Modern Hebrew, Esperanto, and the Quest for a Universal Language," *Jewish Social Studies* 19, no. 1 (2012): 1–33.
8. Boulton, *Zamenhof*; Peter G. Forster, *The Esperanto Movement* (The Hague: Mouten, 1982), chapter 2; Korzhenkov, *Zamenhof*; Privat, *Life of Zamenhof*. Authored by specialists working outside the field of Russian history, even the best of recent revisionist studies of Esperanto's early history do not endeavor to historicize Zamenhof in his broader imperial Russian context. Garvia, *Esperanto and Its Rivals*; Lins, *Dangerous Language*; and Schor, *Bridge of Worlds*.
9. I borrow this useful phrase from Joseph Bradley, *Voluntary Associations in Tsarist Russia: Science, Patriotism, and Civil Society* (Cambridge, MA: Harvard University Press, 2009), 5.
10. Sara Bender, *The Jews of Bialystok during World War II and the Holocaust*, trans. by YaVa Murciano (Lebanon, NH: Brandeis University Press, 2008), 17. The nineteenth century witnessed a dramatic growth of tsarist Russia's Jewish population generally,

leading to stunning demographic changes in cities throughout the Pale and, by century's end, a markedly "young and mobile" Russian Jewry. Benjamin Nathans, "The Jews," in *The Cambridge History of Russia. Volume II: Imperial Russia, 1689-1917* (Cambridge: Cambridge University Press, 2006), 191-2.
11. Bender, *Jews of Bialystok*, 4-13.
12. On the introduction of state-sponsored Jewish schools in the Pale and their intended goals of Jewish integration into the imperial Russian social order, see Benjamin Nathans, *Beyond the Pale: The Jewish Encounter with Late Imperial Russia* (Berkeley: University of California Press, 2002), 35-7.
13. Korzhenkov, *Zamenhof*, 8.
14. Boulton, *Zamenhof*, quotes on pp. 74 and 1.
15. Quoted in Lins, *Dangerous Language*, 5.
16. See Nathans, *Beyond the Pale*, quote on 67. For an excellent and remarkably concise account of how proponents of Haskalah and tsarist bureaucrats struggled to achieve Jewish integration in imperial Russian life see also Nathans, "The Jews."
17. Schor, *Bridge of Words*, 28.
18. "Esperanto and Jewish Ideals: Interview for the Jewish Chronicle with Dr. Zamenhof," *The Jewish Chronicle* (London), September 6, 1907: 16.
19. Rebecca Kobrin, *Jewish Bialystok and its Diaspora* (Bloomington: Indiana University Press, 2010).
20. Korzhenkov claims that at the time, Mark Zamenhof was "one of only three Jews teaching in Warsaw's schools." See his *Zamenhof*, 10.
21. L. L. Zamenhof, *The Birth of Esperanto: Extract of a Private Letter from L. L. Zamenhof to N. Borovko* (Fort Lee, NJ: Esperanto Association of North America, 1931), 8. Italics as in the original.
22. Leon Zamengof, *Iz biografii D-ra Liudovika Zamengofa*, trans. K. K. Petriaevskii (Saratov: Eldono de Esperanta Biblioteka Georg Davidov, 1918), 5.
23. Nathans, *Beyond the Pale*, 215.
24. Ibid., chapter 6.
25. Ibid.
26. Privat, *Life of Zamenhof*, 22-3.
27. Schor, *Bridge of Words*, 67.
28. "Esperanto and Jewish Ideals," 17.
29. Boulton, *Zamenhof*, 19.
30. See Schor, *Bridge of Words*, 66; "Esperanto and Jewish Ideals," 17; and Korzhenkov, *Zamenhof*, 11.
31. John Doyle Klier, *Russians, Jews, and the Pogroms of 1881-1882* (Cambridge: Cambridge University Press, 2014); Nathans, *Beyond the Pale*, esp. 186-98; Jonathan Frankel, "The Crisis of 1881-1882 as a Turning Point in Modern Jewish History," in *The Legacy of Jewish Migration: 1881 and Its Impact*, ed. David Berger (New York: Columbia University Press, 1983): 9-22.
32. Boulton, *Zamenhof*, 23-4.
33. Gamzefon, "Chto zhe nakonets delat'?" *Razsvet*, nos. 2-5 (January-February 1882), reproduced in Adolf Holzhaus, *Doktoro kaj Lingvo Esperanto* (Helsinki: Fondumo Esperanto, 1969), 91-114.
34. Ibid., 102.
35. Ibid., 106.
36. Ibid., 114. A delegation of Jews had recently departed imperial Russia and, in 1881, set up a colony at Sicily Island, Louisiana. Their excessively optimistic reports about their

progress were publicized in Russia's Jewish press. It seems likely that these reports inspired Zamenhof's vision of Lousiana as a promised land. On the short-lived Sicily Island colony, see Klier, *Russians, Jews, and the Pogroms*, 276-7.
37. Gamzefon, "Chto zhe nakonets delat'," 112.
38. Theodore R. Weeks, *Nation and State in Late Imperial Russia: Nationalism and Russification on the Western Frontier, 1863-1914* (DeKalb: Northern Illinois University Press, 1996), 118-19.
39. On the quota system and its impacts, see Nathans, *Beyond the Pale*, esp. 266-81.
40. Ibid., 198.
41. "Esperanto and Jewish Ideals," 17.
42. Boulton, *Zamenhof*, 25-32; Schor, *Bridge of Words*, 67-9; Gamzefon, "Pod obshchee znamia!" *Razsvet*, nos. 13 (March 26, 1882), reproduced in Holzhaus, *Doktoro kaj Lingvo Esperanto*, 115-20; Shulamit Laskov, "Zamenhof's Letter to the Bilium," *Zionism* 1, no. 2 (1980): 151-7.
43. Richard Stites, *Revolutionary Dreams: Utopian Vision and Experimental Life in the Russian Revolution* (New York: Oxford University Press, 1991), chapter 1.
44. Boulton, *Zamenhof*, 27.
45. Ibid., 32.
46. Holzhaus, *Doktoro kaj lingvo Esperanto*, 275. As for the *Unua Libro*'s English edition, Esther Schor notes that the first version was "so faulty—and so much in demand— that it had to be redone a year later." Schor, *Bridge of Words*, 72.
47. Korzhenkov, *Zamenhof*, 16.
48. Quoted in ibid., 28.
49. "Esperanto and Jewish Ideals," 16.
50. Zamenhof, *Mezhdunarodnyi iazyk*, 5.
51. Ibid., 5.
52. Zamenhof, *Mezhdunarodnyi iazyk*, 30-4.
53. See "Vsemirnyi iazyk Esperanto," *Niva* no. 45 (1888): 1135. See also Holzhaus, *Doktoro kaj lingvo*, 76-86.
54. Holzhaus, *Doktoro kaj lingvo*, 266. The full list of the one thousand names and addresses has been reproduced online at https://eo.wikisource.org/wiki/Adresaro_de_la_personoj_kiuj_ellernis_la_lingvon_%22Esperanto%22/Serio_I (accessed September 11, 2017).
55. Holzhaus, *Doktoro kaj lingvo*, 269.
56. Schor, *Bridge of Words*, 72.
57. See Korzhenkov, *Zamenhof*, 22-5. In 1892, the journal simplified its name to simply *Esperantisto*. Many of its articles have been reproduced in L. L. Zamenhof, *Originala Verkaro. Antauparoloj, Gazetartikoloj, Traktajoj, Paroladoj, Leteroj, Poemoj* (Leipzig: Ferdinand Hirt & Sohn, 1929), 55-214.
58. "Al novaj landoj!" *La Esperantisto* no. 70 (1893): 45, as reprinted in Zamenhof, *Originala Verkaro*, 171.
59. Zamenhof, *Birth of Esperanto*, 4. Italics as in original.
60. Borovko was the founder of Odessa's Esperanto society and in the 1890s worked energetically to advance the language, most notably by writing original fiction for *La Esperantisto*. Borovko is said to have learned Esperanto in 1889 while exiled in Siberia. See Geoffrey Sutton, *Concise Encyclopedia of the Original Literature of Esperanto, 1887-2007* (New York: Mondial, 2008), 38.
61. Published in Sweden, *Lingvo Internacia* began publication in late 1895 and operated independently from Zamenhof. Korzhenkov, *Zamenhof*, 31.

62. Zamenhof, *Birth of Esperanto*, 4.
63. Ibid., 4.
64. Ibid., 6, 8.
65. Ibid., 10.
66. Ibid., 12.
67. Ibid., 14.
68. Ibid., 6.
69. On the widening politics and institutionalization of nationality (ethnicity) in late imperial Russia, see Juliette Cadiot, "Searching for Nationality: Statistics and National Categories at the End of the Russian Empire (1897–1917)," *The Russian Review* 64, no. 3 (2005): 440–55; Charles Steinwedel, "To Make a Difference: the Category of Ethnicity in Late Imperial Russian Politics, 1861–1917," in *Russian Modernity*, ed. David L. Hoffmann and Yanni Kotsonis (New York: St. Martin's, 2000), 67–86; Charles Steinwedel, "Making Social Groups, One Person at a Time: The Identification of Individuals by Estate, Religious Confession, and Ethnicity in Late Imperial Russia," in *Documenting Individual Identity: The Development of State Practices since the French Revolution*, ed. Jane Caplan and John Torpey (Princeton, NJ: Princeton University Press, 2000), 67–82; and Weeks, *Nation and State in Late Imperial Russia*. In an argument that Zamenhof would have surely appreciated, Paul Werth has shown how the late imperial politicization of ethnicity was entangled in long-standing imperial conceptions of faith as constitutive of peoples. See his *The Tsar's Foreign Faiths: Toleration and the Fate of Religious Freedom in Imperial Russia* (New York: Oxford University Press, 2014), especially chapter 6. On how increasingly elusive were the parameters of a collective Jewish identity in late imperial Russia, and how this reality complicated tsarist efforts to document and institutionalize nationality in the late nineteenth and early twentieth centuries, see Eugene M. Avrutin, *Jews and the Imperial State: Identification Politics in Tsarist Russia* (Ithaca, NY: Cornell University Press, 2010).
70. Cadiot, "Searching for Nationality."
71. Gomo Sum [Zamenhof], *Gillelizm: Proekt resheniia evreiskogo voprosa* (Warsaw: Tip. M. Veidenfel'd i Ig. Khel'ter, 1901). On the Jewish philosophers who appear to have inspired Zamenhof's formulation of Hillelism, see Garvia, "Religion and Artificial Languages," especially 54–63.
72. "Esperanto and Jewish Ideals," 17.
73. Zamenhof, *Gillelizm*, 4.
74. Ibid., 9.
75. Zamenhof scoffed at the notion that ancient Hebrew could be considered the Jews' national language, as they did not speak it in contemporary times. He also disqualified Yiddish as the Jews' national language, owing to its status as a "jargon." Ibid., 10–11.
76. Ibid., 8.
77. "Esperanto and Jewish Ideals," 17.
78. Zamenhof praised the United States as a place where Jews at the very least enjoyed equal rights and civic belonging. See Zamenhof, *Gillelizm*, 52.
79. Ibid., 17.
80. Schor, *Bridge of Words*, chapter 3; idem., "L.L. Zamenhof and the Shadow People," *Language Problems and Language Planning* 34, no. 2 (2010): 183–92.
81. Zamenhof, *Gillelizm*, 8.
82. "Esperanto and Jewish Ideals," 17.
83. Zamenhof, *Gillelizm*, 41.

84. Ibid., 52.
85. Ibid., 55–7, quote on 57. His objections to Hebrew and Yiddish are repeated at various points in the text.
86. Ibid., 58–9.
87. Ibid., 64.
88. Ibid., 71–3.
89. On Zamenhof as a "prophet of idealism," see Privat's hagiographic account, *Life of Zamenhof,* quote on 50. Privat argues that Russia's Jewish Esperantists regarded Zamenhof's Hillelism as "too idealistic" (53).
90. Ibid., 54.
91. Quoted in Boulton, *Zamenhof,* 78–9.
92. Quoted in Esther Schor, *Bridge of Words,* 87.
93. Quoted in ibid., 59.
94. Ibid., 86.
95. Quoted in ibid., 87.
96. See Boulton, *Zamenhof,* 78; Schor, *Bridge of Words,* 87.
97. Quoted in Boulton, *Zamenhof,* 79.
98. Quoted in ibid., 80–1.
99. The Boulogne Declaration can be read online at https://web.archive.org/web/20140506075349/http://aktuale.info/en/biblioteko/dokumentoj/1905 (accessed July 7, 2017).
100. Quoted in Boulton, *Zamenhof,* 85. Esther Schor has deconstructed the mistaken but popular idea that Esperantism was thus defined as politically neutral. She argues that "Esperanto is *essentially* political…. It was created to enable diverse peoples to talk not only past their differences but also about them." See her *Bridge of Words* (quote on 10). On how Esperantists have variously understood and at times contested Zamenhof's principle of neutrality, see Federico Gobbo, "Beyond the Nation-State? The Ideology of the Esperanto Movement between Neutralism and Multilingualism," *Social Inclusion* 5, no. 4 (2017): 38–47.
101. Quoted in Boulton, *Zamenhof,* 82.
102. Schor, *Bridge of Words,* 87.
103. The backstory to the Boulogne events has only recently been given adequate treatment in Esther Schor's *Bridge of Words,* 82–91.
104. The exceptions were during the First and Second World Wars. In 2020, the 105th World Esperanto Congress scheduled to take place in Montreal was canceled owing to the COVID-19 pandemic and replaced with virtual programming.
105. Berdichevsky, "Zamenhof and Esperanto," *Ariel,* p. 58.
106. Garvia, *Esperanto and Its Rivals,* chapter 10 (quote on 79).
107. Russian Esperantists appreciated the coincidence of the separate international meetings in Boulogne and Portsmouth in August 1905. The editors of the journal *Ruslanda Esperantisto* speculated openly that the Portsmouth proceedings could only have gone more smoothly had Esperanto been deployed as a language of diplomacy. See "La Bulona Kongreso," *Ruslanda Esperantisto* 1, no. 3–4 (September–October 1905): 82–3.
108. Quoted in Boulton, *Zamenhof,* 98–9.
109. These figures are borrowed from Robert Weinberg, "Workers, Pogroms, and the 1905 Revolution in Odessa," *The Russian Review* 46, no. 1 (1987), 53. On the Bialystok pogrom of June 1906, see "From Kishineff to Bialystok: A Table of Pogroms from 1903 to 1906," *American Jewish Year Book* 8 (September 20, 1906): 34–89. See

also Shlomo Lambroza, "The Pogroms of 1903–1906," in *Pogroms: Anti-Jewish Violence in Modern Russian History*, ed. John D. Klier and Shlomo Lambroza (Cambridge: Cambridge University Press, 1992), 195–247.
110. Jane Burbank, "An Imperial Rights Regime: Law and Citizenship in the Russian Empire," *Kritika: Explorations in Russian and Eurasian History* 7, no. 3 (2006): 397–431.
111. Yanni Kotsonis, *States of Obligation: Taxes and Citizenship in the Russian Empire and Early Soviet Republic* (Toronto: University of Toronto Press, 2014) and Joshua A. Sanborn, *Drafting the Nation: Military Conscription, Total War, and Mass Politics, 1905–1925* (Dekalb: Northern Illinois University Press, 2003).
112. Stites, *Revolutionary Dreams*, chapter 1.
113. [Zamenhof], "Dogmaty Gillelizma / Dogmoj de Hilelismo," *Ruslanda Esperantisto* 2, no, 1 (January 1906): 1–2.
114. Ibid., 2–3.
115. Ibid., 3. The "Tenets of Hillelism," authored by Zamenhof, were purported by him to be the work of a circle of Hillelists and were presented as such to the readers of *Ruslanda Esperantisto*. It is doubtful he fooled anyone.
116. Ibid., 4.
117. Ibid., 5–11.
118. Quoted in Boulton, *Zamenhof*, 107–8.
119. Quoted in ibid., 108–9.
120. Schor, "Zamenhof and the Shadow People," 188. See also her *Bridge of Words*, 91–4.
121. P-ro A. Dombrovski, "Kelkaj rimarkoj pri hilelismo," *Ruslanda Esperantisto* 2, no. 3 (March 1906): 50.
122. [Zamenhof], "Prilozhenie k 'Dogmatam Gillelizma' / Aldono al la 'Dogmoj de Hilelismo,'" *Ruslanda Esperantisto* 2, no. 2 (February 1906): 27. This rebranding did little to further his cause. To avoid confusion, I will continue in the text to refer to Zamenhof's programmatic vision as Hillelism.
123. "Esperanto and Jewish Ideals," 17.
124. Quoted in Privat, *Life of Zamenhof*, 79.
125. Ido means "offspring" in Esperanto and its proponents were often decried as "Idiots" (and worse) by diehard Esperantists. On the Ido split and controversy, see Boulton, *Zamenhof*, 122–35; Foster, *The Esperanto Movement*, chapter 4; Garvia, *Esperanto and Its Rivals*, chapter 16; Schor, *Bridge of Words*, 94–9.
126. On Zamenhof's prodigious translation efforts, see Boulton, *Zamenhof*, 167–77.
127. L. L. Zamenhof, "International Language," in *Papers on Inter-Racial Problems Communicated to the First Universal Races Congress*, ed. G. Spiller (London: P. S. King & Son, 1911), 430.
128. L. L. Zamenhof, "After the Great War: An Appeal to Diplomatists," *The British Esperantist* no. 123 (1915): 51.
129. Boulton, *Zamenhof*, 192.
130. Schor, "Zamenhof and the Shadow People," 190.

2 Pen Pals, Dreamers, and Globe-Trotters

1. RGIA f. 776 o. 12 d. 56 l. 2.
2. Ibid., l. 4.

3. Ibid., l. 5.
4. Ibid., l. 6.
5. Ibid., l. 6ob.
6. Ibid., l. 7ob.
7. Ibid., l. 9.
8. Forster, *The Esperanto Movement*, 66.
9. Joseph Rhodes, "Progress and Prospects of Esperanto," *North American Review* 184, no. 608 (1907): 282.
10. Historians of Russia have effectively dismantled this long-standing claim, yet it persists in popular and in some scholarly accounts. See Bradley, *Voluntary Associations in Tsarist Russia*, especially chapter 1 (quote on 5).
11. See Rosenberg, *Transnational Currents*, especially chapter 2.
12. Quoted in Lins, *Dangerous Language* 1: 10.
13. Zinoviev, *Mezhdunarodnyi iazyk "Esperanto"* (St. Petersburg: Muller and Bogel'man, 1890), 3.
14. Ibid., 10. As Osterhammel notes, even "to think in terms of networks was a nineteenth-century development" and systems of communication, transportation, commerce, and public utilities were never so newly networked as they were in the years between the Crimean and First World Wars. See Osterhammel, *Transformation of the World*, 710–11 (quote on 711).
15. Zinoviev, *Mezhdunarodnyi iazyk*, 10–12 (quote on 12).
16. V. L. Kravtsov, *Vazhnoe delo* (Boguchar: I. Ivanova, 1891), 5–6.
17. Ibid., 12–13.
18. Ibid., quote on 15.
19. Leon Trotsky, *My Life: An Attempt at an Autobiography* (New York: Charles Scribner's Sons, 1931), 16.
20. Educated urbanites in fin de siècle Russia were very self-conscious of the modernity of their times, and they agonized over catastrophe even while they dreamed of modernity's promises of liberation. See Mark D. Steinberg, *Petersburg Fin de Siècle* (New Haven, CT: Yale University Press, 2011).
21. See, for example, Simone M. Muller, *Wiring the World: The Social and Cultural Creation of Global Telegraph Networks* (New York: Columbia University Press, 2015); Marsha Siefert, "'Chingis-Khan with the Telegraph': Communications in the Russian and Ottoman Empires," in *Comparing Empires: Encounters and Transfers in the Long Nineteenth Century*, ed. Jorn Leonhard and Ulrike von Hirschhausen (Gottingen: Vandenhoeck and Ruprecht, 2011): 78–108; Ogle, *Global Transformation of Time*, especially chapter 6; Graham Murdock and Michael Pickering, "The Birth of Distance: Communications and changing conceptions of elsewhere," in *Narrating Media History*, ed. Michael Bailey (London: Routledge, 2008): 171–83; Tom Standage, *The Victorian Internet: The Remarkable Story of the Telegraph and the Nineteenth Century's On-line Pioneers* (New York: Walker and Company, 1998); Roland Wenzlhuemer, *Connecting the Nineteenth-Century World: The Telegraph and Globalization* (Cambridge: Cambridge University Press, 2012).
22. For an excellent case study in this global competition to build and dominate a "world wireless network," see Heidi Tworek, *News from Germany: The Competition to Control World Communications, 1900–1945* (Cambridge, MA: Harvard University Press, 2019), especially chapter 2.

23. Simone M. Muller and Heidi J. S. Tworek, "'The Telegraph and the Bank': On the Interdependence of Global Communications and Capitalism, 1866–1914," *Journal of Global History* 10, no. 2 (2015): 259–83.
24. Peter A. Shulman, "Ben Franklin's Ghost: World Peace, American Slavery, and the Global Politics of Information before the Universal Postal Union." *Journal of Global History* 10, no. 2 (2015): 212–34; Léonard Laborie, Global Commerce in Small Boxes: Parcel Post, 1878–1913." *Journal of Global History* 10, no. 2 (2015): 235–58.
25. David M. Henkin, *The Postal Age: The Emergence of Modern Communications in Nineteenth-Century America* (Chicago: University of Chicago Press, 2006).
26. Ibid., 172–3. It was renamed the Universal Postal Union in 1878.
27. *Adresaro de la Esperantistoj. Serio XVI.* (Warsaw: A. Gins, 1896).
28. RGIA f. 776 o. 8 d. 1902 l. 2.
29. D. V. Vlasov, *Istoriia primeneniia Esperanto v Rossii: pechat', radioveshchanie, perepiska, samizdat* (Moscow: Impeto, 2014), 22.
30. D. V. Vlasov, *Esperanto: polveka tsenzury. Razvitie Esperanto-dvizheniia i ego zhurnalistiki v usloviiakh tsenzury v Rossiiskoi imperii i SSSR (1887–1938 gg.)* (Moscow: Impeto, 2011), 16.
31. Quoted in ibid., 17.
32. RGIA f. 776 o. 8 d. 873 ll. 1–1ob.
33. Vlasov, *Esperanto: polveka tsenzury*, 20–21 (quote on 21).
34. Marianna Tax Choldin, *A Fence around the Empire: Russian Censorship of Western Ideas under the Tsars* (Durham, NC: Duke University Press, 1985), quote on 26.
35. Charles A. Ruud, *Fighting Words: Imperial Censorship and the Russian Press, 1804–1906* (Toronto: University of Toronto Press, 1982), 137.
36. Ibid., 150.
37. Ibid., esp. chapter 12.
38. L. N. Tolstoi, "Ob iazyke Esperanto," in N. Kabanov, *Vspomogatel'nyi iazyk Esperanto* (Moscow: Posrednik, 1909), 4.
39. "Letter to V. V. Maynov," in L. N. Tolstoy, *Tolstoy's Letters Volume II, 1880–1910*, ed. and trans. by R. F. Christian (New York: Scribner's Sons 1978), 446–7.
40. Garvia, *Esperanto and Its Rivals*, 74–5 (quote on 75).
41. Secret police memo to the Main Administration of Press Affairs (January 3, 1895), reprinted in G. Demidiuk, "Esperanto—vovse ne iazyk!," *Izvestiia TsK SESR* 6 (1928): 332.
42. Memo from censor Geispits (January 10, 1895), reprinted in ibid.
43. "Reason and Religion," in Leo Tolstoy, *Essays and Letters*, trans. by Aylmer Maude (London: Henry Frowde, 1911): 155–9.
44. Lins, *Dangerous Language* 1: 15–17; Demidiuk, "Esperanto—vovse ne iazyk," 333; and Vlasov, *Esperanto: polveka tsenzury*, 26–8.
45. L. N. Tolstoi, *Polnoe sobranie sochinenii*, third series, volume 68 (Moscow: Gosudarstvennoe izdatel'stvo khudozhestvennoi literatury, 1954), 89.
46. Lins, *Dangerous Language* 1: 17.
47. Ruud, *Fighting Words*, 227.
48. Lins, *Dangerous Language* 1:17; Vlasov, too, accepts the hypothesis that Esperantists in this period were suppressed in their efforts to publish Esperanto texts largely because of bureaucratic fear that it was a language of subversion with dangerous revolutionary potential. Many of the archival sources Vlasov himself examined, however, do not support the thesis and Vlasov acknowledges that the first Esperanto-language

publication in Russia received official sanction before the 1905 Revolution. See his, *Esperanto: polveka tsenzury*, esp. 32–6.
49. RGIA f. 776 o. 8 d. 1832 l. 1.
50. Ibid., l. 1ob.
51. Ibid., l. 2.
52. Ibid., ll. 8–19ob.
53. Ibid., l. 13.
54. Ibid., l. 19ob. On this being the era of competing international language projects at the near height of the idea's popularity, see Garvia, *Esperanto and Its Rivals*.
55. RGIA f. 776 o. 8 d. 1832 ll. 2–2ob.
56. Ibid., l. 27.
57. Ibid., ll. 31–2.
58. Ibid., ll. 35–35ob, 37.
59. Ruud, *Fighting Words*, 207.
60. Ibid., chapter 13.
61. P. Stoian and V. Neshinskii, eds., *Neobkhodimye svedeniia ob Esperanto* (St. Petersburg: K. P. Shrader, 1912), 14–15. In the years following the 1905 Revolution, the broader Russian press exploded. Literacy rates were on the rise, censorship restrictions were discontinued, and the Russian public craved debate and discussion about civic affairs. By 1912, Mark Steinberg notes, and in St. Petersburg alone, more than five hundred journals and more than one hundred newspapers were produced. See his *Petersburg*, esp. 35.
62. A. A. Postnikov, *O mezhdunarodnomy iazyke Esperanto* (St. Petersburg: Tip. A. S. Suvorina, 1911), 1.
63. Benedict Anderson, *Imagined Communities: Reflections on the Origins and Spread of Nationalism* (New York: Verso, 2006).
64. On how the aggressive imagining of nation-states helped simultaneously to inspire new imagined international communities, see Iriye, *Cultural Internationalism*, especially chapter 1 and Sluga, *Internationalism*, especially 152–8.
65. On how travelogues helped to arouse excitement and support for European imperialist projects and stimulate a Eurocentric yet "planetary consciousness," see Mary Louise Pratt, *Imperial Eyes: Travel Writing and Transculturation* (London: Routledge, 2007). On how travelogues and popular scientific illustrated journals in late imperial Russia helped to reinforce a global and even interplanetary consciousness, see Anindita Banerjee, *We Modern People: Science Fiction and the Making of Russian Modernity* (Middleton, CT: Wesleyan University Press, 2012), chapter 1; Bojanowska, *A World of Empires*.
66. Stoian, *Neobkhodimye svedeniia*, 25.
67. A. A. Postnikov, *O mezhdunarodnom iazyke Esperanto* (St. Petersburg: Tip. A. S. Suvorina, 1911), 5.
68. GARF f. A626 o.1 d. 6 ll. 38–380b.
69. Vlasov, *Esperanto: polveka tsenzury*, 41.
70. "Al samideanoj," *Ruslanda Esperantisto* 1, no. 1 (April 1905): 1.
71. E. Radvan-Ripinskii, "Kratkii istoricheskii ocherk idei mezhdunarodnogo iayzka voobshche i iazyka Esperanto," *Ruslanda Esperantisto* 1, no. 1 (April 1905): 6.
72. "Koresponda fako," *Ruslanda Esperantisto* 1, no. 1 (April 1905): 49–56.
73. "Ad for St. Petersburg's 'Esperanto' Society," *Ruslanda Esperantisto* no. 1 (1909), inside back cover.
74. Banerjee, *We Modern People*, 18.

75. Ibid., 52.
76. On Bitner and his Esperantist awakening, see D. V. Vlasov, "Izdatel' V.V. Bitner i ego sotrudnichestvo s Esperanto-dvizheniem," http://www.mediascope.ru/node/1177 (accessed June 11, 2015).
77. Ibid.
78. V. V. Bitner, "O zhurnale 'Espero,' " *Vestnik znaniia* no. 1 (1908): 5–7 (quote on 6).
79. On this emerging proletarian intelligentsia, see Mark D. Steinberg, *Proletarian Imagination: Self, Modernity, and the Sacred in Russia, 1910–1925* (Ithaca, NY: Cornell University Press, 2002), especially chapters 1–2.
80. V. Bitner, "Ot redaktsii," *Espero* 1 (1908): 1–6.
81. V. Bitner, "Proshchaite Esperantisty—da zdravstvuet Esperanto! Adiau esperantistoj—vivu Esperanto!" *Espero* 12 (1908): 453–6.
82. Vlasov, *Esperanto: polveka tsenzury*; Lins, *Dangerous Language*; Forster, *The Esperanto Movement*, esp. 65–6.
83. Schor, *Bridge of Words*, 320–1.
84. "La liberiga movado kaj niaj esperoj," *Ruslanda Esperantisto* 6 (1905): 129.
85. D-ro A. I. Asnes, "Rapidu," *Ruslanda Esperantisto* 6 (1905): 152.
86. Joseph Bradley, "Voluntary Associations, Civic Culture, and Obshchestvennost' in Moscow," in *Between Tsar and People: Educated Society and the Quest for Public Identity in Late Imperial Russia*, ed. Edith W. Clowes, Samuel D. Kassow, and James L. West (Princeton, NJ: Princeton University Press, 1991), 131. These associations and their political and social significance are explored in depth in Bradley, *Voluntary Associations in Tsarist Russia*.
87. Steinberg, *Proletarian Imagination*.
88. Kotsonis, *States of Obligation*.
89. "Perepiska chitatelei," *Espero* 4 (1908): 179.
90. "Perepiska," *Espero* 5 (1908): 221.
91. "Perepiska," *Espero* 9 (1908): 878.
92. "Perepiska chitatelei," *Espero* 12 (1908): 462.
93. Case, *Age of Questions*.
94. Schor, *Bridge of Words*, 100.
95. "Ustav Rossisskoi Ligi Esperantistov," *Ruslanda Esperantisto* 1 (1910): 14.
96. *Ustav Tomskago Obshchestva Esperantistov* (Tomsk: Tipografiia Doma Trudoliubiia, 1912), 7.
97. P.E. Stoian, *Slavianstvo i Esperanto* (Saratov: B. L. Rabinovich, 1914), 5.
98. "Ot redaktsii," *Ruslanda Esperantisto* 1 (1909): 4.
99. R.F. Brandt, *O mezhdunarodnykh iazykakh voobshche i v chastnosti ob Esperanto* (Moscow: Esperanto, 1909), 19.
100. M. Mul'tanovskii, *Primenenie Esperanto dlia perepiski s inostrantsami* (Saratov: B. L. Rabinovich, 1915), 9, 10.
101. Quoted in Tobie Mathew, *Greetings from the Barricades: Revolutionary Postcards in Imperial Russia* (London: Four Corners Books, 2019), 388.
102. Mul'tanovskii, *Primenenie Esperanto*, 11.
103. A. P. Andreev, *Mezhdunarodnyi iazyk Esperanto. Ego nastoiashchee, proshedshee i budushchee* (Tiflis': Tipografiia "Esperanto," 1913), 81.
104. Brandt, *O mezhdunarodnykh iazykakh voobshche*, 17.
105. S. P. Rantov, *Mezhdunarodnyi iazyk i sovremennaia zhizn'* (Saratov: B. L. Rabinovich, 1914), 8.
106. Ibid., 9.

107. V. A. Kolosov, *Mezhdunarodnyi iazyk Esperanto, ego vozniknovenie, sostav, stroi, znachenie i rasprostranenie* (Simbirsk: Tip. Gubernskogo Pravleniia, 1911), 1.
108. Andreev, *Mezhdunarodnyi iazyk Esperanto*, 87.
109. L. A. [Lev Agurtin], *Esperanto i uchashchaiasia molodezh'* (Saratov: B.L. Rabinovich, 1914).
110. Lev Agurtin, *Mezhdunarodnyi iazyk. Internacia Lingvo* (Saratov: B. L. Rabinovich, 1914), 14.
111. "50-letie izobretatelia 'Esperanto,'" *Priroda i liudi* 9 (1910): 142.
112. N. Kabanov, *Vspomogatel'nyi mezhdunarodnyi iazyk Esperanto* (Moscow: I. N. Kushnerev, 1913), 6.
113. "K russkim Esperantistam," *Ruslanda Esperantisto* 2 (1909): 1.
114. Vsevolod Loiko, "Narodnyia massy i Esperanto," *Ruslanda Esperantisto* 3 (1909): 3–5.
115. A. A. Postnikov, *O mezhdunarodnom iazyke Esperanto* (St. Petersburg, 1911), 7.
116. "La Bulona Kongreso," *Ruslanda Esperantisto* 3–4 (1905): 82.
117. "II-a Esperantista Festo de l'interpopola frateco ("nash kongress'"), *Ruslanda Esperantisto* 8 (1906): 146.
118. Leo Belmont', "Pervyi kongress esperantistov," in *Na puti bratstvu narodov*, ed. A. A. Sakharov (Kazan: Pervaia esperantskaia tipografiia, 1907): 87–103.
119. Ibid., 99.
120. "Dni kongressa (V Zheneve, 1906g.)," *Ruslanda Esperantisto* 9 (1906): 172–6.
121. See Bojanowska, *A World of Empires*.
122. See, for example, Osterhammel, *The Transformation of the World*, esp. 510–12; Ogle, *The Global Transformation of Time*; and Iriye, *Cultural Internationalism and World Order*, chapter 1.
123. Madeleine Herren, "Governmental Internationalism and the Beginnings of a New World Order in the Late Nineteenth Century," in *The Mechanics of Internationalism: Culture, Society, and Politics from the 1840s to the First World War*, ed. Martin H. Geyer and Johannes Paulmann (New York: Oxford University Press): 121–44.
124. Iriye, *Cultural Internationalism*, esp. chapter 1; Sluga, *Internationalism in the Age of Nationalism*.
125. Postnikov, *O mezhdunarodnom iazyke Esperanto*, 11. In a shocking twist, Postnikov was arrested in 1911 and found guilty of espionage on behalf of Austria-Hungary, Germany, and Japan. While his spying activities appear unrelated to his Esperantist activities, his downfall cast a negative shadow over the Esperantist movement in late imperial Russia. See Vlasov, *Esperanto: polveka tsenzury*, 49–50.
126. Otdel Torgovli Ministerstva Torgovli i Promyshlennosti, *Otchet o VII vsemirnom kongresse esperantistov v gor. Antverpen, c 7 po 14 avgusta n.s. 1911 goda* (St. Petersburg, 1912).
127. A. Nedoshivin, *Novyi iazyk dlia mezhdunarodnykh snoshenii. Kratkii ocherk esperantskogo dvizheniia* (Petrograd: Sila, 1916), 16–20.
128. On Eroshenko, see especially, Sho Konishi, *Anarchist Modernity: Cooperation and Japanese-Russian Intellectual Relations in Modern Japan* (Cambridge, MA: Harvard University Press, 2013, chapter 5; Sho Konishi, "Translingual World Order: Language without Culture in Post-Russo-Japanese War Japan," *Journal of Asian Studies* 72, no. 1 (2013): 91–114; Gotelind Muller and Gregor Benton, "Esperanto and Chinese Anarchism in the 1920s and 1930s," *Language Problems and Language Planning* 30, no. 2 (2006): 173–92.
129. Konishi, "Translingual World Order," 106.

130. After his deportation, Esperantists again came to Eroshenko's aid. His contacts within the Esperanto Association in China helped him to find work lecturing on Russian literature and Esperanto at Peking University. See Konishi, *Anarchist Modernity*, 291.
131. Petr Vasil'kovskii, "V Saratov," *Ruslanda Esperantisto* 4 (1909): 4.
132. Ibid., 5.
133. Margaret L. Jones, *The Esperanto Manual* (London: British Esperanto Association, 1908), 9.
134. "Perepiska chitatelei," *Espero* 4 (1908): 179.
135. See, for example, "Korespondada fako" *La Ondo de Esperanto* 4 (1910): 15 and "Korespondada fako" *La Ondo de Esperanto* 12 (1910): 17.
136. "Biographical Information," Gennadii Ivanovich Tupitsyn Papers, Box 1, Hoover Institution Archives [hereafter, Tupitsyn Papers, HIA].
137. "Postcard from George L. Howe to G. I. Tupitsyn, 19 April 1912," Tupitsyn Papers, Box 4, HIA.
138. "Postcard from A. H. Johnson to G. I. Tupitsyn, 1 April 1912," Tupitsyn Papers, Box 4, HIA.
139. N. O. Chulkov, *Rech', proisnesennaia pri otkrytii Arkhangel'skogo otdeleniia S-Peterburgskogo Obshchestva 'Espero' 21 Noiabria 1898 goda* (Arkhangelsk: Arkhang. Gub. Tip.,1898), 10.
140. Ibid., 598.
141. Kim, "Constructing a Global Identity," 135.
142. V. Zavialov, *Putevodnaia zvezda. (Vpechatleniia ot poezdki v Parizh na X-I Vsemirnyi Kongress Esperantistov)* (Saratov: O-va Knigopechatnikov, 1915).
143. Ibid., 6–9.
144. Ibid., 11.
145. Ibid., 16.
146. Sluga, *Internationalism*, 14.
147. GARF f. A626 o. 1 d. 5 l. 21.
148. Xavier Alcalde, "The Practical Internationalism of Esperanto," *Peace in Progress* 24 (2015): http://www.icip-perlapau.cat/numero24/articles_centrals/article_central_5/ (accessed March 7, 2018).
149. Ia. Shapiro, *Voina narodov i Esperanto* (Saratov: Tip. O-va knigopechatnikov, 1915), 13.

3 Bolshevik Tower of Babel

1. Thomas Bell, *Pioneering Days* (London: Lawrence and Wishart, 1941), 231.
2. J. T. Murphy, *New Horizons* (London: John Lane, 1941), 111.
3. See especially Kirschenbaum, *International Communism*; McGuire, *Red at Heart*; and Studer, *Transnational World*.
4. For a thoughtful review of the evolution of Comintern historiography, its recent rejuvenation, and prospects for further research, see Lisa Kirschenbaum, "Reframing Slavic Studies and the Global Impacts of 1917," in *The Global Impacts of Russia's War and Revolution, Book 2, Part 2: The Wider Arc of the Revolution*, ed. Choi Chatterjee, Steven G. Marks, Mary Neuburger, and Steven Sabol (Bloomington, IN: Slavica, 2019), 345–58. See also Oleksa Drachewych and Ian McKay's introduction to

their edited volume, *Left Transnationalism: The Communist International and The National, Colonial, and Racial Questions* (Montreal: McGill-Queen's University Press, 2019), 3–45.

5. On the West, and Europe in particular, as the primary focal point of (early) Soviet internationalism, see especially Gilburd, *To See Paris and Die*; Clark, *Moscow The Fourth Rome*; and David-Fox, *Showcasing the Soviet Experiment*. The Bolsheviks' early internationalism was also oriented toward "the East"— their blanket category for the oppressed colonial peoples of the Middle East, Asia, Africa, and even the Americas. Yet the West, and Europe, took first priority. On the early Bolshevik conceptions of and strategies toward the foreign "East," see Masha Kirasirova, "The 'East' as a Category of Bolshevik Ideology and Comintern Administration," *Kritika: Explorations in Russian and Eurasian History* 18, no. 1 (2017): 7–34. Of course, revolutionary activists throughout the colonial world attached their own meanings to the Bolsheviks' Revolution and what it might mean for their own futures in ways that the Eurocentric Comintern could not control. See S. A. Smith, "The Russian Revolution, National Self-Determination, and Anti-Imperialism, 1917–1927," in *Left Transnationalism: the Communist International and the National, Colonial, and Racial Questions*, ed. Oleksa Drachewych and Ian McKay (Montreal: McGill-Queens University Press, 2019): 73–98.
6. Quoted in Steinberg, *The Russian Revolution*, 23.
7. Quoted in ibid., 22.
8. Rossiiskii gosudarstvennyi arkhiv sotsial'no-politicheskoi istorii (RGASPI) f. 495 o. 99 d. 66 l. 43.
9. Orlando Figes and Boris Kolonitskii, *Interpreting the Russian Revolution: the Language and Symbols of 1917* (New Haven, CT: Yale University Press, 1999). As Michael Gorham has shown, the Bolsheviks' struggle to clarify, standardize, and effectively disseminate an authoritative revolutionary vocabulary and Soviet manner of speaking would extend into the 1930s. Soviet citizens were at first still "speaking in tongues" even as they were learning to "speak Bolshevik." Michael Gorham, *Speaking in Soviet Tongues: Language Culture and the Politics of Voice in Revolutionary Russia* (Dekalb: Northern Illinois Press, 2003); Stephen Kotkin, *Magnetic Mountain: Stalinism as Civilization* (Berkeley: University of California Press, 1995), chapter 5.
10. R. Tsyvinskii and T. Sikora, *Manifest soiuza sotsialistov-Esperanistov* (Vyborg: Estra, 1917).
11. Born in 1884, Tsyvinskii became an Esperantist in 1908 and had been broadly active in prerevolutionary Esperantist circles. Although nothing came of his attempt to establish a Universal League of Socialist Esperantists, Tsyvinskii remained an active Esperantist in the 1920s and 1930s. His fate was that of many prominent Soviet Esperantists in the years of Stalin's Terror. Arrested in 1936 on charges of espionage, Tsyvinskii entered the Gulag with a ten-year sentence and was never heard from again. See A. V. Sidorov, *Esperanto-dvizhenie na Severo-Zapade Rossii* (St. Petersburg: n.p., 2014), 123–4.
12. Tsyvinskii and Sikora, *Manifest*, 2.
13. Ibid., 5.
14. Ibid., 6.
15. Ibid., 14.
16. Ibid., 16.

17. I borrow this notion of the "cultural ecosystem" as a useful frame for examining the Russian revolution and its cultural parameters from Katerina Clark, *Petersburg: Crucible of Cultural Revolution* (Cambridge, MA: Harvard University Press, 1995).
18. Schor, *Bridge of Words*, 10.
19. Gleb J. Albert, "From 'World Revolution' to 'Fatherland of all Proletarians.' Anticipated World Society and Global Thinking in Early Soviet Russia," *Interdisciplines* 1 (2012): 90.
20. V. A. Dmitriev and P. D. Medem, *Mezhdunarodnyi vspomogatel'nyi iazyk Esperanto: Ego primenenie i rasprostranenie* (Petrograd: Sila, 1918), 3.
21. Ibid., 8.
22. B. Breslau, *Mezhdunarodnyi iazyk i proletariat* (Saratov: Tip. P. N. Sibrina, 1918), 3.
23. Ibid., 6.
24. These documents have been reproduced on the "Breslav Kh.V-M" page of the "Esperanto en Rusio" website, which serves as a digital repository of archival documents and other materials relating to the history of Esperanto in Russia and the USSR: http://historio.ru/breslav.php (accessed 14 March 2018).
25. "Breslau, B. M.," http://historio.ru/breslaux.php (accessed March 15, 2018).
26. "Bakushinskii, R. N." http://historio.ru/bakushin.php (accessed March 15, 2018).
27. GARF f. 9550 o. 14 d. 19 l. 1.
28. "Kak ia stal Esperantistom," http://historio.ru/bajxenov.php (accessed March 15, 2018).
29. RGASPI f. 495 o. 99 d. 66 ll. 43-43ob (quote on l. 43).
30. RGASPI f. 495 o. 99 d. 65 l. 7. See also, for example, RGASPI f. 495 o. 99 d. 66 l. 20.
31. RGASPI f. 495 o. 99 d. 65 ll. 7–11.
32. "Vozzvanie tsentral'nogo biuro vserossiiskogo soiuza iunykh Esperantistov," *Zhizn' i tvorchestvo russkoi molodezhi* no. 22 (1919), 4; reproduced online at http://historio.ru/zanovyj.php (accessed 9/5/2015).
33. GARF f. A-2307 o. 2 d. 438 ll. 1-27ob.
34. Ibid., l. 6. In 1918, the British Prime Minister appointed a committee to consider the teaching of international languages, Esperanto in particular, in UK schools. This committee arrived at a conclusion very similar to that of Narkompros. See *The Modern Languages Committee and Artificial Languages* (London: British Esperanto Association, 1918).
35. GARF f. A-2306 o. 15 d. 425 l. 28; RGASPI f. 495 o. 99 d. 66 l. 21.
36. RGASPI f. 495 o. 99 d. 66 l. 21.
37. John Riddell, ed., *Founding the Communist International: Proceedings and Documents of the First Congress, March 1919* (New York: Pathfinder, 1987), 99–100.
38. John Riddell, ed. *The German Revolution and the Debate on Soviet Power* (New York: Pathfinder, 1986), 441–3 (quote on 442).
39. On the improvised nature of the first Congress's convening, see Aleksandr Vatlin, *Komintern: idei, resheniia, sudy'by* (Moscow: Rosspen, 2009), 53–8. On the delegates to the first Comintern Congress, see Riddell, *Founding the Communist International*, 8–19.
40. Ibid., 13.
41. Branko Lazitch and Milorad M. Drachovitch, *Lenin and the Comintern, Volume I* (Stanford, CA: Hoover Institution Press, 1972), 80.
42. Duncan Hallas, *The Comintern* (Chicago: Haymarket Books, 2008), 10.
43. Arthur Ransome, *Russia in 1919* (New York: B. W. Huebsch, 1919), 214.

44. Quoted in Riddell, *Founding the Communist International*, 19–20.
45. Ransome, *Russia in 1919*, 215.
46. Ibid.
47. Riddell, *Founding the Communist International*, 204. In his speech at the festivities concluding the congress, Bukharin made much of Liu Shaozhou's having spoken Chinese at the start of his report. "It is no accident," Bukharin declared, "that at the first congress of our Communist International for the first time we heard a speech of our Communist International in the Chinese language. This is a profound historical symbol, a symbol of unity between revolutionary proletarian forces under capitalism and the efforts of colonial peoples who are liberating themselves." Ibid., 308.
48. Mark Gamsa, "Mixed Marriages in Russian-Chinese Manchuria," in *Entangled Histories: The Transcultural Past of Northeast China*, Dan Ben-Canaan et al. ed. (Cham: Springer, 2014), 56.
49. Riddell, *Founding the Communist International*, 24.
50. Ibid., 149.
51. Ibid., 220.
52. Angelica Balabanoff, *My Life as a Rebel* (New York: Greenwood Press, [1938] 1968), 87. The Bolsheviks, in their effort to bury the Second International, were also replicating its modes of dealing with language diversity at its international conferences. The Second International adopted three working languages—French, German, and English—and offered consecutive interpretation of speeches. In the decade and a half prior to the outbreak of World War I, some delegates argued in vain that the Second International needed to adopt an international auxiliary language for its work. See Kevin J. Callahan, *Demonstration Culture: European Socialism and the Second International, 1889–1914* (Leicester: Troubador, 2010), 11–15.
53. See Lunarcharskii's "revolutionary silhouette" of Lenin, https://www.marxists.org/archive/lunachar/works/silhouet/lenin.htm (accessed July 12, 2018); Beatrice Farnsworth, *Aleksandra Kollontai: Socialism, Feminism, and the Bolshevik Revolution* (Stanford, CA: Stanford University Press, 1980), 60.
54. Even when firmly in power, Stalin was self-conscious of the disadvantage, recognizing how his lack of foreign language abilities hamstringed his efforts to compete with his political opponents in the Party no less than to engage foreign visitors without an interpreter. As Sheila Fitzpatrick has noted, Stalin and other Party elites who lacked strong foreign language skills (Molotov, Mikoian, and Kaganovich, for example) burned with a certain degree of anxiety and even embarrassment—especially when criticized or mocked by an intellectual showboat like Trotsky. Sheila Fitzpatrick, *On Stalin's Team: The Years of Living Dangerously in Soviet Politics* (Princeton, NJ: Princeton University Press, 2015), 96–7.
55. Ronald Grigor Suny, "A Journeyman for Revolution: Stalin and the Labour Movement in Baku, June 1907–May 1908," *Soviet Studies* 23, no. 3 (1972), 393. Fellow prisoners in Baku recalled how Stalin would justify his study of Esperanto by claiming that other major European languages like German, French, and English were "fleeting phenomena in a capitalist age." See Essad Bey, *Stalin: The Career of a Fanatic*, trans. Huntley Paterson (New York: Viking, 1932), 143; Vladimir Lebedeff, "Stalin's Days in Prison," *New York Times* (January 24, 1937).
56. Even after being exiled from the USSR, Trotsky was intent on highlighting Stalin's inability to master foreign languages as indicative of his inability to steer the Communist Party of the Soviet Union through the challenges they faced in a decidedly hostile geopolitical environment. Stalin's "ignorance of foreign languages,"

Trotsky wrote in his autobiography, "compels him to follow the political life of other countries at second-hand." Trotsky, *My Life*, 506.

57. Stephen Kotkin, *Stalin: Waiting for Hitler, 1929–1941* (New York: Penguin, 2017), 34.
58. Lisa Kirschenbaum, "Michael Gruzenberg/Mikhail Borodin: The Making of an International Communist," in *The Global Impacts of Russia's War and Revolution, Book 2, Part 1: The Wider Arc of the Revolution*, ed. Choi Chatterjee, Steven G. Marks, Mary Neuburger, and Steven Sabol (Bloomington, IN: Slavica, 2019): 337–65.
59. Trotsky, *My Life*, 118.
60. Riddell, *Founding the Communist International*, 311.
61. An American journalist who attended the Fourth Comintern Congress at which this legendary feat was achieved reported that Trotsky spoke for a total of seven and a half hours "with only two brief intermissions." He described Trotsky's German as "exquisite" and his French as "fluent, rich." Louis Fischer, *Men and Politics: Europe between the Two World Wars* (New York: Harper & Row, 1966 [1941]), 56. Joseph Freeman, the *New Masses* editor, who worked as a Comintern translator in the 1920s, was awed by Trotsky's oratorical skills in at least three languages. He recalled how at one Comintern plenum, French delegates begged Trotsky to translate his own remarks for them in French. See his *An American Testament: A Narrative of Rebels and Romantics* (New York: Farrar and Rinehart, 1936), 629–30.
62. Riddell, *Founding the Communist International*, 312.
63. Ibid., 315.
64. Victor Serge, *Memoirs of a Revolutionary*, translated by Peter Sedgwick with George Paizis (New York: New York Review Books, 2012), 83.
65. Ibid., 90.
66. Ibid., 92.
67. Leon Trotsky, *The First Five Years of the Communist International. Volume I*, translated and edited by John G. Wright (New York: Pioneer Publishers, 1945), 85.
68. The widespread grassroots activism inspired by the Comintern's founding has been largely overlooked by historians. A welcome exception is Gleb J. Albert, "'Esteemed Comintern!': The Communist International and World-Revolutionary Charisma in Early Soviet Society," *Twentieth-Century Communism* 8 (2015): 10–39.
69. V. P. Artiushkin-Kormilitsyn, *Mezhdunarodnyi iazyk revoliutsionnogo proletariata Esperanto* (Petrograd: n.p., 1919), 7.
70. Ibid., 14.
71. RGASPI f. 495 o. 99 d. 65 ll. 14ob-16ob; f. 495 o. 99 d. 66 l. 1.
72. RGASPI f. 495 o. 99 d. 66 l. 8ob.
73. GARF f. A-2306 o. 2 d. 591 l. 20.
74. RGASPI f. 495 o. 99 d. 66 l. 22.
75. Ibid., l. 3.
76. The appeals from the British League of Esperantist Socialists and La Maison de l'Esperanto in Paris can be found at RGASPI f. 495 o. 99 d. 66 l. 16 and ll. 27–8.
77. John Riddell, ed. *Workers of the World and Oppressed Peoples, Unite! Proceedings and Documents of the Second Congress*, 2 vols. (New York: Pathfinder Press, 1991), especially the introduction. For a first-hand account of the Congress and related festivities as remembered by a British delegate, see Murphy, *New Horizons*, chapters 6–9.
78. Riddell, *Workers of the World* 1: 421.
79. Charles Shipman, *It Had to Be Revolution: Memoirs of an American Radical* (Ithaca, NY: Cornell University Press, 1993), 115.
80. Riddell, *Workers of the World* 1: 182.

81. Ibid., 270. Murphy's memoir details a variety of slights and inconveniences endured by those who did not speak Russian or German at the Congress. He specifically recalled how Zinoviev responded to him with visible annoyance upon their first meeting, expressing his disapproval that Murphy "could converse only in English." See his *New Horizons*, quote on 139.
82. Quoted in James W. Hulse, *The Forming of the Communist International* (Stanford, CA: Stanford University Press, 1964), 195.
83. Riddell, *Workers of the World* 1: 421.
84. Ibid., 2: 622.
85. The Twenty-One Conditions can be read in English translation online at https://www.marxists.org/archive/lenin/works/1920/jul/x01.htm (accessed March 26, 2018).
86. On the Twenty-One Conditions and their meaning for Bolshevik authority over the Comintern, see A. James McAdams, *Vanguard of the Revolution: The Global Idea of the Communist Party* (Princeton, NJ: Princeton University Press, 2017), 102–5; Halles, *The Comintern*, 28–34; Hulse, *Forming of the Communist International*, 205–11; Jon Jacobson, *When the Soviet Union Entered World Politics* (Berkeley: University of California Press, 1994), 34–6; and Lazitch and Drachovitch, *Lenin and the Comintern*, 318–34.
87. Quoted in Halles, *The Comintern*, 29.
88. Francisco J. Romero Salvadó, "Report on the action taken by the delegate Angel Pestaña at the second congress of the third international which was presented by him to the Confederación Nacional del Trabajo," *Revolutionary Russia* 8, no. 1 (1995): 68.
89. M. N. Roy, *M. N. Roy's Memoirs* (Bombay: Allied Publishers, 1964), 372.
90. Salvadó, "Report on the Action," 69.
91. Riddell, *Workers of the World* 2: 772–3.
92. RGASPI f. 495 o. 99 d. 67 l. 4. It also inspired hope among foreign communist Esperantists. See, for example, Mark Starr, "Communism and an International Language," *Communist Review* 2, no. 4 (February 1922): 265.
93. Advocates of various international language projects competed and argued bitterly with one another in the early twentieth century, yet no rivalry among these projects was as personal or as bitter as that between the Esperantists and the Idists. See Garvia, *Esperanto and its Rivals*, esp. chapter 16.
94. RGASPI f. 495 o. 99 d. 67 l. 9.
95. See, for example, ibid., l. 4.
96. John Riddell, ed. and trans. *To the Masses: Proceedings of the Third Congress of the Communist International, 1921* (Leiden: Brill, 2015), 47.
97. Josephine Fowler, *Japanese and Chinese Immigrant Activists: Organizing in American and International Communist Movements, 1919–1933* (New Brunswick, NJ: Rutgers University Press, 2007), 68. See also McGuire, *Red at Heart*, 79–80. The Comintern's Eurocentric language politics represented the organization's overriding Eurocentric approach to international communism. On the Comintern's Eurocentric priorities, see Oleksa Drachewych, *The Communist International and Racial Equality in the British Dominions* (London: Routledge, 2019).
98. I. Izgur, *Mezhdunarodnyi iazyk na sluzhbe proletariat* (Moscow: Novaia epokha, 1925), 17.
99. One historian has suggested that even at the end of the 1920s, seemingly no one in the Comintern's Far East Bureau could claim competency in Japanese. Sandra Wilson, "The Comintern and the Japanese Communist Party," in *International Communism and the Communist International, 1919–1943*, ed. Tim Rees and Andrew Thorpe (Manchester: Manchester University Press, 1998), 295.

100. RGASPI f. 495 o. 99 d. 67 l. 15.
101. See, for example, GARF f. A-2306 o. 15 d. 425 ll. 15, 23.
102. Ibid., l. 27.
103. Ibid., l. 16.
104. Ibid., l. 49.
105. RGASPI f. 495 o. 99 d. 67 l. 60.
106. GARF f. A-2306 o. 1 d. 622 l. 12.
107. Ibid., l. 12. I'm using the organization's most commonly known acronym, SEU—the one derived from its name in Esperanto, not in Russian.
108. "M. Gor'kii ob Esperanto," *Vestnik rabotnikov iskusstv* no. 7–9 (1921): 37–8.
109. On Gorky as intelligentsia patron see Clark, *Petersburg*, 102.
110. "Theses on the World Situation and the Tasks of the Communist International," in Riddell, *To the Masses*, 901–20.
111. Trotsky, *First Five Years*, 267–8.
112. Lazitch and Drachkovitch, *Lenin and the Comintern*, chapter 12 (quotes on 529).
113. E. Lanti, *The Workers' Esperanto Movement*, trans. H. Stay (London: NCLC Publishing, 1928), 13.
114. Ibid., 29.
115. Lanti, *Away with Neutralism! (For la neutralismon!)*, quoted in Lins, *Dangerous Language* 1: 170.
116. Quoted in Garvia, *Esperanto and its Rivals*, 123.
117. Quoted in Lins, *Dangerous Language* 1: 170.
118. See Garvia, *Esperanto and its Rivals*, 122–4; Schor, *Bridge of Words,* 144; Lins, *Dangerous Language*, 1: 168–70.
119. Quoted in Lins, *Dangerous Language*, 1: 171.
120. RGASPI f. 495 o. 99 d. 67.
121. Souvarine's letter as quoted in "Dezorganizatory," *Biulleten' TsK SESS* 2 (February 1923): 11.
122. RGASPI f. 495 o. 30 d. 168 ll. 41-41ob.
123. Even as the Bolsheviks began to make headway during the Civil War, they took a more hardline stance toward cultural projects they regarded as "utopian luxuries"—the Proletkult movement perhaps the most well-known casualties among them. See Lynn Mally, *Culture of the Future: The Proletkult Movement in Revolutionary Russia* (Berkeley: University of California Press, 1990), especially chapter 7.
124. RGASPI f. 495 o. 99 d. 70 l. 23. See also RGASPI f. 495 o. 30 d. 168 ll. 17–18; 69–70.
125. Riddell, John, ed. *Toward the United Front: Proceedings of the Fourth Congress of the Communist International 1922* (Leiden: Brill, 2011), 1119.
126. See Jacobson, *When the Soviet Union*, chapter 6. On the failure of the German Revolution and its effects on the culture and politics of early Soviet internationalism, see, for example, Albert, "From 'World Soviet;" Albert, "'German October is Approaching': Internationalism, Activists, and the Soviet State in 1923," *Revolutionary Russia* 24, no. 2 (2011): 111–42; Clark, *Petersburg*, esp. 187–92; Kevin McDermott and Jeremy Agnew, *The Comintern: A History of International Communism from Lenin to Stalin* (New York: St. Martin's Press, 1997), esp. chapter 2; Vatlin, *Komintern*; and Alexander Vatlin and Stephen A. Smith, "The Comintern," in *The Oxford Handbook of Communism* (Oxford: Oxford University Press, 2014): 187–202.
127. Warren Lerner, *Karl Radek: The Last Internationalist* (Stanford, CA: Stanford University Press, 1970), 131. This was the first time Stalin participated in any significant way at a Comintern Congress; he did not speak German.

128. Quoted in McGuire, *Red at Heart*, 77. On the Bolshevization of the Comintern's foreign cadres—the attempt to reforge them as New Soviet Men and Women, albeit foreign ones—see Kirschenbaum, *International Communism*, esp. chapter 1 and Studer, *Transnational World*. Studer notes that it was in the 1930s that the Soviet Union began to intensely pressure the Comintern's foreign cadres to learn Russian, the "language of Lenin" (131).
129. See, for example, J. T. Murphy, "The First Year of the Lenin School," *Communist International* IV, 14 (September 30, 1927): 268; Murphy, *New Horizons*, 248; Yueh Sheng, *Sun Yat-sen University in Moscow and the Chinese Revolution: A Personal Account* (Lawrence: University of Kansas, 1971), chapter 5. As McGuire notes in her *Red at Heart*, this coursework was intensive, demanding, and controversial, but not always effective (pp. 71–3, 129–31).
130. Alexander V. Pantov and Daria A. Spichak, "Chinese Stalinists and Trotskyists at the International Lenin School in Moscow, 1926–1938," *Twentieth-Century China* 33, no. 2 (2008): 33.
131. Studer, *Transnational World*, 131. The Soviet state pursued this logic still more aggressively during the Cold War. See Applebaum, "The Rise of Russian."
132. William J. Chase, *Enemies within the Gates? The Comintern and Stalinist Repression, 1934–1939* (New Haven, CT: Yale University Press, 2001), 96–101.
133. Sergei Chernov, "At the Dawn of Simultaneous Interpreting in the USSR: Filling Some Gaps in History," in *New Insights in the History of Interpreting*, ed. Kayoko Takeda and Jesus Baigorri-Jalon (Amsterdam: John Benjamins, 2016): 135–65. The system of simultaneous interpretation used today at the United Nations and many other international organizations is of rather recent origins. In the aftermath of World War I, the need for more effective and time-saving methods of translation and interpretation at international conferences and other events was ever more keenly felt; it was not just the early meetings of the Comintern that witnessed the pains, inefficiencies, and resource costs required of consecutive and "whispering" interpretation. The first experiments with simultaneous interpretation via wired technology, including at the Comintern, were thus conducted in the interwar period. The Nuremberg Trials, however, established the standards for providing and managing simultaneous interpretation at international events. Francesca Gaiba, *The Origins of Simultaneous Interpretation: The Nuremberg Trial* (Ottawa: University of Ottawa Press, 1998), especially chapter 1.
134. Henri Barbusse, *One Looks at Russia*, trans. Warre B. Wells (London: J. M. Dent & Sons, 1931), 18.
135. Markoosha Fischer, *My Lives in Russia* (New York: Harper & Brothers, 1944), 43–4. The Soviet press hailed this as the world's first instance of simultaneous interpretation and a technological boost for order and efficiency at the Comintern. "Tekhnika na sluzhbe kommunisticheskoi revoliutsii," *Krasnaia niva* no. 32 (August 3, 1932).
136. Quoted in McGuire, *Red at Heart*, 80.
137. The phrase is borrowed from Mally, *Culture of the Future*, 192.

4 Comrades with(out) Borders

1. Innokentii Zhukov, *Puteshestvie zvena Krasnoi Zvezdy v stranu chudes* (Kharkov: O-va sodeistviia iunomu Leninitsu, 1924).

2. Ibid., 98.
3. As Roxanne Panchasi notes, a "culture of anticipation" infused much of interwar cultural life in Europe. See her *Future Tense: The Culture of Anticipation in France between the Wars* (Ithaca, NY: Cornell University Press, 2009). On utopian visions in early Soviet popular culture, see Stites, *Revolutionary Dreams*; John McCannon, "Technological and Scientific Utopias in Soviet Children's Literature, 1921–1932," *Journal of Popular Culture* 34, no. 4 (2001): 153–69.
4. In another, *The Bricklayer*, a play written by Proletkultist Pavel Bessal'ko in 1918, the proletariat builds a worldwide commune that overcomes class and national divisions using an international language. Mally, *Culture of the Future*, 141.
5. On Russian science fiction of the revolutionary era as a road map to a future populated by modern and liberated subjects see Banerjee, *We Modern People*.
6. Richard Crossman, ed., *The God That Failed* (New York: Harper & Row, 1963), 205.
7. David-Fox, *Showcasing*, 31.
8. GARF f. 374 o. 27 d. 147 l. 103.
9. "Rezoliutsiia 1-go S'ezda SESS po organizatsionnomu voprosu," *Biulleten' TsK SESS* no. 6 (1923): 4.
10. N. I., "Oboiti molchaniem nel'zia," *Biulleten' TsK SESS* no. 4 (1923): 11–15.
11. The leaflets are archived in the Russian National Library in St. Petersburg.
12. "Nash radio-doklad," *Biulleten' TsK SESS* no. 4 (1923): 16–17. In September 1923, Drezen gave his second Esperanto-Russian address via radio and this time, the SEU received word from comrades in Latvia, Germany, and Belgium that his address was heard by comrades outside of the Soviet Union. "Nash radio–doklad (vtoroi)," *Biulleten' TsK SESS* no. 7 (1923): 3–4.
13. Eugene Lyons, *Assignment in Utopia* (New York: Harcourt, Brace, & Company, 1937), 70.
14. E. Lanti, "Three Weeks in Russia," https://www.marxists.org/archive/lanti/1922/3-weeks.htm (accessed on May 31, 2018).
15. Ibid.
16. See Schor, *Bridge of Words*, 143–4.
17. E. Borsboom, *Vivo de Lanti* (Paris: SAT, 1976), 36.
18. GARF f. 1235 o. 138 d. 1415 l. 5; RGASPI f. 17 o. 85 d. 22 l. 12; A. Sidorov, ed., *Esperanto-dvizhenie: fragmenty istorii* (Moscow: Impeto, 2008), 21; Lins, *Dangerous Language*, 1: 166–7.
19. Schor, *Bridge of Words*, 146–8 (quote on 148).
20. Garvia, *Esperanto and its Rivals*, 124.
21. On these early resentments and scandals, see Lins, *Dangerous Language*, 1: 171–7; Vlasov, *Esperanto: Polveka tsenzury*, 82–6.
22. E. D. [Drezen], "Plan raboty SESS v oblasti mezhdunarodnoi Esperantskoi deiatel'nosti," *Biulleten' TsK SESS* no. 3 (1923): 12.
23. "Ot TsK SESS," *Sovetskii Esperantist* no. 2 (1925): 7.
24. G. D. [Demidiuk], "Za rabotu," *Biulleten' TsK SESS* no. 1 (1924): 9.
25. "The Radio of the Future" in Velimir Khlebnikov, *The King of Time: Selected Writings of Russian Futurism*, trans. Paul Schmidt and Charlotte Douglas (Cambridge, MA: Harvard University Press, 1985): 155–9. In 1919, Khlebnikov also proposed his own universal written language which he called his "common systems of hieroglyphs for the people of our planet." See his "To the Artists of the World" in *The King of Time*, 146–51.

26. Harry A. Epton, *The International Radio Manual* (London: British Esperanto Association, 1925), 3.
27. Steven Lovell, *Russia in the Microphone Age: A History of Soviet Radio, 1919-1970* (Oxford: Oxford University Press, 2015), 12.
28. Ibid., chapter 1.
29. Daniel R. Headrick, *The Invisible Weapon: Telecommunications and International Politics 1851-1945* (New York: Oxford University Press, 1991), esp. chapter 8.
30. Ibid., chapter 11.
31. Paul Schubert, *The Electric Word* (New York: Macmillan, 1928), 250.
32. D.V. Vlasov, "Esperanto v Sovetskom radio-efire v 1920-1930-e gody," *Vestnik Sankt-Peterburgskogo Universiteta* 9, no. 4 (2013): 154.
33. RGASPI f. 495 o. 99 d. 77 ll. 24-6.
34. S. Podkaminer, "Radio i Esperanto," *Vestnik znaniia* no. 12 (1926): 796.
35. Epton, *International Radio Manual*, 75.
36. Ibid., 56-7.
37. Reuben Algot Tanquist, "A Study of the Social Psychology of the Diffusion of Esperanto with Special Reference to the English Speaking Peoples," Master's Thesis (University of Minnesota, 1927), 6.
38. Epton, *International Radio Manual*, 81.
39. Lowell, *Russia in the Microphone Age*, chapter 2.
40. Vlasov, "Esperanto v Sovetskom radio-efire," 155.
41. Lowell, *Russia in the Microphone Age*, chapters 2 and 3; Vlasov, "Esperanto v Sovetskom radio-efire."
42. S. Rublev, *Kruzhok Esperanto: Prakticheskoe posobie dlia gruppovykh zaniatii* (Moscow: Izdanie TsK SESR, 1936), 3.
43. Ibid., 4.
44. Ibid., 14.
45. On the origins of worker correspondence, see Matthew Lenoe, *Closer to the Masses: Stalinist Culture, Social Revolution, and Soviet Newspapers* (Cambridge, MA: Harvard University Press, 2004), 32.
46. Lenoe, *Closer to the Masses*, especially chapter 4; Jeremy Hicks, "Worker Correspondents: between Journalism and Literature," *Russian Review* 66, no. 4 (2007): 568-85.
47. Hicks, "Worker Correspondents," 576.
48. Leon Trotsky, *Problems of Everyday Life* (New York: Pathfinder, 1973), 214.
49. Ibid., 215.
50. Hicks, "Worker Correspondents," 579.
51. Lenoe, *Closer to the Masses*, 159.
52. M. I. Ul'ianova, *Rabkorskoe dvizhenie za granitsei i mezhdunarodnaia sviaz'* (Moscow: Izdatel'stvo 'Pravda' i "Bednota," 1928), 114.
53. Ibid., 116. Ulianova directed the international worker correspondence bureau for the Soviet newspaper *Pravda* in the 1920s.
54. GARF f. 5451 o. 10 d. 469 l. 3.
55. Trotsky, *Problems of Everyday Life*, 197-8.
56. Ibid., 206.
57. RGASPI f. 495 o. 99 d. 77 l. 4.
58. V. Svistunov, *Elementy Esperanto* (Moscow: Izdanie TsK SESR, 1932), 23.
59. GARF f. 5451 o. 10 d. 469 l. 5ob.

60. "Abortoj en Sovetio," *Sennaciulo* 2, no. 41 (July 8, 1926): 7; "Britia Sindikata Delegitaro en Moskvo," *Sennaciulo* 1, no. 11 (December 11, 1924): 5; G. Filipov, "El sovetlanda urbeto," *Sennaciulo* 1, no. 38 (June 18, 1925): 3–4 and 1, 39 (25 June 1925): 3–4; G. Teterin, "Virino en Sovetio," *Sennaciulo* 1, no. 33 (May 14, 1925): 3.
61. N. Usov, "El la vivo de soveta instruisto," *Sennaciulo* 5, no. 238 (April 25, 1929): 279.
62. V. Fedorovski, "Tago El Mia Vivo," *Sennaciulo* 6, no. 281 (February 20, 1930): 238.
63. GARF f. 5451 o. 10 d. 469 l. 3; E. Sazonova, *Kratkie svedeniia ob Esperanto* (Moscow: TsK SESR, 1930), 19–22.
64. I. Izgur, *Ogon' v konvertakh* (Kiev: Molodoi bol'shevik, 1934).
65. GARF f. 3316 o. 19 d. 340 l. 4.
66. RGASPI f. 495 o.99 d. 78 l. 10.
67. RGASPI f. 17 o. 85 d. 22 l. 11.
68. M. Ul'ianova, "Inostrannye iazyki ili Esperanto?" *Raboche-krest'ianskii korrespondent* no. 21 (November 15, 1928): 9.
69. Quoted in "Na putiakh k priznaniiu," *Izvestiia TsK SESR* no. 7–8 (1928): 236.
70. D. Ikhok, "Za ili protiv Esperanto?" *Raboche-krest'ianskii korrespondent* no. 7–8 (April 15–30, 1928): 22.
71. V. Fin, "Khoroshie slova nado pretvorit' v delo," *Raboche-krest'ianskii korrespondent* no. 22 (November 30, 1928): 20.
72. R. Nikol'skii, "Esperanto i mezhdunarodnoe rabkorstvo," *Mezhdunarodnyi iazyk* no. 20–22 (1926): 19.
73. "Korespondado," *Sennacieca Revuo* 3 (December 1923): 16; "Korespondado," *Sennacieca Revuo* no. 7–8 (April-May 1924): 20.
74. "Sostoianie esperdvizhenie v Smolenske," *Mezhdunarodnyi iazyk* no. 15 (1926): 7.
75. Matthias Neumann, "Youthful Internationalism in the Age of 'Socialism in One Country': Komsomol'tsy, Pioneers and 'World Revolution' in the Interwar Period," *Revolutionary Russia* 31, no. 2 (2018): 279–303.
76. P. Nikol'skii, "Esperanto i mezhdunarodnoe rabkorstvo," *Mezhdunarodnyi iazyk* nos. 20–2 (1926): 17.
77. Lev Kopelev, *The Education of a True Believer* trans. Gary Kern (New York: Harper and Row, 1980), 97.
78. Ibid., 98.
79. Ibid., 99.
80. R. Skribemulo, "Neobdumannye pis'ma," *Izvestiia TsK SESS* no. 1–2 (1926–7): 22–4.
81. Fin, "Khoroshie slova," 22.
82. Sazonova, *Kratkie svedeniia,* 21.
83. P. Tilin, "Na novyi kurs!" *Mezhdunarodnyi iazyk* no. 6 (1930): 280–2 (quote on 281).
84. See, for example, "Poleznye fakty i tsifry dlia pisem za granitsu," *Izvestiia TsK SESR* no. 11–12 (1928): 353–6.
85. P. Nikol'skii, "Neobdumannye pis'ma," *Izvestiia TsK SESR* no. 1–2 (1926–7): 25.
86. N. Intsertov, "Vopros ob esperantskikh-odinochkakh," *Mezhdunarodnyi iazyk* no. 6 (1929): 337–8.
87. Neumann, "Youthful Internationalism," 286.
88. GARF f. 7668 o. 1 d. 445 l. 33.
89. N. Intsertov, *Kak dolzhna rabotat' iacheika SESR* (Moscow: TsK SESR, 1930), 24.
90. Ibid., 98.
91. I. Lisichnik, *Tovarishch Shatov–Tovarishchu Tak-Milanu* (Moscow: Profizdat, 1933), 57.
92. Ibid., 58.

93. V. Gorazeev, "O kachestve pis'ma i 'kachestvakh' zagranichnogo korrespondenta," *Mezhdunarodnyi iazyk* no. 11–12 (1933): 238.
94. P. Kiriushin, "Moi zagranichnye 'sobkory,'" *Mezhdunarodnyi iazyk* no. 3 (1929): 149–50.
95. Juliane Fürst, *Stalin's Last Generation: Soviet Post-War Youth and the Emergence of Mature Socialism* (New York: Oxford University Press, 2010), 254.
96. See GARF f. 1235 o. 97. D. 17 ll. 5, 8. In 1925, when the annual SAT world congress was held in Vienna, the Austrian government refused to grant visas to Soviet delegates, fearing the "dangerous propaganda" of Bolshevik rabble-rousers in Esperantist disguise. S. Podkaminer, "Radio i Esperanto," *Vestnik znaniia* 12 (1926): 796.
97. The most comprehensive and compelling account is David-Fox, *Showcasing*.
98. GARF f. 5446 o. 7 d. 958 l. 10.
99. RGASPI f. 495 o. 99 d. 76 l. 5ob; GARF f. 3316 o. 19 d. 340 l. 9ob.
100. L. S. Ozerov, *Stroitel'stvo sotsializma v SSSR i mezhdunarodnaia proletarskaia solidarnost' (1921–1937g.g.)* (Moscow: Mysl', 1972), esp. 155–90.
101. N. V. Kiseleva, *Iz istorii bor'by sovetskoi obshchestvennosti za proryv kul'turnoi blokady SSSR* (Rostov on the Don, 1991), esp. chapter 1; David-Fox, *Showcasing*.
102. Raisa Orlova, *Memoirs*, trans. Samuel Cioran (New York: Random House, 1983), 107.
103. Podkaminer, "Proletarskaia revoliutsiia," 386.
104. RGASPI f. 495 o. 30 d. 168 l. 185.
105. E. Drezen, "K VI kongressu SAT," *Mezhdunarodnyi iazyk* no. 11 (1926): 4.
106. *Mezhdunarodnyi iazyk,* no. 16 (1926): 16.
107. G. D., "Pochtovaia marka k VI Kongressu SAT," *Mezhdunarodnyi iazyk* no. 20–2 (1926): 2.
108. "Karavan nemetskikh rabochikh esperantistov na congress SAT v Leningrade," *Mezhdunarodnyi iazyk* no. 17 (1926): 1; "Estimaj gekamaradoj!" *Mezhdunarodnyi iazyk* no. 18 (1926): 1.
109. P. Kiriushin, "Inostrannye Sat-ovtsy v Minske," *Mezhdunarodnyi iazyk* no. 20–2 (1926): 7.
110. RGASPI f. 495 o. 99 d. 76 l. 17.
111. "VI-I mezhdunarodnyi s'ezd soiuza rabochikh esperantistov edinogo fronta," *Leningradskaia pravda* no. 179 (August 6, 1926): 1.
112. RGASPI f. 495 o. 99 d. 76 l. 17.
113. Ibid.; G. Demidiuk, "Posle s'ezdov. Itogi, perespektivy, i zadachi," *Mezhdunarodnyi iazyk* no. 23 (1926): 2.
114. "Protokolo de la VI-a Kongreso de Sennacieca Asocio Tutmonda Leningrado, 6–10 Augusto 1926," *Sennaciulo*, ekstra numero (November 1926): 6–7.
115. "Privetstviia mezhdunarodnomu kongressu rabochikh esperantistov," *Leningradskaia pravda* no. 179 (August 6, 1926): 4.
116. G. Demidjuk, "Ekskursoj," *Sennaciulo* 2, no. 46 (August 19, 1926): 3; "Na s'ezd esperantistov," *Leningradskaia pravda* (August 1, 1926), 4; "Khronika kongressa," *Leningradskaia pravda* no. 176 (August 3, 1926), 4.
117. "Khronika kongressa," *Leningradskaia pravda* no. 177 (August 4, 1926): 5; "Khronika kongressa," *Leningradskaia pravda* no. 181 (August 10, 1926): 4.
118. RGASPI f. 495 o. 99 d. 76 l. 17ob.
119. See, for example, "Movement for an International Language in the USSR," *VOKS Weekly News Bulletin* 28–9 (July 22, 1927): 10; G. Demidiuk, "Pod znakom Edinburga i Leningrada," *Izvestiia TsK SESR* no. 3–4 (1926–7): 93–4.

120. Lins, *Dangerous Language*, 1: 183.
121. Quoted in ibid., 183.
122. G. Demidiuk, "Pod znakom Edinburga i Leningrada," *Izvestiia TsK SESR* no. 3–4 (1926–7): 93.
123. "Educational Director, International Ladies' Garment Workers' Union Mark Starr," 1946; Mark Starr Papers; TAM 019; Tamiment Library/Robert F. Wagner Labor Archive, New York University, Box 25.
124. Mark Starr, "Senkasaj Impresoj Pri Sovetio," *Sennaciulo* 106 (October 7, 1926): 5. My thanks to Ulrich Lins for sharing a copy of this article with me.
125. Stefan Zweig, *The World of Yesterday: An Autobiography* (Lincoln, NE: University of Nebraska Press, 1964), 335.
126. Ibid., 331.
127. Ibid., 337.
128. David-Fox, *Showcasing*, 25.
129. Frederick C. Corney, *Telling October: Memory and the Making of the Bolshevik Revolution* (Ithaca, NY: Cornell University Press, 2004), 175.
130. David-Fox, *Showcasing*, 123.
131. Corney, *Telling October*, chapter 7.
132. Sylvia R. Margulies, *The Pilgrimage to Russia: The Soviet Union and the Treatment of Foreigners 1924–1937* (Madison: University of Wisconsin Press, 1968), 152.
133. "Preparations for the Tenth Anniversary of the October Revolution," *VOKS Weekly News Bulletin* 36–8 (September 23, 1927): 20.
134. Kiseleva, *Iz istorii bo'rby*, 123.
135. "Preparations for the Tenth Anniversary," 19.
136. "October Guests in USSR," *VOKS Weekly News Bulletin* 2 (January 14, 1928): 11; GARF f. 5283 o. 8 d. 26 l. 3.
137. Ibid., l. 15.
138. Ibid., l. 10.
139. Ibid., l. 3.
140. Paul Hollander, *Political Pilgrims: Travels of Western Intellectuals to the Soviet Union, China, and Cuba 1928–78* (New York: Oxford University Press, 1981) chapter 4; Margulies, *The Pilgrimage*, especially chapters 4–5, Shawn Connelly Salmon, "To the Land of the Future: A History of Intourist and Travel to the Soviet Union, 1929–1991," PhD diss. (University of California-Berkeley, 2008).
141. Fitzpatrick, "Foreigners Observed," 225.
142. Silas B. Axtell, "Russia, and Her Foreign Relations," *The Annals of the American Academy of Political and Social Science* 138, no. 1 (July 1928): 86.
143. Salmon, "To the Land of the Future," xv.
144. "Foreign Delegates in USSR," *VOKS Weekly News Bulletin* 47–8 (December 2, 1927): 10.
145. P. Kiriushin, *Mezhdunarodnaia sviaz' na Esperanto* (Moscow: Izdanie TsK SESR, 1930), 13.
146. Ibid., 11–14 (quote on 14).
147. "In the Streets of Moscow," *VOKS Weekly News Bulletin* 47–8 (December 2, 1927): 15.
148. Malte Rolf, *Soviet Mass Festivals, 1917–1991*, trans. Cynthia Klohr (Pittsburgh, PA: University of Pittsburgh Press, 2013), 45.
149. "In the Red Square," *VOKS Weekly News Bulletin* 47–8 (December 2, 1927): 17.
150. GARF f. 5283 o. 8 d. 26 ll. 8, 20.

151. Ibid., l. 21.
152. Ibid., ll. 20-3.
153. On these surveillance reports as a fundamental aspect of the VOKS guide-interpreters' work, see Michael David-Fox, *Showcasing*, chapter 1; idem., "The Fellow Travelers Revisited," esp. 306-20; Fitzpatrick, "Foreigners Observed," esp. 222-4; and Ludmila Stern, "Moscow 1937: The Interpreter's Story," *Australian Slavonic and East European Studies* 21, no. 1-2 (2007), esp. 75-6.
154. David-Fox, "Fellow Travelers Revisited," 314.
155. GARF f. 5283 o. 8 d. 26 ll. 3-13; 20-3; 30-9.
156. "Per Propraj Okuloj," *Sennaciulo* 4, no. 171 (January 12, 1928): 118.
157. GARF f. 5283 o. 8 d. 26 ll. 4-5.
158. Ibid., l. 15.
159. Ibid., l. 10.
160. Ibid., l. 35.
161. Ibid., l. 10.
162. Ibid., l. 31.
163. "Per Propraj Okuloj," 118.
164. GARF f. 5283 o. 8 d. 26 l. 37.
165. Ibid., l. 38.
166. Ibid., l. 10.
167. Ibid., ll. 26, 33.
168. Ibid., l. 34.
169. Ibid., ll. 10-11.
170. Ibid., l. 40.
171. Ibid., l. 20.
172. Ibid., l. 12.
173. Ibid., ll. 12-13.
174. Amy S. Jennings, "How to Travel in Soviet Russia," *Nation* 136, no. 3540 (May 10, 1933): 528.
175. David-Fox, *Showcasing*, 1.
176. Hollander, *Political Pilgrims*; Margulies, *Pilgrimage to Russia*; and Frederick C. Barghoorn, *The Soviet Cultural Offensive: The Role of Cultural Diplomacy in Soviet Foreign Policy* (Princeton, NJ: Princeton University Press, 1960).
177. Hollander, *Political Pilgrims*.
178. See, for example, David-Fox, *Showcasing*; Fitzpatrick, "Foreigners Observed;" and Ludmila Stern, *Western Intellectuals and the Soviet Union, 1920-1940: From Red Square to the Left Bank* (London: Routledge, 2007). For an account of leftist cultural diplomacy in the interwar years that de-centers the Soviet Union and emphasizes the forging of transnational proletarian solidarity, see Kasper Brasken, *The International Workers' Relief, Communism, and Transnational Solidarity* (Houndsmills: Palgrave Macmillan, 2015). For a larger history of foreign tourism to the Soviet Union from the 1920s through the 1980s, see I. B. Orlov and A. D. Popov, *Skvoz' "zheleznyi zanaves." See USSR! Inostrannye turisty i prizrak potemkinskikh dereven'* (Moscow: Izdatel'skii dom Vysshei shkoly ekonomiki, 2018).
179. Liam O'Flaherty, *I Went to Russia* (New York: Harcourt, Brace, and Company, 1931), 255.
180. Ruth Epperson Kennell, *Theodore Dreiser and the Soviet Union, 1927-1945* (New York: International Publishers, 1969), 32-3.
181. P. L. Travers, *Moscow Excursion* (New York: Reynal and Hitchcock, 1934), 9.

182. Ibid., 52.
183. Ibid., 61.
184. Ibid., 29.
185. Ibid., 95.
186. Hubert Griffith, *Seeing Soviet Russia: An Informative Record of the Cheapest Trip in Europe* (London: John Lane, 1932), 137.
187. Ibid., 86–7.
188. Ibid., 9.
189. Ibid., 42–3. As Margulies noted, one of the USSR's techniques of hospitality was to allow privileged foreign guests the "illusion" of freedom of movement and freedom from surveillance. Even when allowed to "wander" on their own as Griffith described it, Margulies pointed out, the foreign visitors were often kept under "subtle surveillance." Those foreign visitors who spoke no Russian were allowed some small measure of latitude to explore Moscow on their own. Given their presumed inability to freely converse with Soviet citizens in the absence of a guide-interpreter, little danger was seen in their limited autonomous exploration. Margulies, *The Pilgrimage to Russia*, 115–17 (quote on 115). Fitzpatrick, however, has noted that attempts to "discourage" foreign visitors "from wandering round the streets on their own" was at least as much about preventing them from losing their way as it was "to prevent them from seeing too much of the underside of Soviet everyday life." See her "Foreigners Observed," 220.
190. Griffith, *Seeing Soviet Russia*, 43.
191. Ibid., 48.
192. Jennings, "How to Travel in Soviet Russia," 530.
193. David-Fox, *Showcasing*, 126.
194. Ibid.
195. Margulies, *The Pilgrimage*, 124–5. Andrew Smith, an American worker who traveled to the USSR to help build socialism but quickly grew disillusioned by the Soviet experiment, wrote a scathing memoir in which he described the efforts to deceive foreign delegations as the "the greatest show on earth." The authorities would even go so far, he claimed, as to have party propagandists play the role of workers on the occasion of foreigners' guided tours to Soviet factories. See Andrew Smith, *I Was a Soviet Worker* (New York: E. P. Dutton & Co, 1936), 74–80.
196. Waldo Frank, *Dawn in Russia: The Record of a Journey* (New York: Scribner & Sons, 1932), 139.
197. David-Fox, *Showcasing*, 105–6.
198. Ibid., 119.
199. Ibid., 54.
200. Tamara Solonevich, *Zapiski sovetskoi perevodchitsy* (originally published in Sofia in 1937), available online at https://www.litmir.me/br/?b=137611 (accessed July 8, 2019).
201. Orlov and Popov, *Skvoz' "Zheleznyi zanaves,"* 239.
202. On the stresses these VOKS guides endured, see Sheila Fitzpatrick, "Australian Visitors to the Soviet Union: the View from the Soviet Side," in *Political Tourists: Travellers from Australia to the Soviet Union in the 1920s-1940s*, ed. Sheila Fitzpatrick and Carolyn Rasmussen (Carlton: Melbourne University Press, 2008), esp. 14–15.
203. David-Fox, *Showcasing*, 42, 57–60.

204. N. Semper (Sokolova), "Portrety i peizazhi: Chastnye vospominaniia o XX veke," *Druzhba narodov* 2, no. 2 (1997): 73–115, here 107–15.
205. Sheila Fitzpatrick, "Australian Visitors," 20.
206. Alexander Wicksteed, *My Russian Neighbors: Recollections of Ten Years in Soviet Moscow* (New York: McGraw Hill, 1934), 29.
207. David-Fox, *Showcasing*, 118–20; 188–9; Orlov and Popov, *Skvoz' "Zheleznyi zanaves,"* 237–5.
208. Quoted in Stern, "Moscow 1937," 74.
209. A. V. Golubev and V. A. Nevezhin, "VOKS v 1930-1940-e gody," *Minuvshee*, 14 (1993): 349–50 (quote on 350).
210. Fitzpatrick, "Foreigners Observed," 229; Margulies, *The Pilgrimage*, 143.
211. See, for example, Fitzpatrick, "Australian Visitors," 8.
212. A. I. Matiushkin-Gerke i Rozenblit, *Izuchaite inostrannye iazyki* (Leningrad: Molodaia gvardiia, 1931), 17–18.
213. For an illuminating analysis of the significance of the at times especially intimate bonds between Soviet cultural mediators and their foreign charges and contacts, see Michael David-Fox, *Crossing Borders: Modernity, Ideology, and Culture in Russia and the Soviet Union* (Pittsburgh: Pittsburgh University Press, 2015), chapter 6 (quote on 164).
214. GARF f. 374 o. 27 d. 147 l. 96.
215. Ibid., 100.
216. Ibid., l. 96.
217. Ibid., l. 91.
218. For example, RGASPI f. 495 o. 99 d. 77 ll. 20–21, 27.

5 Language Revolutions and Their Discontents

1. M. Ul'ianova, "Inostrannye iazyki ili Esperanto?" *Raboche-krest'ianskii Korrespondent* 21 (November 15, 1928), 6–9. On Soviet Esperantists' angry and scandalized responses to Ul'ianova's provocation, see "D. Ikhok., "Za ili protiv Esperanto?" *Raboche-krest'ianskii Korrespondent* 21 (April 15–30, 1929), 21–2.
2. Matiushkin-Gerke, *Izuchaite inostrannye iazyki*, 3–12.
3. David-Fox, *Showcasing*, 175.
4. M. I. Ul'ianova, *Rabkorskoe dvizhenie*, 107–8.
5. L.V. Shcherba, *Iazykovaia sistema i rechevaia deiatel'nost'* (Leningrad: Nauka, 1974), 344–65 (quote on 348).
6. Kiseleva, *Istoriia bor'by*, 130.
7. Matiushkin-Gerke, *Izuchaite inostrannye iazyki*.
8. O. Kameneva, "Inostrannyi iazyk v massy," *Revoliutsiia i kul'tura* no. 3–4 (1928): 98.
9. VOKS, *Fakty i tsyfry* (Moscow: Mospoligraf, 1930), 43.
10. G. Demidiuk, "Esperanto i kampaniia za inostrannye iazyki," *Izvestiia TsK SESR* no. 7–8 (1928): 241–2.
11. Kiseleva, *Iz istorii bor'by*, 130–1.
12. Ibid., 132–4.
13. Quoted in Demidiuk, "Esperanto i kampaniia za inostrannye iazyki," 243.
14. The directive is reproduced in M. Sergievskii and Iu. Vikhert, *Inostrannye iazyki v massy* (Moscow: Narkompros, 1930), 31–2.

15. Iu. Larin, "Boevye voprosy narodnogo obrazovaniia," *Revoliutsiia i kul'tura* no. 14 (1929): 14–15.
16. Quoted in E. Drezen, "Dialektika razvitiia iazyka i protivniki Esperanto," in *Novye problemy iazykoznaniia*, ed. Internatsional'naia proletarskaia Esperanto-lingvisticheskaia komissiia (TsK SESR: Moscow, 1933), 30.
17. G. Demidiuk, "Esperanto i kampaniia za inostrannye iazyki," *Izvestiia TsK SESR* 7–8 (1928): 241–4.
18. V. N. Engel'gardt, *Shkola, uchitel'stvo i Esperanto* (Moscow: TsK SESR, 1930), 14.
19. Quoted in Ikhok., "Za ili protiv Esperanto," 21–2.
20. Kiriushin, *Mezhdunarodnaia rabochaia sviaz'*, 4–8.
21. G. M. Filippov, "Esperanto i izuchenie inostrannykh iazykov," *Izvestiia TsK SESR* no. 9–10 (1928): 272–4.
22. Demidiuk, "Esperanto i kampaniia za inostrannye iazyki," 242.
23. N. Intsertov, "Esperanto–na sluzhbu tekhnike!" *Mezhdunarodnyi iazyk* no. 2 (1931): 87.
24. GARF f. 7668 o. 1 d. 445 ll. 4–12 (quote on 7).
25. Intsertov, "Esperanto–na sluzhbu tekhnike," 85–9.
26. E. Ivnitskii, *Esperantskii traktor / Esperantista traktoro* (Moscow: TsK SEU, 1930).
27. "Chto poslat' svoemu zagranichnomu korrespondentu," *Mezhdunarodnyi iazyk* no. 2–3 (1930): 162.
28. Lins, *Dangerous Language* 2: 41.
29. "Stat' na put'," *Mezhdunarodnyi iazyk* no. 4 (1931): 179–80.
30. "Pomozhem mekhanizatsii Donbassa. K revoliutsionnym rabochim-gorniakam vsego mira (Iz obrashcheniia-pis'ma stalinskikh esperantistov)," *Mezhdunarodnyi iazyk* no. 3 (1931): 180–2.
31. D. Snezhko, "Krupitsy tsenneishego opyta," *Mezhdunarodnyi iazyk* no. 3 (1931): 143–4.
32. GARF f. 7668 o. 1 d. 445 ll. 29–30.
33. Ibid., ll. 32–7.
34. I. Zabelyshinskii, *Inostrannye iazyki v massy* (Moscow: Uchpedgiz, 1931), 11.
35. Matiushkin-Gerke, *Izuchaite inostrannye iazyki*, no. 9–12 (quote on 9).
36. Ibid., 57.
37. Morton Benson, "The New Soviet Foreign Language Program," *Modern Language Journal* 40, no. 4 (1956): 173.
38. GARF f. 7668 o. 1 d. 445 ll. 3, 50.
39. Ibid., ll. 54-54ob.
40. RGASPI f. 558 o. 11 d. 852 l. 77-77ob.
41. GARF f. 7668 o. 1 d. 445 l. 49ob.
42. Quoted in Garvia, *Esperanto and its Rivals*, 124.
43. RGASPI f. 495 o. 99 d. 70 l. 18.
44. Ibid., l. 119.
45. Lins, *Dangerous Language* 1: 176–7; Garvia, *Esperanto and its Rivals*, 124–5.
46. Sidorov, *Esperanto-dvizhenie: fragmenty istorii*, 123.
47. Garvia, *Esperanto and its Rivals*, 125: Lins, *Dangerous Language* 1: 176.
48. Vlasov, *Esperanto: polveka tsenzury*, 106.
49. "IX Mezhdunarodnyi kongress Vnenatsional'nogo Vsemirnogo Soiuza (SAT)," *Mezhdunarodnyi iazyk* no. 3 (1929): 129–31 (quote on 131). For more on Lanti's alleged heresy, see Lins, *Dangerous Language*, 1: 206–10.

50. Matthew Worley, "Courting Disaster? The Communist International in the Third Period," in *In Search of Revolution: International Communist Parties in the Third Period*, ed. Matthew Worley (London: I.B. Tauris, 2014): 1–17.
51. "IX Mezhdunarodnyi congress SAT v Leiptsige," *Mezhdunarodnyi iazyk* no. 4–5 (1929): 195–9.
52. For greater detail on how the conflict evolved, see Lins, *Dangerous Language*, 1: 210–20.
53. P. Kiriushin, "Litso klassovogo vraga," *Mezhdunarodnyi iazyk* no. 3 (1931): 132.
54. RGASPI f. 495 o. 99 d. 82 l. 3.
55. Schor, *Bridge of Words*, 150; Borsboom, *Vivo de Lanti*, 111–12.
56. Vlasov, *Esperanto: polveka tsenzury*, 106–8.
57. GARF f. 7668 o. 1 d. 445, ll.79–83 (quote on l. 81).
58. Ibid., l. 1.
59. "Ustav Internatsionala Proletarskikh Esperantistov," *Mezhdunarodnyi iazyk* no. 7–8 (1932): 206.
60. RGASPI f. 495 o. 99 d. 82 ll. 16–18.
61. "IPE, SAT, i zadachi SESR," *Mezhdunarodnyi iazyk* no. 7–8 (1932): 194.
62. "Da zdravstvuet IPE," *Mezhdunarodnyi iazyk* no. 6 (1932): 163.
63. "Gniiushchie mrakobesy. SAT—v peredovom otriade mirovoi burzhuazii," *Mezhdunarodnyi iazyk* 1 (1932): 5.
64. Lins, *Dangerous Language*, 1: 219.
65. Schor, *Bridge of Words*, 152.
66. Ibid., 153, 191–2.
67. "Gniiushchie mrakobesy," 7.
68. RGASPI f. 495 o. 99 d. 81 l. 1
69. "Gniiushchie mrakobesy," 8–9.
70. N. Ia. Marr, *Izbrannye raboty*, vol. 1 (Leningrad: GAIMK, 1933), 6.
71. On the downfall of Marr's theory and the Soviet linguistic controversy of 1950, see Ethan Pollock, *Stalin and the Soviet Science* Wars (Princeton, NJ: Princeton University Press, 2006), chapter 5.
72. On Marr and the Soviet development of a "Marxist" linguistics, see Craig Brandist, *The Dimensions of Hegemony: Language, Culture and Politics in Revolutionary Russia* (Leiden: Brill, 2015), chapter 8; Katerina Clark, *Petersburg, Crucible of Cultural Revolution* (Cambridge, MA: Harvard University Press, 1995), 212–23; Valerii Grechko, "Mezhdu utopiei i 'Realpolitik': Marr, Stalin, i vopros o vsemirnom iazyke," *Russian Linguistics* 34, no. 2 (2010): 159–72; Michael G. Smith, *Language and Power in the Creation of the USSR, 1917–1953* (New York: Mouton de Gruyter, 1998), chapter 4; Yuri Slezkine, "N. Ia. Marr and the National Origins of Soviet Ethnogenetics," *Slavic Review* 55, no. 4 (1996): 826–62; Lawrence L. Thomas, *The Linguistic Theories of N. Ja. Marr* (Berkeley: University of California Press, 1957).
73. Marr, *Izbrannye raboty*, 1: 13.
74. Quoted in Slezkine, "Marr and the National Origins," 843.
75. N. Ia. Marr, *Izbrannye raboty*, vol. 2 (Moscow: Tipografiia Akademii Nauk SSR, 1936), 328.
76. Clark, *Petersburg*, 214.
77. Marr, *Izbrannye raboty*, 2: 328.
78. Michael G. Smith, *Language and Power in the Creation of the USSR, 1917–1953* (New York: Mouton de Gruyter, 1998), chapters 3 and 4.
79. Ibid., 76.

80. Michael G. Smith, "For a Rationalization of Language: The Bolshevik Experience with Esperanto" in *The Idea of a Universal* Language, ed. Humphrey Tonkin and Karen Johnson Walker (New York: Center for Research and Documentation on World Language Problems, 1986), 72.
81. Smith, *Language and Power*, esp. 76–80. See also Aleksandr Dulichenko, "Ideia mezhdunarodnogo iskusstvennogo iazyka v debriakh rannei sovetskoi sotsiolingvistiki," *Russian Linguistics* 34, no. 2 (2010): 143–57. Notably, Esperanto also helped to inspire in 1933 the first Soviet proposal for a translation machine. See Gordin, "The Forgetting and Rediscovery," especially pp. 849–64.
82. RGASPI f. 495 o. 99. d. 76 ll. 1–10 (quote on 1).
83. E. Drezen, "O ratsionalizatsii iazyka," *Izvestiia TsK SESR* no. 5–6 (1926–7): 174.
84. E. Drezen, *V poiskakh vseobshchego iazyka* (Moscow: Zemlia i fabrika, 1925), 12.
85. Ibid., 18.
86. E. Drezen, *Za vseobshchim iazykom (tri veka iskanii)* (Moscow: Gosizdat, 1928), 3–9.
87. Ibid., 31.
88. Ibid., 240.
89. E. Drezen, "O zadachakh stoiashchikh pered Esperantistami v periode diktatury proletariata," *Mezhdunarodnyi iazyk*, no. 2–3 (1930): 72.
90. J. V. Stalin, "Political Report of the Central Committee to the Sixteenth Congress of the CPSU (B) June 27, 1930," Marxists Internet Archive, https://www.marxists.org/reference/archive/stalin/works/1930/aug/27.htm (accessed October 31, 2019).
91. J. V. Stalin, "The National Question and Leninism (1929)," Marxists Internet Archive, https://www.marxists.org/reference/archive/stalin/works/1929/03/18.htm (accessed October 31, 2019).
92. Stalin, "Political Report of the Central Committee to the Sixteenth Congress."
93. Thomas, *Linguistic Theories of N. Ja. Marr*, 89.
94. Brandist, *Dimensions of* Hegemony, 194.
95. Smith, *Language and Power*, 97–102. On Soviet linguists' struggle to 'revolutionize' linguistics and the often heated scholarly debates among them in the interwar period, see also Craig Brandist and Katya Chown, ed., *Politics and the Theory of Language in the USSR 1917–1938: The Birth of Sociological Linguistics* (New York: Anthem Press, 2010).
96. "Obrashchenie gruppy Iazykovednyi Front," *Mezhdunarodnyi iazyk* no. 4–5 (1930): 177–8 (quote on 178).
97. GARF f. 7668 o. 1 d. 445 l. 9.
98. E. Spiridovich, "Protsessy internatsionalizatsii iazyka," *Izvestiia TsK SESR* no. 5–6 (1926–7): 161–5; Spiridovich, "Skhema razvitiia iazyka," *Izvestiia TsK SESR* no. 7–8 (1926–1927): 241–6.
99. E. F. Spiridovich, *Iazykoznanie i mezhdunarodnyi iazyk* (Moscow: TsK SESR, 1931), 4. Spiridovich offered a more concise critique of Marr's Japhetic Theory as too vague on the question of international language in his "Akademik Marr i vsemirnyi iazyk budushchego," *Mezhdunarodnyi iazyk* no. 5 (1935): 135–8.
100. Spiridovich, *Iazykoznanie*, 35.
101. Ibid., 50.
102. Ibid., 55.
103. Ibid., 66.
104. Ibid., 91.
105. Ibid., 98.
106. Ibid., 99.

107. See the editor's note in ibid., 66 fn. 1.
108. GARF f. 7668 o. 1 d. 445 ll. 39–48; E. Drezen, "O griadushchem Esperanto. Iazyk natsional'nyi, mezhdunarodnyi i vseobshchii," *Mezhdunarodnyi iazyk* no. 1 (1931): 14–17.
109. GARF f. 7668 o. 1 d. 445 l. 45
110. Ibid., l. 40.
111. Ibid., ll. 42, 44.
112. Ibid., l. 46.
113. E. Drezen, "Mirovaia kuznitsa M. Ia." *Mezhdunarodnyi iazyk* no. 6 (1932): 179.
114. E. Drezen, *Problema mezhdunarodnogo iazyka* (Moscow: TsK SESR, 1932), 34.
115. V. Kolchinskii, "Mezhdunarodnoi tekhnicheskoi sviazi pomoch' delom," *Mezhdunarodnyi iazyk* no. 11–12 (1932): 309.
116. "Krupneishaia pobeda," *Mezhdunarodnyi iazyk* no. 4 (1932): 97–8.
117. "Istoricheskii document. Tesizy o mezhdunarodnom iazyke razrabotany brigadoi iazykovogo stroitel'stva i priniaty plenumom NIIaz," *Mezhdunarodnyi iazyk* no. 4 (1932): 99–102, quote on 100.
118. Ibid., 101.
119. "Krupneishaia pobeda."
120. E. Spiridovich, " 'Istinnyi lozung bor'by' v Markso-Leninskom iazykoznanii," *Mezhdunarodnyi iazyk* no. 11–12 (1932): 338.
121. N. Ia. Zolotov, "Protiv burzhuaznoi kontrabandy v iazykoznanii," in S. Ia. Bykovskii, ed., *Protiv burzhuaznoi kontrabandy v iazykoznanii* (Leningrad: GAIMK, 1932): 12, reproduced online at http://crecleco.seriot.ch/textes/Zolotov32.html (accessed 6 November 2019).
122. F. P. Filin, "Bor'ba za markistsko-leninskoe iazykoznanie i gruppa 'Iazykfront,' in Bykovskii, *Protiv burzhuaznoi kontrabandy*: 38, reproduced online at http://crecleco.seriot.ch/textes/Filin32a.html (accessed November 6, 2019).
123. Smith, *Language and Power*, 101.
124. On Wüster's life and scholarship, see Angela Campo, "The Reception of Eugen Wüster's Work and the Development of Terminology" (PhD diss., Université de Montréal, 2012).
125. E. Drezen, "Normalizatsiia tekhnicheskogo iazyka pri kapitalizme i sotsializme," *Mezhdunarodnyi iazyk* no. 7–8 (1932): 231–6, quote on 231.
126. Ibid., 233.
127. A. P. Andreev, "Sovetskoe iazykoznanie za 15 let," *Mezhdunarodnyi iazyk*, no. 9–10 (1932): 288–91 (quote on 290).
128. E. Spiridovich, "Mesto Esperanto dolzhno byt' naideno," *Mezhdunarodnyi iazyk*, no. 7–8 (1933): 186–8; Solenyi-Rukhimovich, "Sovetskaia obshchestvennost' zhdet otveta," *Mezhdunarodnyi iazyk*, no. 7–8 (1933): 188–9.
129. E. Drezen, "Nad chem vy teper' rabotaete?" *Mezhdunarodnyi iazyk* no. 6 (1934): 149.
130. Brigid O'Keeffe, "The Woman Always Pays: The Lives of Ivy Litvinov," *Slavonic and East European Review* 97, no. 3 (July 2019): 501–28; John Carswell, *The Exile: A Life of Ivy Litvinov* (London: Faber and Faber, 1983).
131. Basic English Postcard Advert, Cambridge University Library, Department of Manuscripts and University Archives, Charles Ogden: Correspondence and Papers [Hereafter, Ogden Papers], MS Add.8312/I.
132. C. K. Ogden, *Basic English Versus the Artificial Languages* (London: Kegan Paul, 1935), 63.

133. C. K. Ogden, *Debabelization, With a Survey of Contemporary Opinion on the Problem of a Universal Language* (London: Kegan Paul, 1931), 144.
134. Basic English Postcard Advert, Ogden Papers.
135. Ogden, *Debabelization*, 166.
136. Ogden to Litvinov, March 21, 1935, Ogden Papers, MS Add.8312/I/107.
137. Litvinov to Ogden, February 23, 1933, Ogden Papers MS Add.8312/I/31.
138. E. Drezen, "Beisik Inglish (Basic English)," *Mezhdunarodnyi iazyk* no. 1 (1934): 8–9.
139. Keable to Litvinov, March 28, 1934, Ogden Papers, MS Add.8312/I/35.
140. Drezen to Litvinov, April 6, 1934, Ogden Papers, MS Add.8312/I/36.
141. Unidentified to Litvinov, May 14, 1934, Ogden Papers, MS Add.8312/I/49.
142. Litvinov to Ogden, May 8, 1934, Ogden Papers, MS Add.8312/I/44; Litvinov to Ogden, April 28, 1934, Ogden Papers, MS Add.8312/I/40.
143. Litvinov to Ogden, April 28, 1934, Ogden Papers, MS Add.8312/I/40.
144. "Perepiska o 'Beisik Inglish,'" *Mezhdunarodnyi iazyk*, no. 4 (1934), 89–92.
145. Ibid., 90–1.
146. Litvinov to Ogden, September 16, 1934, Ogden Papers, MS Add.8312/I/137.
147. Litvinov to Ogden, May 10, 1934, Ogden Papers, MS Add.8312/I/45
148. Litvinov to Ogden, April 28, 1934, Ogden Papers, MS Add.8312/I/40.
149. A. V. Litvinova, *Basic Step by Step. Uchebnik angliiskogo iazyka na osnove "Basic Step by Step" Ch. K. Ogdena* (Moscow: Izdatel'skoe tovarishchestvo inostrannykh rabochikh v SSSR, 1935).
150. Ivy Litvinov, "To Russia With Love," *Observer* (July 25, 1976): 17.
151. Litvinov to Ogden, March 18, 1936, Ogden Papers, MS Add.8312/I/150.
152. Litvinov had her own personal reasons for wanting to leave Moscow at this time. She was humiliated by her husband's very public extramarital affair. See O'Keeffe, "Woman Always Pays," 515–17.
153. Litvinov to Ogden, January 23, 1937, Ogden Papers, MS Add.8312/I/178.
154. Litvinov to Ogden, Ogden Papers, March 14, 1937, MS Add.8312/I/183.
155. *XVII S'ezdu Vsesoiuznoi kommunisticheskoi partii (bol'shevikov). Raport Soiuza esperantistov sovetskikh respublik (SESR)* (Moscow: Put' Oktiabr', 1934), 3.
156. Ibid., 9–10.
157. Ibid., 14.
158. RGASPI f. 495 o. 14 d. 426 l. 23.
159. Vatlin and Smith, "The Comintern," 192–3; Jonathan Haslam, "The Comintern and the Origins of the Popular Front 1934–1935," *Historical Journal* 22, no. 3 (1979): 673–91; Julian Jackson, *The Popular Front in France: Defending Democracy, 1934–1938* (Cambridge: Cambridge University Press, 1988), especially chapter 1.
160. RGASPI f. 495 o. 99 d. 83 l. 1.
161. Schor, *Bridge of Worlds*, 179.
162. Lins, *Dangerous Language* 1: 97–118.
163. RGASPI f. 495 o. 99 d. 86 l. 98.
164. Ibid., l. 104.
165. Vlasov, *Esperanto: polveka tsenzury*, 110, 136, 176.
166. GARF f. 5451 o. 13a d. 614 l. 1
167. Quoted in Lins, *Dangerous Language* 2: 24.
168. RGASPI f. 495 o. 99 d. 86 l. 10.
169. Ibid., l. 107.
170. Ibid., l. 130.
171. Ibid., l. 131.

172. RGASPI f. 495 o. 30 d. 1157 ll. 14–15.
173. RGASPI f. 495 o. 99 d. 87 ll. 51–53.
174. Ibid., l. 57ob.
175. Quoted in Sidorov, *Esperanto-dvizhenie: fragmenty istorii*, 80–1.
176. RGASPI f. 495 o. 30 d. 1157 ll. 35–98.
177. RGASPI f. 495 o. 99 d. 87 l. 6. Here, in the CPSU report, Drezen's words were misquoted/mistranslated. The stenographic record of the Leipzig SAT congress, printed in the pages of *Sennaciulo*, quotes Drezen as having said, "For 22 years, I have been a worse communist than a good Esperantist." The comment was made during discussion of the SEU's struggles with Lanti for ideological leadership within SAT. "Protokoloro de la 9-a SAT-Kongreso 4–10 augusto 1929 en Leipzig," *Sennaciulo* 5, no. 256 (1929): 495.
178. RGASPI f. 495 o. 99 d. 87 l. 7.
179. On the coexistence of xenophobia and internationalism in Soviet ideology and everyday life during these years, see especially Kirschenbaum, *International Communism*.
180. David-Fox, "Foreign Travelers Revisited," 335.
181. David-Fox, *Showcasing*, 300–2 (quote on 302). Ville Laamanen suggests that VOKS was in recovery by 1939. See his "VOKS, Cultural Diplomacy and the Shadow of the Lubianka: Olavi Paavolainen's 1939 Visit to the Soviet Union," *Journal of Contemporary History* 52, no. 4 (2017): 1022–41.
182. William J. Chase, *Enemies within the Gates? The Comintern and Stalinist Repression, 1934–1939* (New Haven, CT: Yale University Press, 2001), quote on 7. On Comintern use and training in ciphered communications, see Fridrikh A. Firsov, Harvey Klehr, and John Earl Haynes, *Secret Cables of the Comintern, 1933–1943*, trans. Lynn Visson (New Haven, CT: Yale University Press, 2014), chapter 1. On the xenophobic purging of the Comintern, see M. M. Panteleev, "Repressii v Kominterne (1937–1938 gg.)," *Otechestvennaia istoriia* 6 (1996): 161–8.
183. Firsov, *Secret Cables*, 24–5 (quote on 24).
184. Fischer, *My Lives in Russia*, 144.
185. Ibid., 153; Fischer, *Men and Politics*, 354.
186. Litvinov to Ogden, May 16, 1936, Ogden Papers, MS Add.8312/I/154.
187. Alexandre Barmine, *Memoirs of a Soviet Diplomat*, trans. Gerard Hopkins (London: Lovat Dickson, 1938), 333–4.
188. Karl Schlogel, *Moscow, 1937*, trans. Rodney Livingstone (Cambridge: Polity, 2012), 65. On NKVD arrests on the basis of foreign names, see also Alexander Vatlin, *Agents of Terror: Ordinary Men and Extraordinary Violence in Stalin's Secret Police*, trans. Seth Bernstein (Madison: University of Wisconsin Press, 2016), 46.
189. J. Arch Getty and Oleg V. Naumov, *The Road to Terror: Stalin and the Self-Destruction of the Bolsheviks* (New Haven, CT: Yale University Press, 1999), 480–1.
190. Terry Martin, "The Origins of Soviet Ethnic Cleansing," *Journal of Modern History* 70, no. 4 (1998): 813–61.
191. Lev Kopelev, *To Be Preserved Forever*, trans. Anthony Austin (Philadelphia, PA: J. B. Lippincott Company, 1977), 112.
192. Sidorov, *Esperanto-dvizhenie: fragmenty istorii*, 85–6.
193. Quoted in ibid., 93.
194. "Muravkin, G. I." http://historio.ru/muravkin.php (accessed August 26, 2019).
195. "Iosif Bata," http://historio.ru/batta.php (accessed August 26, 2019).

196. "Protokol doprosa Bata Iosifa Ivanovicha ot 8-go Fevralia 1938," http://historio.ru/b2.php (accessed August 26, 2019).
197. Lins, *Dangerous Language* 2: 8.
198. Nikolai Stepanov, "Kak eto bylo? Polnyi razgrom sovetskogo Esperanto-dvizheniia v 1938 godu," http://historio.ru/kaketoby.php (accessed August 26, 2019).
199. See Nikolai Rytkov's account of his arrest and interrogation, as quoted in M. S. Abol'skaia, "Presledovaniia Esperantistov," http://historio.ru/abolskaja.php (accessed August 26, 2019).

Epilogue: The Death of Esperanto

1. Nikolai Rytkov's account of his arrest and interrogation, as quoted in M. S. Abol'skaia, "Presledovaniia Esperantistov," http://historio.ru/abolskaja.php (accessed August 26, 2019). In 1965, Rytkov received permission to travel to Vienna for a congress of Esperantists and defected. He died in London in 1973. Aleksandr Khar'kovskii, "Nikolai Ryt'kov: Akter, Zek, Esperantist," http://miresperanto.com/pri_esperantistoj/hharjkovskij_pri_rytjkov.htm (accessed October 22, 2019). On the NKVD's methods of manufacturing testimony regarding fictitious (Trotskyite) spy rings and other crimes, as well as NKVD's violent methods of securing signed confessions from the accused, see Vatlin, *Agents of Terror*, esp. 30–46.
2. Ryt'kov, Nikolai Nikolaevich http://historio.ru/rytjkov.php (accessed August 26, 2019).
3. A. V. Sidorov, *Esperanto-dvizhenie na Severo-Zapade Rossii* (St. Petersburg: n.p., 2014), 124.
4. "Bakushinskii, R. N." http://historio.ru/bakushin.php (accessed March 15, 2018)
5. "Bakushinskii, Ruf Nikolaevich," http://historio.ru/bakusx.php (accessed August 26, 2019).
6. B. Breslau, "Drug chelovechestva," *Mezhdunarodnyi iazyk* no. 5 (1934): 126–7.
7. "Breslau, B. M." http://historio.ru/breslaux.php (accessed August 26, 2019).
8. "Drezen, E. K. (1892–1937)," http://historio.ru/drezen.php (accessed August 26, 2019).
9. Stepanov, "Kak eto bylo?"
10. "Intsertov, Nikolai Iakovlevich," http://historio.ru/incertov.php (accessed August 27, 2019).
11. Ibid.; Stepanov, "Kak eto bylo?"
12. Andrei Sakharov Center, Martirolog zhertv politicheskikh repressii, Elena Konstantinovna Drezen-Sazonova, https://www.sakharov-center.ru/asfcd/martirolog/?t=page&id=19085 (accessed 18 October 2019).
13. Lins, *Dangerous Language* 2: 26, fn. 26.
14. "Smirnova, A.C." http://historio.ru/smirnova.php (accessed August 27, 2019)
15. Gavrilov, Petr Alekseevich," http://historio.ru/gavrilov.php (accessed August 27, 2019).
16. Ibid.
17. "Mastepanov, Sergei Danilovich," http://historio.ru/mastepan.php (accessed August 27, 2019).
18. "Repressii protiv Esperantistov na Ukraine," http://historio.ru/ukraina.php (accessed December 18, 2019).

19. Ibid.
20. Ibid.
21. Robichek, Fyodor Pavlovich http://historio.ru/robicxek.php (accessed August 27, 2019); Andrei Sakharov Center, Martirolog zhertv politicheskikh repressii, Fyodor Pavlovich Robichek https://www.sakharov-center.ru/asfcd/martirolog/?t=page&id=53 (accessed October 18, 2019).
22. "Zykov, V. M.," http://historio.ru/zykov.php (accessed August 29, 2019).
23. Timofeevskii, A. K.," http://historio.ru/timofeevskij.php (accessed August 27, 2019).
24. "Samoilenko, A. T." http://historio.ru/samojlen.php (accessed August 27, 2019).
25. "Novozhilov, Aleksei Andreevich," http://historio.ru/novojxilov.php (accessed August 28, 2019).
26. "Temerin, N. N.," http://historio.ru/temerin.php (accessed August 28, 2019).
27. "Filippov, F. A.," http://historio.ru/filippov.php (accessed August 28, 2019).
28. "Usov, N. P.," http://historio.ru/usov.php (accessed August 28, 2019).
29. "Nevolin, A. N.," http://historio.ru/nevolin.php (accessed August 28, 2019).
30. Sidorov, *Esperanto-dvizhenie na Severo-Zapade Rossii*, 102–4.
31. Valentin Luk'ianin, "Obyknovennaia istoriia, XX vek," originally published in *Ural*, no. 12 (2011); republished online at https://magazines.gorky.media/ural/2011/12/obyknovennaya-istoriya-hh-vek.html (accessed September 4, 2019).
32. Sidorov, *Esperanto-dvizhenie: fragmenty istorii*, 94–6.
33. Quoted in ibid., 110.
34. Lins, *Dangerous Language* 1: 234–5.
35. Lins, *Dangerous Language* 2: 3–5.
36. Varlam Shalamov, *Kolyma Stories. Volume I*, trans. Donald Rayfield (New York: NYRB Books, 2018), quote on 384.
37. I. Lisichnik, "Zhizn' posviashchennaia idee mezhdunarodnoi solidarnosti," http://historio.ru/lisicxnik.php (accessed March 18, 2018).
38. R. Bugeli, "Kogo chto vdokhnovliaet," *Kutaisi* (January 21, 1967), reproduced online at http://historio.ru/lis-6.php (accessed January 7, 2019).
39. "Repressii protiv Esperantistov na Ukraine."
40. Letter from Lisichnik to S.N. Krainov (June 29, 1973), http://historio.ru/lis-5.php (accessed January 7, 2019).
41. Case, *Age of Questions*.
42. Harper, "Empire, Diaspora, and the Language of Globalism," 143.
43. Gilburd, *To See Paris and Die*, 5.
44. In the post-Stalin era, there was a minor revival of Esperantism in the Soviet Union and across the socialist bloc. This late socialist Esperanto movement was small and in no way comparable—either in its aspirations or in the scope of its activity—to the Soviet Esperantist movement of the interwar period. For more on this revival, see Lins, *Dangerous Language* 2: chapters 9–11.
45. On the coexistence of Soviet internationalism and Stalinist xenophobia and isolationism during the Purges and Terror, see Kirschenbaum, *International Communism*.
46. Applebaum, "The Rise of Russian;" Gilburd, *To See Paris and Die*. On how, during the Cold War, English edged out Russian in the race to become the international language of science, see Gordin, *Scientific Babel*, especially chapter 9.

Bibliography

Archives

Russian Federation

Gosudarstvennyi Arkhiv Rossiiskoi Federatsii (GARF). Moscow.

Fond A-626:	Sakharov, Aleksandr Andreevich
Fond A-2306:	Ministerstvo Prosveshcheniia RSFSR
Fond A-2307:	Glavnoe upravlenie nauchnykh i muzeinykh uchrezhdenii
Fond 374:	Tsentral'naia kontrol'naia komissiia VKP(b)—Narodnyi komissariat raboche-krest'ianskoi inspektsii SSSR
Fond 1235:	Vserossiiskii tsentral'nyi ispolnitel'nyi komitet RSFSR
Fond 3316:	Tsentral'nyi ispolnitel'nyi komitet SSSR
Fond 5283:	Vsesoiuznoe obshchestvo kul'turnykh sviazi s zagranitsei (VOKS)
Fond 5446:	Sovet ministrov SSSR
Fond 5451:	Vsesoiuznyi tsentral'nyi sovet professional'nykh soiuzov
Fond 7668:	Komitet po zavedyvaniiu uchenymi i uchebnymi uchrezhdeniiami pri prezidiume verkhovnogo soveta SSSR
Fond 9550:	Kollektsiia listovok sovetskogo perioda

Rossiiskii Gosudarstvennyi Arkhiv Sotsial'no-Politicheskoi Istorii (RGASPI). Moscow.

Fond 17:	Tsentral'nyi komitet KPSS
Fond 495:	Ispolkom Kominterna
Fond 558:	Stalin, Iosif Vissarionovich (1878–1953)

Rossiiskii Gosudarstvennyi Istoricheskii Arkhiv (RGIA). St. Petersburg.

Fond 776:	Glavnoe upravlenie po delam pechati

United Kingdom

Cambridge University Library, Department of Manuscripts and University Archives

    Charles Ogden: Correspondence and Papers

United States

Hoover Institution Archives, Stanford University

    Ivy and Tatiana Litvinov Papers
    Gennadii Ivanovich Tupitsyn Papers

Tamiment Library/Robert F. Wagner Labor Archives, New York University

    Mark Starr Papers

Internet Repositories

Andrei Sakharov Center, Martirolog zhertv politicheskikh repressii, rasstreliannykh i zakhorennykh v Moskve i Moskovskoi Oblasti v 1918–1953 g.g. https://www.sakharov-center.ru/asfcd/martirolog/
Esperanto en Rusio, http://historio.ru/
Marxists Internet Archive, https://www.marxists.org/

Periodicals

Biulleten' TsK SESS
Espero
Izvestiia TsK SESR
Krasnaia niva
La Ondo de Esperanto
Leningradskaia pravda
Mezhdunarodnyi iazyk
Niva
Raboche-krest'ianskii korrespondent
Revoliutsiia i kul'tura
Ruslanda Esperantisto
Sennacieca Revuo
Sennaciulo
Sovetskii Esperantist
Vestnik rabotnikov iskusstv
Vestnik znaniia
VOKS Weekly News Bulletin
Zhizn' i tvorchestvo russkoi molodezhi

Published Primary Sources

Adresaro de la Esperantistoj. Serio XVI. Warsaw: A. Gins, 1896.
Agurtin, L. A. *Esperanto i uchashchaiasia molodezh'*. Saratov: B. L. Rabinovich, 1914.
Agurtin, L. A. *Mezhdunarodnyi iazyk. Internacia Lingvo*. Saratov: B. L. Rabinovich, 1914.
Andreev, A. P. *Mezhdunarodnyi iazyk Esperanto. Ego nastoiashchee, proshedshee i budushchee*. Tiflis': Tipografiia "Esperanto," 1913.
Artiushkin-Kormilitsyn, V. P. *Mezhdunarodnyi iazyk revoliutsionnogo proletariata Esperanto*. Petrograd: n.p., 1919.
Axtell, Silas B. "Russia, and Her Foreign Relations." *Annals of the American Academy of Political and Social Science* 138, no. 1 (July 1928): 85–92.
Balabanoff, Angelica. *My Life as a Rebel*. New York: Greenwood Press, [1938] 1968.
Barbusse, Henri. *One Looks at Russia*. Translated by Warre B. Wells. London: J.M. Dent & Sons, 1931.
Barmine, Alexandre. *Memoirs of a Soviet Diplomat*. Translated by Gerard Hopkins. London: Lovat Dickson, 1938.
Bell, Thomas. *Pioneering Days*. London: Lawrence and Wishart, 1941.
Bey, Essad. *Stalin: The Career of a Fanatic*. Translated by Huntley Paterson. New York: Viking, 1932.

Borsboom, E. *Vivo de Lanti*. Paris: SAT, 1976.
Brandt, R. F. *O mezhdunarodnykh iazykakh voobshche i v chastnosti ob Esperanto*. Moscow: Esperanto, 1909.
Breslau, B. *Mezhdunarodnyi iazyk i proletariat*. Saratov: Tip. P. N. Sibrina, 1918.
Chulkov, N. O. *Rech', proisnesennaia pri otkrytii Arkhangel'skogo otdeleniia S-Peterburgskogo Obshchestva 'Espero' 21 Noiabria 1898 goda*. Arkhangelsk: Arkhang. Gub. Tip., 1898.
Dmitriev, V. A., and P. D. Medem. *Mezhdunarodnyi vspomogatel'nyi iazyk Esperanto: ego primenenie i rasprostranenie*. Petrograd: Sila, 1918.
Drezen, E. *Problema mezhdunarodnogo iazyka*. Moscow: TsK SESR, 1932.
Drezen, E. *V poiskakh vseobshchego iazyka*. Moscow: Zemlia i fabrika, 1925.
Drezen, E. *Za vseobshchim iazykom (tri veka iskanii)*. Moscow: Gosizdat, 1928.
Engel'gardt, V. N. *Shkola, uchitel'stvo i Esperanto*. Moscow: TsK SESR, 1930.
Epton, Harry A. *The International Radio Manual*. London: British Esperanto Association, 1925.
"Esperanto and Jewish Ideals: Interview for the Jewish Chronicle with Dr. Zamenhof." *Jewish Chronicle* (London). September 6, 1907: 16–18.
Filin, F. P. "Bor'ba za markistsko-leninskoe iazykoznanie i gruppa 'Iazykfront.'" In *Protiv burzhuaznoi kontrabandy v iazykoznanii*. Edited by S. Ia. Bykovskii, 28–46. Leningrad: GAIMK, 1932. Reproduced online at http://crecleco.seriot.ch/textes/Filin32a.html. Accessed November 6, 2019.
Fischer, Louis. *Men and Politics: Europe Between the Two World Wars*. New York: Harper & Row, [1941] 1966.
Fischer, Markoosha. *My Lives in Russia*. New York: Harper & Brothers, 1944.
Frank, Waldo. *Dawn in Russia: The Record of a Journey*. New York: Scribner & Sons, 1932.
Freeman, Joseph. *An American Testament: A Narrative of Rebels and Romantics*. New York: Farrar and Rinehart, 1936.
"From Kishineff to Bialystok: A Table of Pogroms from 1903 to 1906." *American Jewish Year Book* 8 (September 20, 1906): 34–89.
Griffith, Hubert. *Seeing Soviet Russia: An Informative Record of the Cheapest Trip in Europe*. London: John Lane, 1932.
Holzhaus, Adolf. *Doktoro kaj Lingvo Esperanto*. Helsinki: Fondumo Esperanto, 1969.
Internatsional'naia proletarskaia Esperanto-lingvisticheskaia komissia. *Novye problemy iazykoznaniia*. TsK SESR: Moscow, 1933.
Intsertov, N. *Kak dolzhna rabotat' iacheika SESR*. Moscow: TsK SESR, 1930.
Ivnitskii, E. *Esperantskii traktor / Esperantista traktoro*. Moscow: TsK SEU, 1930.
Izgur, I. *Mezhdunarodnyi iazyk na sluzhbe proletariat*. Moscow: Novaia epokha, 1925.
Izgur, I. *Ogon' v konvertakh*. Kiev: Molodoi bol'shevik, 1934.
Jennings, Amy S. "How to Travel in Soviet Russia" *Nation* 136, no. 3540 (May 10, 1933): 528–30.
Jones, Margaret L. *The Esperanto Manual*. London: British Esperanto Association, 1908.
Kabanov, N. *Vspomogatel'nyi iazyk Esperanto*. Moscow: Posrednik, 1909.
Kennell, Ruth Epperson. *Theodore Dreiser and the Soviet Union, 1927–1945*. New York: International Publishers, 1969.
Khlebnikov, Velimir. *The King of Time: Selected Writings of Russian Futurism*. Translated by Paul Schmidt and Charlotte Douglas. Cambridge, MA: Harvard University Press, 1985.
Kiriushin, P. *Mezhdunarodnaia sviaz' na Esperanto*. Moscow: Izdanie TsK SESR, 1930.

Kolosov, V. A. *Mezhdunarodnyi iazyk Esperanto, ego vozniknovenie, sostav, stroi, znachenie i rasprostranenie*. Simbirsk: Tip. Gubernskogo Pravleniia, 1911.
Kopelev, Lev. *To Be Preserved Forever*. Translated by Anthony Austin. Philadelphia, PA: J. B. Lippincott, 1977.
Kopelev, Lev. *The Education of a True Believer*. Translated by Gary Kern. New York: Harper and Row, 1980.
Kravtsov, V. L. *Vazhnoe delo*. Boguchar: I. Ivanova, 1891.
Lanti, E. *The Workers' Esperanto Movement*. Translated by H. Stay. London: NCLC Publishing, 1928.
Laskov, Shulamit. "Zamenhof's Letter to the Bilium." *Zionism* 1, no. 2 (1980): 151–7.
Lebedeff, Vladimir. "Stalin's Days in Prison." *New York Times*, January 24, 1937.
Lisichnik, I. *Tovarishch Shatov–Tovarishchu Tak-Milanu*. Moscow: Profizdat, 1933.
Litvinov, Ivy. "To Russia With Love." *Observer*. July 25, 1976.
Litvinova, A. V. *Basic Step by Step. Uchebnik angliiskogo iazyka na osnove 'Basic Step by Step' Ch. K. Ogdena*. Moscow: Izdatel'skoe tovarishchestvo inostrannykh rabochikh v SSSR, 1935.
Luk'ianin, Valentin. "Obyknovennaia istoriia, XX vek," *Ural*, no. 12 (2011); republished online at https://magazines.gorky.media/ural/2011/12/obyknovennaya-istoriya-hh-vek.html. Accessed September 4, 2019.
Lyons, Eugene. *Assignment in Utopia*. New York: Harcourt, Brace, & Company, 1937.
Margulies, Sylvia R. *The Pilgrimage to Russia: The Soviet Union and the Treatment of Foreigners 1924–1937*. Madison: University of Wisconsin Press, 1968.
Marr, N. Ia. *Izbrannye raboty*. Volume 1. Leningrad: GAIMK, 1933.
Marr, N. Ia. *Izbrannye raboty*. Volume 2. Moscow: Tipografiia Akademii Nauk SSR, 1936.
Matiushkin-Gerke i Rozenblit. *Izuchaite inostrannye iazyki*. Leningrad: Molodaia gvardiia, 1931.
Mul'tanovskii, M. *Primenenie Esperanto dlia perepiski s inostrantsami*. Saratov: B. L. Rabinovich, 1915.
Murphy, J. T. *New Horizons*. London: John Lane, 1941.
Murphy, J. T. "The First Year of the Lenin School." *Communist International* IV, 14 (September 30, 1927): 267–9.
Nedoshivin, A. *Novyi iazyk dlia mezhdunarodnykh snoshenii. Kratkii ocherk esperantskogo dvizheniia*. Petrograd: Sila, 1916.
Ogden, C. K. *Basic English versus the Artificial Languages*. London: Kegan Paul, 1935.
Ogden, C. K. *Debabelization, with a Survey of Contemporary Opinion on the Problem of a Universal Language*. London: Kegan Paul, 1931.
O'Flaherty, Liam. *I Went to Russia*. New York: Harcourt, Brace, and Company, 1931.
Orlova, Raisa. *Memoirs*. Translated by Samuel Cioran. New York: Random House, 1983.
Otdel Torgovli Ministerstva Torgovli i Promyshlennosti. *Otchet o VII vsemirnom kongresse esperantistov v gor. Antverpen, c 7 po 14 avgusta n.s. 1911 goda*. St. Petersburg, 1912.
Postnikov, A. A. *O mezhdunarodnom iazyke Esperanto*. St. Petersburg: Tip. A. S. Suvorina, 1911.
Ransome, Arthur. *Russia in 1919*. New York: B. W. Huebsch, 1919.
Rantov, S. P. *Mezhdunarodnyi iazyk i sovremennaia zhizn'*. Saratov: B. L. Rabinovich, 1914.
Rhodes, Joseph. "Progress and Prospects of Esperanto." *North American Review* 184, no. 608 (1907): 282–91.
Riddell, John ed., *Founding the Communist International: Proceedings and Documents of the First Congress, March 1919*. New York: Pathfinder, 1987.

Riddell, John. *The German Revolution and the Debate on Soviet Power.* New York: Pathfinder, 1986.
Riddell, John. *To the Masses: Proceedings of the Third Congress of the Communist International, 1921.* Leiden: Brill, 2015.
Riddell, John. *Toward the United Front: Proceedings of the Fourth Congress of the Communist International 1922.* Leiden: Brill, 2011.
Riddell, John. *Workers of the World and Oppressed Peoples, Unite! Proceedings and Documents of the Second Congress.* 2 vols. New York: Pathfinder Press, 1991.
Roy, M. N. *M. N. Roy's Memoirs.* Bombay: Allied Publishers, 1964.
Rublev, S. *Kruzhok Esperanto: Prakticheskoe posobie dlia gruppovykh zaniatii.* Moscow: Izdanie TsK SESR, 1936.
Sakharov, A. A. *Na puti bratstvu narodov: sbornik statei o mezhdunarodnom iazyke Esperanto.* Kazan: Pervaia esperantskaia tipografiia, 1907.
Sazonova, E. *Kratkie svedeniia ob Esperanto.* Moscow: TsK SESR, 1930.
Salvadó, Francisco J. Romero. "Report on the action taken by the delegate Angel Pestaña at the second congress of the third international which was presented by him to the Confederación Nacional del Trabajo." *Revolutionary Russia* 8, no. 1 (1995): 39–103.
Schubert, Paul. *The Electric Word.* New York: Macmillan, 1928.
XVII S'ezdu Vsesoiuznoi kommunisticheskoi partii (bol'shevikov). Raport Soiuza esperantistov sovetskikh respublik (SESR). Moscow: Put' Oktiabr', 1934.
Semper (Sokolova), N. "Portrety i peizazhi: chastnye vospominaniia o XX veke." *Druzhba narodov* 2, no. 2 (1997): 73–115.
Serge, Victor. *Memoirs of a Revolutionary.* Translated by Peter Sedgwick with George Paizis. New York: New York Review Books, 2012.
Sergievskii M., and Iu. Vikhert. *Inostrannye iazyki v massy.* Moscow: Narkompros, 1930.
Shalamov, Varlam. *Kolyma Stories. Volume I.* Translated by Donald Rayfield. New York: NYRB Books, 2018.
Shapiro, Ia. *Voina narodov i Esperanto.* Saratov: Tip. O-va knigopechatnikov, 1915.
Shcherba, L. V. *Iazykovaia sistema i rechevaia deiatel'nost'.* Leningrad: Nauka, 1974.
Sheng, Yueh. *Sun Yat-sen University in Moscow and the Chinese Revolution: A Personal Account.* Lawrence: University of Kansas, 1971.
Shipman, Charles. *It Had to Be Revolution: Memoirs of an American Radical.* Ithaca, NY: Cornell University Press, 1993.
Smith, Andrew. *I Was a Soviet Worker.* New York: E. P. Dutton & Co, 1936.
Solonevich, Tamara. *Zapiski sovetskoi perevodchitsy* (1937). https://www.litmir.me/br/?b=137611 . Accessed July 8, 2019.
Spiridovich, E. F. *Iazykoznanie i mezhdunarodnyi iazyk.* Moscow: TsK SESR, 1931.
Starr, Mark. "Communism and an International Language," *Communist Review* 2, no. 4 (February 1922): 264–7.
Stoian, P., and V. Neshinskii, eds. *Neobkhodimye svedeniia ob Esperanto.* St. Petersburg: K. P. Shrader, 1912.
Stoian, P. E. *Slavianstvo i Esperanto.* Saratov: B.L. Rabinovich, 1914.
Svistunov, V. *Elementy Esperanto.* Moscow: Izdanie TsK SESR, 1932.
Tanquist, Reuben Algot. "A Study of the Social Psychology of the Diffusion of Esperanto with Special Reference to the English Speaking Peoples." Master's Thesis. University of Minnesota, 1927.
The Modern Languages Committee and Artificial Languages. London: British Esperanto Association, 1918.

Tolstoy, L. N. *Essays and Letters*. Translated by Aylmer Maude. London: Henry Frowde, 1911.
Tolstoy, L. N. *Polnoe sobranie sochinenii*. Third series, volume 68. Moscow: Gosudarstvennoe izdatel'stvo khudozhestvennoi literatury, 1954.
Tolstoy, L. N. *Tolstoy's Letters Volume II, 1880–1910*. Edited and translated by R. F. Christian. New York: Scribner's Sons, 1978.
Travers, P. L. *Moscow Excursion*. New York: Reynal and Hitchcock, 1934.
Trotsky, Leon. *My Life: An Attempt at an Autobiography*. New York: Charles Scribner's Sons, 1931.
Trotsky, Leon. *The First Five Years of the Communist International. Volume I*. Translated and edited by John G. Wright. New York: Pioneer Publishers, 1945.
Trotsky, Leon. *Problems of Everyday Life*. New York: Pathfinder, 1973.
Tsyvinskii, R., and T. Sikora. *Manifest soiuza sotsialistov-Esperanistov*. Vyborg: Estra, 1917.
Ul'ianova, M. I. *Rabkorskoe dvizhenie za granitsei i mezhdunarodnaia sviaz'* (Moscow: Izdatel'stvo 'Pravda' i 'Bednota,' 1928), 1928.
Ustav Tomskago Obshchestva Esperantistov. Tomsk: Tipografiia Doma Trudoliubiia, 1912.
VOKS. *Fakty i tsyfry*. Moscow: Mospoligraf, 1930.
Wicksteed, Alexander. *My Russian Neighbors: Recollections of Ten Years in Soviet Moscow*. New York: McGraw Hill, 1934.
XVII S'ezdu Vsesoiuznoi kommunisticheskoi partii (bol'shevikov). Raport Soiuza esperantistov sovetskikh respublik (SESR). Moscow: Put' Oktiabr', 1934.
Zabelyshinskii, I. *Inostrannye iazyki v massy*. Moscow: Uchpedgiz, 1931.
Zamengof, Leon. *Iz biografii D-ra Liudovika Zamengofa*. Translated by K. K. Petriaevskii. Saratov: Eldono de Esperanta Biblioteka Georg Davidov, 1918.
Zamenhof, L. L. *Mezhdunarodnyi iazyk: Predislovie i polnyi uchebnik [por Rusoj]*. Warsaw: Tipo-Litografiia Kh. Khel'tera, 1887. [Reprinted in facsimile, Moscow: Moskva Gazeto, 1992].
Zamenhof, L. L. *Gillelizm: Proekt resheniia evreiskogo voprosa*. Warsaw: Tip. M. Veidenfel'd i Ig. Khel'ter, 1901.
Zamenhof, L. L. "International Language," In *Papers on Inter-Racial Problems Communicated to the First Universal Races Congress*. Edited by G. Spiller, 425–32. London: P.S. King & Son, 1911.
Zamenhof, L. L. "After the Great War: An Appeal to Diplomatists." *British Esperantist* no. 123 (1915): 51–5.
Zamenhof, L. L. *Originala Verkaro. Antauparoloj, Gazetartikoloj, Traktajoj, Paroladoj, Leteroj, Poemoj*. Leipzig: Ferdinand Hirt & Sohn, 1929.
Zamenhof, L. L. *The Birth of Esperanto: Extract of a Private Letter from L. L. Zamenhof to N. Borovko*. Fort Lee, NJ: Esperanto Association of North America, 1931.
Zavialov, A. *Putevodnaia zvezda. (Vpechatleniia ot poezdki v Parizh na X-I Vsemirnyi Kongress Esperantistov)*. Saratov: O-va Knigopechatnikov, 1915.
Zhukov, Innokentii. *Puteshestvie zvena Krasnoi Zvezdy v stranu chudes*. Kharkov: O-va sodeistviia iunomu Leninitsu, 1924.
Zinoviev. *Mezhdunarodnyi iazyk "Esperanto."* St. Petersburg: Muller and Bogel'man, 1890.
Zolotov, N. Ia. "Protiv burzhuaznoi kontrabandy v iazykoznanii." In *Protiv burzhuaznoi kontrabandy v iazykoznanii*. Edited by S. Ia. Bykovskii, 7–27. Leningrad: GAIMK, 1932. Reproduced online at http://crecleco.seriot.ch/textes/Zolotov32.html. Accessed November 6, 2019.

Zweig, Stefan. *The World of Yesterday: An Autobiography*. Lincoln: University of Nebraska Press, 1964.

Secondary Sources

Albert, Gleb J. "'German October is Approaching': Internationalism, Activists, and the Soviet State in 1923." *Revolutionary Russia* 24, no. 2 (2011): 111–42.

Albert, Gleb J. "From 'World Revolution' to 'Fatherland of all Proletarians:' Anticipated World Society and Global Thinking in Early Soviet Russia." *Interdisciplines* 1 (2012): 85–119.

Albert, Gleb J. "'Esteemed Comintern!': The Communist International and World-Revolutionary Charisma in Early Soviet Society." *Twentieth-Century Communism* 8 (2015): 10–39.

Alcalde, Xavier. "The Practical Internationalism of Esperanto." *Peace in Progress* 24 (2015). http://www.icip-perlapau.cat/numero24/articles_centrals/article_central_5/

Anderson, Benedict. *Imagined Communities: Reflections on the Origins and Spread of Nationalism*. New York: Verso, 2006.

Antic, Ana, Johanna Conterio, and Dora Vargha. "Conclusion: Beyond Liberal Internationalism." *Contemporary European History* 25, no. 2 (2016): 359–71.

Applebaum, Rachel. "The Friendship Project: Socialist Internationalism in the Soviet Union and Czechoslovakia in the 1950s and 1960s." *Slavic Review* 74, no. 3 (2015): 484–507.

Applebaum, Rachel. *Empire of Friends: Soviet Power and Socialist Internationalism*. Ithaca, NY: Cornell University Press, 2019.

Applebaum, Rachel. "The Rise of Russian in the Cold War: How Three Worlds Made a World Language." *Kritika: Explorations in Russian and Eurasian History* 21, no. 2 (2020): 347–70.

Avrutin, Eugene M. *Jews and the Imperial State: Identification Politics in Tsarist Russia*. Ithaca, NY: Cornell University Press, 2010.

Bayly, C. A. *The Birth of the Modern World, 1780–1914: Global Connections and Comparisons*. Oxford: Blackwell, 2004.

Banerjee, Anindita. *We Modern People: Science Fiction and the Making of Russian Modernity*. Middletown, CT: Wesleyan University Press, 2012.

Barghoorn, Frederick C. *The Soviet Cultural Offensive: the Role of Cultural Diplomacy in Soviet Foreign Policy*. Princeton: Princeton University Press, 1960.

Bender, Sara. *The Jews of Bialystok during World War II and the Holocaust*. Translated by YaVa Murciano. Lebanon, NH: Brandeis University Press, 2008.

Benson, Morton. "The New Soviet Foreign Language Program." *Modern Language Journal* 40, no. 4 (1956): 173–4.

Berdichevsky, Norman. "Zamenhof and Esperanto." *Ariel* no. 64 (1986): 58–71.

Bojanowska, Edyta M. *A World of Empires: The Russian Voyage of the Frigate Pallada*. Cambridge, MA: Harvard University Press, 2018.

Boulton, Marjorie. *Zamenhof: Creator of Esperanto*. London: Routledge and Paul, 1960.

Bradley, Joseph. "Voluntary Associations, Civic Culture, and Obshchestvennost' in Moscow." In *Between Tsar and People: Educated Society and the Quest for Public Identity in Late Imperial Russia*. Edited by Edith W. Clowes, Samuel D. Kassow, and James L. West, 131–48. Princeton, NJ: Princeton University Press, 1991.

Bradley, Joseph. *Voluntary Associations in Tsarist Russia: Science, Patriotism, and Civil Society*. Cambridge, MA: Harvard University Press, 2009.

Brandist, Craig. *The Dimensions of Hegemony: Language, Culture and Politics in Revolutionary Russia*. Leiden: Brill, 2015.

Brandist, Craig, and Katya Chown, editors. *Politics and the Theory of Language in the USSR 1917–1938: The Birth of Sociological Linguistics*. New York: Anthem Press, 2010.

Brasken, Kasper. *The International Workers' Relief, Communism, and Transnational Solidarity*. Houndsmills: Palgrave Macmillan, 2015.

Burbank, Jane. "An Imperial Rights Regime: Law and Citizenship in the Russian Empire." *Kritika: Explorations in Russian and Eurasian History* 7, no. 3 (2006): 397–431.

Cadiot, Juliette. "Searching for Nationality: Statistics and National Categories at the End of the Russian Empire (1897–1917)." *Russian Review* 64, no. 3 (2005): 440–55.

Callahan, Kevin J. *Demonstration Culture: European Socialism and the Second International, 1889–1914*. Leceister: Troubador, 2010.

Campo, Angela. "The Reception of Eugen Wüster's Work and the Development of Terminology." PhD diss., Université de Montréal, 2012.

Carswell, John. *The Exile: A Life of Ivy Litvinov*. London: Faber and Faber, 1983.

Case, Holly. *The Age of Questions: Or, a First Attempt at an Aggregate History of the Eastern, Social, Woman, American, Jewish, Polish, Bullion, Tuberculosis, and Many Other Questions over the Nineteenth Century, and Beyond*. Princeton, NJ: Princeton University Press, 2018.

Chase, William J. *Enemies within the Gates? The Comintern and Stalinist Repression, 1934–1939*. New Haven, CT: Yale University Press, 2001.

Chatterjee, Choi. "Imperial Subjects in the Soviet Union: M.N. Roy, Rabindranath Tagore, and Re-Thinking Freedom and Authoritarianism." *Journal of Contemporary History* 52, no. 4 (2017): 913–34.

Chatterjee, Choi, Steven G. Marks, Mary Neuberger, and Steven Sabol, editors. *The Global Impact of Russia's Great War and Revolution, Book 2: The Wider Arc of the Russian Revolution*. 2 vols. Bloomington, IN: Slavica, 2019.

Chernov, Sergei. "At the Dawn of Simultaneous Interpreting in the USSR: Filling Some Gaps in History." In *New Insights in the History of Interpreting*. Edited by Kayoko Takeda and Jesus Baigorri-Jalon, 135–65. Amsterdam: John Benjamins Publishing Company, 2016.

Choldin, Marianna Tax. *A Fence around the Empire: Russian Censorship of Western Ideas under the Tsars*. Durham, NC: Duke University Press, 1985.

Clark, Katerina. *Moscow The Fourth Rome: Stalinism, Cosmopolitanism, and the Evolution of Soviet Culture, 1931–1941*. Cambridge, MA: Harvard University Press, 2011.

Clark, Katerina. *Petersburg, Crucible of Cultural Revolution*. Cambridge, MA: Harvard University Press, 1995.

Corney, Frederick C. *Telling October: Memory and the Making of the Bolshevik Revolution*. Ithaca, NY: Cornell University Press, 2004.

Crossman, Richard, ed. *The God That Failed*. New York: Harper & Row, 1963.

David-Fox, Michael. *Crossing Borders: Modernity, Ideology, and Culture in Russia and the Soviet Union*. Pittsburgh: Pittsburgh University Press, 2015.

David-Fox, Michael. *Showcasing the Great Experiment: Cultural Diplomacy and Western Visitors to the Soviet Union, 1921–1941*. New York: Oxford University Press, 2011.

David-Fox, Michael. "The Fellow Travelers Revisited: The 'Cultured' West through Soviet Eyes." *Journal of Modern History* 75, no. 2 (2003): 300–35.

Drachewych, Oleksa. *The Communist International and Racial Equality in the British Dominions*. London: Routledge, 2019.
Drachewych, Oleksa, and Ian McKay, ed. *Left Transnationalism: The Communist International and the National, Colonial, and Racial Questions*. Montreal: McGill-Queen's University Press, 2019.
Dulichenko, Aleksandr. "Ideia mezhdunarodnogo iskusstvennogo iazyka v debriakh rannei sovetskoi sotsiolingvistiki." *Russian Linguistics* 34, no. 2 (2010): 143–57.
Farnsworth, Beatrice. *Aleksandra Kollontai: Socialism, Feminism, and the Bolshevik Revolution*. Stanford, CA: Stanford University Press, 1980.
Figes, Orlando, and Boris Kolonitskii. *Interpreting the Russian Revolution: The Language and Symbols of 1917*. New Haven, CT: Yale University Press, 1999.
Firsov, Fridrikh A., Harvey Klehr, and John Earl Haynes. *Secret Cables of the Comintern, 1933–1943*. Translated by Lynn Visson. New Haven, CT: Yale University Press, 2014.
Fitzpatrick, Sheila. "Australian Visitors to the Soviet Union: the View from the Soviet Side." In *Political Tourists: Travellers from Australia to the Soviet Union in the 1920s–1940s*. Edited by Sheila Fitzpatrick and Carolyn Rasmussen, 1–39. Carlton: Melbourne University Press, 2008.
Fitzpatrick, Sheila. "Foreigners Observed: Moscow Visitors in the 1930s Under the Gaze of their Soviet Guides." *Russian History/Histoire Russe* 35, no. 1–2 (2008): 215–34.
Fitzpatrick, Sheila. *On Stalin's Team: The Years of Living Dangerously in Soviet Politics*. Princeton, NJ: Princeton University Press, 2015.
Forster, Peter G. *The Esperanto Movement*. The Hague: Mouten, 1982.
Fowler, Josephine. *Japanese and Chinese Immigrant Activists: Organizing in American and International Communist Movements, 1919–1933*. New Brunswick, NJ: Rutgers University Press, 2007.
Frankel, Jonathan. "The Crisis of 1881–1882 as a Turning Point in Modern Jewish History." In *The Legacy of Jewish Migration: 1881 and its Impact*. Edited by David Berger, 9–22. New York: Columbia University Press, 1983.
Fürst, Juliane. *Stalin's Last Generation: Soviet Post-War Youth and the Emergence of Mature Socialism*. New York: Oxford University Press, 2010.
Gaiba, Francesca. *The Origins of Simultaneous Interpretation: The Nuremberg Trial*. Ottawa: University of Ottawa Press, 1998.
Gamsa, Mark. "Mixed Marriages in Russian-Chinese Manchuria." In *Entangled Histories: The Transcultural Past of Northeast China*. Edited by Dan Ben-Canaan et al., 47–58. Cham: Springer, 2014.
Garvia, Roberto. *Esperanto and its Rivals: The Struggle for an International Language*. Philadelphia: University of Pennsylvania Press, 2015.
Garvia, Roberto. "Religion and Artificial Languages at the Turn of the Twentieth Century: Ostwald and Zamenhof." *Language Problems and Language Planning* 37, no. 1 (2013): 47–70.
Getty, J. Arch, and Oleg V. Naumov. *The Road to Terror: Stalin and the Self-destruction of the Bolsheviks, 1932–1939*. Annals of Communism. New Haven, CT: Yale University Press, 1999.
Gilburd, Eleonory. *To See Paris and Die: The Soviet Lives of Western Culture*. Cambridge, MA: Harvard University Press, 2018.
Gobbo, Federico. "Beyond the Nation-State? The Ideology of the Esperanto Movement between Neutralism and Multilingualism." *Social Inclusion* 5, no. 4 (2017): 38–47.
Golubev, A. V., and V. A. Nevezhin. "VOKS v 1930-1940-e gody." *Minuvshee*, 14 (1993): 313–64.

Gordin, Michael D. *Scientific Babel: How Science Was Done Before and After Global English*. Chicago: University of Chicago Press, 2015.
Gordin, Michael D. "The Forgetting and Rediscovery of Soviet Machine Translation." *Critical Inquiry* 46 (Summer 2020): 835–66.
Gorham, Michael. *Speaking in Soviet Tongues: Language Culture and the Politics of Voice in Revolutionary Russia*. Dekalb: Northern Illinois Press, 2003.
Grechko, Valerii. "Mezhdu utopiei i 'Realpolitik': Marr, Stalin, i vopros o vsemirnom iazyke." *Russian Linguistics* 34, no. 2 (2010): 159–72.
Hallas, Duncan. *The Comintern*. Chicago: Haymarket Books, 2008.
Halperin, Liora R. "Modern Hebrew, Esperanto, and the Quest for a Universal Language." *Jewish Social Studies* 19, no. 1 (2012): 1–33.
Harper, T. N. "Empire, Diaspora, and the Languages of Globalism, 1850–1914." In *Globalization in World History*. Edited by A. G. Hopkins, 141–66.
New York: Norton, 2002.
Haslam, Jonathan. "The Comintern and the Origins of the Popular Front 1934–1935." *Historical Journal* 22, no. 3 (1979): 673–91.
Headrick, Daniel R. *The Invisible Weapon: Telecommunications and International Politics 1851–1945*. New York: Oxford University Press, 1991.
Henkin, David M. *The Postal Age: The Emergence of Modern Communications in Nineteenth-Century America*. Chicago: University of Chicago Press, 2006.
Herren, Madeleine. "Governmental Internationalism and the Beginnings of a New World Order in the Late Nineteenth Century." In *The Mechanics of Internationalism: Culture, Society, and Politics from the 1840s to the First World War*. Edited by Martin H. Geyer and Johannes Paulmann, 121–44. New York: Oxford University Press.
Hicks, Jeremy. "Worker Correspondents: Between Journalism and Literature." *Russian Review* 66, no. 4 (2007): 568–85.
Hollander, Paul. *Political Pilgrims: Travels of Western Intellectuals to the Soviet Union, China, and Cuba 1928–1978*. New York: Oxford University Press, 1981.
Hulse, James W. *The Forming of the Communist International*. Stanford, CA: Stanford University Press, 1964.
Iriye, Akira. *Cultural Internationalism and World Order*. Baltimore, MD: John Hopkins University Press, 1997.
Jackson, Julian. *The Popular Front in France: Defending Democracy, 1934–1938*. Cambridge: Cambridge University Press, 1988.
Jacobson, Jon. *When the Soviet Union Entered World Politics*. Berkeley: University of California Press, 1994.
Khar'kovskii, Aleksandr. "Nikolai Ryt'kov: Akter, Zek, Esperantist." http://miresperanto.com/pri_esperantistoj/hharjkovskij_pri_rytjkov.htm. Accessed October 22, 2019.
Kim, Young S. "Constructing a Global Identity: The Role of Esperanto." In *Constructing World Culture: International Nongovernmental Organizations Since 1875*, Edited by John Boli and George M. Thomas, 127–48. Stanford, CA: Stanford University Press, 1999.
Kirasirova, Masha. "The 'East' as a Category of Bolshevik Ideology and Comintern Administration." *Kritika: Explorations in Russian and Eurasian History* 18, no. 1 (2017): 7–34.
Kirschenbaum, Lisa. *International Communism and the Spanish Civil War: Solidarity and Suspicion*. Cambridge: Cambridge University Press, 2015.

Kirschenbaum, Lisa. "Michael Gruzenberg/Mikhail Borodin: The Making of an International Communist." In *The Global Impacts of Russia's War and Revolution, Book 2, Part 1: The Wider Arc of the Revolution*. Edited by Choi Chatterjee, Steven G. Marks, Mary Neuburger, and Steven Sabol, 337–65. Bloomington, IN: Slavica, 2019.

Kirschenbaum, Lisa. "Reframing Slavic Studies and the Global Impacts of 1917." In *The Global Impacts of Russia's War and Revolution, Book 2, Part 2: The Wider Arc of the Revolution*. Edited by Choi Chatterjee, Steven G. Marks, Mary Neuburger, and Steven Sabol, 345–58. Bloomington, IN: Slavica, 2019.

Kiseleva, N. V. *Iz istorii bor'by sovetskoi obshchestvennosti za proryv kul'turnoi blokady SSSR*. Rostov-na-Donu, 1991.

Klier, John Doyle. *Russians, Jews, and the Pogroms of 1881–1882*. Cambridge: Cambridge University Press, 2014.

Kobrin, Rebecca. *Jewish Bialystok and its Diaspora*. Bloomington, IN: Indiana University Press, 2010.

Konishi, Sho. *Anarchist Modernity: Cooperation and Japanese-Russian Intellectual Relations in Modern Japan*. Cambridge, MA: Harvard University Press, 2013.

Konishi, Sho. "Translingual World Order: Language without Culture in Post-Russo-Japanese War Japan." *Journal of Asian Studies* 72, no. 1 (2013): 91–114.

Korzhenkov, Aleksandr. *Zamenhof: The Life, Works and Ideas of the Author of Esperanto*. Translated by Ian M. Richmond. New York: Mondial, 2009.

Kotkin, Stephen. *Magnetic Mountain: Stalinism as Civilization*. Berkeley: University of California Press, 1995.

Kotkin, Stephen. *Stalin: Waiting for Hitler, 1929–1941*. New York: Penguin, 2017.

Kotsonis, Yanni. *States of Obligation: Taxes and Citizenship in the Russian Empire and Early Soviet Republic*. Toronto: University of Toronto Press, 2014.

Laamanen, Ville. "VOKS, Cultural Diplomacy and the Shadow of the Lubianka: Olavi Paavolainen's 1939 Visit to the Soviet Union." *Journal of Contemporary History* 52, no. 4 (2017): 1022–41.

Laborie, Léonard. "Global Commerce in Small Boxes: Parcel Post, 1878–1913." *Journal of Global History* 10, no. 2 (2015): 235–58.

Lambroza, Shlomo. "The Pogroms of 1903–1906." In *Pogroms: Anti-Jewish Violence in Modern Russian History*. Edited by John D. Klier and Shlomo Lambroza, 195–247. Cambridge: Cambridge University Press, 1992.

Lazitch, Branko, and Milorad M. Drachovitch. *Lenin and the Comintern. Volume I*. Stanford, CA: Hoover Institution Press, 1972.

Lenoe, Matthew. *Closer to the Masses: Stalinist Culture, Social Revolution, and Soviet Newspapers*. Cambridge, MA: Harvard University Press, 2004.

Lerner, Warren. *Karl Radek: The Last Internationalist*. Stanford, CA: Stanford University Press, 1970.

Lins, Ulrich. *Dangerous Language: Esperanto under Hitler and Stalin*. Translated by Humphrey Tonkin. 2 vols. London: Palgrave Macmillan, 2016.

Lovell, Steven. *Russia in the Microphone Age: A History of Soviet Radio, 1919–1970*. Oxford: Oxford University Press, 2015.

Mally, Lynn. *Culture of the Future: The Proletkult Movement in Revolutionary Russia*. Berkeley: University of California Press, 1990.

Martin, Terry. "The Origins of Soviet Ethnic Cleansing." *Journal of Modern History* 70, no. 4 (1998): 813–61.

Mathew, Tobie. *Greetings from the Barricades: Revolutionary Postcards in Imperial Russia.* London: Four Corners Books, 2019.
McAdams, A. James. *Vanguard of the Revolution: The Global Idea of the Communist Party.* Princeton, NJ: Princeton University Press, 2017.
McCannon, John. "Technological and Scientific Utopias in Soviet Children's Literature, 1921-1932." *Journal of Popular Culture* 34, no. 4 (2001): 153-69.
McGuire, Elizabeth. "Sino-Soviet Every Day: Chinese Revolutionaries in Moscow Military Schools." In *Everyday Life in Russia Past and Present.* Edited by Choi Chatterjee, David L. Ransel, Mary Cavender, and Karen Petrone, 329-49. Bloomington: Indiana University Press, 2014.
McGuire, Elizabeth. *Red at Heart: How Chinese Communists Fell in Love with the Russian Revolution.* New York: Oxford University Press, 2017.
McDermott, Kevin, and Jeremy Agnew. *The Comintern: A History of International Communism from Lenin to Stalin.* New York: St. Martin's Press, 1997.
Mëhilli, Elidor. *From Stalin to Mao: Albania in the Socialist World.* Ithaca, NY: Cornell University Press, 2017.
Mickenberg, Julia L. *American Girls in Red Russia: Chasing the Soviet Dream.* Chicago: University of Chicago Press, 2017.
Muller, Gotelind, and Gregor Benton. "Esperanto and Chinese Anarchism in the 1920s and 1930s." *Language Problems and Language Planning* 30, no. 2 (2006): 173-92.
Muller, Simone M., and Heidi J. S. Tworek. "'The Telegraph and the Bank': On the Interdependence of Global Communications and Capitalism, 1866-1914." *Journal of Global History* 10, no. 2 (2015): 259-83.
Muller, Simone M. *Wiring the World: The Social and Cultural Creation of Global Telegraph Networks.* New York: Columbia University Press, 2015.
Murdock, Graham, and Michael Pickering. "The Birth of Distance: Communications and Changing Conceptions of Elsewhere." In *Narrating Media History.* Edited by Michael Bailey, 171-83. London: Routledge, 2008.
Nathans, Benjamin. *Beyond the Pale: The Jewish Encounter with Late Imperial Russia.* Berkeley: University of California Press, 2002.
Nathans, Benjamin. "The Jews." In *The Cambridge History of Russia. Volume II: Imperial Russia, 1689-1917*, 184-201. Cambridge: Cambridge University Press, 2006.
Neuberger, Mary. "The 100th Anniversary of the Russian Revolution: Introduction." *Journal of Contemporary History* 52, no. 4 (2017): 807-15.
Neumann, Matthias. "Youthful Internationalism in the Age of 'Socialism in One Country': Komsomol'tsy, Pioneers and 'World Revolution' in the Interwar Period." *Revolutionary Russia* 31, no. 2 (2018): 279-303.
Ogle, Vanessa. *The Global Transformation of Time 1870-1950.* Cambridge, MA: Harvard University Press, 2015.
O'Keeffe, Brigid. "The Woman Always Pays: The Lives of Ivy Litvinov." *Slavonic and East European Review* 97, no. 3 (July 2019): 501-28.
Orent, Akira. *In the Land of Invented Languages: Esperanto Rock Stars, Klingon Poets, Loglan Lovers, and the Mad Dreamers Who Tried to Build a Perfect Language.* New York: Spiegel & Grau, 2009.
Orlov, I. B., and A. D. Popov. *Skvoz' "zheleznyi zanaves." See USSR! Inostrannye turisty i prizrak potemkinskikh dereven'.* Moscow: Izdatel'skii dom Vysshei shkoly ekonomiki, 2018.
Osterhammel, Jürgen. *The Transformation of the World: A Global History of the Nineteenth Century.* Princeton, NJ: Princeton University Press, 2014.

Ozerov, L. S. *Stroitel'stvo sotsializma v SSSR i mezhdunarodnaia proletarskaia solidarnost' (1921-1937g.g.)*. Moscow: Mysl', 1972.
Panchasi, Roxanne. *Future Tense: The Culture of Anticipation in France Between the Wars*. Ithaca, NY: Cornell University Press, 2009.
Panteleev, M. M. "Repressii v Kominterne (1937-1938 gg.)." *Otechestvennaia istoriia* 6 (1996): 161-8.
Pantov, Alexander V., and Daria A. Spichak. "Chinese Stalinists and Trotskyists at the International Lenin School in Moscow, 1926-1938." *Twentieth-Century China* 33, no. 2 (2008): 29-50.
Pollock, Ethan. *Stalin and the Soviet Science Wars*. Princeton, NJ: Princeton University Press, 2006.
Pratt, Mary Louise. *Imperial Eyes: Travel Writing and Transculturation*. Second Edition. London: Routledge, 2007.
Privat, Edmond. *The Life of Zamenhof*. Translated by Ralph Elliot. London: George Allen & Unwin, 1931.
Qualls, Karl. *Stalin's Niños: Educating Spanish Civil War Refugee Children in the Soviet Union, 1937-1951*. Toronto: University of Toronto Press, 2020.
Reinisch, Jessica. "Introduction: Agents of Internationalism." *Contemporary European History* 25, no. 2 (2016): 195-205.
Rolf, Malte. *Soviet Mass Festivals, 1917-1991*. Translated by Cynthia Klohr. Pittsburgh, PA: University of Pittsburgh Press, 2013.
Rosenberg, Emily S. *Transnational Currents in a Shrinking World 1870-1945*. Cambridge, MA: Harvard University Press, 2012.
Ruud, Charles A. *Fighting Words: Imperial Censorship and the Russian Press, 1804-1906*. Toronto: University of Toronto Press, 1982.
Salmon, Shawn Connelly. "To the Land of the Future: A History of Intourist and Travel to the Soviet Union, 1929-1991," PhD diss., University of California-Berkeley, 2008.
Sanborn, Joshua A. *Drafting the Nation: Military Conscription, Total War, and Mass Politics, 1905-1925*. Dekalb: Northern Illinois University Press, 2003.
Schlogel, Karl. *Moscow, 1937*. Translated by Rodney Livingstone. Cambridge: Polity, 2012.
Schor, Esther. "L.L. Zamenhof and the Shadow People." *Language Problems and Language Planning* 34, no. 2 (2010): 183-92.
Schor, Esther. *Bridge of Words: Esperanto and the Dream of a Universal Language*. New York: Metropolitan Books, 2016.
Shulman, Peter A. "Ben Franklin's Ghost: World Peace, American Slavery, and the Global Politics of Information before the Universal Postal Union." *Journal of Global History* 10, no. 2 (2015): 212-34.
Sidorov, A., ed. *Esperanto-dvizhenie: fragmenty istorii*. Moscow: Impeto, 2008.
Sidorov, A. V. *Esperanto-dvizhenie na Severo-Zapade Rossii*. St. Petersburg: n.p., 2014.
Siefert, Marsha. "'Chingis-Khan with the Telegraph': Communications in the Russian and Ottoman Empires." In *Comparing Empires: Encounters and Transfers in the Long Nineteenth Century*. Edited by Jorn Leonhard and Ulrike von Hirschhausen, 78-108. Gottingen: Vandenhoeck and Ruprecht, 2011.
Slezkine, Yuri. "N. Ia. Marr and the National Origins of Soviet Ethnogenetics." *Slavic Review* 55, no. 4 (1996): 826-62.
Sluga, Glenda. *Internationalism in the Age of Nationalism*. Philadelphia: University of Pennsylvania Press, 2015.
Smith, Michael G. "For a Rationalization of Language: The Bolshevik Experience with Esperanto." In *The Idea of a Universal Language*, 69-76. Edited by Humphrey Tonkin

and Karen Johnson Walker. New York: Center for Research and Documentation on World Language Problems, 1986.
Smith, Michael G. *Language and Power in the Creation of the USSR, 1917–1953*. New York: Mouton de Gruyter, 1998.
Smith, S. A. "The Russian Revolution, National Self-Determination, and Anti-Imperialism, 1917–1927." In *Left Transnationalism: The Communist International and the National, Colonial, and Racial Questions*. Edited by Oleksa Drachewych and Ian McKay, 73–98. Montreal: McGill-Queens University Press, 2019.
Standage, Tom. *The Victorian Internet: The Remarkable Story of the Telegraph and the Nineteenth Century's On-line Pioneers*. New York: Walker and Company, 1998.
Stearns, Peter S. *Globalization in World History*. 2nd edition. New York: Routledge, 2016.
Steinberg, Mark D. *Proletarian Imagination: Self, Modernity, and the Sacred in Russia, 1910–1925*. Ithaca, NY: Cornell University Press, 2002.
Steinberg, Mark D. *Petersburg Fin de Siècle*. New Haven, CT: Yale University Press, 2011.
Steinberg, Mark D. *The Russian Revolution 1905–1921*. New York: Oxford University Press, 2017.
Steinwedel, Charles. "Making Social Groups, One Person at a Time: The Identification of Individuals by Estate, Religious Confession, and Ethnicity in Late Imperial Russia." In *Documenting Individual Identity: The Development of State Practices since the French Revolution*. Edited by Jane Caplan and John Torpey, 67–82. Princeton, NJ: Princeton University Press, 2000.
Steinwedel, Charles. "To Make a Difference: The Category of Ethnicity in Late Imperial Russian Politics, 1861–1917." In *Russian Modernity*. Edited by David L. Hoffmann and Yanni Kotsonis, 67–86. New York: St. Martin's, 2000.
Stern, Ludmila. "Moscow 1937: The Interpreter's Story." *Australian Slavonic and East European Studies* 21, no. 1–2 (2007): 73–95.
Stern, Ludmila. *Western Intellectuals and the Soviet Union, 1920–1940: From Red Square to the Left Bank*. London: Routledge, 2007.
Stites, Richard. *Revolutionary Dreams: Utopian Vision and Experimental Life in the Russian Revolution*. New York: Oxford University Press, 1991.
Studer, Brigitte. *The Transnational World of the Cominternarians*. Translated by Dafydd Rees Roberts. London: Palgrave Macmillan, 2015.
Suny, Ronald Grigor. "A Journeyman for Revolution: Stalin and the Labour Movement in Baku, June 1907–May 1908." *Soviet Studies* 23, no. 3 (1972): 373–94.
Sutton, Geoffrey. *Concise Encyclopedia of the Original Literature of Esperanto, 1887–2007*. New York: Mondial, 2008.
Thomas, Lawrence L. *The Linguistic Theories of N. Ja. Marr*. Berkeley: University of California Press, 1957.
Tworek, Heidi. *News from Germany: The Competition to Control World Communications, 1900–1945*. Cambridge, MA: Harvard University Press, 2019.
Vatlin, Alexander. *Komintern: idei, resheniia, sud'by*. Moscow: Rosspen, 2009.
Vatlin, Alexander, and Stephen A. Smith. "The Comintern." In *The Oxford Handbook of Communism*, 187–202. Oxford: Oxford University Press, 2014.
Vatlin, Alexander. *Agents of Terror: Ordinary Men and Extraordinary Violence in Stalin's Secret Police*. Translated by Seth Bernstein. Madison: University of Wisconsin Press, 2016.

Vlasov, D. V. *Esperanto: Polveka tsenzury. Razvitie Esperanto-dvizheniia i ego zhurnalistiki v usloviiakh tsenzury v Rossiiskoi imperii i SSSR (1887–1938 gg.)*. Moscow: Impeto, 2011.

Vlasov, D. V. "Esperanto v Sovetskom radio-efire v 1920-1930-e gody," *Vestnik Sankt-Peterburgskogo Universiteta* 9, no. 4 (2013): 154–61.

Vlasov, D. V. *Istoriia primeneniia Esperanto v Rossii: pechat', radioveshchanie, perepiska, samizdat*. Moscow: Impeto, 2014.

Weeks, Theodore R. *Nation and State in Late Imperial Russia: Nationalism and Russification on the Western Frontier, 1863–1914*. DeKalb: Northern Illinois University Press, 1996.

Weinberg, Robert. "Workers, Pogroms, and the 1905 Revolution in Odessa." *Russian Review* 46, no. 1 (1987): 53–75.

Wenzlhuemer, Roland. *Connecting the Nineteenth-Century World: The Telegraph and Globalization*. Cambridge: Cambridge University Press, 2012.

Werth, Paul. *The Tsar's Foreign Faiths: Toleration and the Fate of Religious Freedom in Imperial Russia*. New York: Oxford University Press, 2014.

Wilson, Sandra. "The Comintern and the Japanese Communist Party." In *International Communism and the Communist International, 1919–1943*. Edited by Tim Rees and Andrew Thorpe, 285–307. Manchester: Manchester University Press, 1998.

Worley, Matthew. "Courting Disaster? The Communist International in the Third Period." In *In Search of Revolution: International Communist Parties in the Third Period*. Edited by Matthew Worley, 1–17. London: I.B. Tauris, 2014.

Young, Glennys. *The Communist Experience in the Twentieth Century: A Global History through Sources*. New York: Oxford University Press, 2012.

Index

Adresaro (Directory) 28, 52, 61
age of questions 5, 6, 65, 188
Alexander II 17, 19, 21, 39, 54
Alexander III 23, 39
All-Union Society for Cultural Ties Abroad (VOKS) *See* VOKS
Arosev, A. Ia. 143, 176
Artiushkin-Kormilitsyn, V. P. 96–7
Asnes, A. I. 63–4
authoritarian essentialism 16, 48
autocracy *See* imperial Russia

Bakushinskii, R. N. 87, 181
Balabanova, Anzhelika 93
Barbusse, Henri 109
Barmine, Alexander 177
Basic English 168–72, 177, 186
Bata, Iosif 178–9
Bazhenov, I. L. 87–8
Bell, Thomas 81
Belmont, Leo 69–70
Bialystok 17–18, 20, 29–30, 38, 39, 41–2
Bitner, V. V. 61–5
Bolsheviks
  attitude toward Esperanto 9, 110–11
  cultural conservatism 110
  multilingualism 93–5
Borovko, N. A. 29–30, 53, 197 n.60
Boulogne Declaration 34, 36, 63, 106
Breslau, Boris 86–7, 181–2
Bukharin, N. I. 94, 98, 110, 157, 209 n.47

Case, Holly 5, 65
censorship 47–8, 53–4, 56–9, 63, 202 n.48, 203 n.61
census (1897 imperial Russian) 30, 33
Clark, Katerina 160, 208 n.17
Cold War 11, 190–1, 229 n.46
Comintern (Communist International)
  Bolshevization 108

Communications Service 177
consecutive interpretation 98–9, 100
delegates 81, 90, 98, 101–2
demonization of social democrats 157
Esperanto 96–8, 101, 107, 110–11, 116
Eurocentrism 101–2, 110, 207 n.5, 211 n.97
Fifth World Congress (1924) 108
First World Congress (1919) 90–3, 95
Fourth World Congress (1922) 107
historiography 82
interpreters and translators 93, 95, 109
Popular Front 172–3
Purge and Terror 176–7
Second World Congress (1920) 81, 98–101
SEU 111, 173–5
Seventh World Congress (1935) 172
simultaneous interpretation 109, 213 n.133, 213 n.135
Sixth World Congress (1928) 109
Stalin, I. V. 108, 212 n.127
Third Period (1928–34) 157, 172
Third World Congress (1921) 81, 101, 104–5
Twenty-One Conditions 99–100, 107
united front policy 118, 157
working languages 91–3, 98, 99, 107, 108
Communist University for the Toilers of the East (KUTV) 108
comradeship 129
Congress of Friends of the Soviet Union 134
COVID-19 pandemic 1, 199 n.104
cultural diplomacy, Soviet
  Esperanto 114, 119, 125, 129, 131, 136–9, 144
  goals 12–13, 114, 130, 133, 134, 135–6, 148
  historiography 139–40

language barriers 114–15, 139, 140–5
surveillance 136, 141, 143
see also VOKS

David-Fox, Michael 114, 134, 136, 139, 142, 144, 176
Demidiuk, G. P. 185
Dmitriev, V. A. 85–6
Dreiser, Theodore 140–1
Drezen, E. K.
 alleged espionage 175–6, 178–9, 182, 183, 185
 arrest and execution 179, 182
 background 116, 182
 foreign travel 130, 157, 175, 182
 linguistics 159, 161–8, 170
 relationship with Lanti 115, 116–17, 156, 158
 relationship with SAT 118, 156–9

Eggers, Boris 183
Eriukhin, A. P. 184
Eroshenko, Vasilii 72, 77, 206 n.130
Esperantists
 Comintern lobbying 89–90, 96–8, 110, 173–5
 exemplars of globalization 2, 4, 188
 Nazi persecution 173, 174
 patriotic cosmopolitanism 8, 60–1, 188
 Purge and Terror 175–6, 178–9, 181–7
 self-fashioning as global citizens 61, 67, 75–7, 123
 social networking 52, 61, 65, 67, 74–7, 126
 treatment by historians 2–3, 5–6, 63, 78, 188
 world congresses 43, 69–70, 77–8
Esperanto
 auxiliary language (definition) 7, 35
 design 7–8, 15, 29–30
 Eurocentrism 7–8, 30
 French period 37, 38
 governmental internationalism 70–1
 historiography 5–6, 16, 37, 38, 48
 incubation in imperial Russia 28, 52
 inner idea 34, 36, 42–3, 84, 86, 87
 mediator 47, 188
 moral community 16, 32–3, 42, 45, 188

neutrality (myth of) 63–4, 65–6, 84–5, 106
perceived language of espionage and subversion 9–10, 181–7, 114, 178–9
perceived threat to nations and nationalism 7–8, 50, 77
proletarian international language 9, 85–6, 88, 97, 109–10
proposed reforms 44, 55
Esperantoland
 armchair travel 70, 72–3, 75
 definition 38, 43
 Esperanto world congresses 36, 69–70, 78
Esperkor 123–4
Espero (organization) 39, 52–3, 60, 62–4, 65, 68, 83
"Espero" (periodical) 62–3, 65
Eurocentrism
 Comintern 101–2, 110, 207 n.5, 211 n.97
 Esperanto 7–8, 30
 globalization 8

February Revolution 45, 82–4, 109
Filippov, F. A. 184
First Universal Congress of Races (1911) 44
Fischer, Louis 114, 177, 210 n.61
Fischer, Markoosha 109, 177
Foreign Languages to the Masses! 13, 148–52, 154
foreign tourism *See* VOKS
friendship 74, 129
Fürst, Juliane 129

Gavrilov, P. A. 183
German October 82, 108, 110
Global English 7, 11, 170
globalization
 definition 4
 Eurocentrism 8
 global identities 8
 "self-reflective" 5
globalizing Russian history 4, 10–11, 82
Goebbels, Joseph 173
Gordin, Michael 7
Gorky, Maxim 103–4
governmental internationalism 70–1

Griffith, Hubert 141–2
Gruzenberg, Mikhail (Borodin) 94
guides *See* tour guides

Hebrew 25, 32–3, 198 n.75
Hibbat Zion (Lovers of Zion) 20, 23, 30
Hillelism 30–6, 39–46
Hitler, Adolf 172–3, 190
Homaranism 43, 200 n.122 (*see also* Hillelism)

Iazykfront 164–8
Ido 44, 101, 200 n.125
imperial Russia
    anti-Semitism 20–2, 33, 38
    autocracy 22, 39, 57
    censorship of Esperantist texts 48, 53–4, 56–9
    ethnic diversity 30–1
    obshchestvennost' (civic spirit) 64
intelligentsia 16, 23, 39, 46, 62–3, 64
international education 123, 149
international language question 2–8, 9, 11, 58, 88–9
International of Proletarian Esperantists (IPE) 158, 172–4, 175, 178
International Radio Association 120
internationalism
    agents 2, 6, 193 n.3
    governmental 70–1
    late imperial Russia 16, 60–3, 67–8, 78
    relationship with nationalism 6–7
    socialist 10–11
    Soviet 10–11, 190
interpreters and interpretation
    Comintern 93, 95, 109, 110
    consecutive 98–9, 100
    simultaneous 109, 213 n.133, 213 n.135
    VOKS 134–5, 140–4
Intsertov, N. Ia. 153, 176, 178, 182
IPE *See* International of Proletarian Esperantists (IPE)

Japhetic theory 159–61, 163–5, 168, 224 n.99
Jewish Question 3, 5, 20–3, 25, 31–4, 36, 45
Johnson, A. H. 75–6

Kameneva, O. D. 149, 150
Keable, W. G. 170–1
Khlebnikov, Velimir 118–19, 214 n.25
Kiriushin, Pavel 129, 131, 136, 152
Kirschenbaum, Lisa 10
Klein, Martin 137
Kollontai, Aleksandra 93, 94
Kopelev, Lev 127, 177
Kravtsov, V. L. 49–50
Krupskaia, N. D. 151

Lanti, Eugene 105–6, 115–17, 156–9, 178, 185
La Esperantisto 28, 55, 56–7
La Ondo de Esperanto 74, 86
Lenin, V. I.
    Comintern 81, 93, 100
    death 108
    foreign language capabilities 94, 95
    on language politics 170
    opinion of Esperanto 147
Lerchner, Richard 137–8
linguistics, Soviet
    Esperanto 161–3, 165–8
    Iazykfront 164–8
    Marr's dominance 159–61, 164, 167
    universal language of communism 160, 162, 164, 168
Lins, Ulrich 57, 133, 186
Lisichnik, Ida 128, 186–7
Litvinov, Ivy 94, 168–72, 177
Litvinov, Maksim 94, 168–9, 171
Liubi, G. N. 58
Luk'ianin, V. P. 185
Luk'ianin, P. M. 185
Lunacharskii, A.V. 132–3
Lux Hotel (Moscow) 116

MacAlpine, Eadmon 99
Main Administration of Press Affairs 47–8, 56–8
Manifesto of the Union of Socialist Esperantists (1917) 83–4, 181
Margulies, Sylvia 142, 220 n.189
Marr, N. Ia. 159–65, 167–9
Mastepanov, Sergei 183
Medem, P. D. 85–6
Michaux, Alfred 34–5
Mul'tanovskii, M. 66–7

Muravkin, G. I. 173–5, 178
Murphy, Jack 81, 99, 211 n.81

Narkompros *See* People's Commissariat of Enlightenment
Nathans, Benjamin 18, 20, 22
nationalism 6–7, 45, 68, 105
nationality (in late imperial Russia) 30–2
neutrality *See* Esperanto
Nedoshivin, A. M. 71
Nevolin, A. N. 184
New Economic Policy (NEP) 12, 104, 107, 113, 130, 139
Nicholas II 38, 39, 59
1905 Revolution 37–9, 41, 53–4, 57, 59–60, 63–6
NKVD (Soviet security police)
  arrest and execution of Esperantists 175–6, 178–9, 181–7
  surveillance of Esperantists 177–8
  surveillance of foreign tourists 143
Novozhilov, A. A. 184

O'Flaherty, Liam 140
Ogden, Charles 169–72, 177
Ostrovskii, I. D. 57–9

Pale of Settlement 17–20, 21, 22, 38
pen pal correspondence
  alleged evidence of espionage 181, 183–5
  collective v. individual 125–30
  perceived threat of subversion 125–6, 129, 175–6
  prerevolutionary 52, 65, 67, 73–7
  solicitation of technical expertise 153–4, 172
  surveillance 128, 145, 178
  worker correspondence 122–5
People's Commissariat of Enlightenment (Narkompros) 88–9, 96, 111, 116, 150
Pestana, Angel 100–1
Podkaminer, S. N. 120, 130, 185–6
pogroms 18, 21–2, 25, 30, 31, 38–9, 42
Popular Front 172–3
postal services 51–2
postcards 67, 75–6, 122, 127, 177
Postnikov, A. A. 69, 71, 205 n.125
Priroda i liudi 62, 68

Radio
  Comintern 90
  Esperanto broadcasting 115, 119–21, 136, 138, 186, 214 n.12
  government regulation 119, 120–1
  visions of the future 113, 118–20
Rakosi, M. 116
Ransome, Arthur 91
Rantov, S. P. 67
Reed, John 99
revolutionary Russia (author's periodization) 14
Robichek, Fyodor 184
Roy, M. N. 100
Ruslanda Esperantisto 39–40, 43, 60–1, 63–4, 68, 70
Russian
  Cold War 190–1
  Comintern 91–2, 108
  lingua franca of socialist internationalism 82, 108–9, 190–1
  litmus test of loyalty to Bolsheviks 108–9
  world language 191
Russian Civil War 85–5, 87–90, 98, 102, 110–11, 115
Russo-Japanese War 37, 60, 72, 199 n.107
Ruud, Charles A. 54, 57, 59
Rytkov, Nikolai 181, 228 n.1

Sadoul, Jacques 90, 91
Samoilenko, A. T. 184
SAT *See* Sennacieca Asocio Tutmonda (SAT)
Sazonova, Elena 182
Schleyer, Johann 6
Schor, Esther 18, 43, 63, 84, 158, 199 n.100
science fiction 113
Scientific Research Institute for Linguistics (NIIaZ) 166–7
Second International 209 n.52
Sennacieca Asocio Tutmonda (SAT)
  anti-nationalism 105–6
  founding 105
  Leningrad Congress (1926) 9, 131–4
  membership 105, 106–7, 155–6, 158
  publications 124, 126, 156
  relationship with SEU 106–7, 115, 116–18, 155–9
  schism 155, 157–9

Sennaciulo 124, 126, 133, 137, 155–8
SEU *See* Union of Soviet Esperantists (SEU)
Semper, Natalia 143
Serge, Victor 95–6
Shalamov, Varlam 186
Shaozhou, Liu (Lin Zerong) 92, 209 n.47
Shcherba, L. V. 149
Shumilov, P. N. 182
simultaneous interpretation 109, 213 n.133, 213 n.135
Sixth World Congress of Proletarian Esperantists (Leningrad) 9, 131–4
Sluga, Glenda 6
Smirnova, A. S. 182–3
Smith, Andrew 220 n.195
social networks *See* Esperantists
socialism in one country 82, 108, 123, 147, 164
Solonevich, Tamara 143
Spanish Civil War 10
Spiridovich, E. F. 165–7, 224 n.99
Stalin, I. V.
  Comintern 108, 212 n.127
  Esperantists' appeals to 155, 173–4
  Esperanto study 94, 209 n.55
  foreign language capabilities 94, 209 n.54, 209 n.56, 212 n.127
  language policy 164, 166
Starr, Mark 133
Stites, Richard 23

Taylorism 161
techniques of hospitality 135, 144, 220 n.189
telegraphy 25, 50–1, 60, 74
Temerin, N. N. 184
Temporary Laws (1882) 22
Tenth Anniversary Celebration of the October Revolution 134–9
terminology science 167–8
Third International *See* Comintern
Timofeevskii, A. K. 184
Tolstoy, Lev 55–7
tour guides
  surveillance 143
  tactics 139–4
  training 134–5, 142

translation of technical expertise 147–50, 153–4
Travers, P. L. 141
Trotsky, Lev
  Comintern 100, 104, 108
  foreign language capabilities 93–5, 210 n.61
  on international education 123
  telegraphy 50
  worker correspondence 122
Tsyvinskii, Richard 83–4, 181, 207 n.11
Tupitsyn, G. I. 74–5, 77
Twenty-One Conditions 99–100, 107

Ulianova, Maria 122–3, 125, 147–9, 215 n.53
Union of Soviet Esperantists (SEU)
  founding (1921) 102–3
  Leningrad Congress (1926) 9, 131–4
  relationship with Comintern 111, 173–5
  relationship with SAT 106–7, 115, 116–18, 155–9
Universal Esperanto Association (UEA) 65–6, 79
Unua Libro (First Book) 15, 25–7, 52, 54, 197 n.46
Usov, N. P. 184

Vestnik znaniia 61–3
Viktorov-Chekhovich, Dmitrii 183
virtual tourism 67, 70, 73, 75–7, 121–2
VOKS (All-Union Society for Cultural Ties Abroad)
  Esperanto 130, 136–7, 144, 149
  foreign language courses 149–50
  foreign tourism 130, 135–6
  guides 134–5, 140–4
  Purge and Terror 176
  surveillance 136, 140–1, 143
  tactics 135–7, 140–4
Volapük 6, 50, 55
Voyage of the Red Star Pioneer Troop to Wonderland (1924) 113
Vozdvizhenskii, Veniamin 183–4

worker correspondence 122–5
World Esperanto Congress
  Antwerp (1911) 71

Boulogne-sur-Mer (1905) 34–8, 40, 69–70
Geneva (1906) 40, 41–2, 70
Paris (1914) 44, 77–8
Washington, D.C. (1910) 71
See also Esperantoland
World Postal Union 51
World War I 44–5, 77–9, 83, 88, 119, 189
worldism 72
Worldwide October
  anticipation 9, 96, 98
  Bolsheviks' timetable 82, 104–5, 108, 110
Wüster, Eugen 167–8, 179

xenophobia 4, 10, 148, 176–7, 190

Yezhov, N. I. 174, 176
Yiddish 18, 19, 25, 30, 32–3, 198 n.75

Zamenhof, L. L.
  "Appeal to the Diplomatists" (1915) 44–5, 79
  celebrity 37
  childhood 17–19
  critique of Russian autocracy 41, 45
  death 45

Esperanto world congresses 34–6, 41–2, 43, 44, 69
finances 25, 31, 55
globalization 6
historiography 16
International Language (1887) 15, 25–6, 54
Jewish Question 20–3, 25, 31–3, 36
marriage 25
multilingualism 18–19
(proto-)Zionism 20, 23, 25, 31
publishing ventures 25, 28, 44, 47, 56–7
"Tenets of Hillelism" (1906) 39–41, 43
university days 20–1, 30
"What, Ultimately, is to be Done?" (1882) 21–2
World War I 44–5
Zamenhof, Mark 17–20, 25
Zavialov, V. 77–8
Zhukov, Innokentii 113
Zilbernik, Klara 23, 25
Zinoviev, G. E. 90, 96, 99, 101, 107, 108, 176, 211 n.81
Zionism 20, 22, 23, 25, 31
Zweig, Stefan 134
Zykov, V. M. 184

www.ingramcontent.com/pod-product-compliance
Lightning Source LLC
Chambersburg PA
CBHW072137290426
44111CB00012B/1899